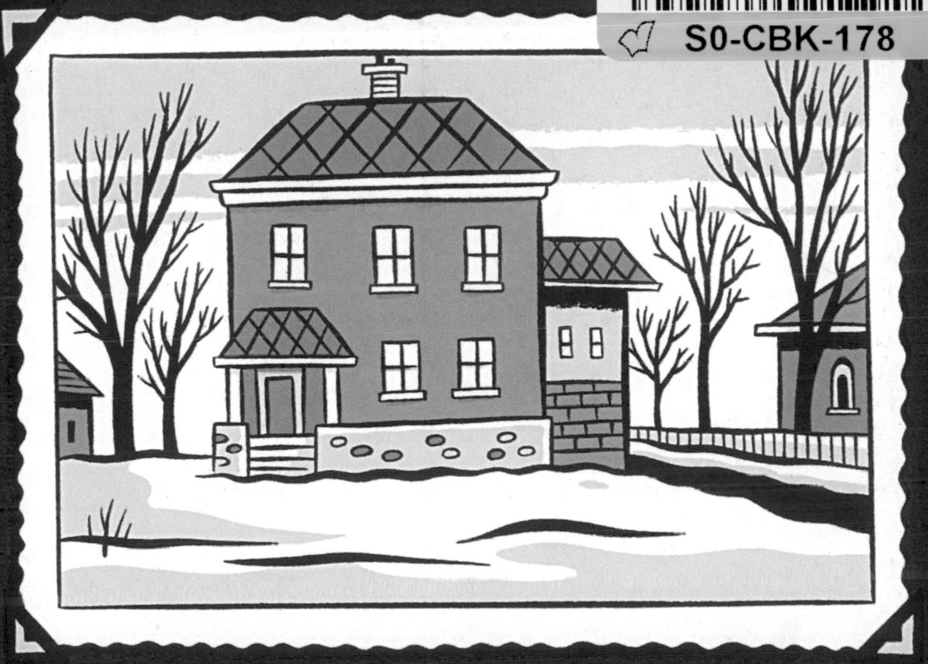

Home — 1960

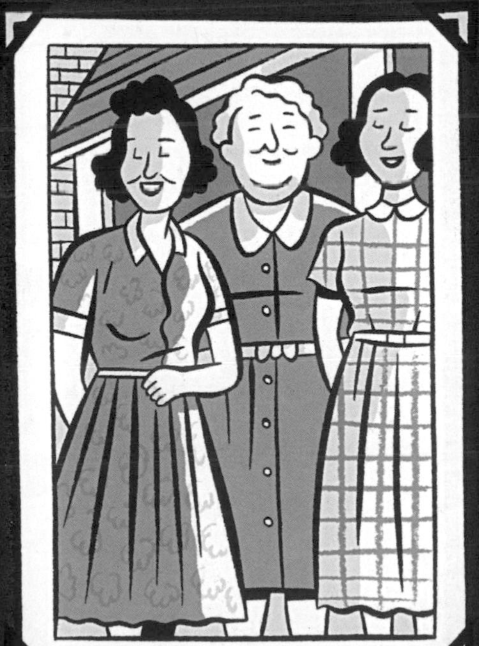

Doris, Mrs. Wright + Helen

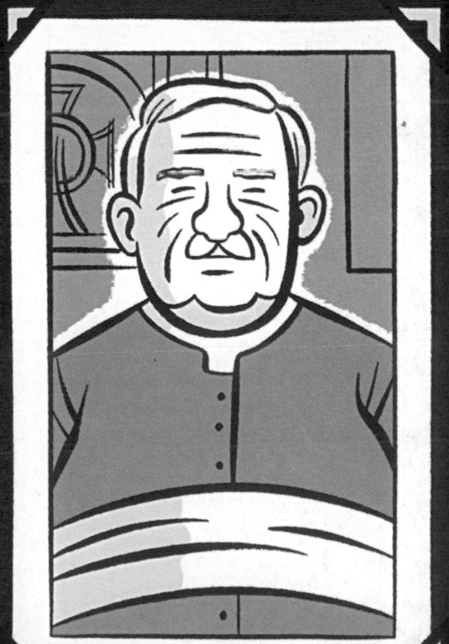

Father Matthew

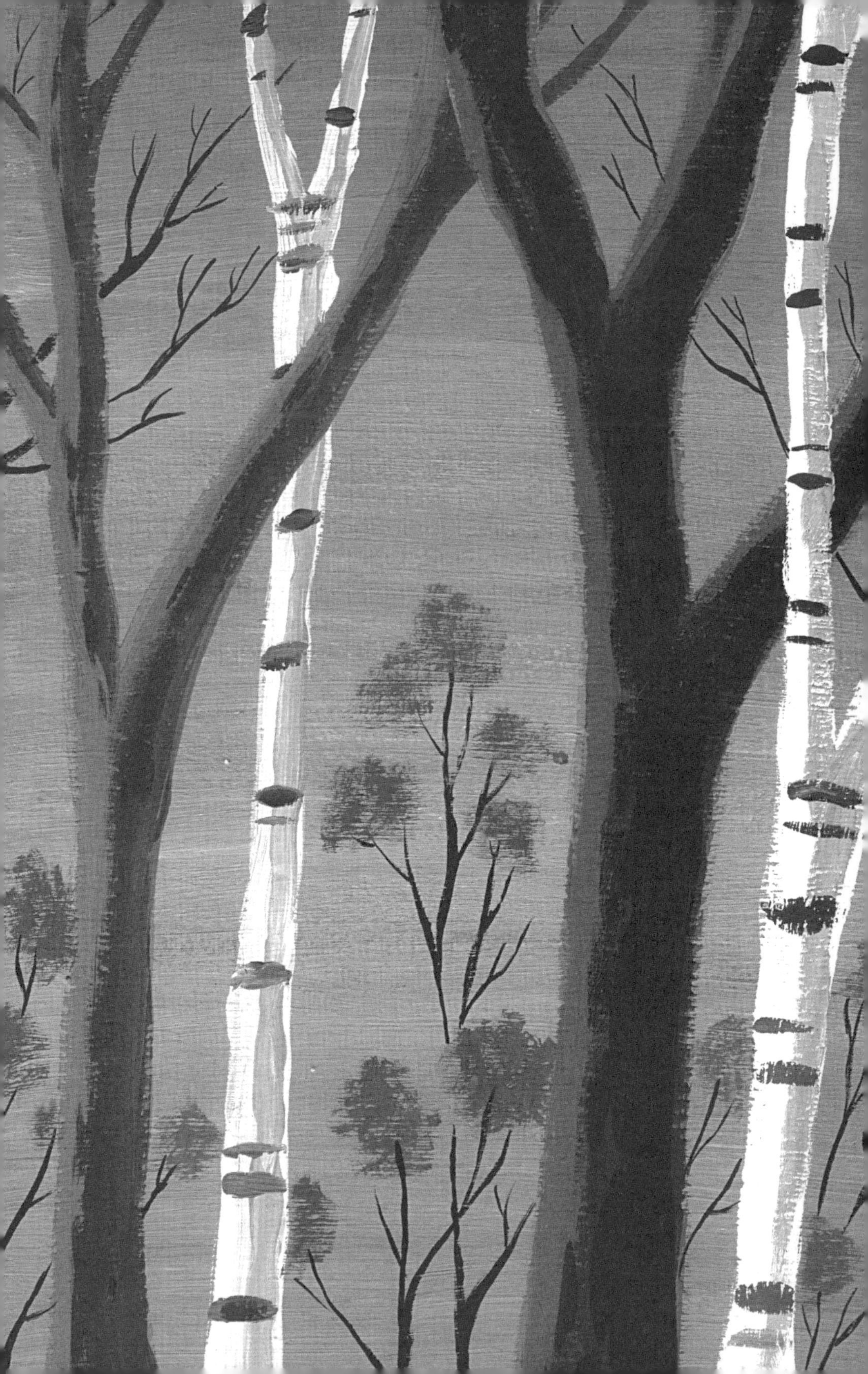

IT'S A GOOD LIFE, IF YOU DON'T WEAKEN

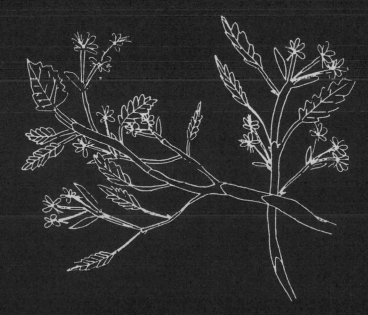

SPECIAL THANKS TO:
Maggie Mortimer, Chester Brown,
Joe Matt, Sarah Evans, Alan Hunt,
and Chris Oliveros

THE STORY PRESENTED HERE WAS ORIGINALLY SERIALIZED IN ISSUES
FOUR THRU NINE OF THE COMIC BOOK SERIES, PALOOKAVILLE.

FIRST CLOTH AND PAPERBACK EDITIONS PUBLISHED IN SEPTEMBER 1996.
5TH PAPERBACK PRINTING: OCTOBER 2011. PRINTED IN SINGAPORE.

NATIONAL LIBRARY OF CANADA CATALOGUING IN PUBLICATION.
SETH, 1962—
IT'S A GOOD LIFE, IF YOU DON'T WEAKEN/BY SETH

ISBN 1-896597-31-9 (BOUND)--ISBN 1-896597-70-X (PBK)
I. CANADIAN WIT AND HUMOUR, PICTORIAL. I. TITLE.
NC 1449. S43177 2003
C 2003-900115-6

10 9 8 7 6 5

DRAWN & QUARTERLY PUBLICATIONS.
POST OFFICE BOX 48056,
MONTREAL, QUEBEC,
CANADA, H2V 4S8
www.drawnandquarterly.com

DISTRIBUTED BY FARRAR, STRAUS AND GIROUX
18 WEST 18TH ST, NEW YORK, NY 10011   800·330·8477
DISTRIBUTED IN CANADA BY RAINCOAST BOOKS,
2440 VIKING WAY, RICHMOND, BC, CANADA
V6V 1N2   800·663·5714

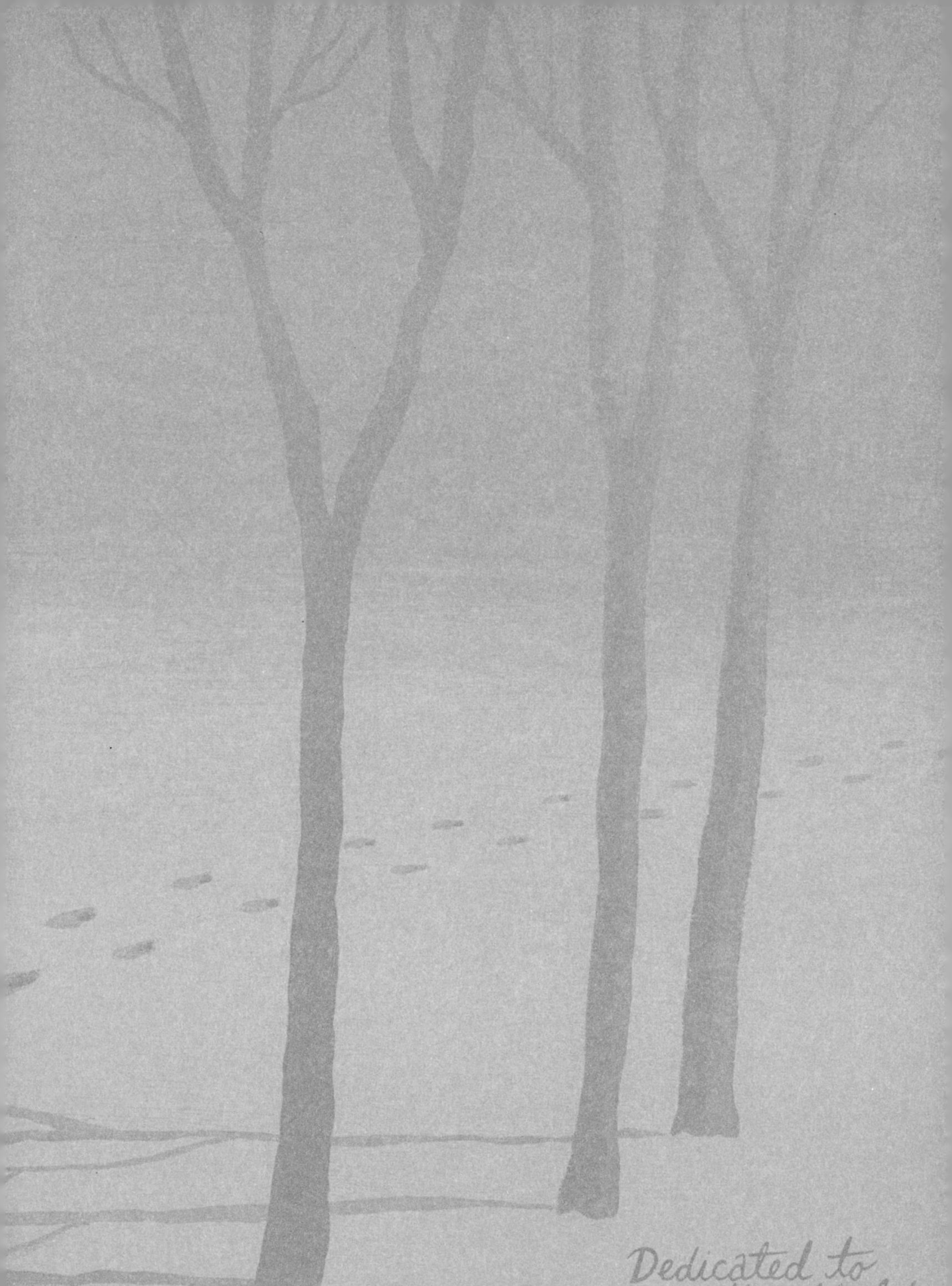

Dedicated to
my mother Violet,
from whom I often
heard the title of
this book

IT'S A GOOD LIFE, IF YOU DON'T WEAKEN

by Seth

DRAWN & QUARTERLY
(MONTREAL · CANADA)

Part One

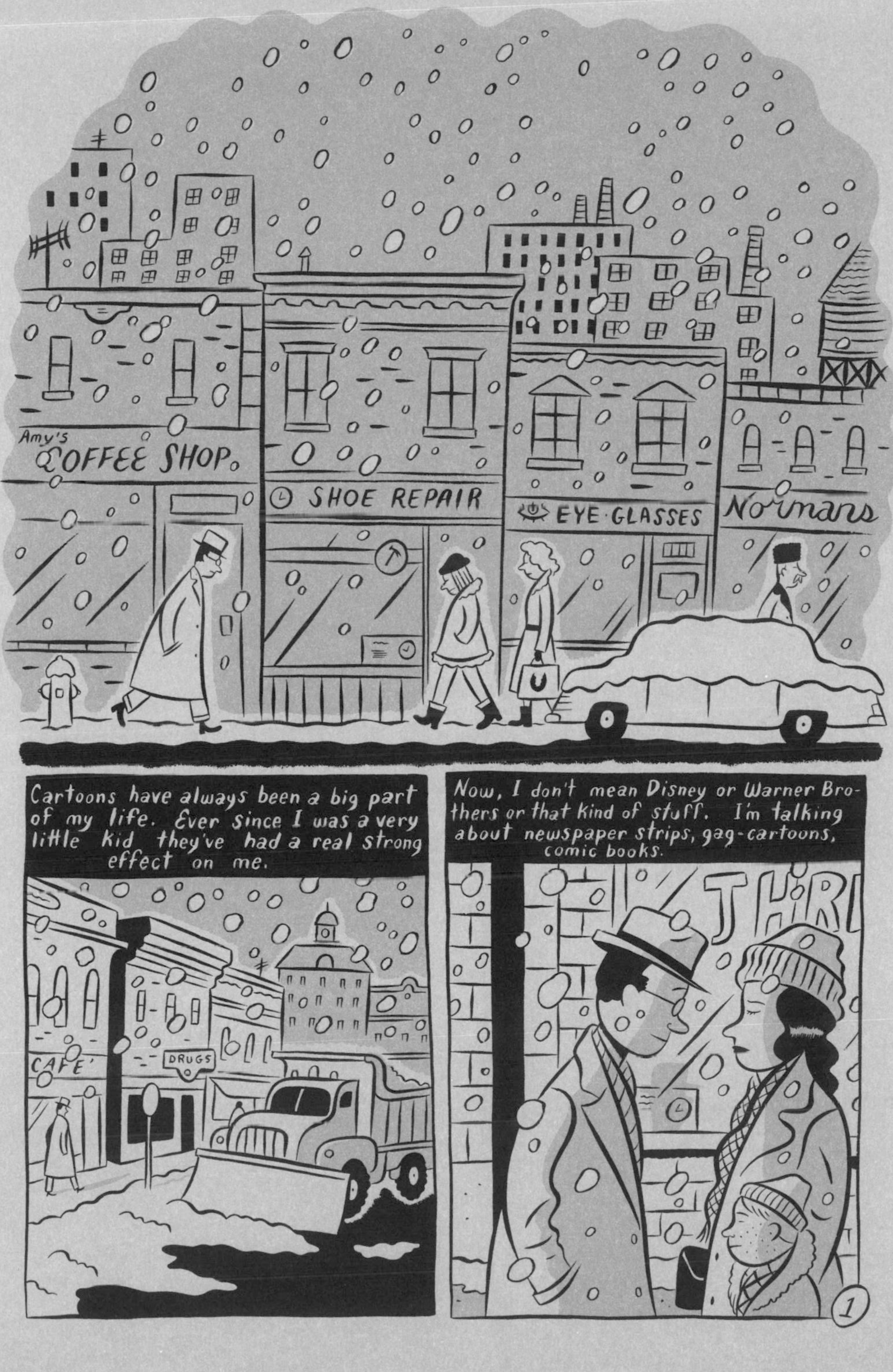
Amy's
COFFEE SHOP
SHOE REPAIR
EYE GLASSES
Normans
Cartoons have always been a big part of my life. Ever since I was a very little kid they've had a real strong effect on me.
CAFE'
DRUGS
Now, I don't mean Disney or Warner Brothers or that kind of stuff. I'm talking about newspaper strips, gag-cartoons, comic books.
THR
1

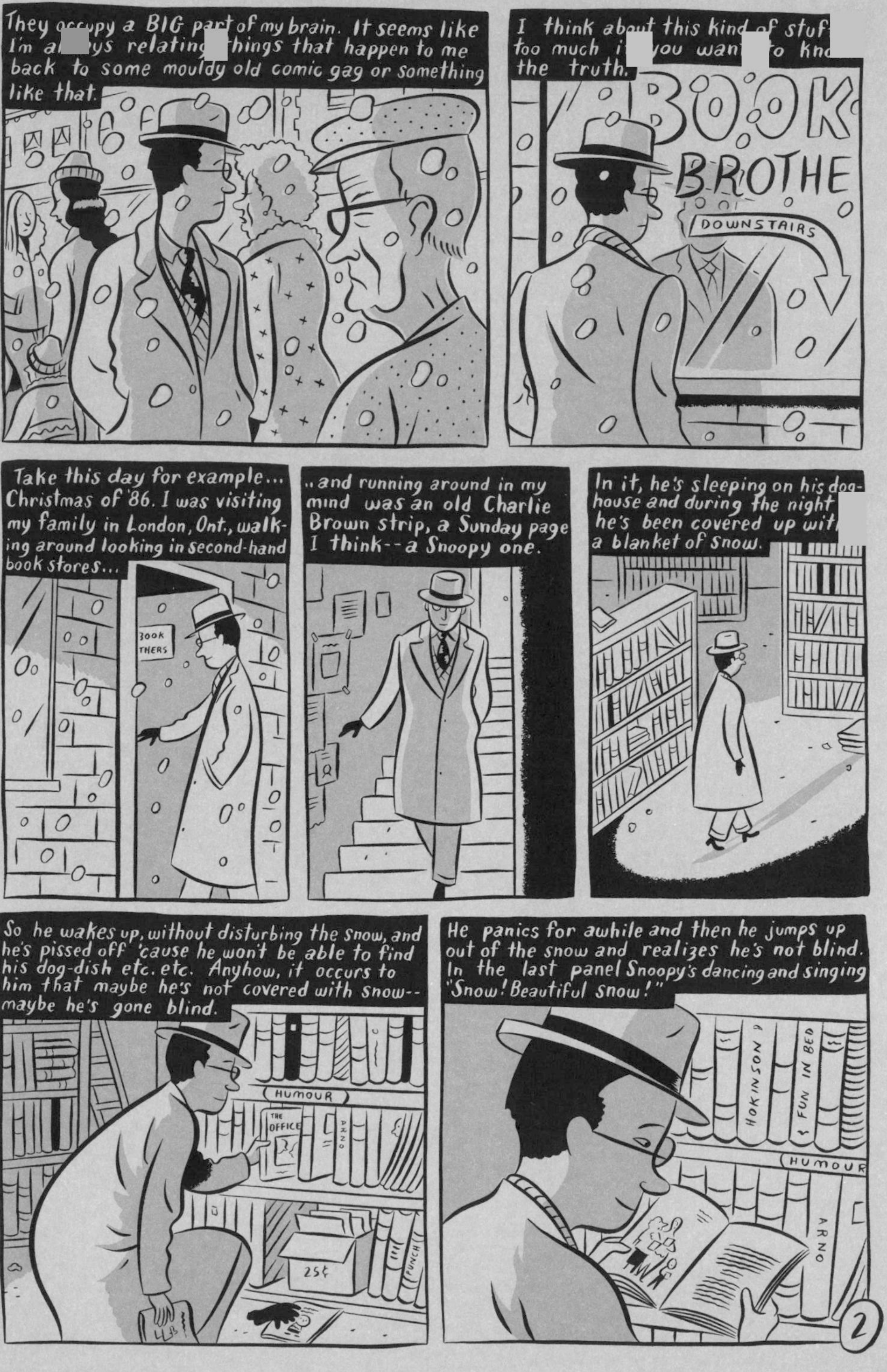
They occupy a BIG part of my brain. It seems like I'm al ys relating things that happen to me back to some mouldy old comic gag or something like that.
I think about this kind of stuf too much i you wan o kn the truth.
BOOK
BROTHE
DOWNSTAIRS
Take this day for example... Christmas of '86. I was visiting my family in London, Ont., walking around looking in second-hand book stores...
BOOK
THERS
..and running around in my mind was an old Charlie Brown strip, a Sunday page I think--a Snoopy one.
In it, he's sleeping on his dog-house and during the night he's been covered up wit a blanket of snow.
So he wakes up, without disturbing the snow, and he's pissed off 'cause he won't be able to find his dog-dish etc. etc. Anyhow, it occurs to him that maybe he's not covered with snow--maybe he's gone blind.
HUMOUR
THE OFFICE
ARNO
25¢
PUNCH
He panics for awhile and then he jumps up out of the snow and realizes he's not blind. In the last panel Snoopy's dancing and singing "Snow! Beautiful snow!"
HOKINSON
FUN IN BED
HUMOUR
ARNO

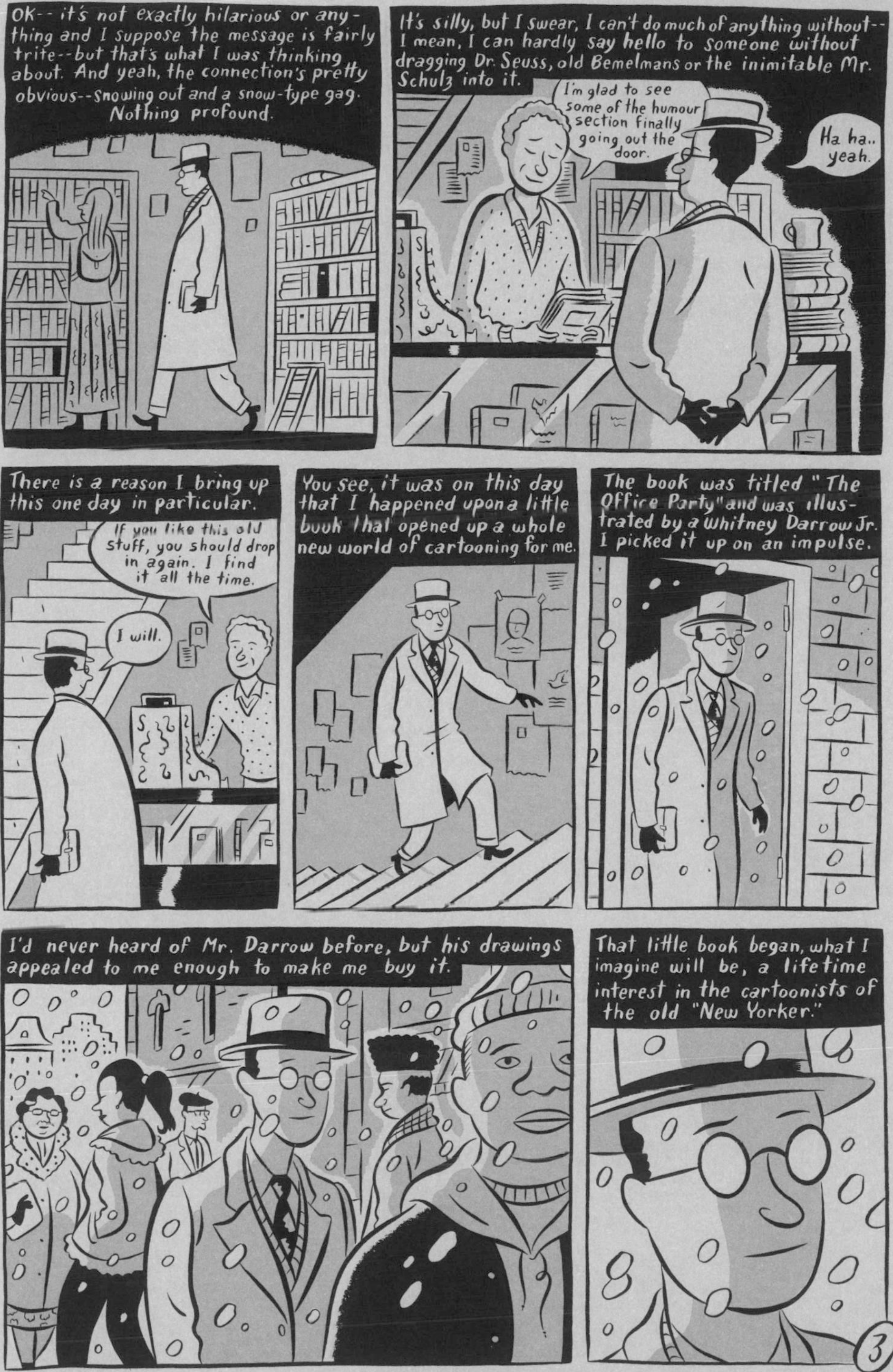
OK-- it's not exactly hilarious or anything and I suppose the message is fairly trite--but that's what I was thinking about. And yeah, the connection's pretty obvious--snowing out and a snow-type gag. Nothing profound.
It's silly, but I swear, I can't do much of anything without-- I mean, I can hardly say hello to someone without dragging Dr. Seuss, old Bemelmans or the inimitable Mr. Schulz into it.
I'm glad to see some of the humour section finally going out the door.
Ha ha.. yeah.
There is a reason I bring up this one day in particular.
If you like this old stuff, you should drop in again. I find it all the time.
I will.
You see, it was on this day that I happened upon a little book that opened up a whole new world of cartooning for me.
The book was titled "The Office Party" and was illustrated by a Whitney Darrow Jr. I picked it up on an impulse.
I'd never heard of Mr. Darrow before, but his drawings appealed to me enough to make me buy it.
That little book began, what I imagine will be, a lifetime interest in the cartoonists of the old "New Yorker."
3

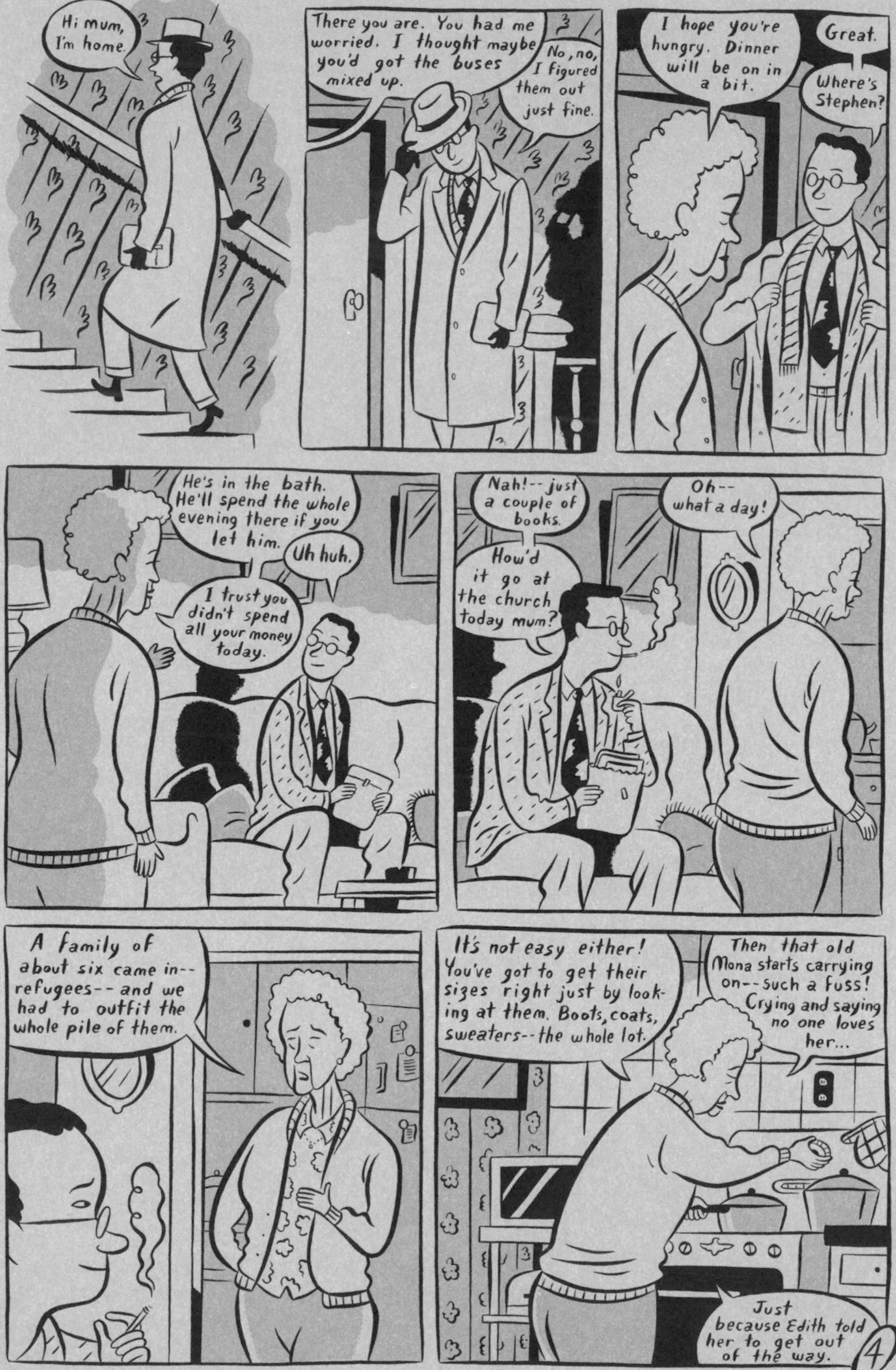

Hi mum, I'm home.
There you are. You had me worried. I thought maybe you'd got the buses mixed up.
No, no, I figured them out just fine.
I hope you're hungry. Dinner will be on in a bit.
Great.
Where's Stephen?
He's in the bath. He'll spend the whole evening there if you let him.
Uh huh.
I trust you didn't spend all your money today.
Nah!-- just a couple of books.
How'd it go at the church today mum?
Oh-- what a day!
A family of about six came in-- refugees-- and we had to outfit the whole pile of them.
It's not easy either! You've got to get their sizes right just by looking at them. Boots, coats, sweaters-- the whole lot.
Then that old Mona starts carrying on-- such a fuss! Crying and saying no one loves her...
Just because Edith told her to get out of the way.

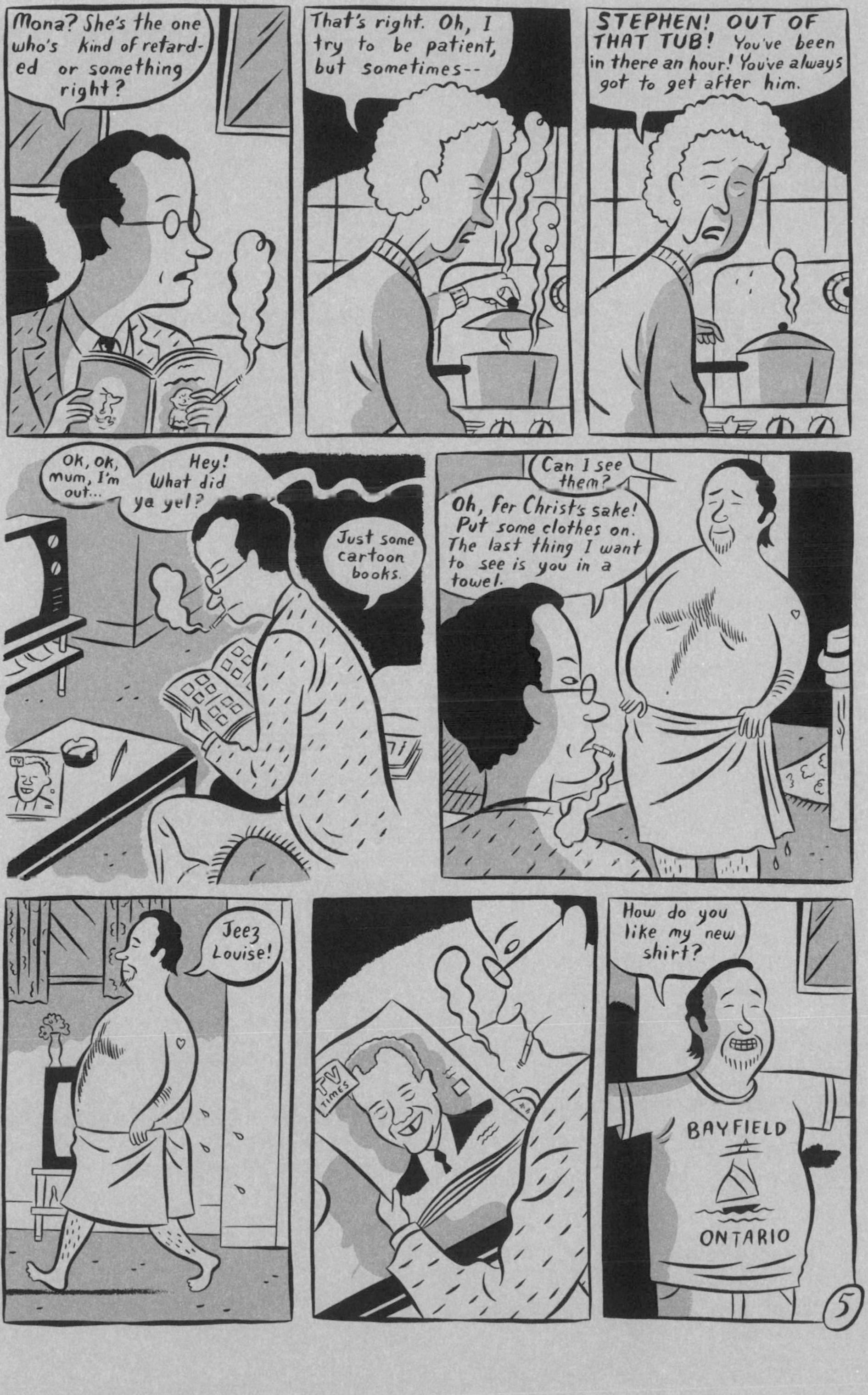
Mona? She's the one who's kind of retard-ed or something right?
That's right. Oh, I try to be patient, but sometimes--
STEPHEN! OUT OF THAT TUB! You've been in there an hour! You've always got to get after him.
Hey! What did ya yel?
OK, OK, mum, I'm out...
Just some cartoon books.
Can I see them?
Oh, fer Christ's sake! Put some clothes on. The last thing I want to see is you in a towel.
Jeez Louise!
TV TIMES
How do you like my new shirt?
BAYFIELD
ONTARIO

Yeah, sure... nice.
Mike got it for me down at the harbour.
Wanna hear a joke--a dry one?
BAYFIELD
ONTARIO
No thank you.
This Newfie, he's calling from a pay-phone see. He goes "I just bought a car from you guys and now I've locked the keys in it.."
BAYFIELD
ONTARIO
And the car dealer, he goes "Ok, we'll send someone over in about a half an hour or so."
BAYFIELD
So the Newfie says "You'd better hurry it up boys, it's starting to rain and I've got the top down!"
HA HA HA HA
That's a hoot Steve.
Well, they all thought it was funny down at the station-- even the Chief laughed.
He said "yer one of a kind Steve."
I'll bet.
Once, I was mopping up the cells and one of the officers locked me in... said I was a menace to society.
Heard it. You already told me.
CLICK

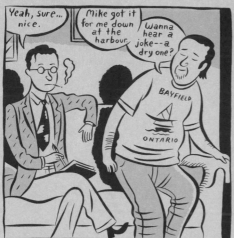

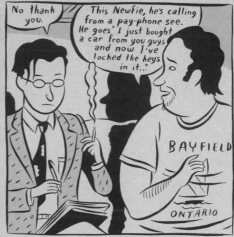

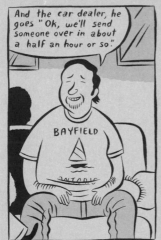

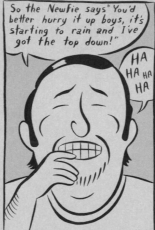

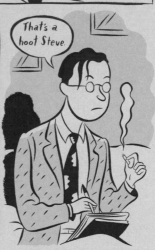

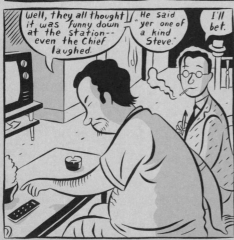

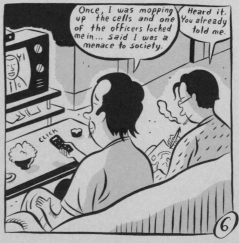

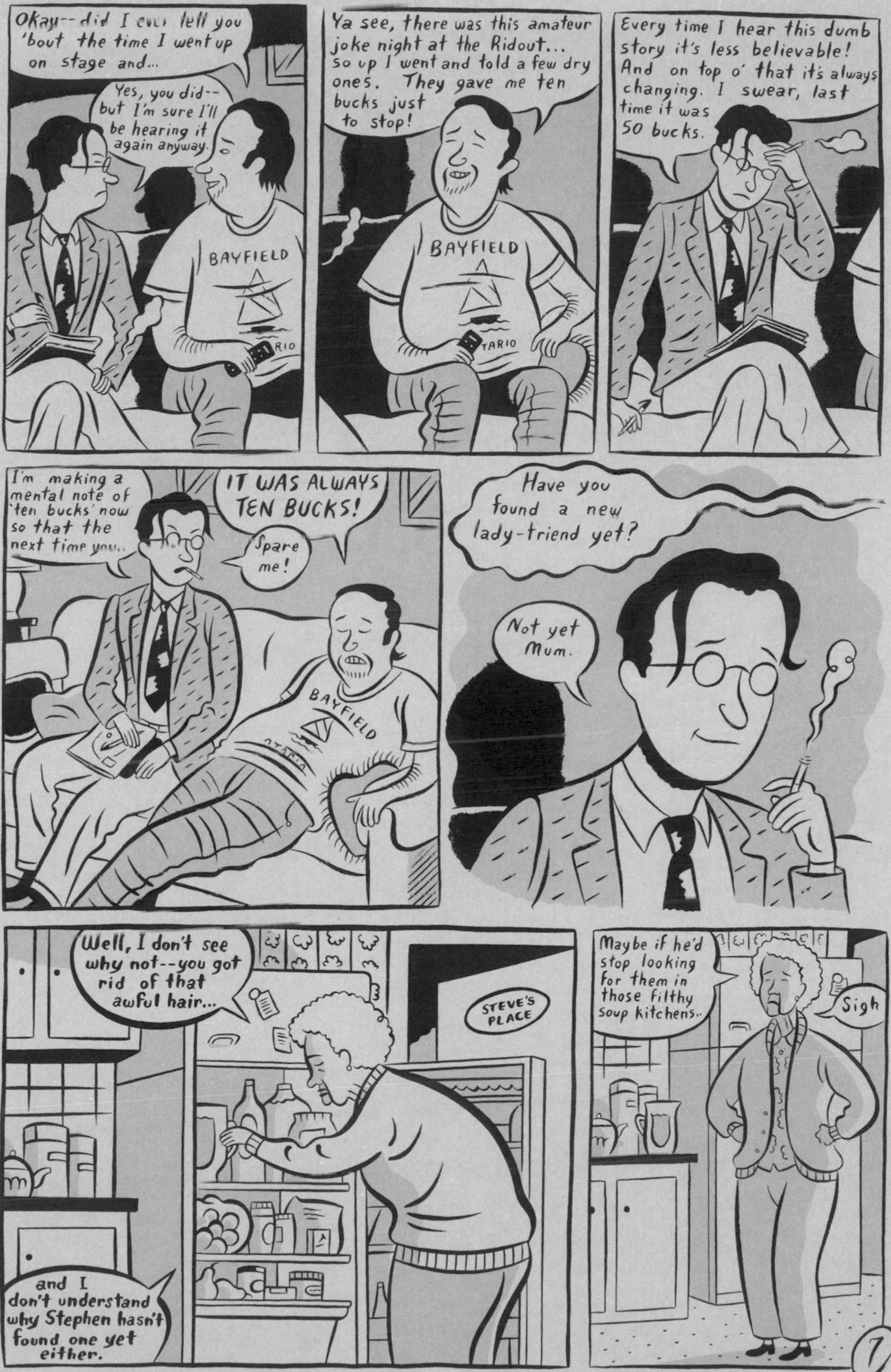

Okay--did I ever tell you 'bout the time I went up on stage and...
Yes, you did-- but I'm sure I'll be hearing it again anyway.
BAYFIELD
Ya see, there was this amateur joke night at the Ridout... so up I went and told a few dry ones. They gave me ten bucks just to stop!
BAYFIELD
Every time I hear this dumb story it's less believable! And on top o' that it's always changing. I swear, last time it was 50 bucks.
I'm making a mental note of 'ten bucks' now so that the next time you...
IT WAS ALWAYS TEN BUCKS!
Spare me!
BAYFIELD
Have you found a new lady-friend yet?
Not yet Mum.
Well, I don't see why not--you got rid of that awful hair...
STEVE'S PLACE
and I don't understand why Stephen hasn't found one yet either.
Maybe if he'd stop looking for them in those filthy soup kitchens...
Sigh

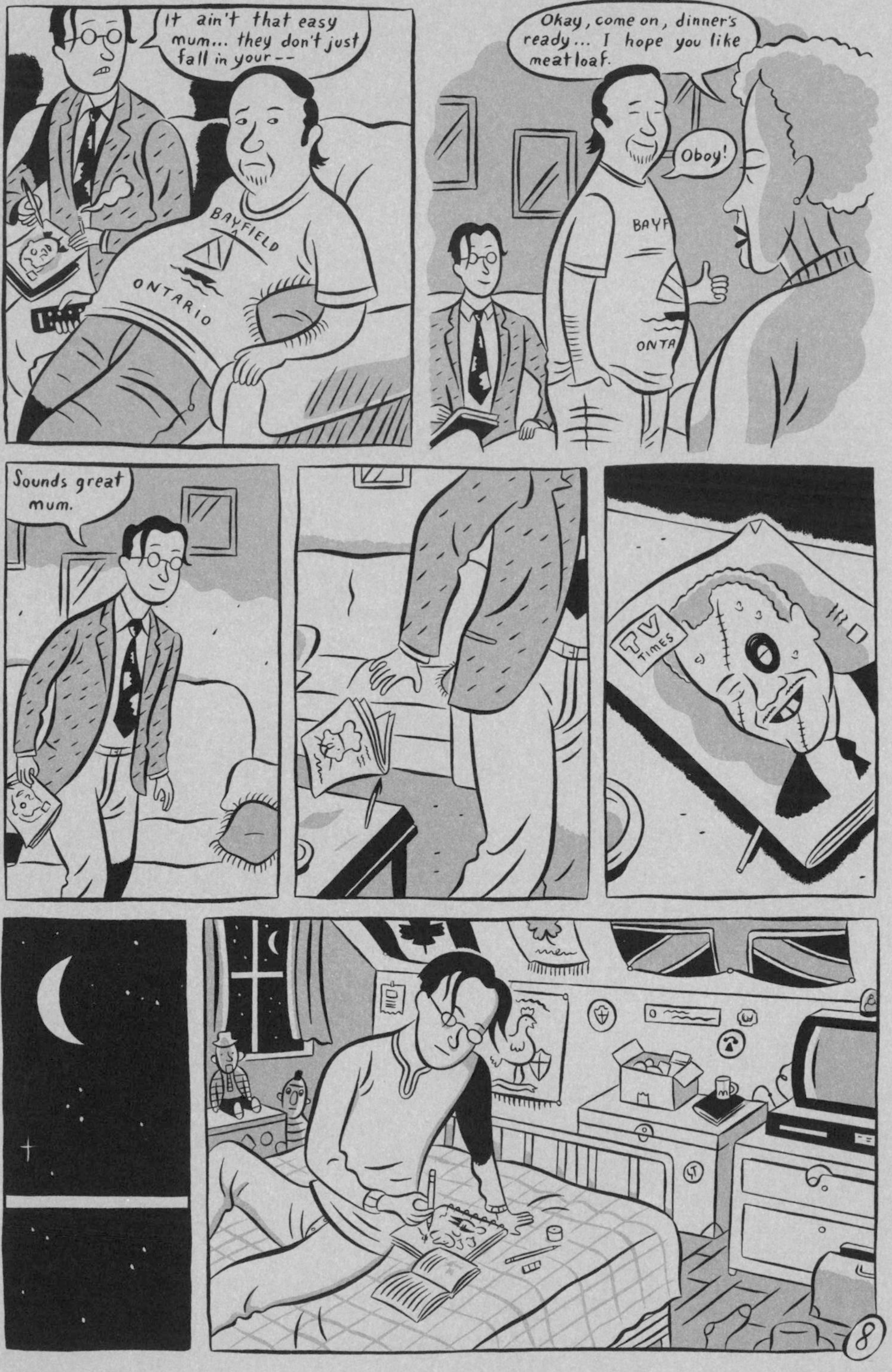
It ain't that easy mum... they don't just fall in your--
BAYFIELD
ONTARIO
Okay, come on, dinner's ready... I hope you like meatloaf.
Oboy!
BAYF
ONTA
Sounds great mum.
TV TIMES
8

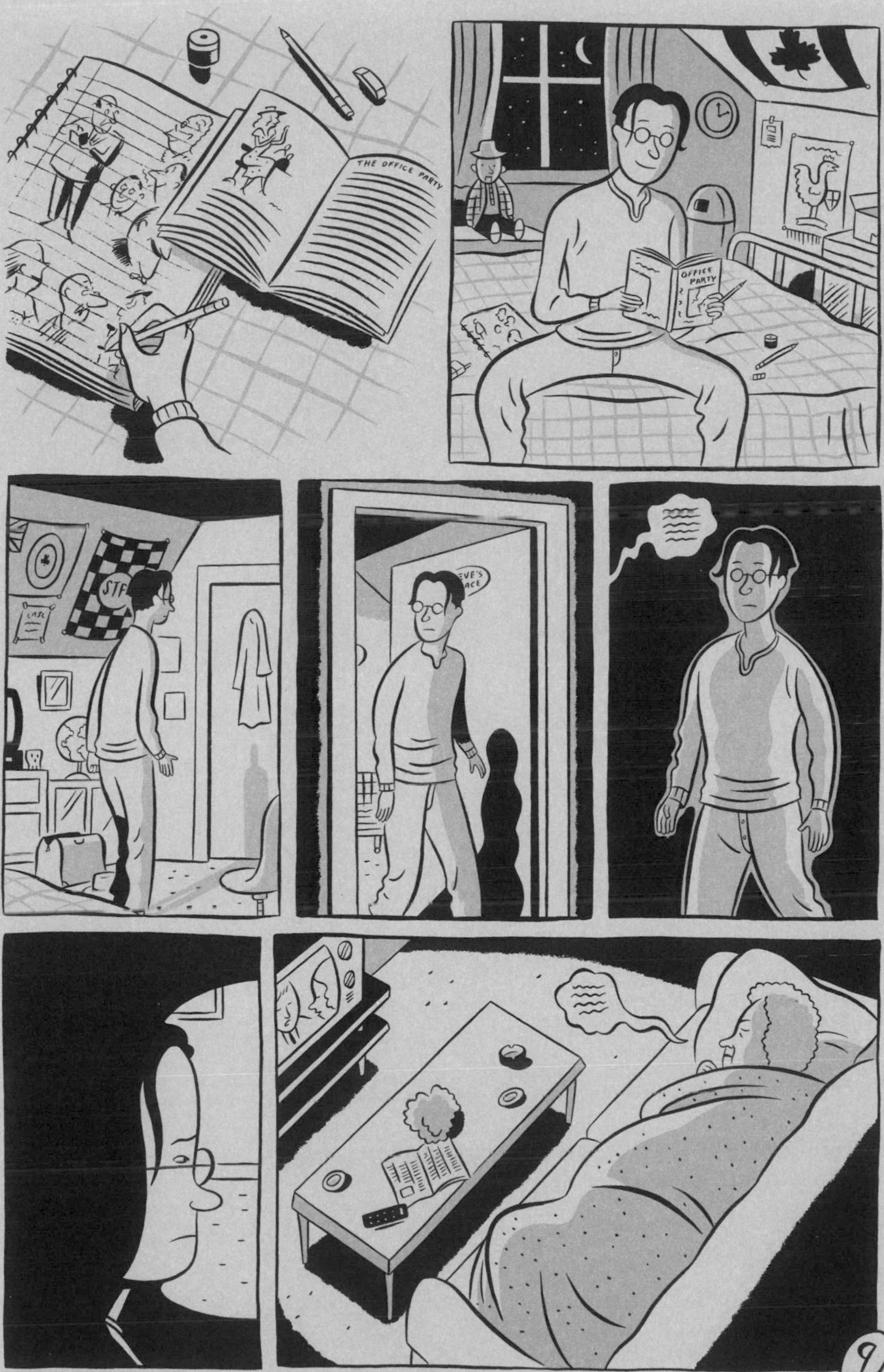
THE OFFICE PARTY
OFFICE PARTY

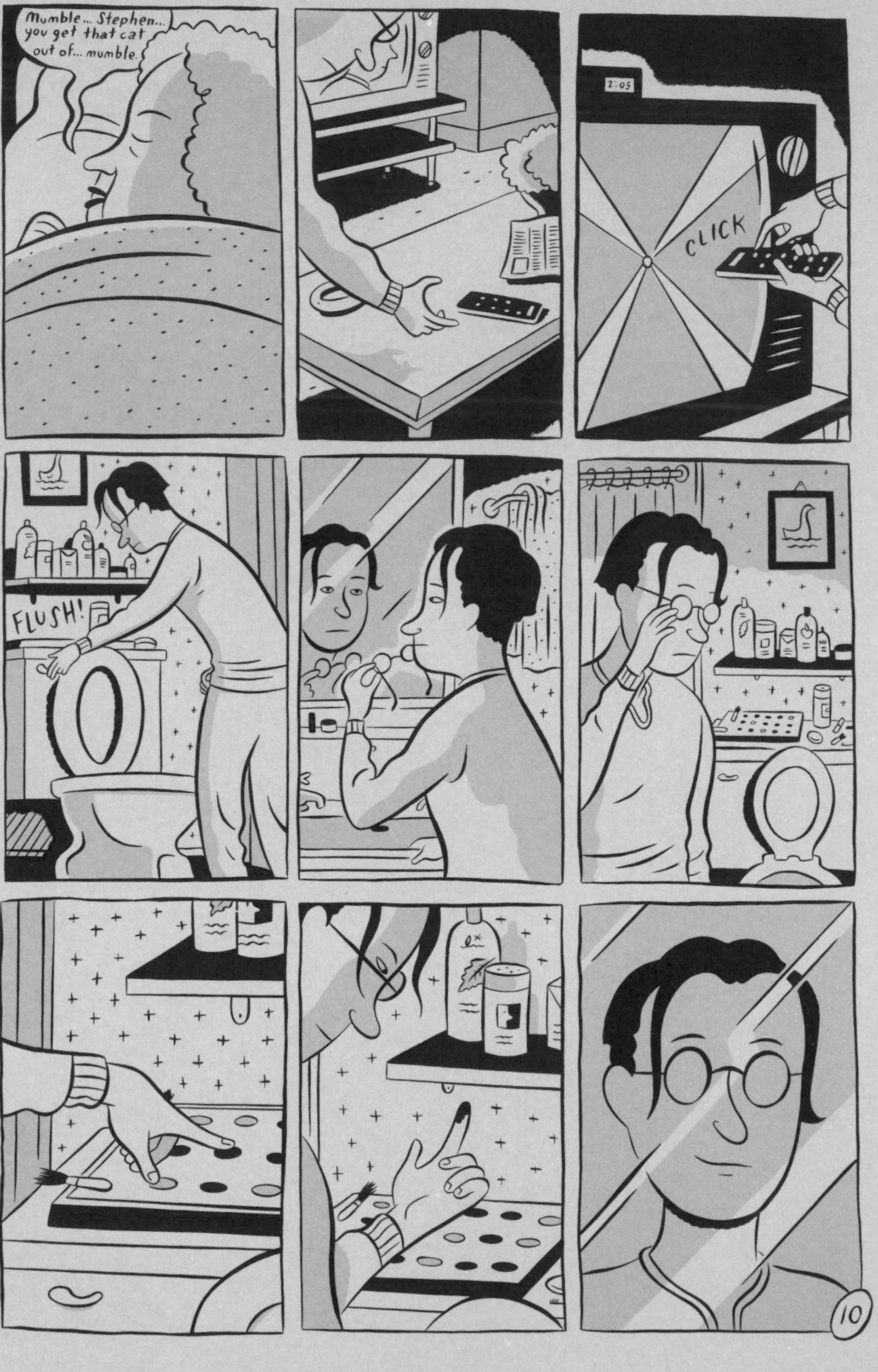
Mumble... Stephen... you get that cat out of... mumble.
2:05
CLICK
FLUSH!
10

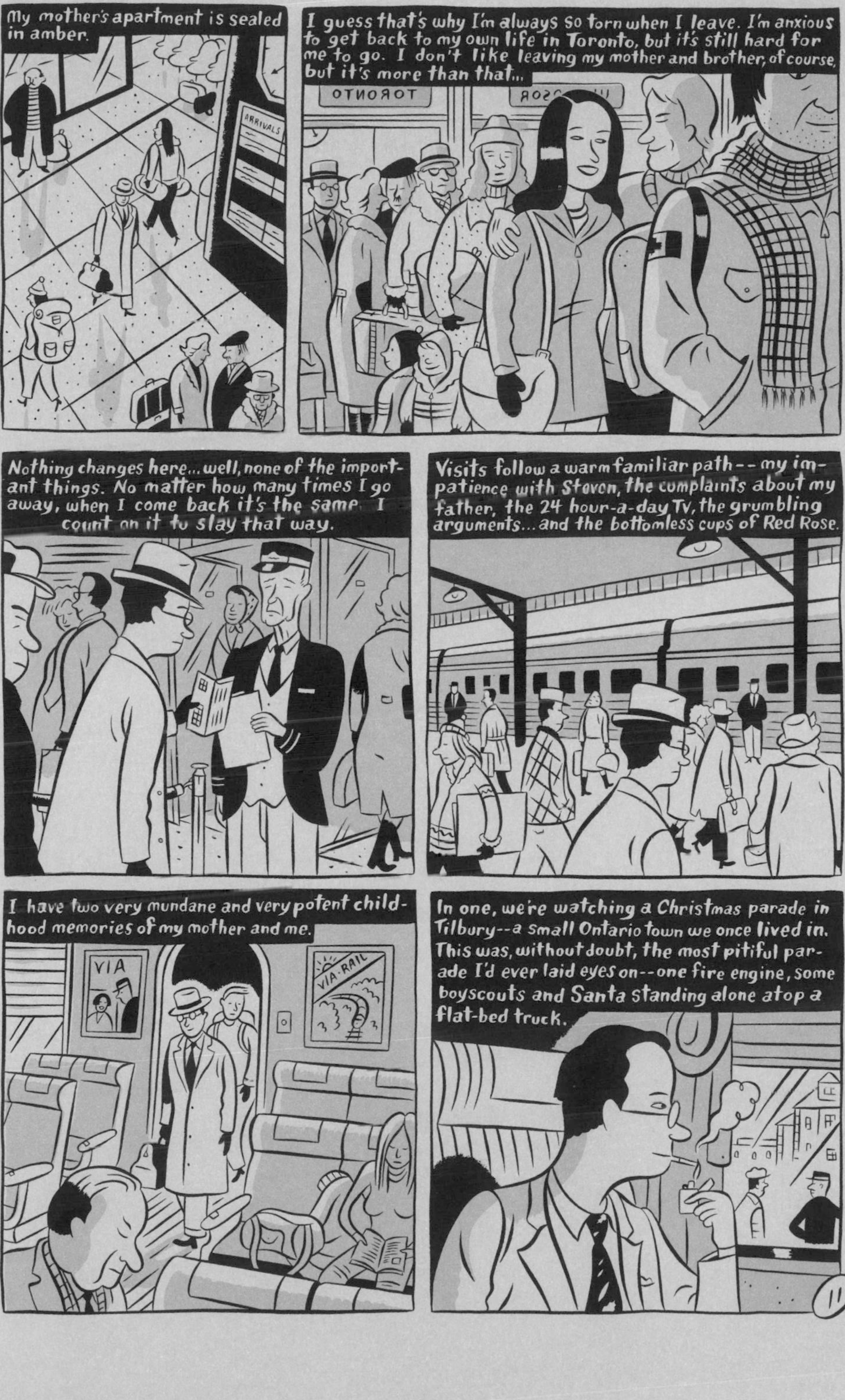
My mother's apartment is sealed in amber.
ARRIVALS
I guess that's why I'm always so torn when I leave. I'm anxious to get back to my own life in Toronto, but it's still hard for me to go. I don't like leaving my mother and brother, of course, but it's more than that...
TORONTO
Nothing changes here... well, none of the important things. No matter how many times I go away, when I come back it's the same. I count on it to stay that way.
Visits follow a warm familiar path-- my impatience with Steven, the complaints about my father, the 24 hour-a-day TV, the grumbling arguments... and the bottomless cups of Red Rose.
I have two very mundane and very potent childhood memories of my mother and me.
VIA
VIA·RAIL
In one, we're watching a Christmas parade in Tilbury--a small Ontario town we once lived in. This was, without doubt, the most pitiful parade I'd ever laid eyes on--one fire engine, some boyscouts and Santa standing alone atop a flat-bed truck.

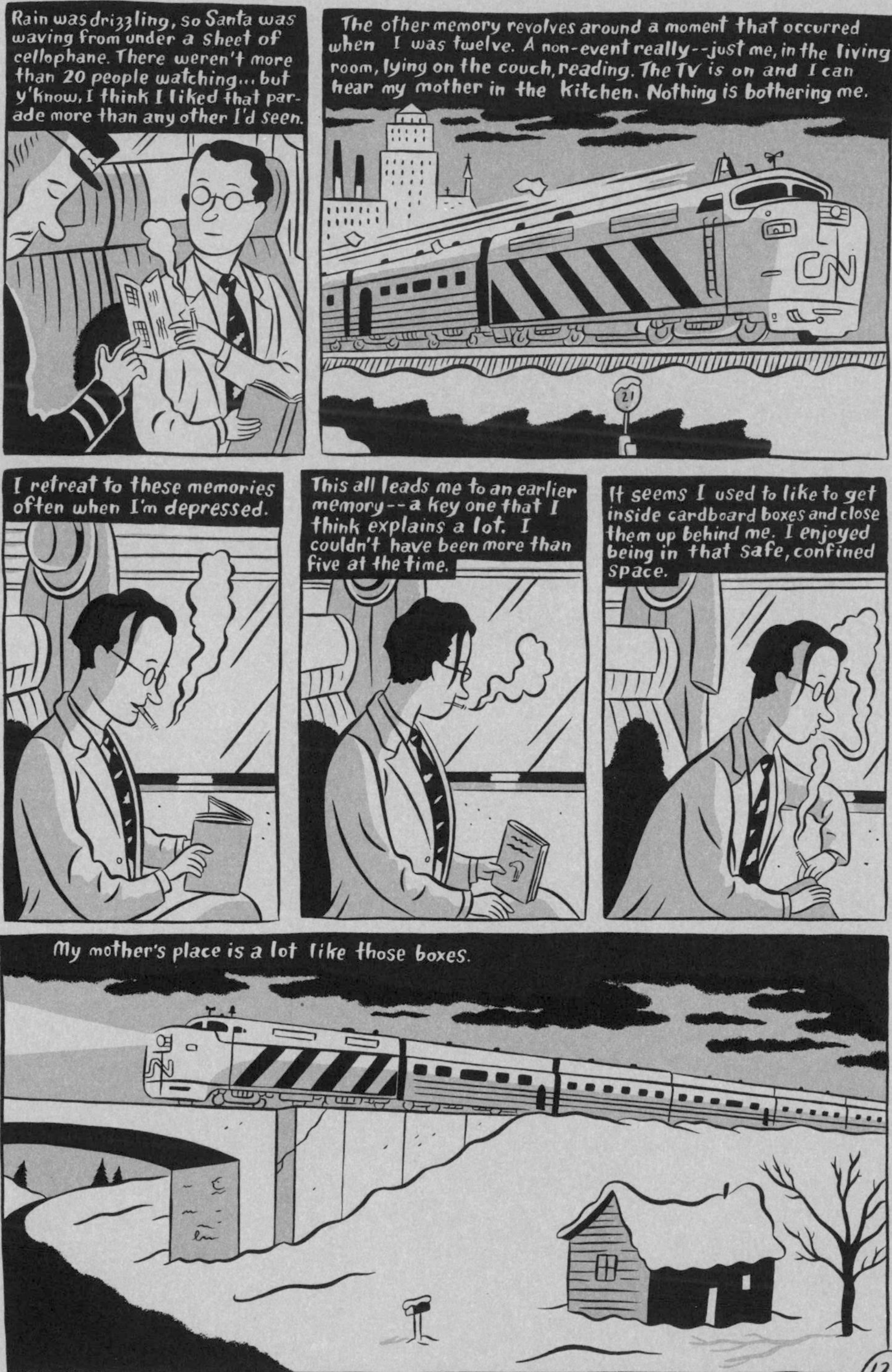

Rain was drizzling, so Santa was waving from under a sheet of cellophane. There weren't more than 20 people watching... but y'know, I think I liked that parade more than any other I'd seen.
The other memory revolves around a moment that occurred when I was twelve. A non-event really--just me, in the living room, lying on the couch, reading. The TV is on and I can hear my mother in the kitchen. Nothing is bothering me.
CN
21
I retreat to these memories often when I'm depressed.
This all leads me to an earlier memory--a key one that I think explains a lot. I couldn't have been more than five at the time.
It seems I used to like to get inside cardboard boxes and close them up behind me. I enjoyed being in that safe, confined space.
My mother's place is a lot like those boxes.

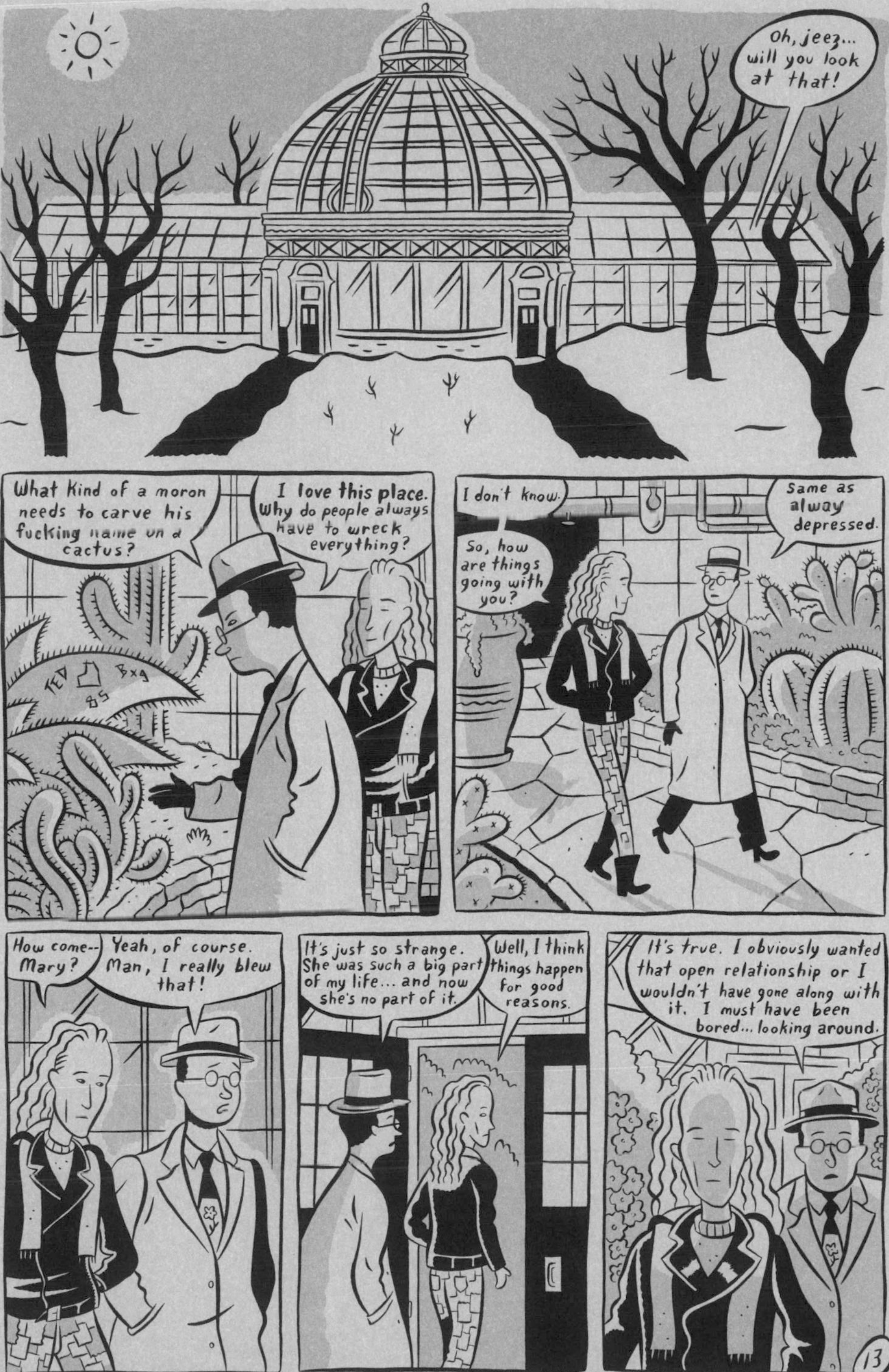

Oh, jeez... will you look at that!
What kind of a moron needs to carve his fucking name on a cactus?
I love this place. Why do people always have to wreck everything?
TEV Bxg 85
I don't know.
So, how are things going with you?
Same as alway depressed.
How come-- Mary?
Yeah, of course. Man, I really blew that!
It's just so strange. She was such a big part of my life... and now she's no part of it.
Well, I think things happen for good reasons.
It's true. I obviously wanted that open relationship or I wouldn't have gone along with it. I must have been bored... looking around.

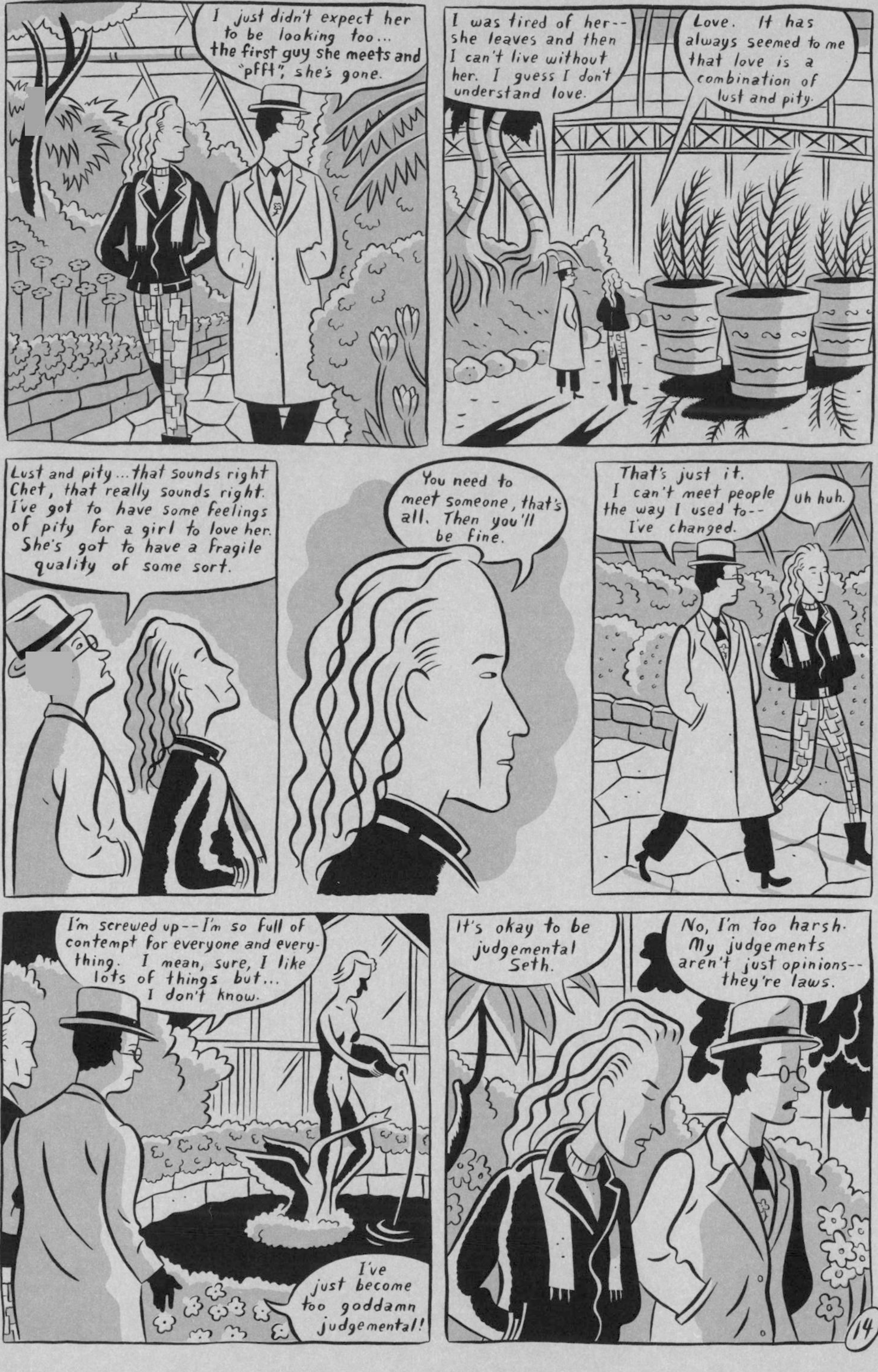
I just didn't expect her to be looking too... the first guy she meets and "pfft", she's gone.
I was tired of her-- she leaves and then I can't live without her. I guess I don't understand love.
Love. It has always seemed to me that love is a combination of lust and pity.
Lust and pity... that sounds right Chet, that really sounds right. I've got to have some feelings of pity for a girl to love her. She's got to have a fragile quality of some sort.
You need to meet someone, that's all. Then you'll be fine.
That's just it. I can't meet people the way I used to-- I've changed.
Uh huh.
I'm screwed up--I'm so full of contempt for everyone and everything. I mean, sure, I like lots of things but... I don't know.
I've just become too goddamn judgemental!
It's okay to be judgemental Seth.
No, I'm too harsh. My judgements aren't just opinions-- they're laws.

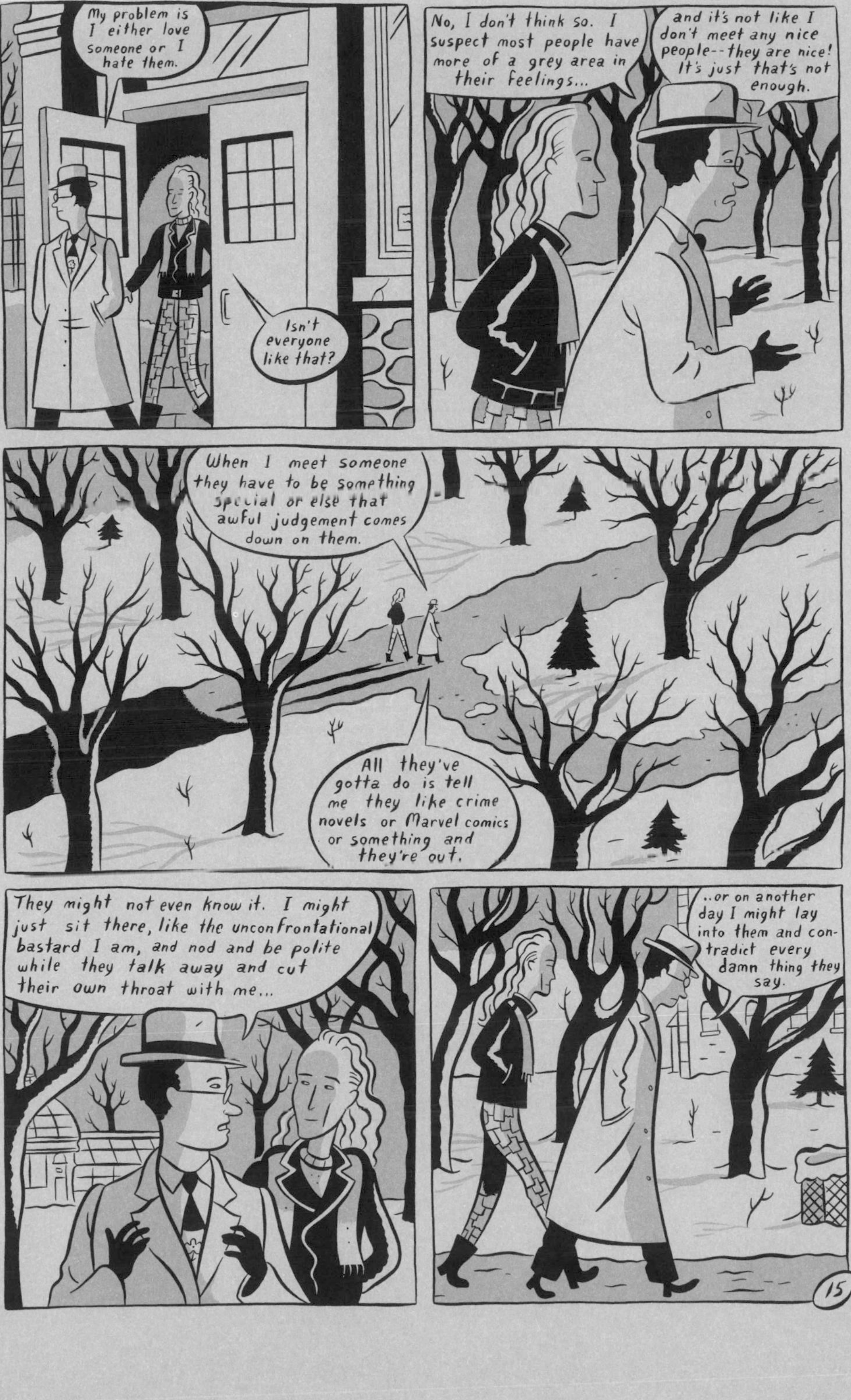
My problem is I either love someone or I hate them.
Isn't everyone like that?
No, I don't think so. I suspect most people have more of a grey area in their feelings...
and it's not like I don't meet any nice people--they are nice! It's just that's not enough.
When I meet someone they have to be something special or else that awful judgement comes down on them.
All they've gotta do is tell me they like crime novels or Marvel comics or something and they're out.
They might not even know it. I might just sit there, like the unconfrontational bastard I am, and nod and be polite while they talk away and cut their own throat with me...
..or on another day I might lay into them and contradict every damn thing they say.
15

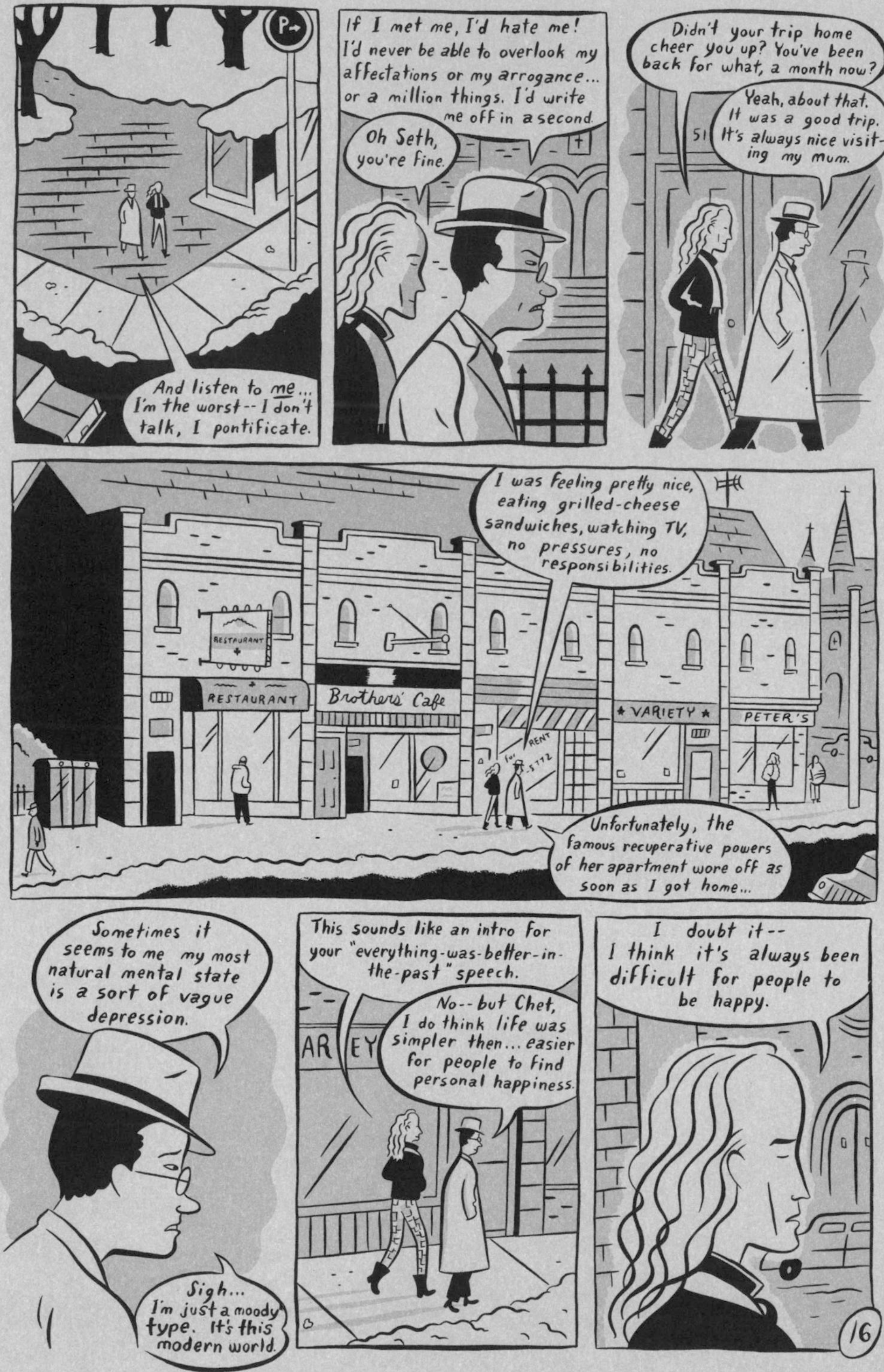
And listen to me... I'm the worst--I don't talk, I pontificate.
If I met me, I'd hate me! I'd never be able to overlook my affectations or my arrogance... or a million things. I'd write me off in a second.
Oh Seth, you're fine.
Didn't your trip home cheer you up? You've been back for what, a month now?
Yeah, about that. It was a good trip. It's always nice visiting my mum.
51
I was feeling pretty nice, eating grilled-cheese sandwiches, watching TV, no pressures, no responsibilities.
RESTAURANT
RESTAURANT
Brothers' Cafe
FOR RENT
VARIETY
PETER'S
Unfortunately, the famous recuperative powers of her apartment wore off as soon as I got home...
Sometimes it seems to me my most natural mental state is a sort of vague depression.
Sigh... I'm just a moody type. It's this modern world.
This sounds like an intro for your "everything-was-better-in-the-past" speech.
No--but Chet, I do think life was simpler then... easier for people to find personal happiness.
I doubt it-- I think it's always been difficult for people to be happy.
16

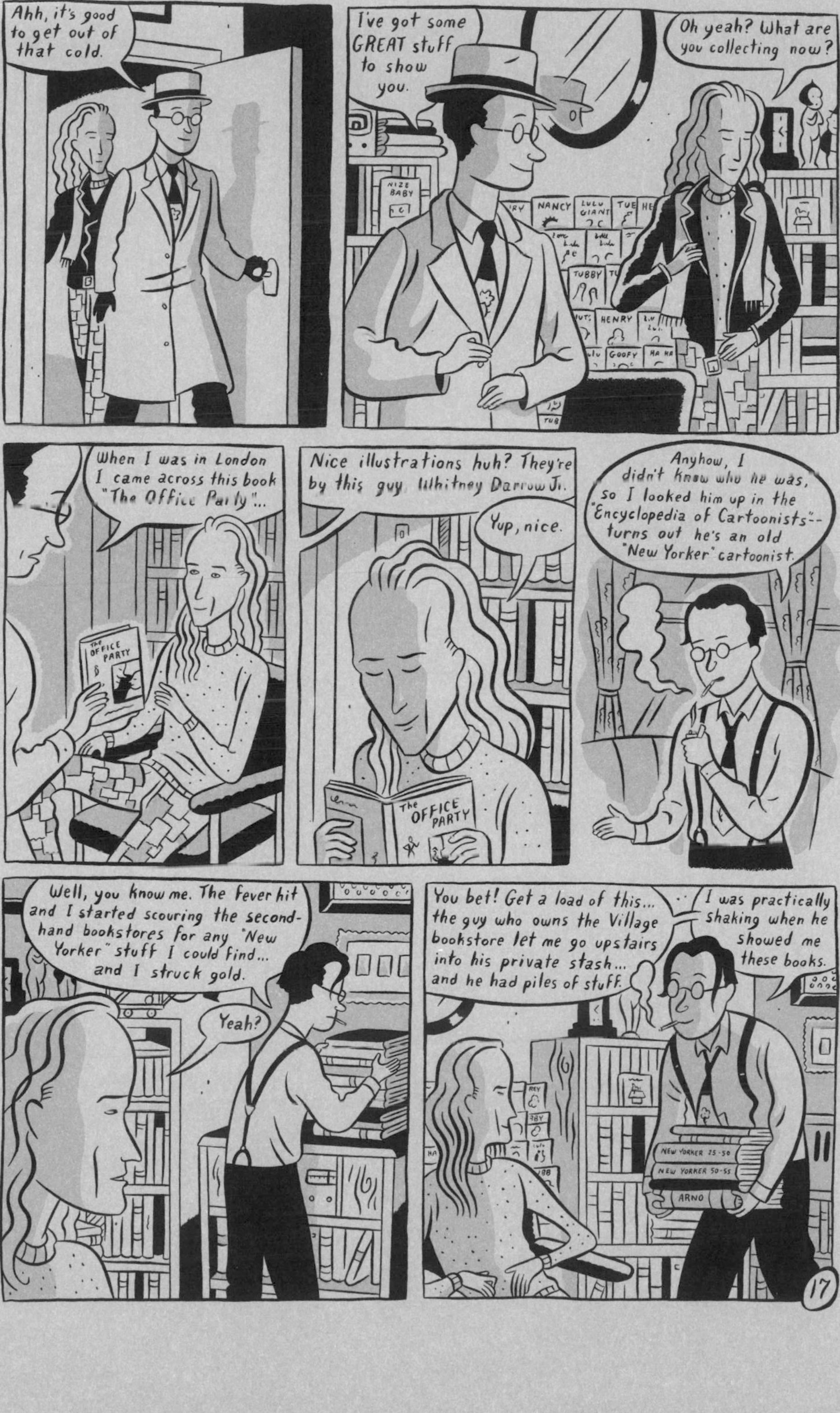
Ahh, it's good to get out of that cold.
I've got some GREAT stuff to show you.
Oh yeah? What are you collecting now?
NIZE BABY
NANCY
LULU GIANT
TUBBY
HENRY
GOOFY
HA HA
When I was in London I came across this book "The Office Party"...
THE OFFICE PARTY
Nice illustrations huh? They're by this guy Whitney Darrow Jr.
Yup, nice.
THE OFFICE PARTY
Anyhow, I didn't know who he was, so I looked him up in the "Encyclopedia of Cartoonists"-- turns out he's an old "New Yorker" cartoonist.
Well, you know me. The fever hit and I started scouring the second-hand bookstores for any "New Yorker" stuff I could find... and I struck gold.
Yeah?
You bet! Get a load of this... the guy who owns the Village bookstore let me go upstairs into his private stash... and he had piles of stuff.
I was practically shaking when he showed me these books.
NEW YORKER 25-50
NEW YORKER 50-55
ARNO

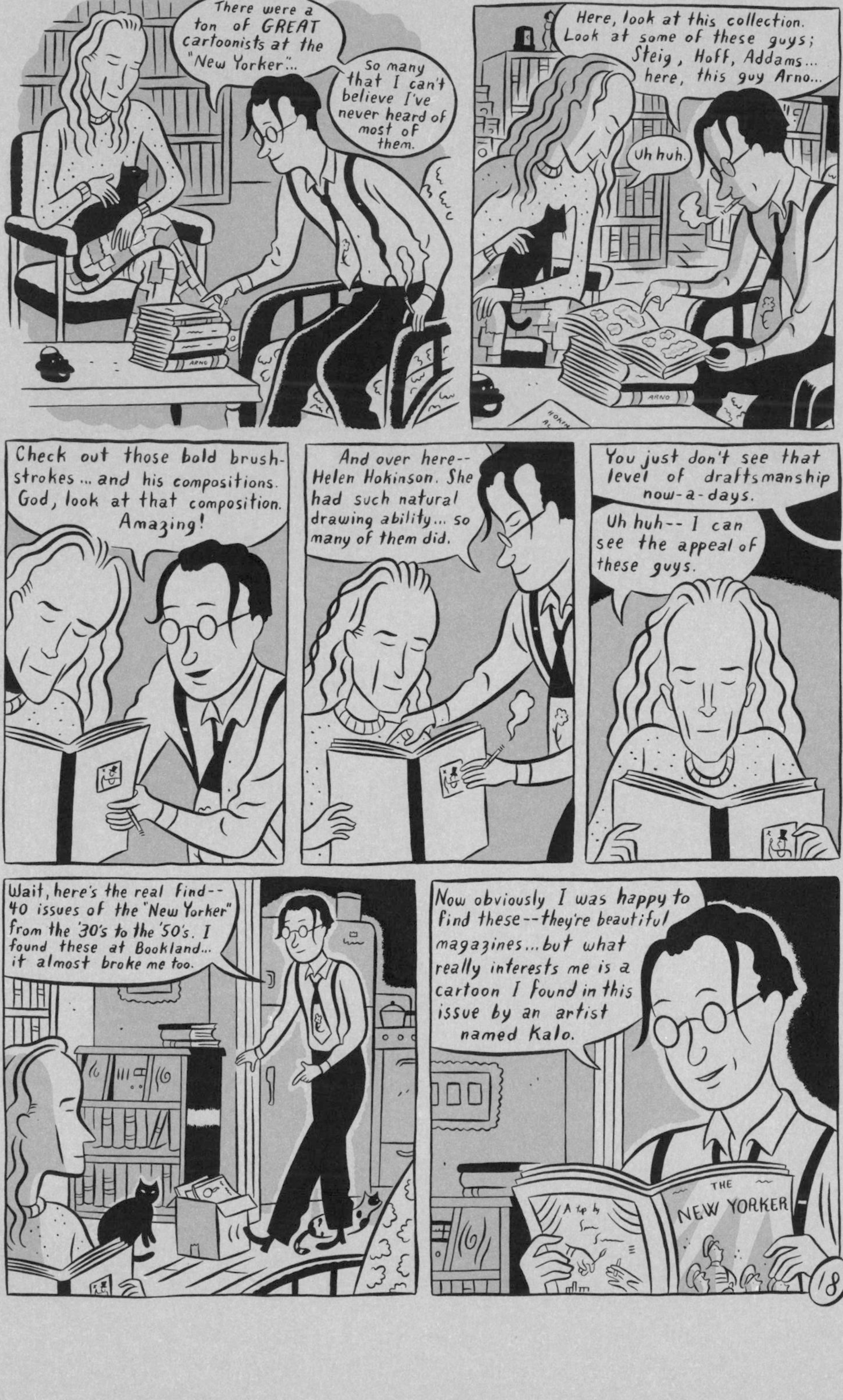

There were a ton of GREAT cartoonists at the "New Yorker"...
So many that I can't believe I've never heard of most of them.
ARNO
Here, look at this collection. Look at some of these guys; Steig, Hoff, Addams... here, this guy Arno...
Uh huh.
ARNO
Check out those bold brush-strokes... and his compositions. God, look at that composition. Amazing!
And over here-- Helen Hokinson. She had such natural drawing ability... so many of them did.
You just don't see that level of draftsmanship now-a-days.
Uh huh-- I can see the appeal of these guys.
Wait, here's the real find-- 40 issues of the "New Yorker" from the '30's to the '50's. I found these at Bookland... it almost broke me too.
Now obviously I was happy to find these--they're beautiful magazines... but what really interests me is a cartoon I found in this issue by an artist named Kalo.
THE NEW YORKER

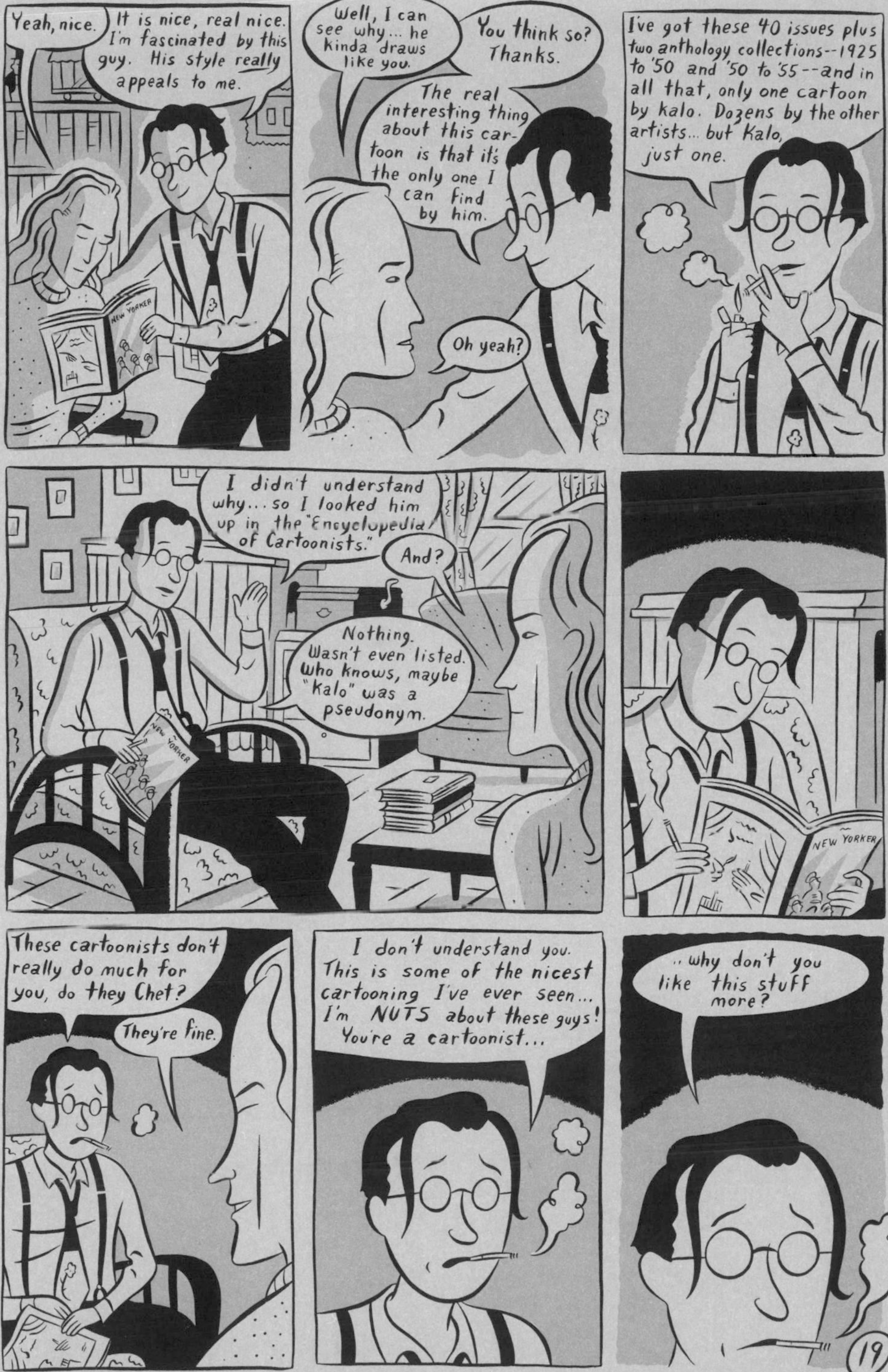

Yeah, nice.
It is nice, real nice. I'm fascinated by this guy. His style really appeals to me.
Well, I can see why... he kinda draws like you.
You think so? Thanks.
The real interesting thing about this cartoon is that it's the only one I can find by him.
Oh yeah?
I've got these 40 issues plus two anthology collections--1925 to '50 and '50 to '55--and in all that, only one cartoon by kalo. Dozens by the other artists... but Kalo, just one.
I didn't understand why... so I looked him up in the "Encyclopedia of Cartoonists."
And?
Nothing. Wasn't even listed. Who knows, maybe "kalo" was a pseudonym.
These cartoonists don't really do much for you, do they Chet?
They're fine.
I don't understand you. This is some of the nicest cartooning I've ever seen... I'm NUTS about these guys! You're a cartoonist...
..why don't you like this stuff more?

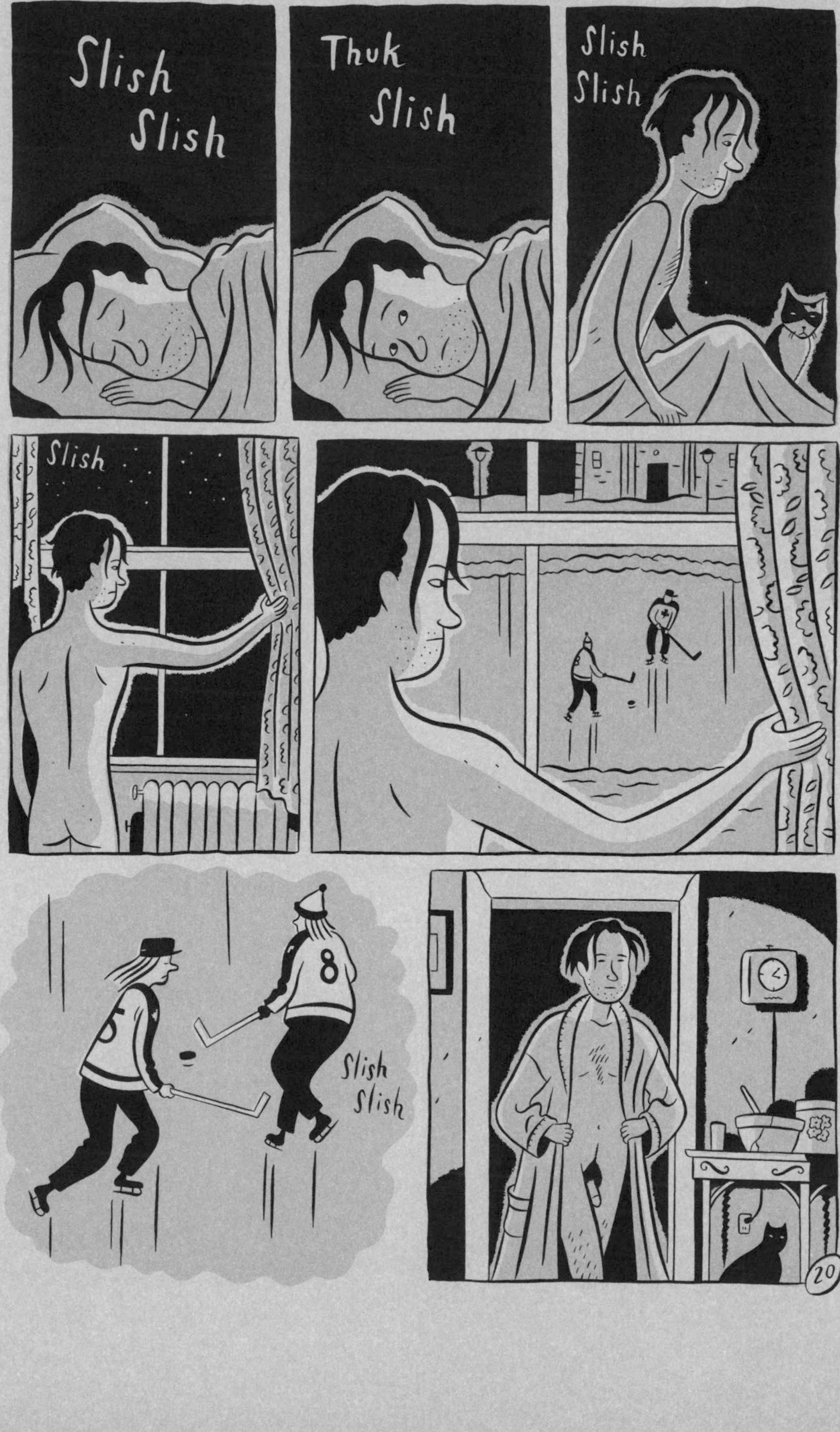
Slish
Slish
Thuk
Slish
Slish
Slish
Slish
Slish
Slish

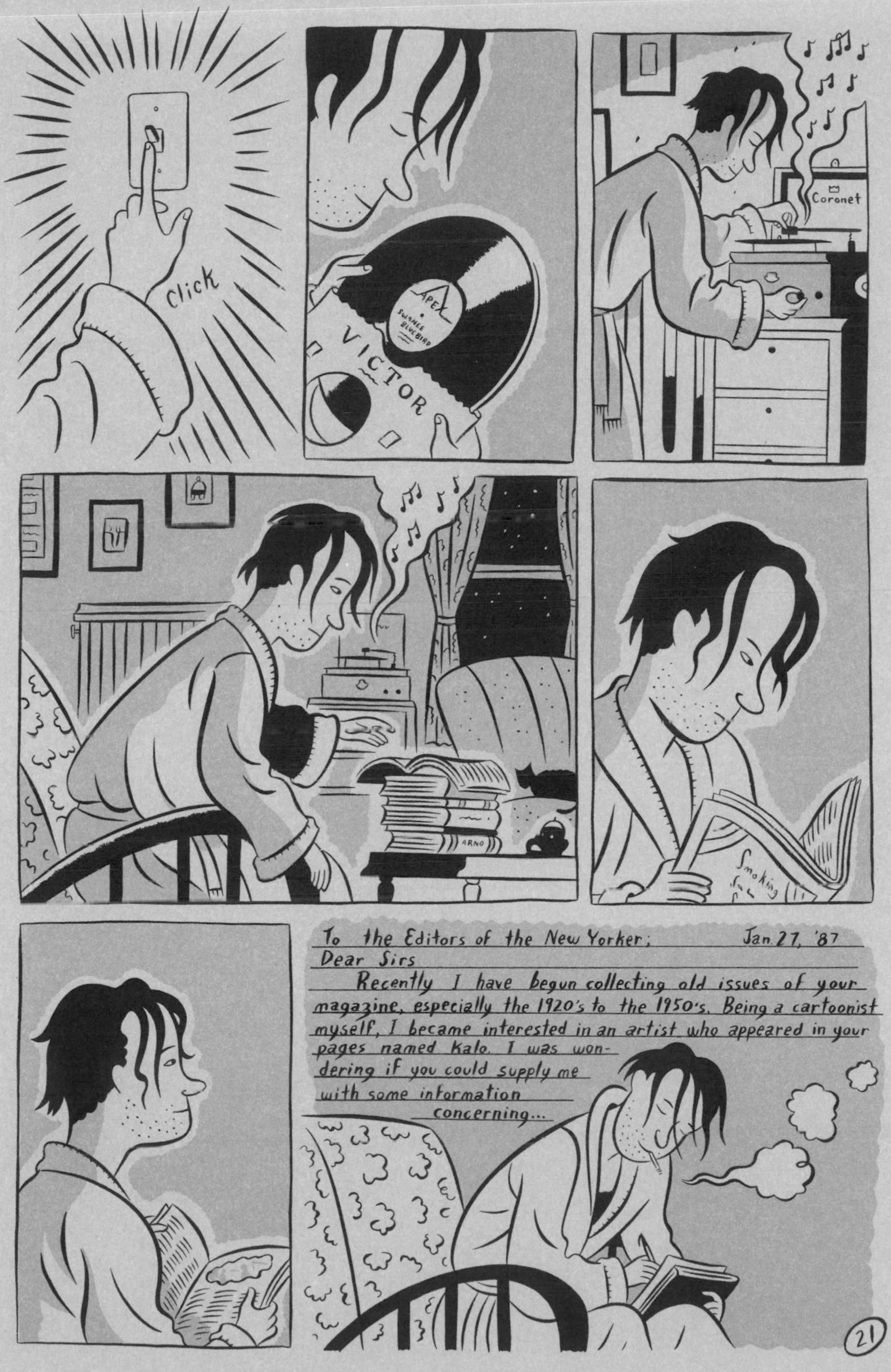
Click
APEX
SWANEE BLUEBIRD
VICTOR
Coronet
ARNO
To the Editors of the New Yorker; Jan. 27, '87
Dear Sirs
Recently I have begun collecting old issues of your magazine, especially the 1920's to the 1950's. Being a cartoonist myself, I became interested in an artist who appeared in your pages named Kalo. I was wondering if you could supply me with some information concerning...

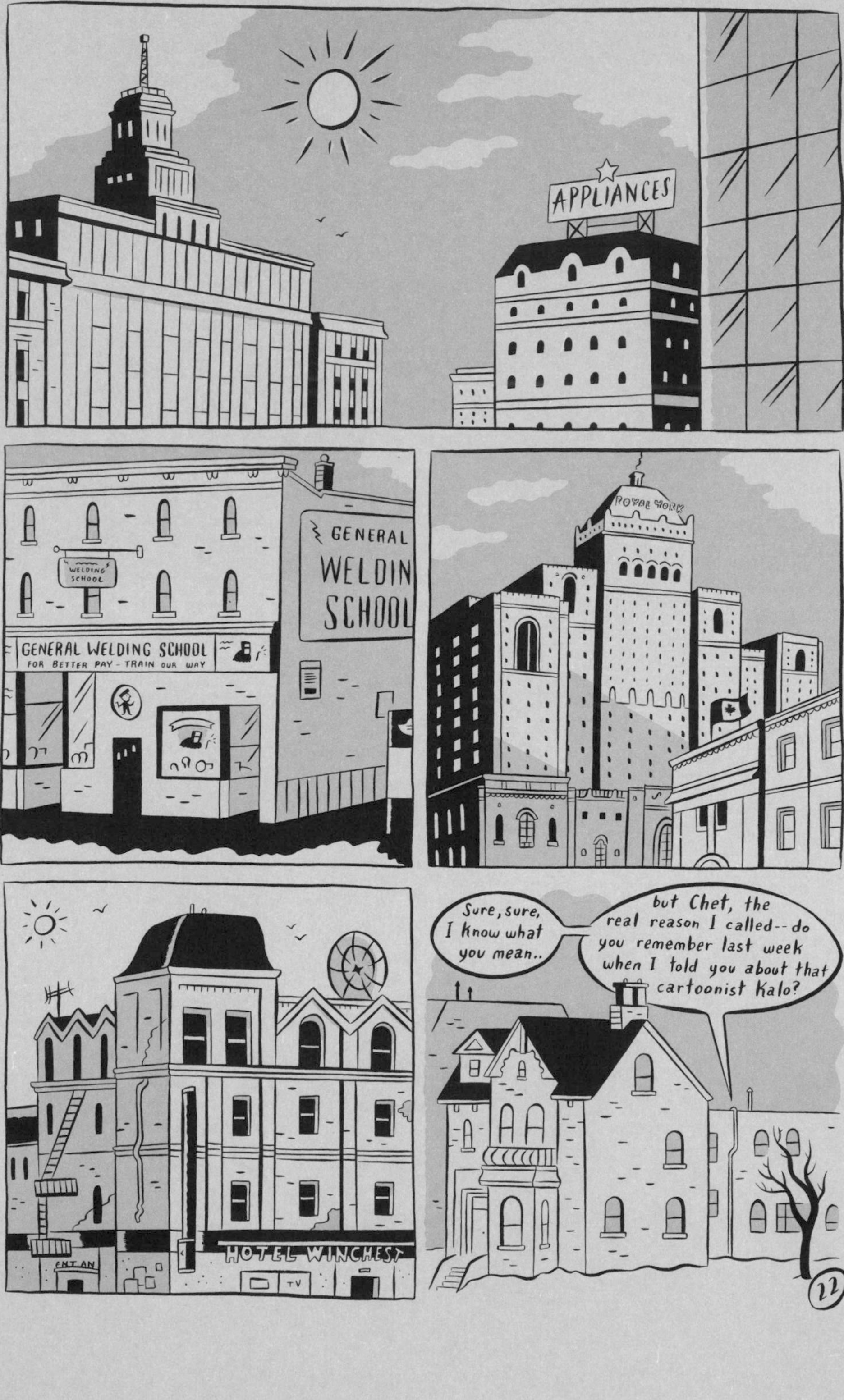
APPLIANCES
GENERAL WELDING SCHOOL
WELDING SCHOOL
GENERAL WELDING SCHOOL
FOR BETTER PAY - TRAIN OUR WAY
ROYAL YORK
HOTEL WINCHEST
TV
Sure, sure, I know what you mean..
but Chet, the real reason I called-- do you remember last week when I told you about that cartoonist Kalo?
22

Uh huh, well, I went out looking for more gag cartoon stuff. I decided to branch out and start buying other old magazines.

You guessed it... a terrific find! It's an old gag magazine from '48. An anthology-- a few cartoons by each guy. And get this--three full-page cartoons by Kalo.

One's even a strip.

Yeah, beautiful stuff. I also found two more "New Yorker" collections, one 35 to 65 and the other one is sports gags. No Kalos in them at all.

I tell you, there's something very interesting about this guy. I don't know what it is but I intend to find out.

Oh, I have a couple of ideas.

Okay Chet, I guess I'll let you go. Talk to you later-- bye bye.

MROW

Boris... what is it? You feelin' lonely boy?

Look at you Bo-bo... you big ol' fat cat you.

What would I do without you? You're the best thing that ever happened to me.

23

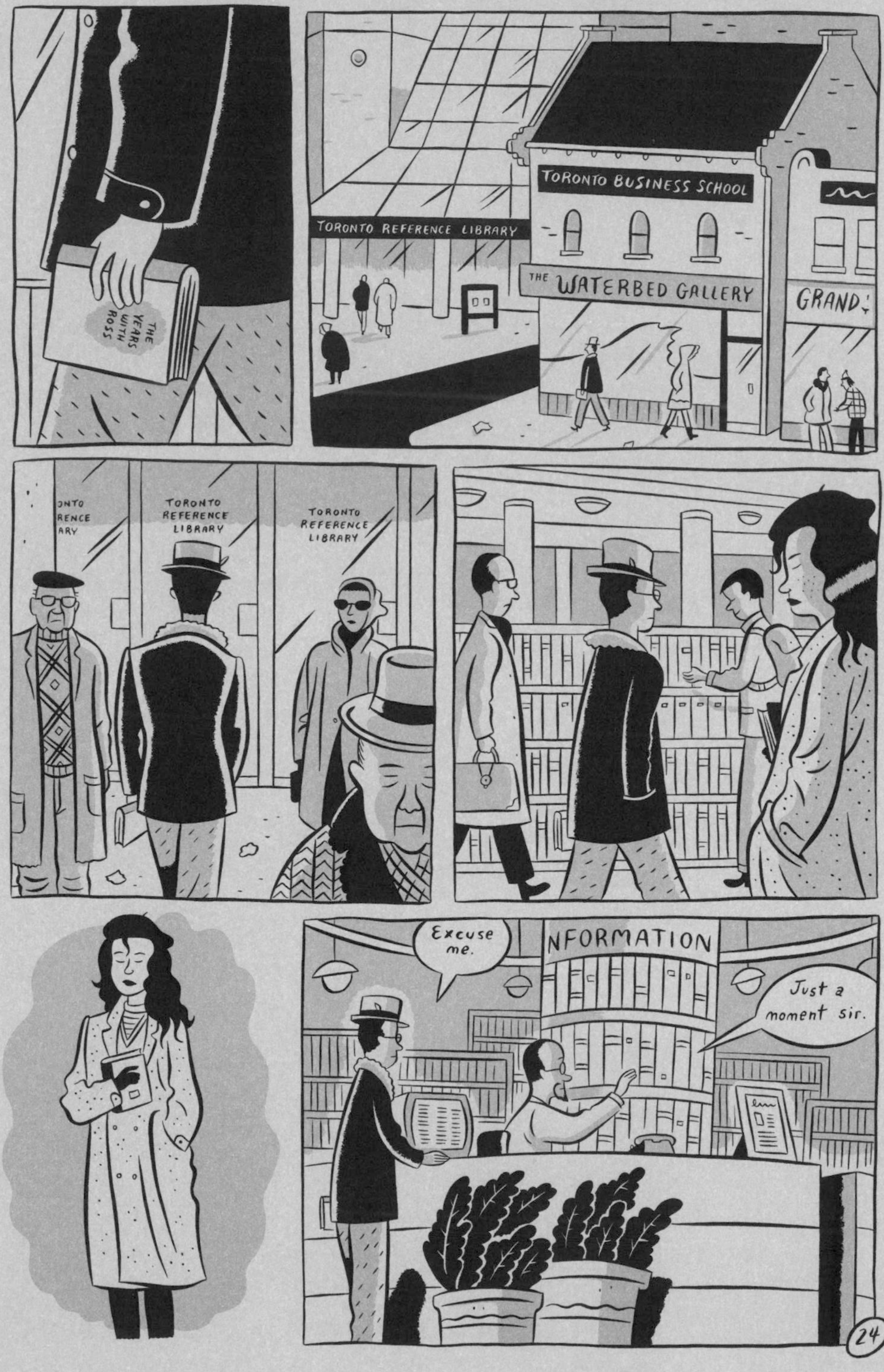
THE YEARS WITH ROSS
TORONTO REFERENCE LIBRARY
TORONTO BUSINESS SCHOOL
THE WATERBED GALLERY
GRAND
TORONTO REFERENCE LIBRARY
TORONTO REFERENCE LIBRARY
Excuse me.
NFORMATION
Just a moment sir.

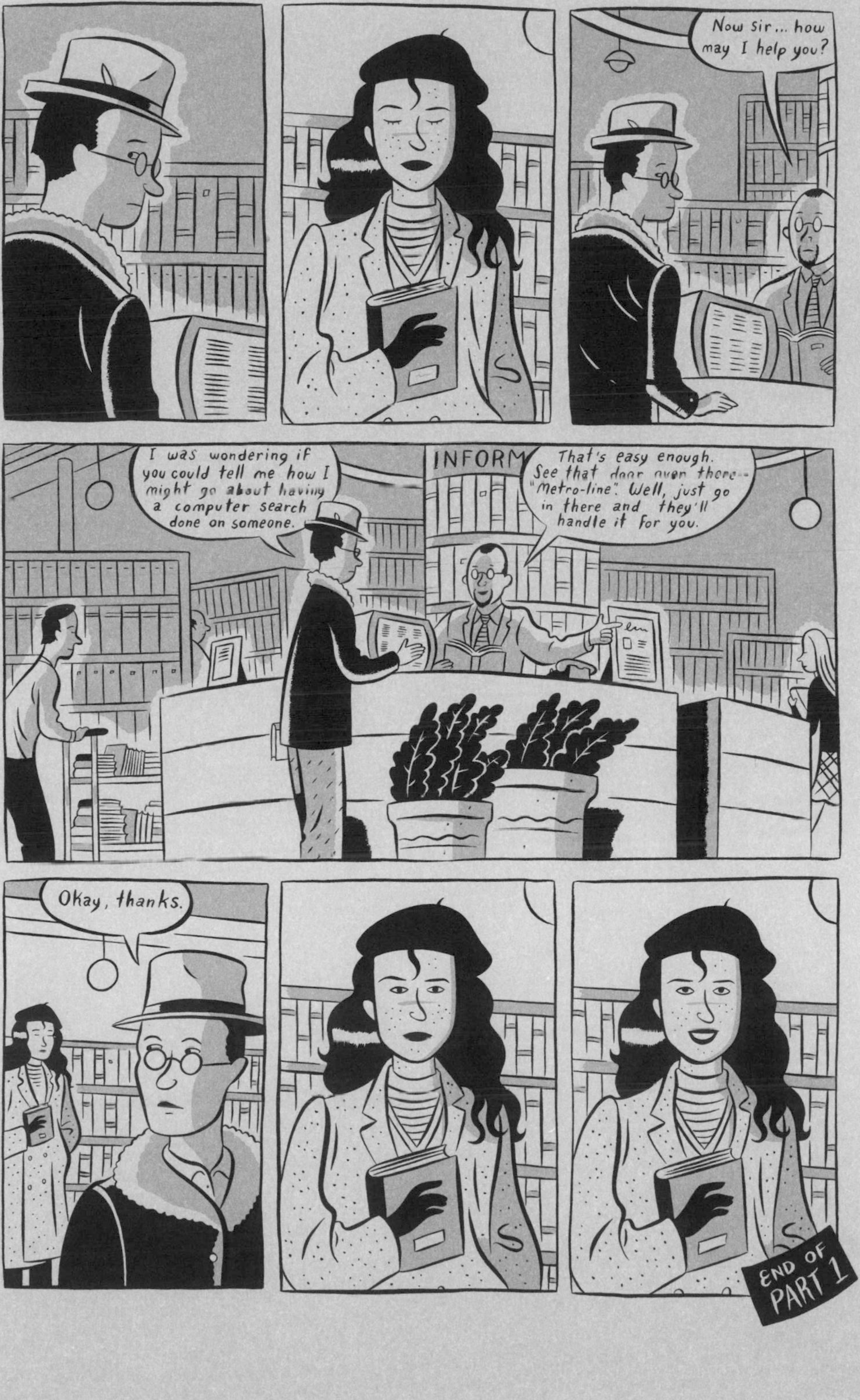
Now sir... how may I help you?
I was wondering if you could tell me how I might go about having a computer search done on someone.
INFORM
That's easy enough. See that door over there-- "Metro-line". Well, just go in there and they'll handle it for you.
Okay, thanks.
END OF PART 1

Part Two

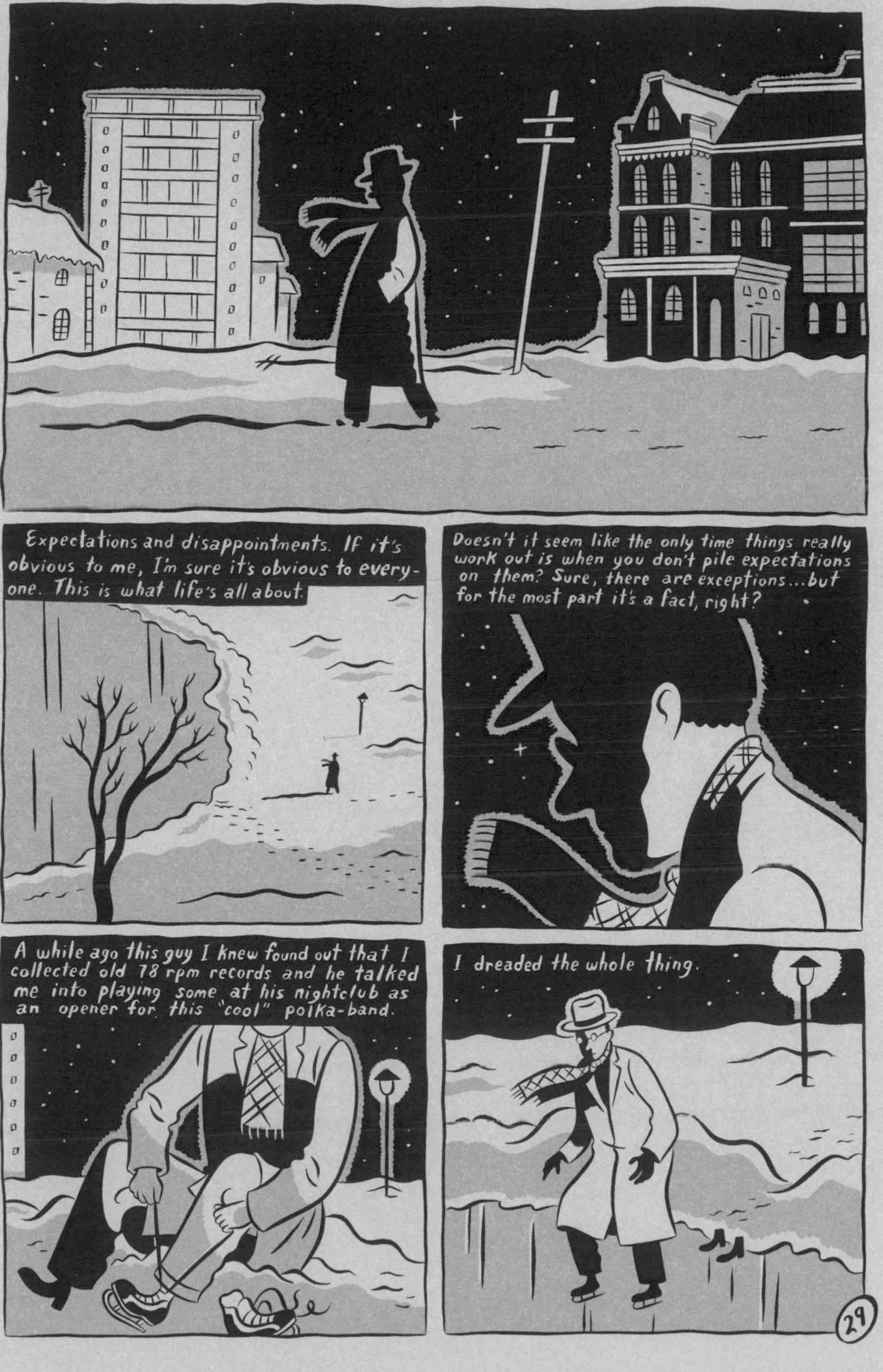
Expectations and disappointments. If it's obvious to me, I'm sure it's obvious to everyone. This is what life's all about.
Doesn't it seem like the only time things really work out is when you don't pile expectations on them? Sure, there are exceptions...but for the most part it's a fact, right?
A while ago this guy I knew found out that I collected old 78 rpm records and he talked me into playing some at his nightclub as an opener for this "cool" polka-band.
I dreaded the whole thing.
29

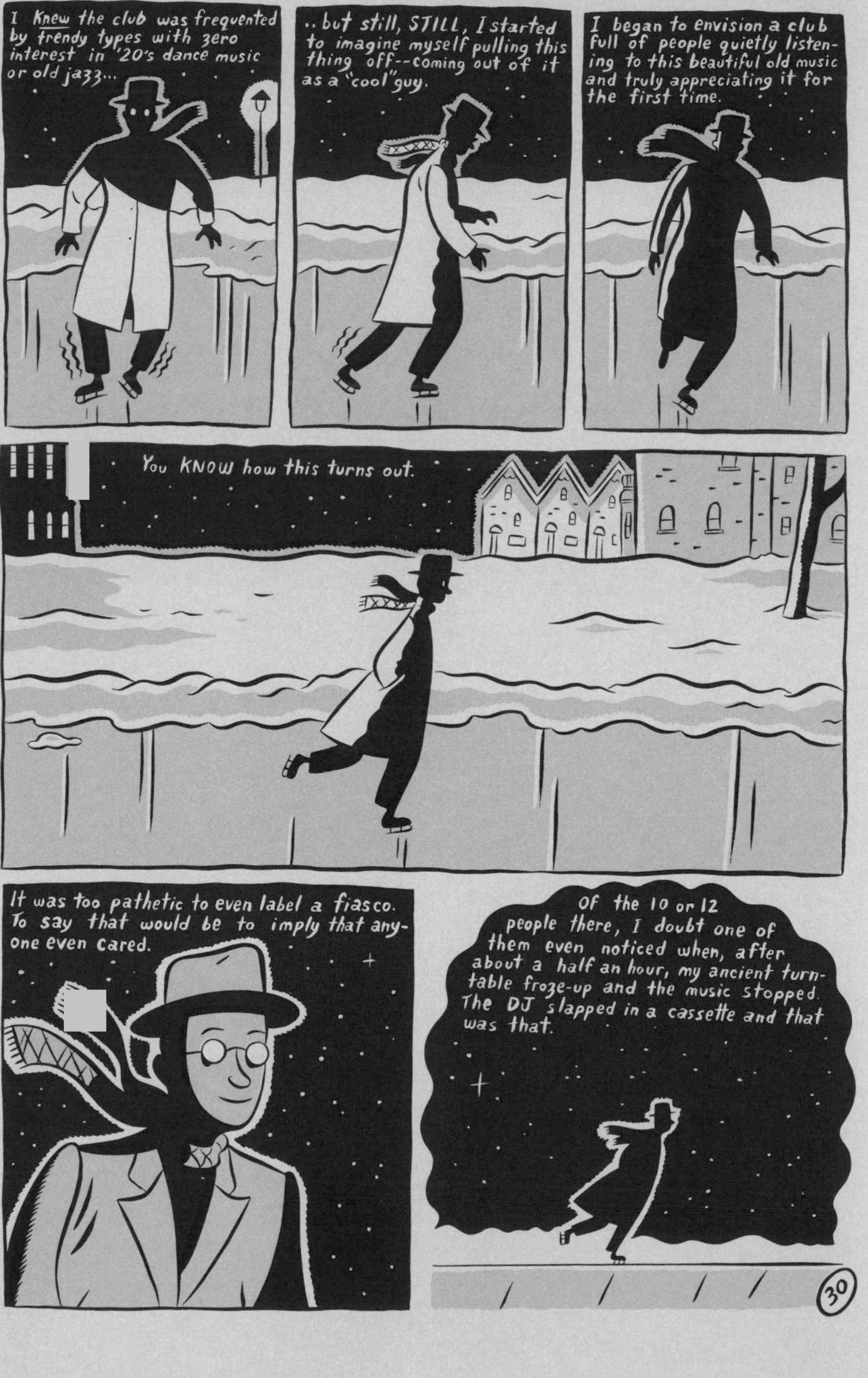
I Knew the club was frequented by trendy types with zero interest in '20's dance music or old jazz...
.. but still, STILL, I started to imagine myself pulling this thing off--coming out of it as a "cool" guy.
I began to envision a club full of people quietly listening to this beautiful old music and truly appreciating it for the first time.
You KNOW how this turns out.
It was too pathetic to even label a fiasco. To say that would be to imply that anyone even cared.
Of the 10 or 12 people there, I doubt one of them even noticed when, after about a half an hour, my ancient turntable froze-up and the music stopped. The DJ slapped in a cassette and that was that.

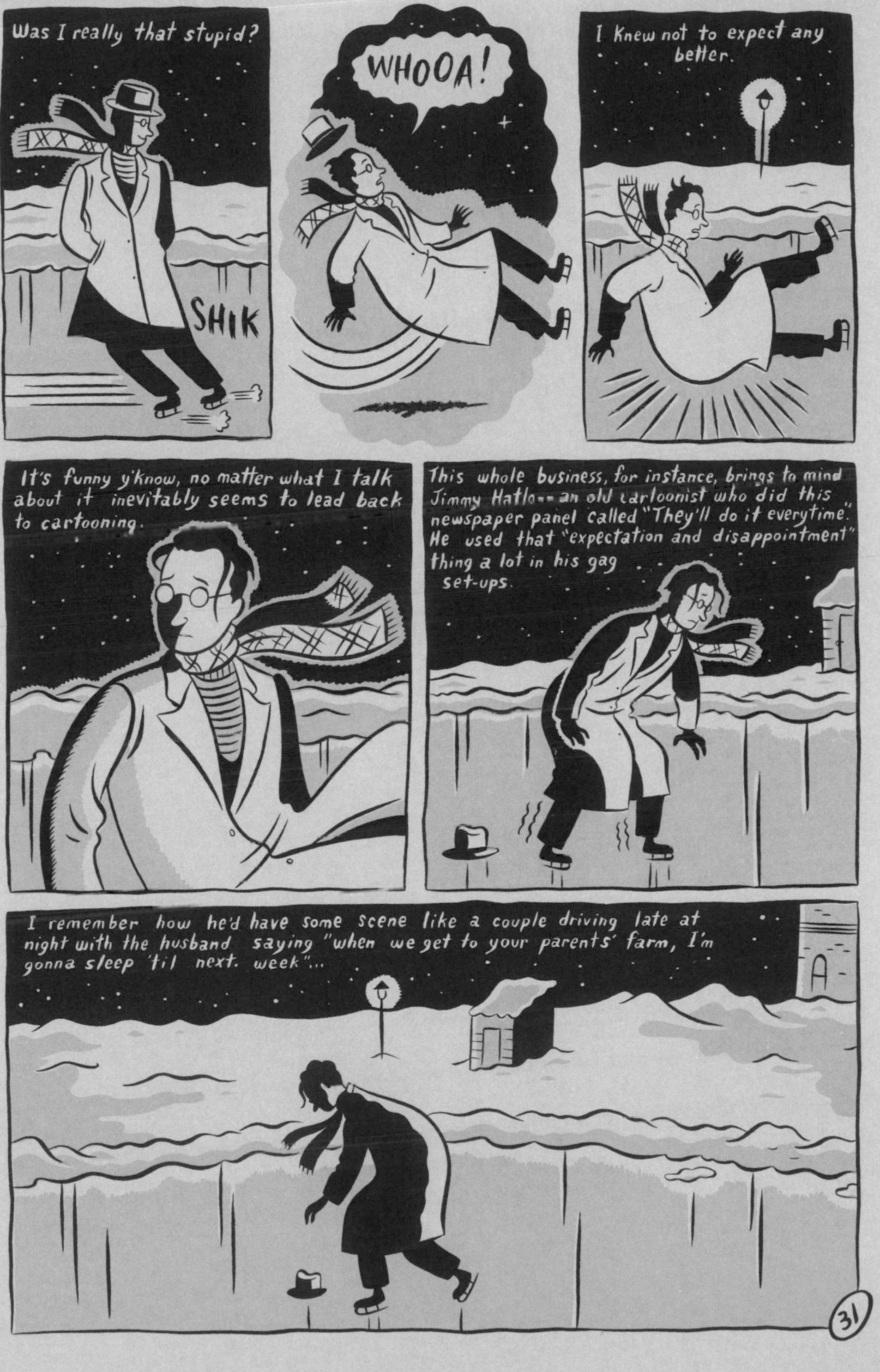

Was I really that stupid?
SHIK
WHOOA!
I knew not to expect any better.
It's funny y'know, no matter what I talk about it inevitably seems to lead back to cartooning.
This whole business, for instance, brings to mind Jimmy Hatlo -- an old cartoonist who did this newspaper panel called "They'll do it everytime". He used that "expectation and disappointment" thing a lot in his gag set-ups.
I remember how he'd have some scene like a couple driving late at night with the husband saying "when we get to your parents' farm, I'm gonna sleep 'til next. week"...

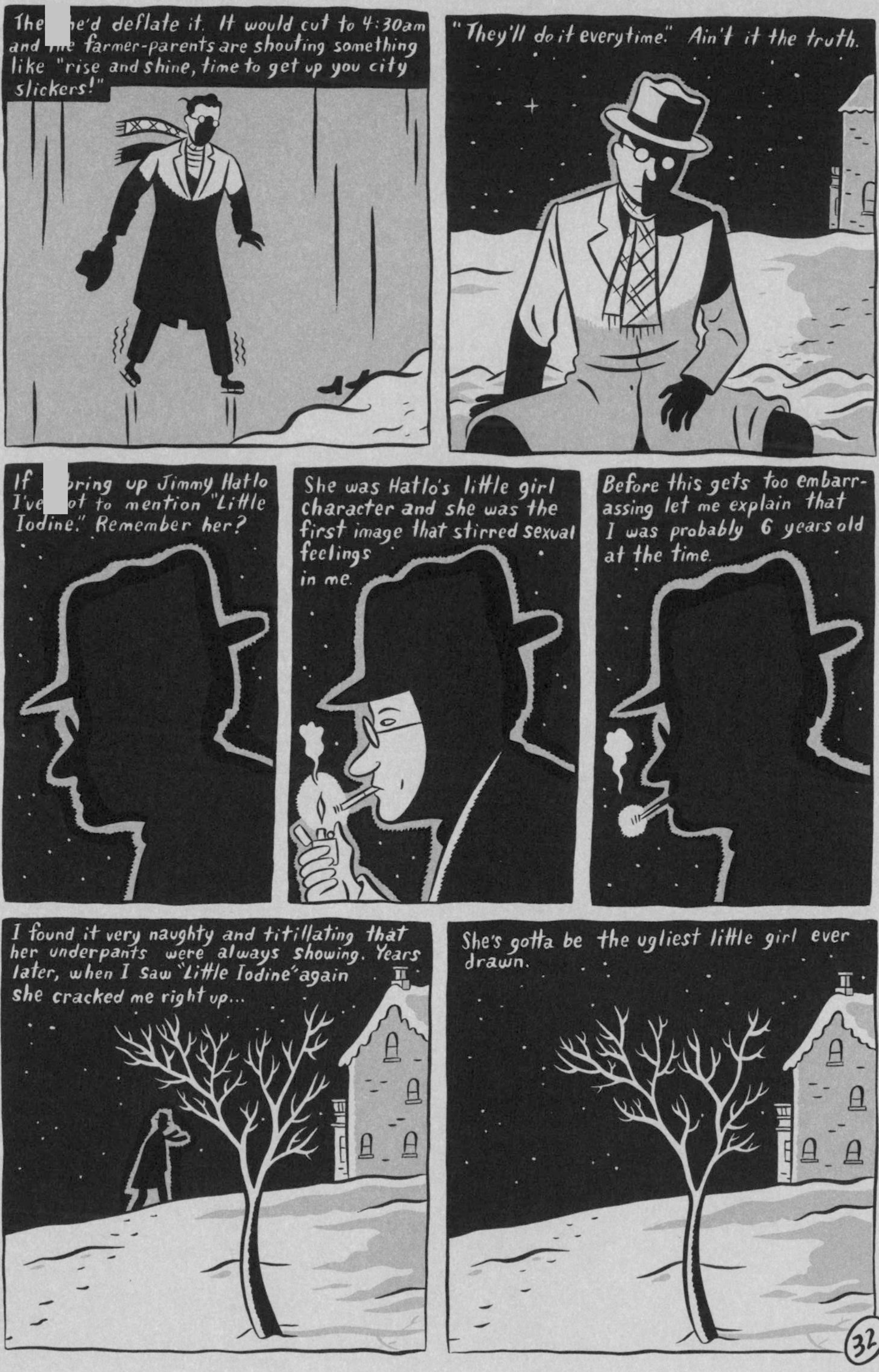
The he'd deflate it. It would cut to 4:30am and the farmer-parents are shouting something like "rise and shine, time to get up you city slickers!"
"They'll do it everytime." Ain't it the truth.
If bring up Jimmy Hatlo I've ot to mention "Little Iodine." Remember her?
She was Hatlo's little girl character and she was the first image that stirred sexual feelings in me.
Before this gets too embarrassing let me explain that I was probably 6 years old at the time.
I found it very naughty and titillating that her underpants were always showing. Years later, when I saw "Little Iodine" again she cracked me right up...
She's gotta be the ugliest little girl ever drawn.

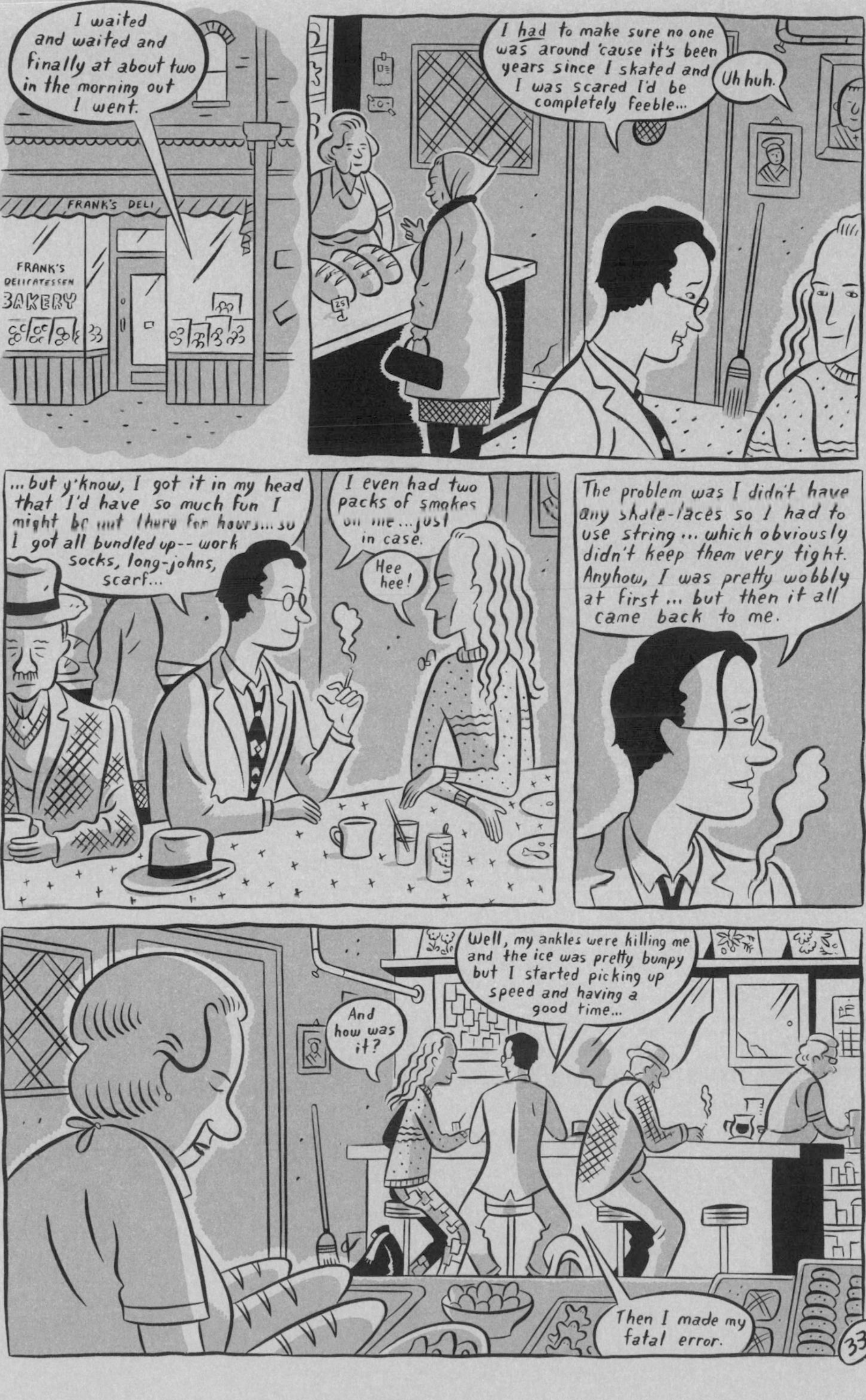

I waited and waited and finally at about two in the morning out I went.
FRANK'S DELI
FRANK'S DELICATESSEN BAKERY
I had to make sure no one was around 'cause it's been years since I skated and I was scared I'd be completely feeble...
Uh huh.
...but y'know, I got it in my head that I'd have so much fun I might be out there for hours... so I got all bundled up-- work socks, long-johns, scarf...
I even had two packs of smokes on me... just in case.
Hee hee!
The problem was I didn't have any skate-laces so I had to use string... which obviously didn't keep them very tight. Anyhow, I was pretty wobbly at first... but then it all came back to me.
Well, my ankles were killing me and the ice was pretty bumpy but I started picking up speed and having a good time...
And how was it?
Then I made my fatal error.

I go to make a fast stop--y'know, twist the ankles quickly...

Uh huh.

...and *WHOOOA*-- I go flying right on my ass!

WHEE HEE HEE!

Yeah, it was pathetic. I bet'cha I wasn't out there ten minutes.

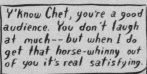

Hee hee.

Y'know Chet, you're a good audience. You don't laugh at much--but when I do get that horse-whinny out of you it's real satisfying.

Uh huh?

So, did you hear from the "New Yorker" yet?

34

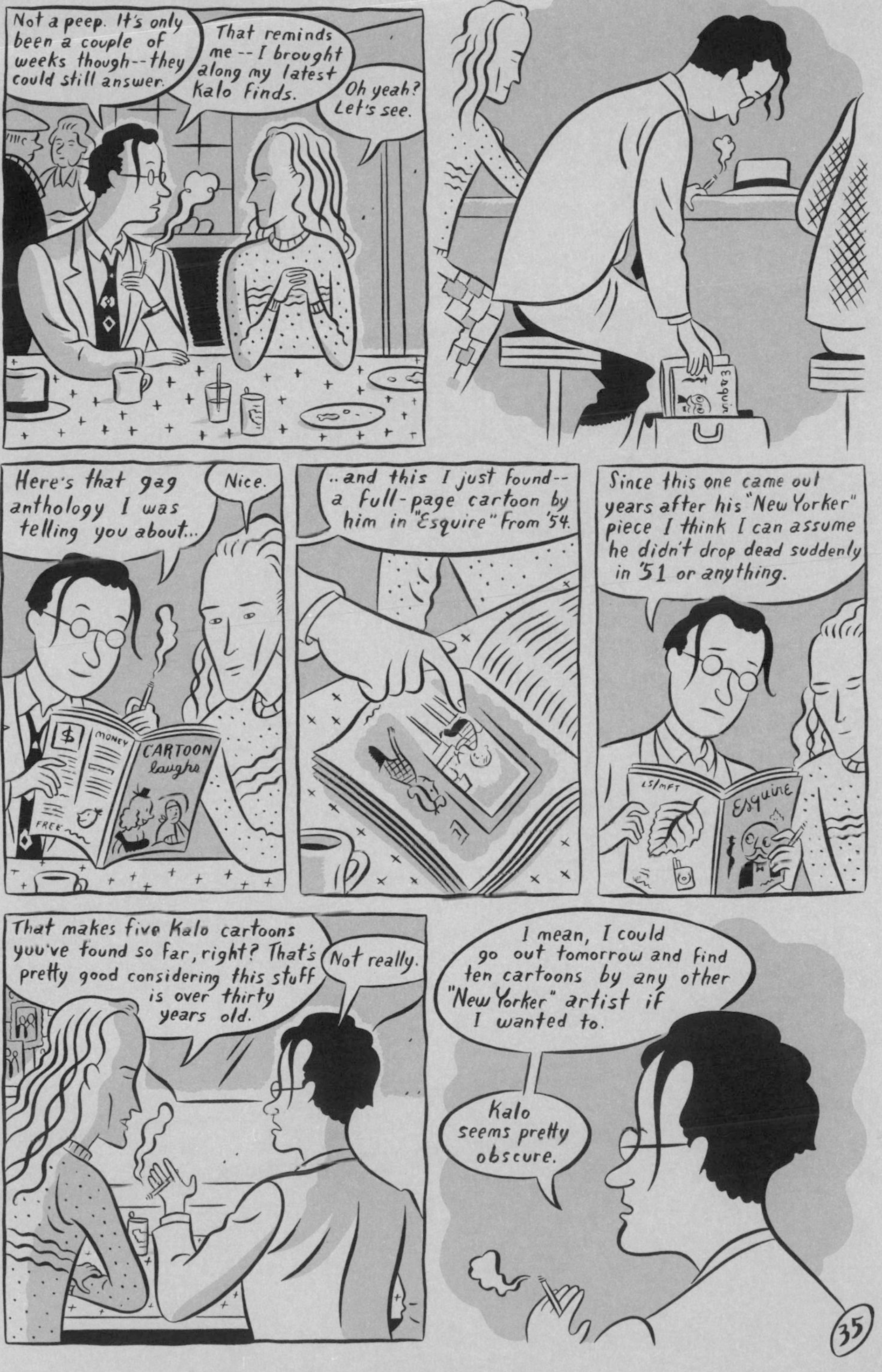
Not a peep. It's only been a couple of weeks though--they could still answer.
That reminds me--I brought along my latest Kalo finds.
Oh yeah? Let's see.
Esquire
Here's that gag anthology I was telling you about...
Nice.
MONEY
CARTOON laughs
FREE
..and this I just found--a full-page cartoon by him in "Esquire" from '54.
Since this one came out years after his "New Yorker" piece I think I can assume he didn't drop dead suddenly in '51 or anything.
LS/MFT
Esquire
That makes five Kalo cartoons you've found so far, right? That's pretty good considering this stuff is over thirty years old.
Not really.
I mean, I could go out tomorrow and find ten cartoons by any other "New Yorker" artist if I wanted to.
Kalo seems pretty obscure.

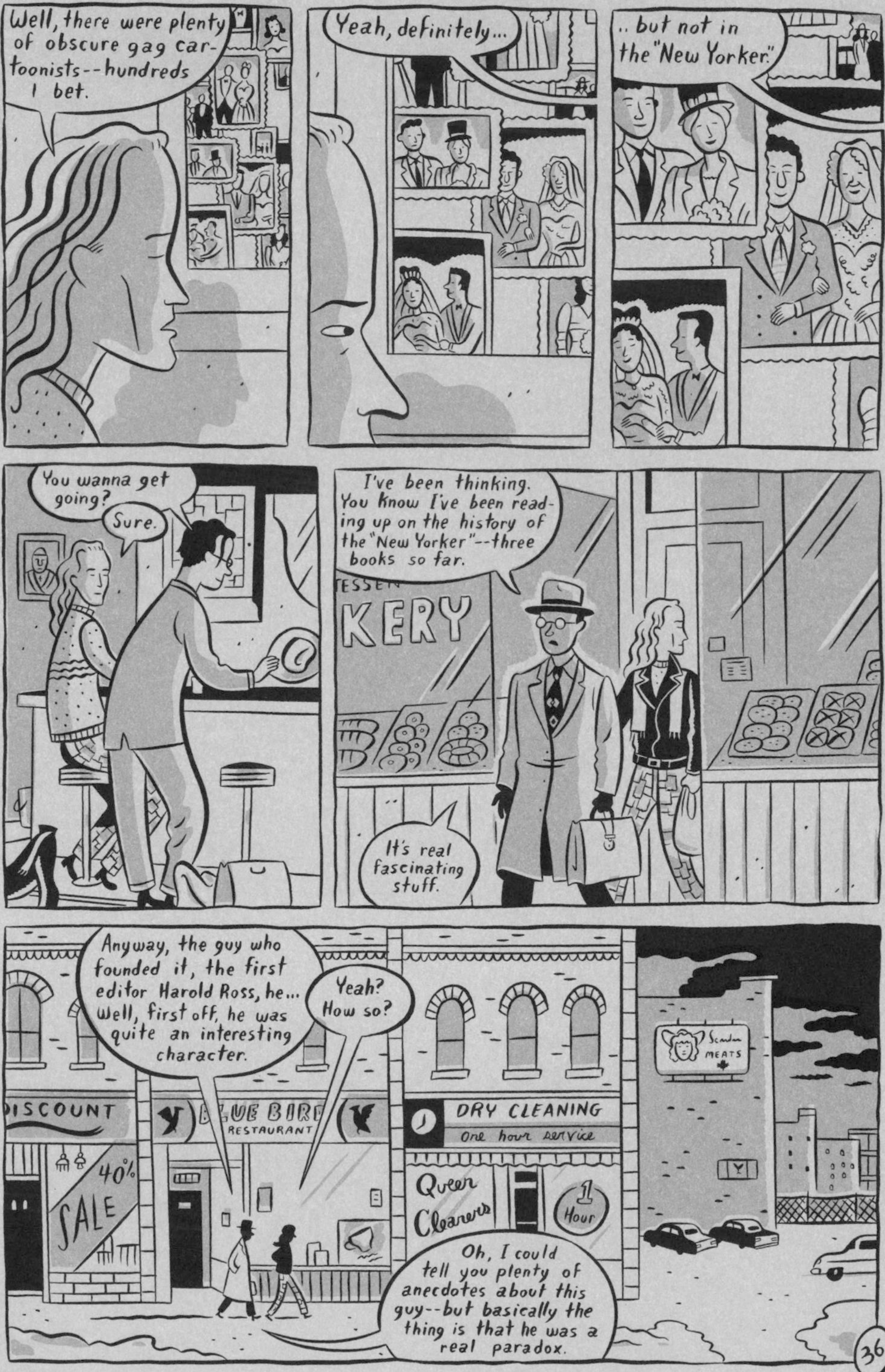

Well, there were plenty of obscure gag cartoonists--hundreds I bet.
Yeah, definitely...
.. but not in the "New Yorker."
You wanna get going?
Sure.
I've been thinking. You know I've been reading up on the history of the "New Yorker"--three books so far.
KERY
It's real fascinating stuff.
Anyway, the guy who founded it, the first editor Harold Ross, he... Well, first off, he was quite an interesting character.
Yeah? How so?
DISCOUNT
BLUE BIRD RESTAURANT
DRY CLEANING
One hour service
40% SALE
Queen Cleaners
1 Hour
MEATS
Oh, I could tell you plenty of anecdotes about this guy--but basically the thing is that he was a real paradox.

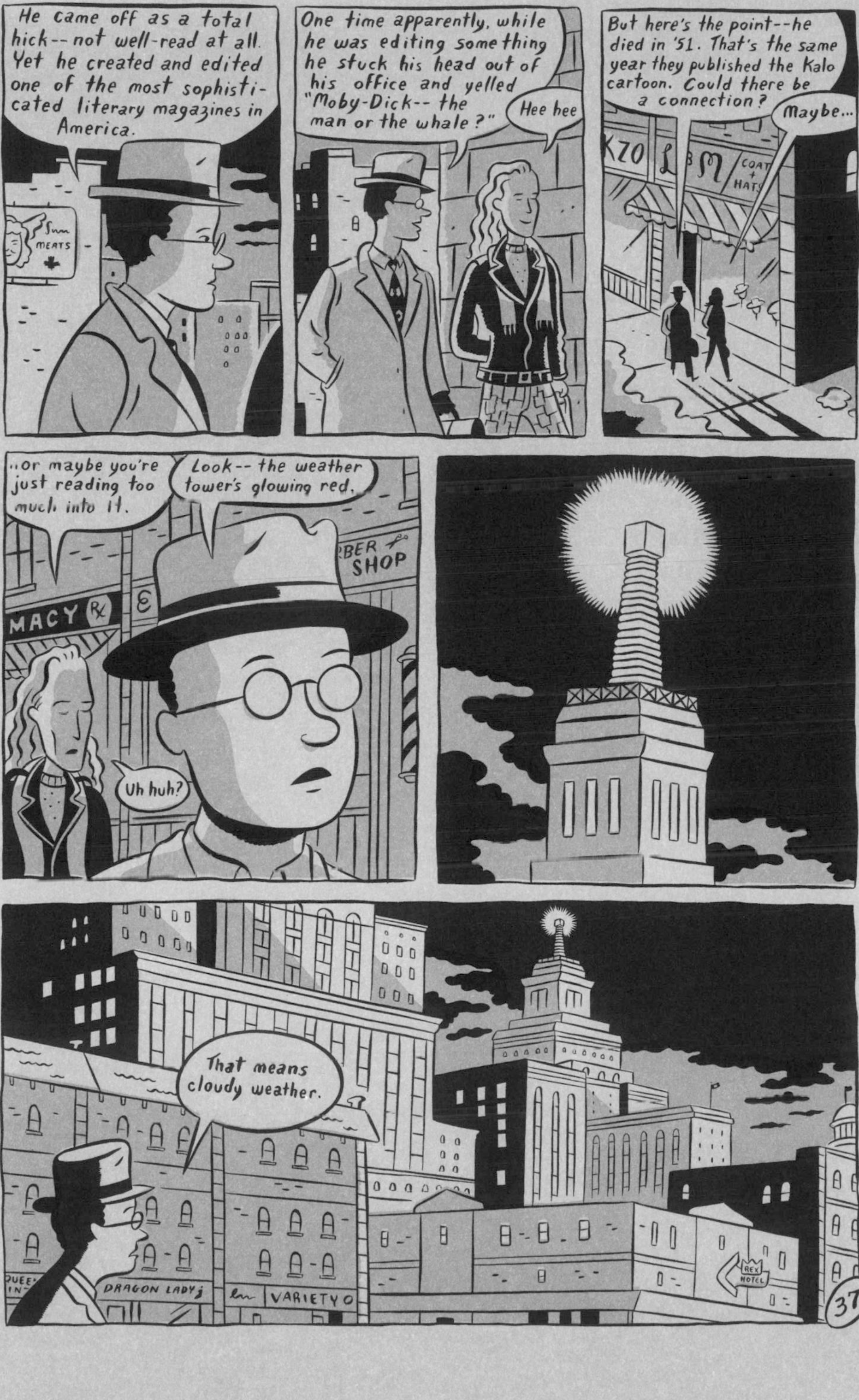
He came off as a total hick--not well-read at all. Yet he created and edited one of the most sophisticated literary magazines in America.
SMM MEATS
One time apparently, while he was editing something he stuck his head out of his office and yelled "Moby-Dick-- the man or the whale?"
Hee hee
But here's the point--he died in '51. That's the same year they published the Kalo cartoon. Could there be a connection?
Maybe...
KZO
COAT + HATS
..or maybe you're just reading too much into it.
Look-- the weather tower's glowing red.
BER SHOP
MACY
Uh huh?
That means cloudy weather.
DRAGON LADY
VARIETY
REX HOTEL

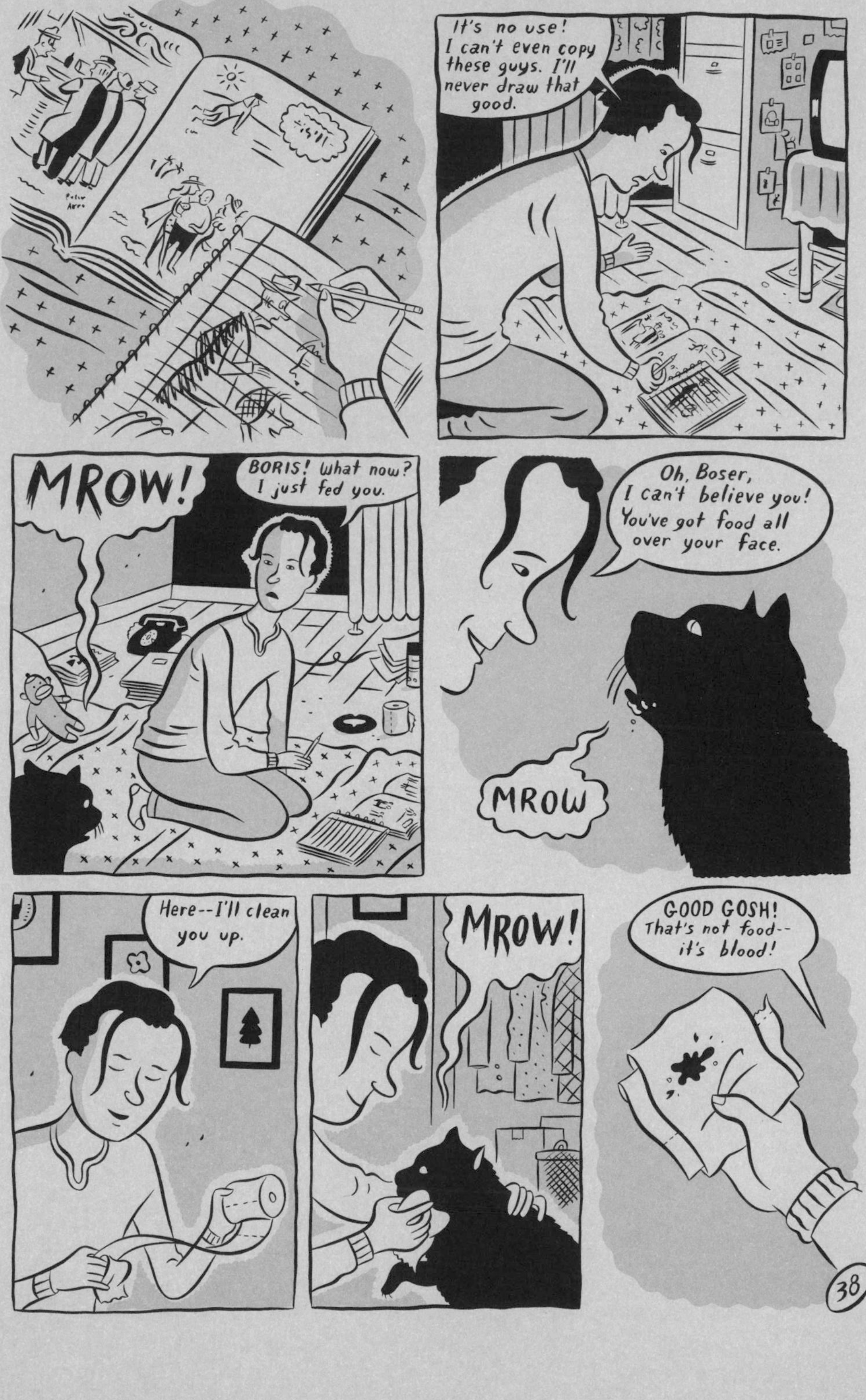
Peter Arno
It's no use! I can't even copy these guys. I'll never draw that good.
MROW!
BORIS! What now? I just fed you.
Oh, Boser, I can't believe you! You've got food all over your face.
MROW
Here--I'll clean you up.
MROW!
GOOD GOSH! That's not food-- it's blood!

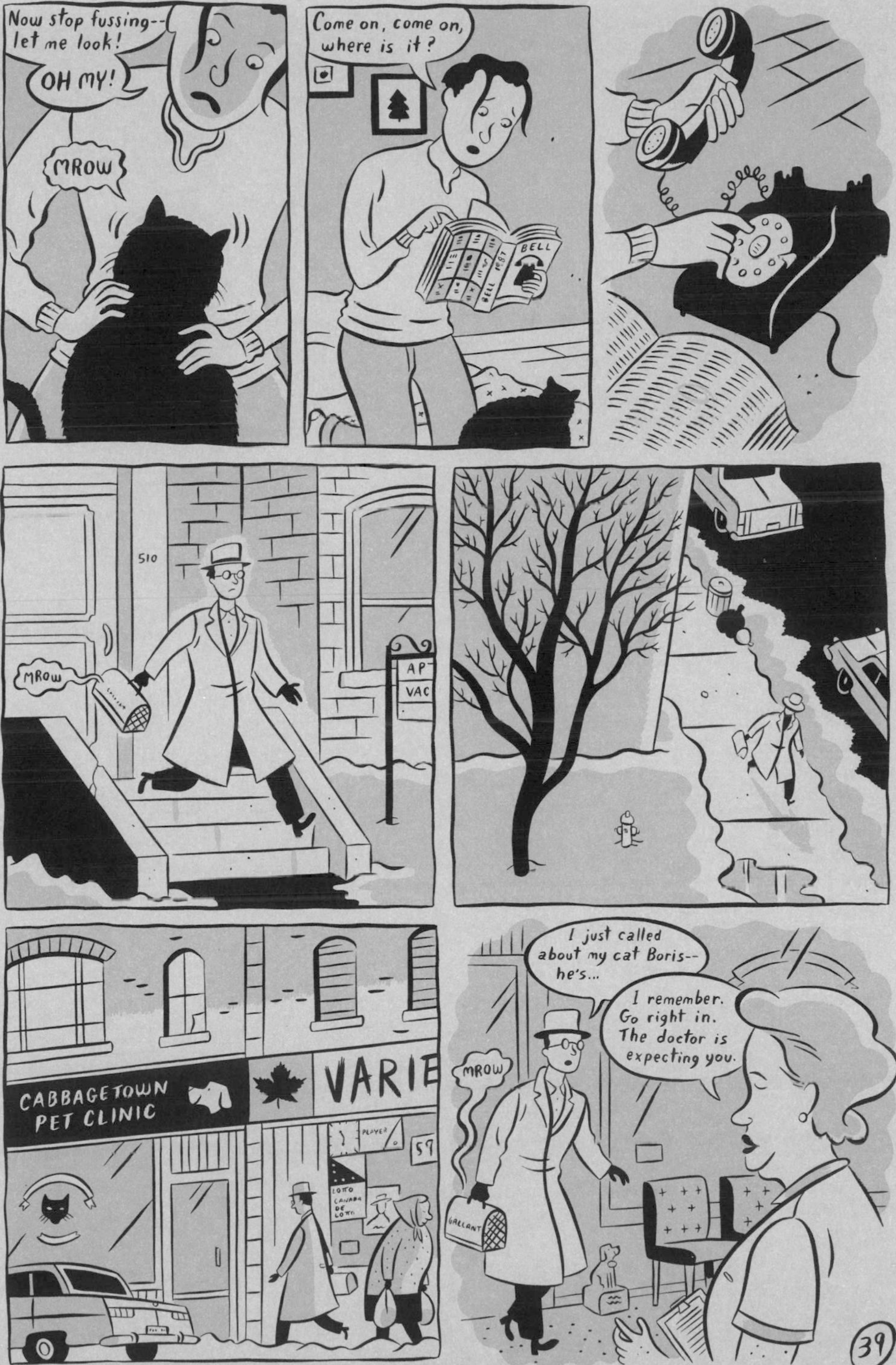
Now stop fussing--
let me look!
OH MY!
MROW
Come on, come on,
where is it?
BELL
510
MROW
AP
VAC
CABBAGETOWN
PET CLINIC
VARIE
PLAYER
57
I just called
about my cat Boris--
he's...
I remember.
Go right in.
The doctor is
expecting you.
MROW
GALLANT

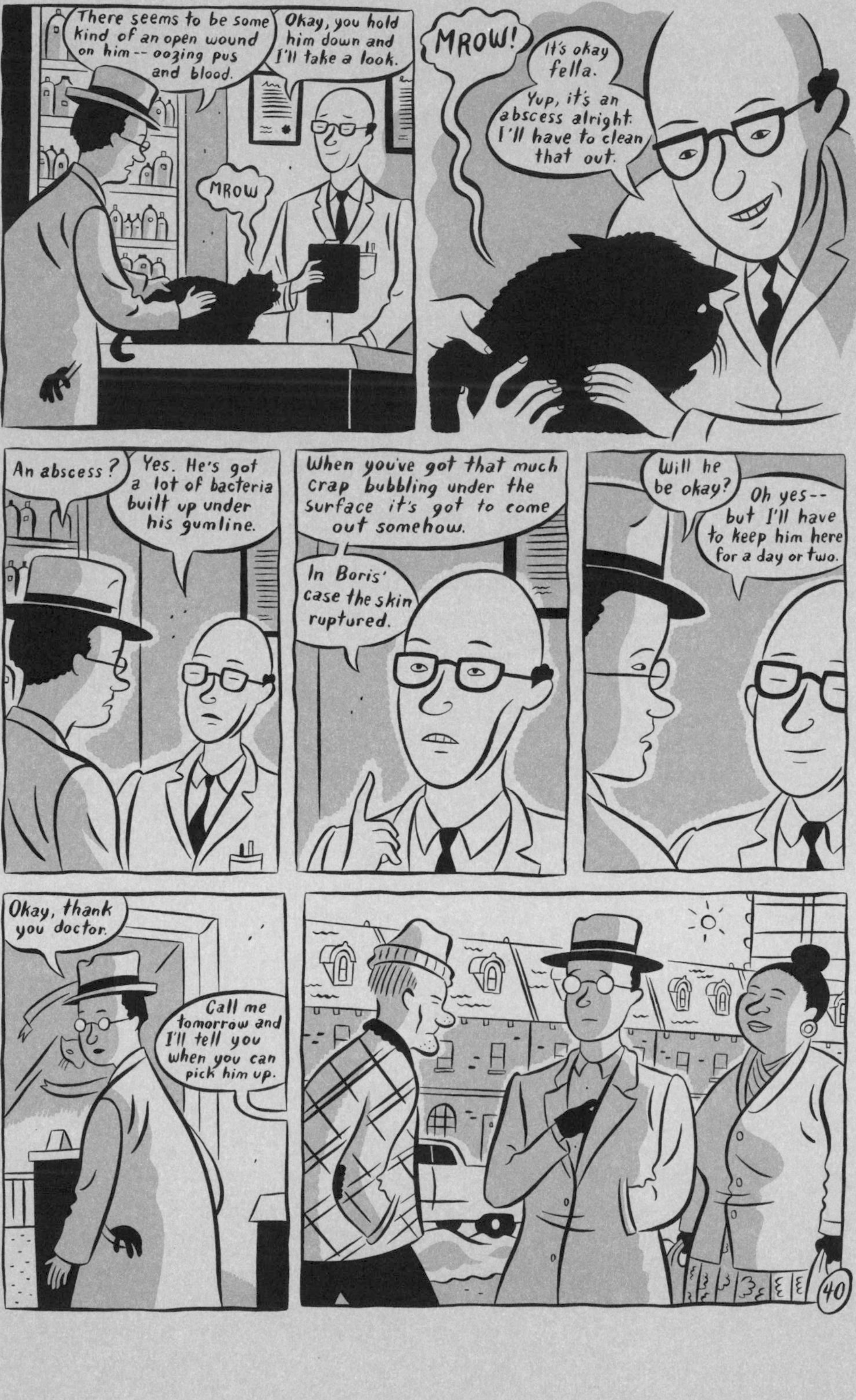
There seems to be some kind of an open wound on him -- oozing pus and blood.
Okay, you hold him down and I'll take a look.
MROW
MROW!
It's okay fella.
Yup, it's an abscess alright. I'll have to clean that out.
An abscess?
Yes. He's got a lot of bacteria built up under his gumline.
When you've got that much crap bubbling under the surface it's got to come out somehow.
In Boris' case the skin ruptured.
Will he be okay?
Oh yes-- but I'll have to keep him here for a day or two.
Okay, thank you doctor.
Call me tomorrow and I'll tell you when you can pick him up.

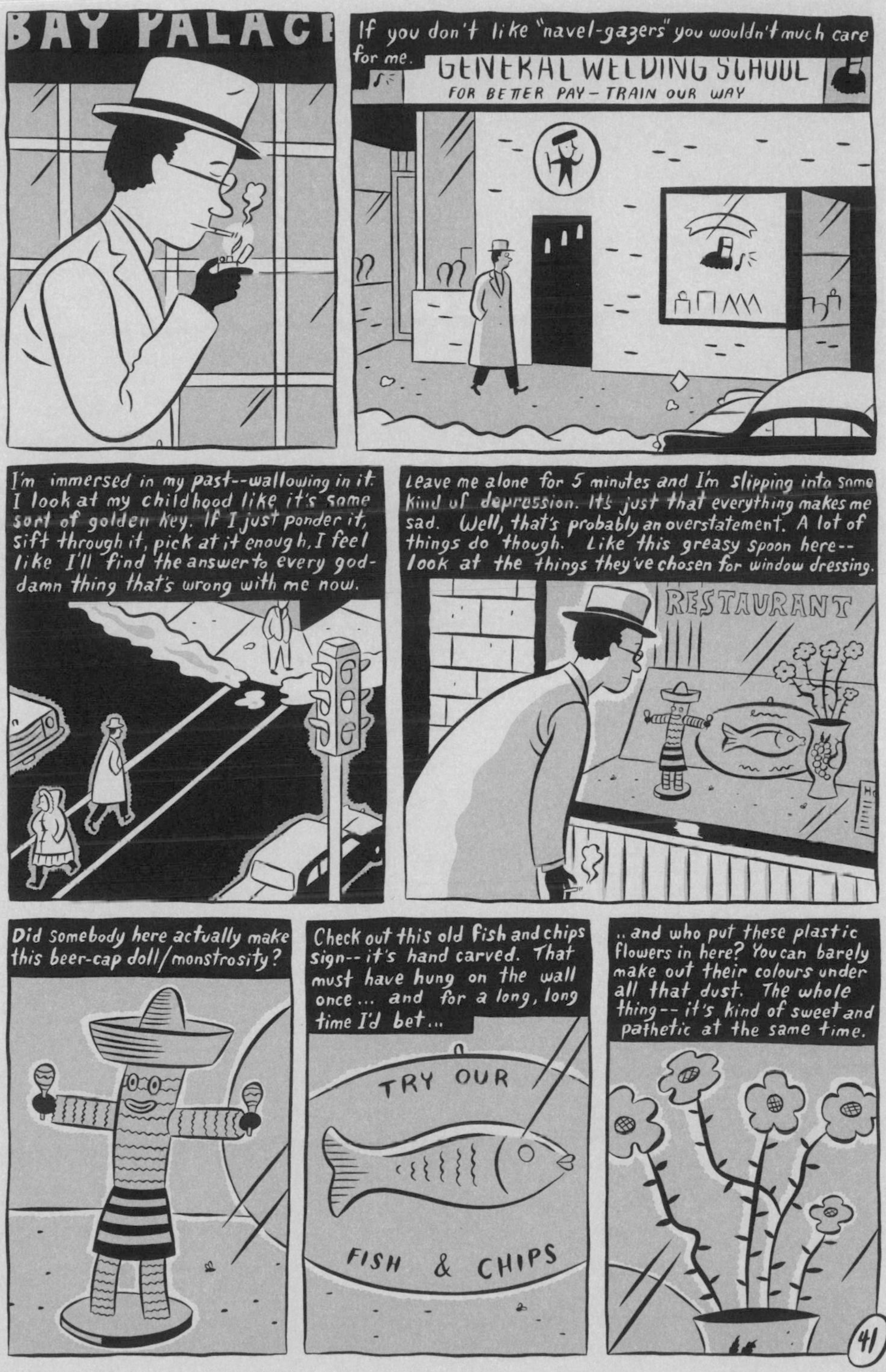
BAY PALACE
If you don't like "navel-gazers" you wouldn't much care for me.
GENERAL WELDING SCHOOL
FOR BETTER PAY — TRAIN OUR WAY
I'm immersed in my past--wallowing in it. I look at my childhood like it's some sort of golden key. If I just ponder it, sift through it, pick at it enough, I feel like I'll find the answer to every god-damn thing that's wrong with me now.
Leave me alone for 5 minutes and I'm slipping into some kind of depression. It's just that everything makes me sad. Well, that's probably an overstatement. A lot of things do though. Like this greasy spoon here-- look at the things they've chosen for window dressing.
RESTAURANT
Did somebody here actually make this beer-cap doll/monstrosity?
Check out this old fish and chips sign-- it's hand carved. That must have hung on the wall once... and for a long, long time I'd bet...
TRY OUR
FISH & CHIPS
..and who put these plastic flowers in here? You can barely make out their colours under all that dust. The whole thing-- it's kind of sweet and pathetic at the same time.
41

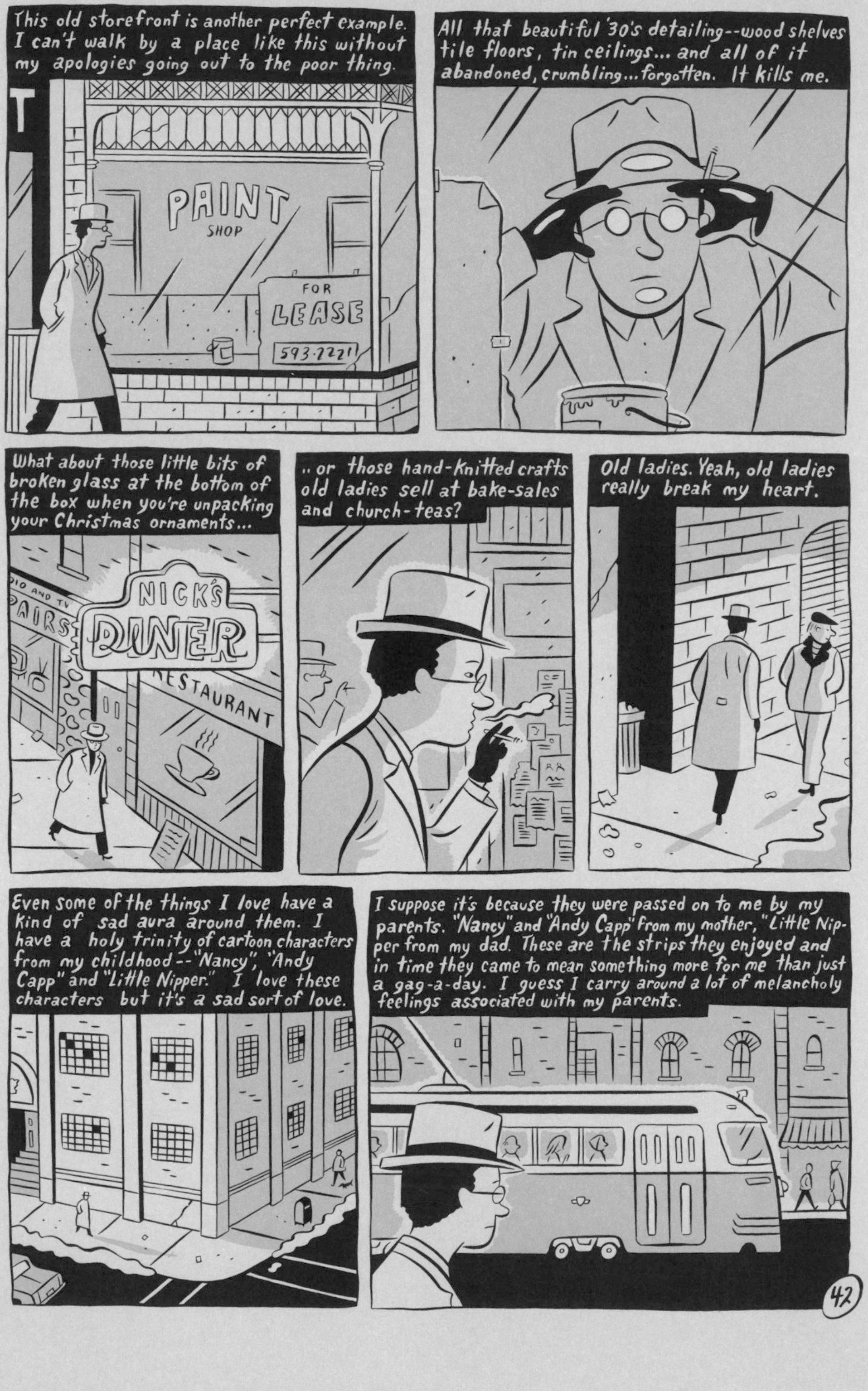
This old storefront is another perfect example. I can't walk by a place like this without my apologies going out to the poor thing.
PAINT
SHOP
FOR
LEASE
593-7221
All that beautiful '30's detailing--wood shelves tile floors, tin ceilings... and all of it abandoned, crumbling... forgotten. It kills me.
What about those little bits of broken glass at the bottom of the box when you're unpacking your Christmas ornaments...
NICK'S
DINER
RESTAURANT
.. or those hand-knitted crafts old ladies sell at bake-sales and church-teas?
Old ladies. Yeah, old ladies really break my heart.
Even some of the things I love have a kind of sad aura around them. I have a holy trinity of cartoon characters from my childhood--"Nancy", "Andy Capp" and "Little Nipper." I love these characters but it's a sad sort of love.
I suppose it's because they were passed on to me by my parents. "Nancy" and "Andy Capp" from my mother, "Little Nipper from my dad. These are the strips they enjoyed and in time they came to mean something more for me than just a gag-a-day. I guess I carry around a lot of melancholy feelings associated with my parents.
42

Maybe I like feeling depressed. I don't know. I've certainly kidded myself about plenty of other stuff.

GENERAL ANTIQUES

For a couple of years I actually had myself convinced that I'd be happier living in the past-- the '20's and '30's specifically.

SELDOM SEEN ANTIQUES

$1 A BUNDLE

OPEN

What a joke. I mean, sure, I really do think lots of things were better in the past.

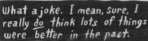

MECHANIX

You've got to admit that the sheer quality of living seems to be getting shoddier and cheaper every year...

..but when I'm truly honest with myself I know I couldn't stand the attitudes or the social conditions back then. I sure wasn't thinking of living through the Depression.

Excuse me.

In hindsight, I was really wishing that some of the better elements of those years had survived into my lifetime.

Just these magazines...

That'll be a buck then.

The world my parents grew up in doesn't seem to fit together with this one. The bits and pieces of that time still lingering around today seem like remnants of some ghost world--a vanished world.

FRUIT SHOP

43

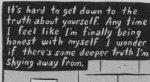

This business of "kidding yourself" worries me. I don't even know how much self-deception I'm involved in.

It's hard to get down to the truth about yourself. Any time I feel like I'm finally being honest with myself I wonder if there's some deeper truth I'm shying away from.

It amazes me how I can know something and avoid it at the same time.

No wonder I get depressed. This neighbourhood! Half the people around here seem like zombies. What keeps them going?

It's like they're killing time, waiting for something better to come along--some lucky break. Just how much are they kidding themselves? Maybe they've faced up to the futility of this life and given up. Who knows, maybe they're just blind and stupid.

Look at this poor bastard--all bent up like an old hinge. Jeez, still hobbling around in that condition. Isn't anyone caring for him?

What's with this lady? What is she thinking? She's wearing that ratty wig like it's a hat or something. Crazy, I guess.

Well, this guy at least seems to have his act together. He's got some dignity about him-- pretty dapper really.

44

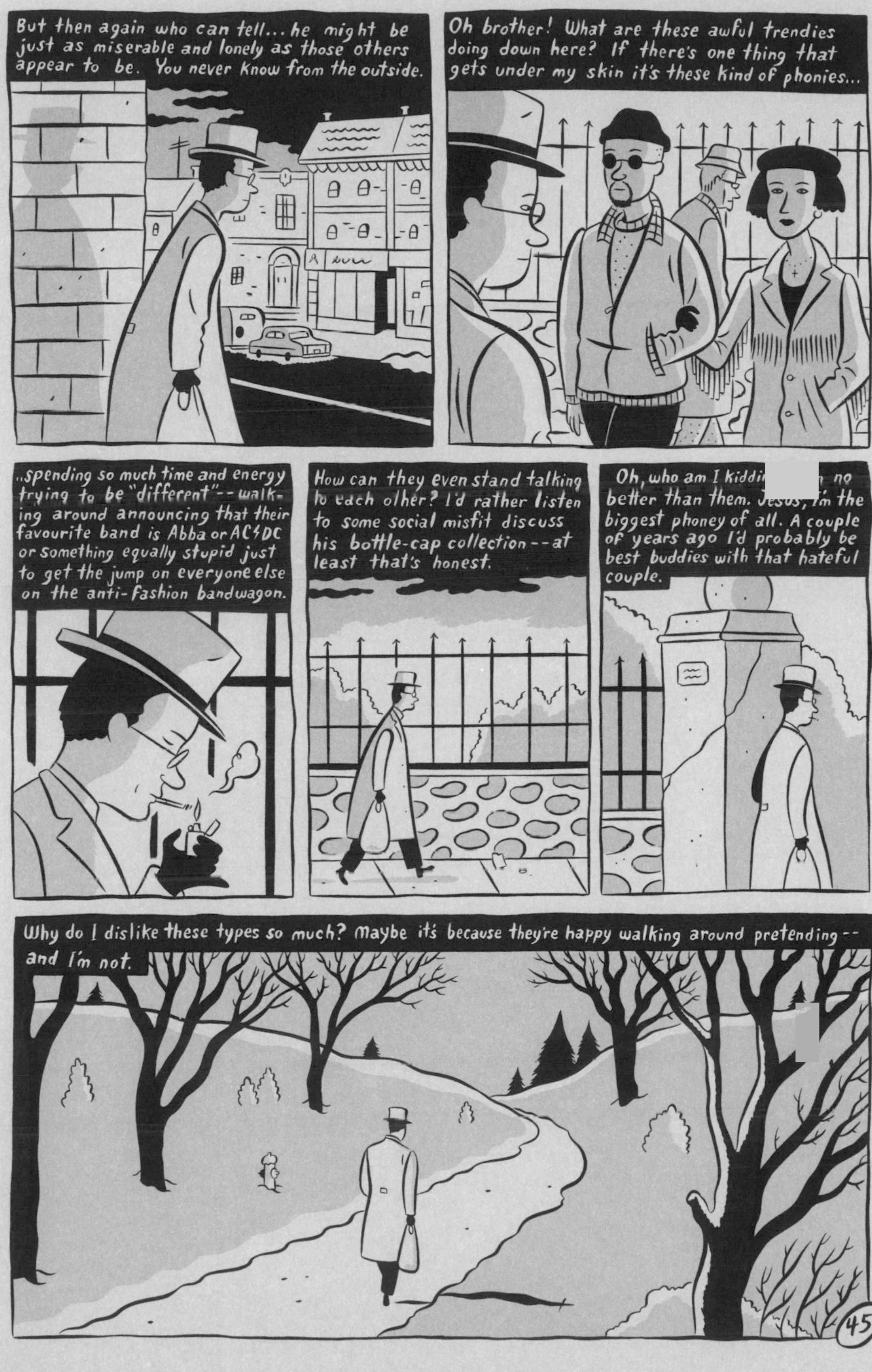
But then again who can tell... he might be just as miserable and lonely as those others appear to be. You never know from the outside.
Oh brother! What are these awful trendies doing down here? If there's one thing that gets under my skin it's these kind of phonies...
..spending so much time and energy trying to be "different"-- walking around announcing that their favourite band is Abba or AC/DC or something equally stupid just to get the jump on everyone else on the anti-fashion bandwagon.
How can they even stand talking to each other? I'd rather listen to some social misfit discuss his bottle-cap collection -- at least that's honest.
Oh, who am I kiddi n no better than them. Jesus, I'm the biggest phoney of all. A couple of years ago I'd probably be best buddies with that hateful couple.
Why do I dislike these types so much? Maybe it's because they're happy walking around pretending -- and I'm not.

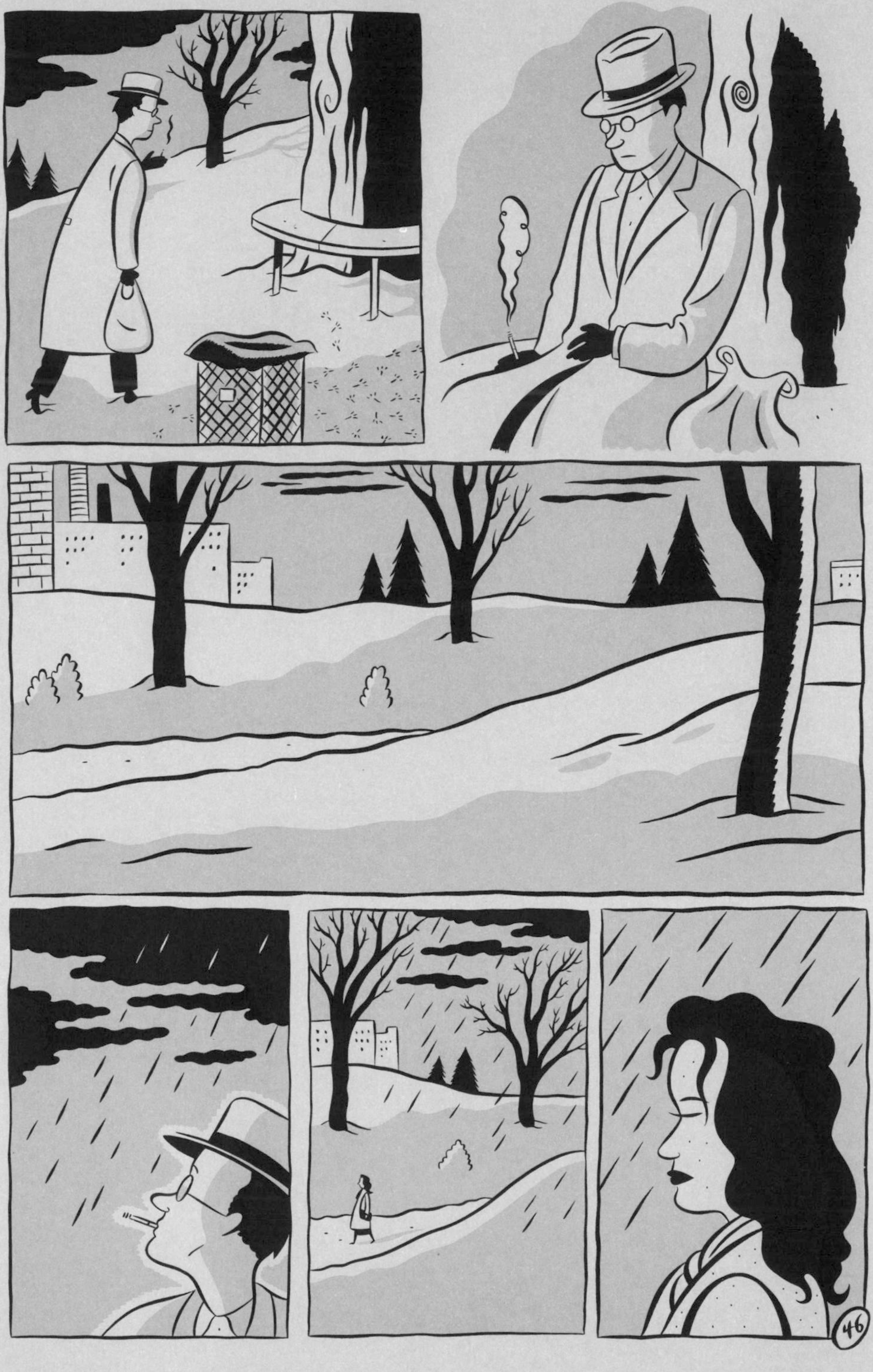

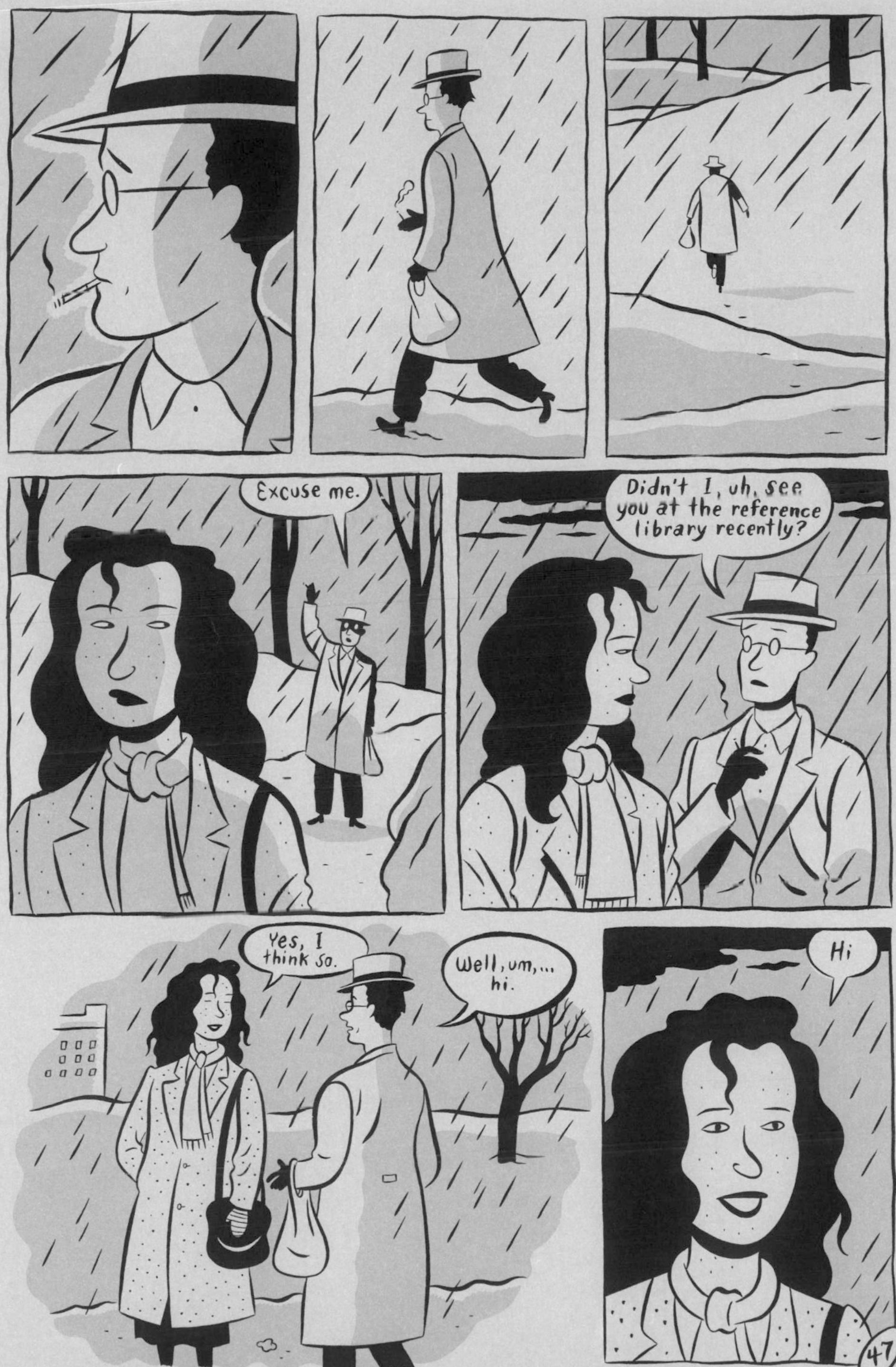

Excuse me.
Didn't I, uh, see you at the reference library recently?
Yes, I think so.
Well, um,... hi.
Hi

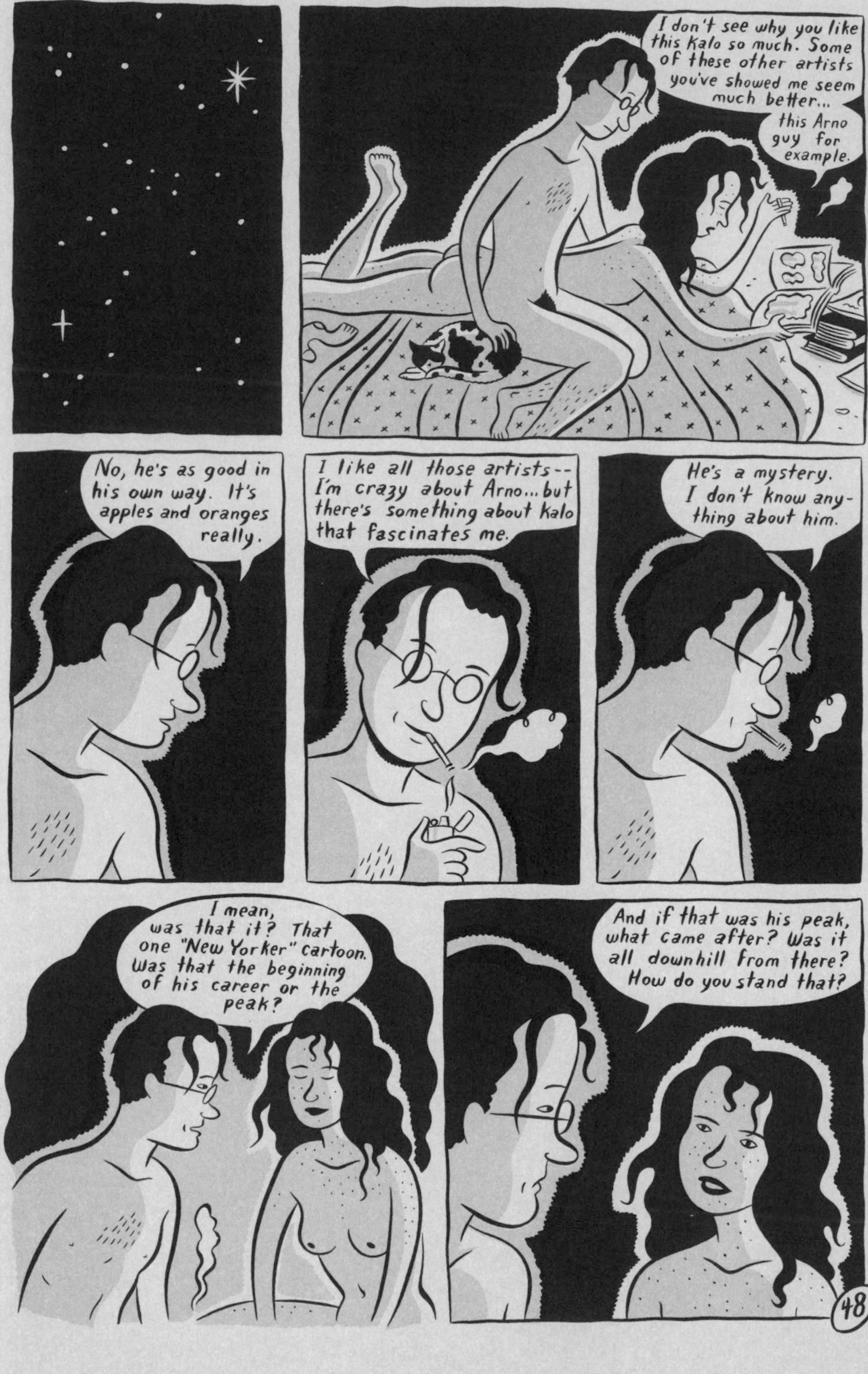
I don't see why you like this Kalo so much. Some of these other artists you've showed me seem much better...
this Arno guy for example.
No, he's as good in his own way. It's apples and oranges really.
I like all those artists-- I'm crazy about Arno... but there's something about Kalo that fascinates me.
He's a mystery. I don't know anything about him.
I mean, was that it? That one "New Yorker" cartoon. Was that the beginning of his career or the peak?
And if that was his peak, what came after? Was it all downhill from there? How do you stand that?
48

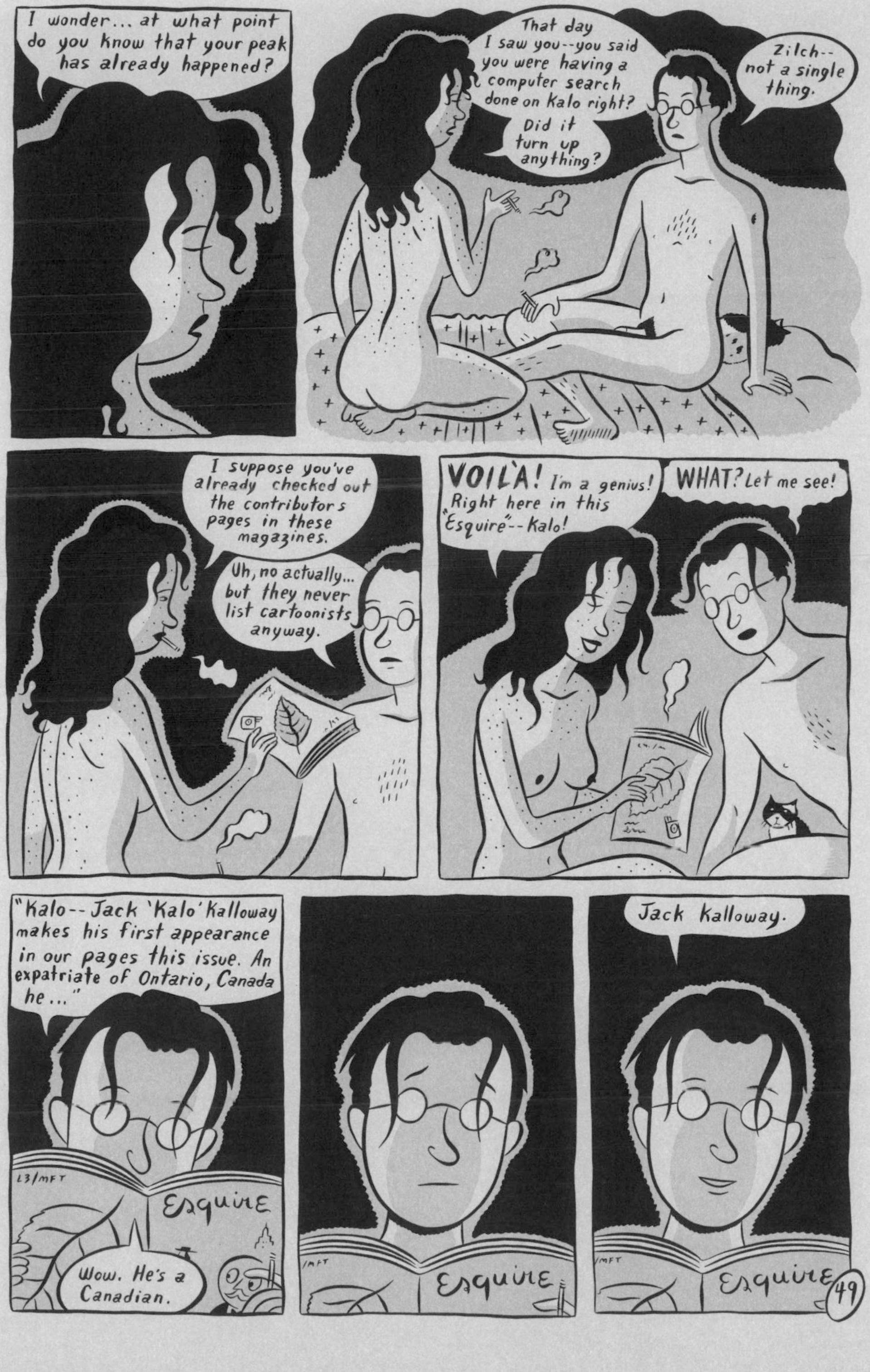
I wonder... at what point do you know that your peak has already happened?
That day I saw you--you said you were having a computer search done on Kalo right?
Did it turn up anything?
Zilch-- not a single thing.
I suppose you've already checked out the contributors pages in these magazines.
Uh, no actually... but they never list cartoonists anyway.
VOILÀ! I'm a genius! Right here in this "Esquire"--Kalo!
WHAT? Let me see!
"Kalo-- Jack 'Kalo' Kalloway makes his first appearance in our pages this issue. An expatriate of Ontario, Canada he..."
Esquire
Wow. He's a Canadian.
Esquire
Jack Kalloway.
Esquire

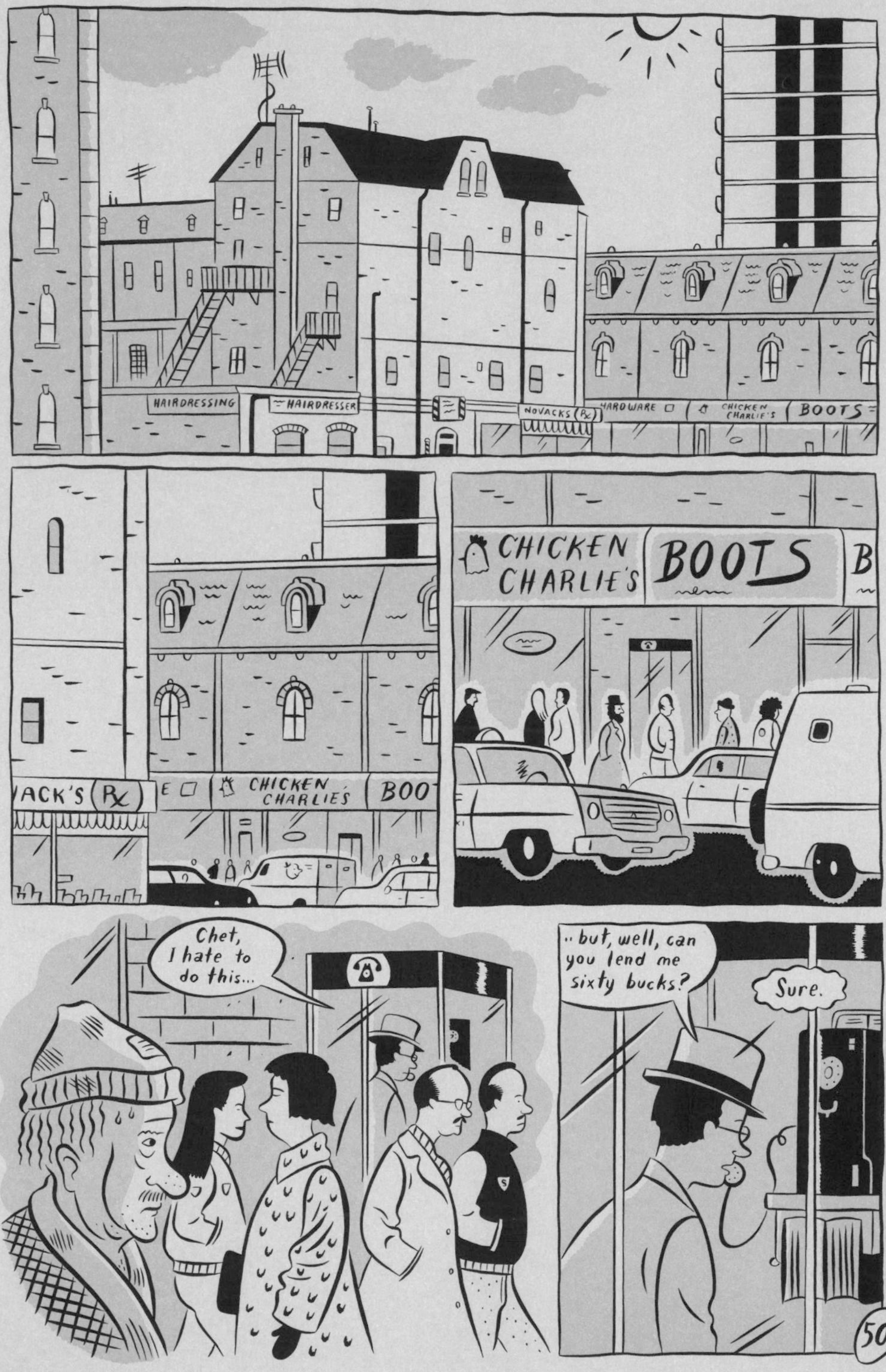
HAIRDRESSING
HAIRDRESSER
NOVACKS Rx
HARDWARE
CHICKEN CHARLIE'S
BOOTS
CHICKEN CHARLIE'S
BOOTS
Chet, I hate to do this...
.. but, well, can you lend me sixty bucks?
Sure.

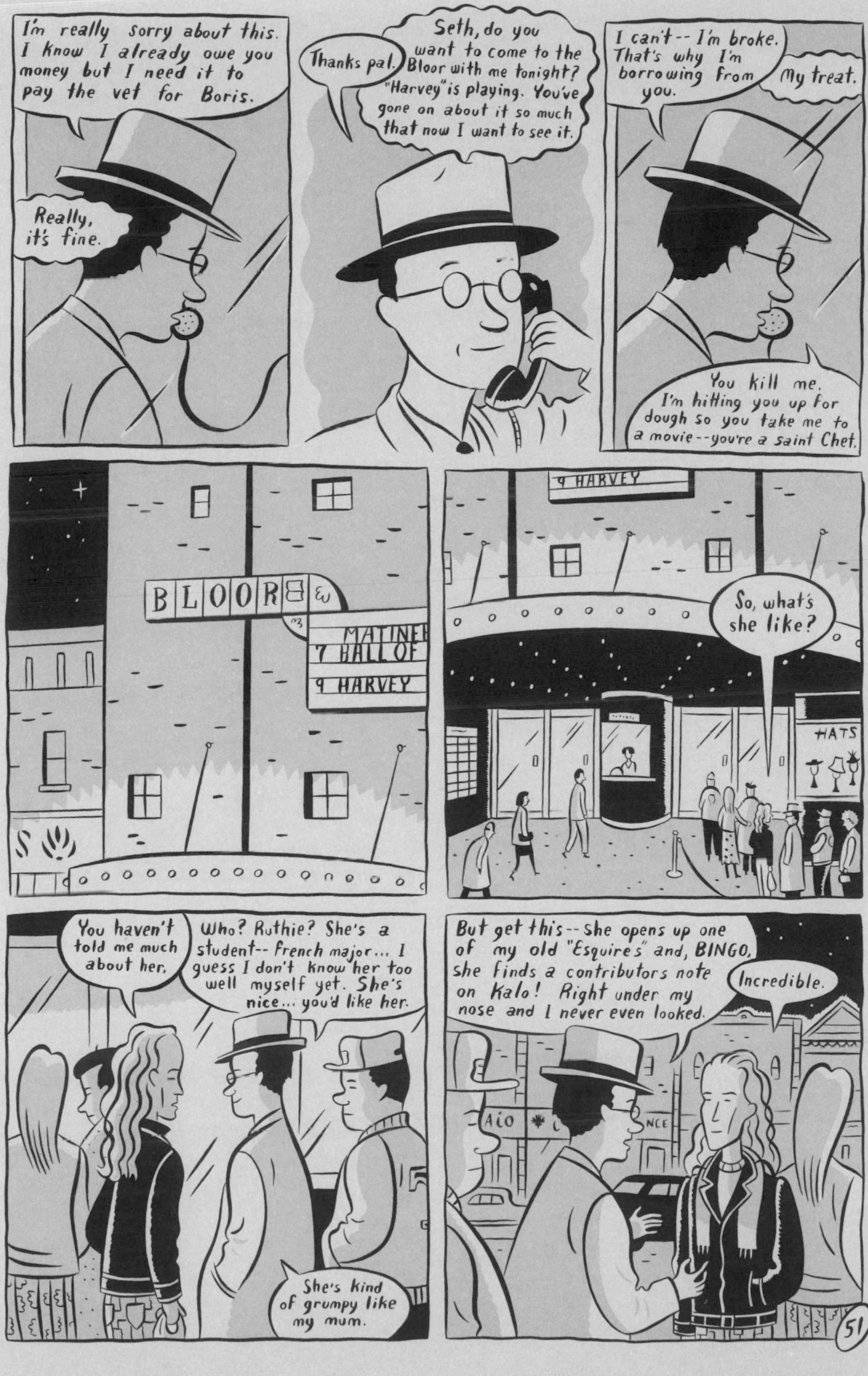
I'm really sorry about this. I know I already owe you money but I need it to pay the vet for Boris.
Really, it's fine.
Thanks pal.
Seth, do you want to come to the Bloor with me tonight? "Harvey" is playing. You've gone on about it so much that now I want to see it.
I can't -- I'm broke. That's why I'm borrowing from you.
My treat.
You kill me. I'm hitting you up for dough so you take me to a movie -- you're a saint Chet.
BLOOR
MATINEE
7 HALL OF
9 HARVEY
9 HARVEY
So, what's she like?
HATS
You haven't told me much about her.
Who? Ruthie? She's a student -- French major... I guess I don't know her too well myself yet. She's nice... you'd like her.
She's kind of grumpy like my mum.
But get this -- she opens up one of my old "Esquire's" and, BINGO, she finds a contributors note on Kalo! Right under my nose and I never even looked.
Incredible.

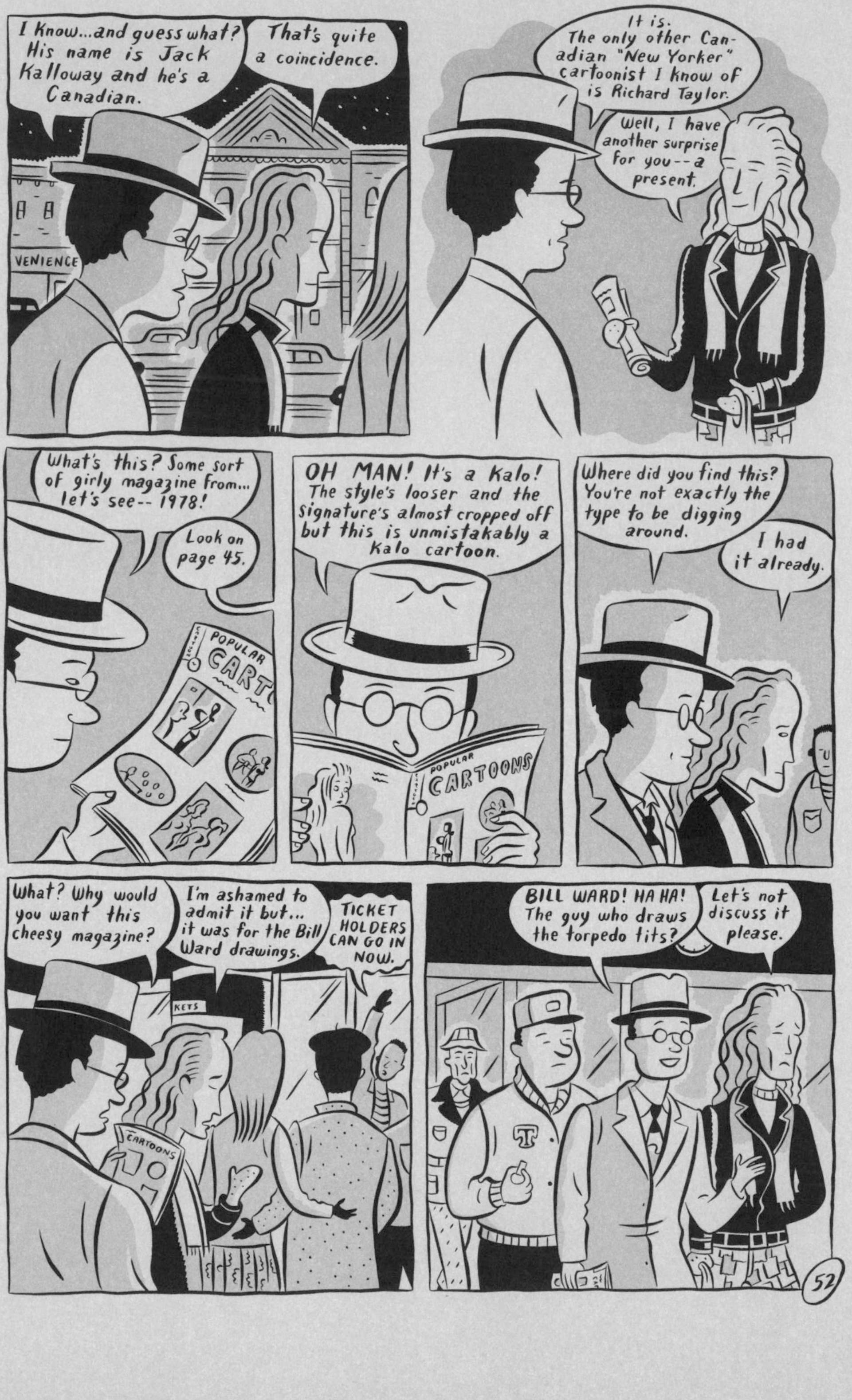
I Know...and guess what? His name is Jack Kalloway and he's a Canadian.
That's quite a coincidence.
VENIENCE
It is. The only other Canadian "New Yorker" cartoonist I know of is Richard Taylor.
Well, I have another surprise for you--a present.
What's this? Some sort of girly magazine from... let's see-- 1978!
Look on page 45.
POPULAR CARTO
OH MAN! It's a Kalo! The style's looser and the signature's almost cropped off but this is unmistakably a Kalo cartoon.
POPULAR CARTOONS
Where did you find this? You're not exactly the type to be digging around.
I had it already.
What? Why would you want this cheesy magazine?
I'm ashamed to admit it but... it was for the Bill Ward drawings.
TICKET HOLDERS CAN GO IN NOW.
KETS
CARTOONS
BILL WARD! HA HA! The guy who draws the torpedo tits?
Let's not discuss it please.

All these cartoons-- Wenzel, DeCarlo--this is all fifties stuff. I'd bet these are all reprints.

See this? It's my next step.

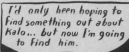

ONTARIO REGISTRAR
P.O. Box 4600
Thunder Bay, ONT.
P7B 6L8

With this letter I should be able to get the date and place of his birth... and death if that's unfortunately the case.

Y'know, all this new information changes everything.

I'd only been hoping to find something out about Kalo... but now I'm going to find him.

Oh, it's starting.

END OF PART 2

Part Three

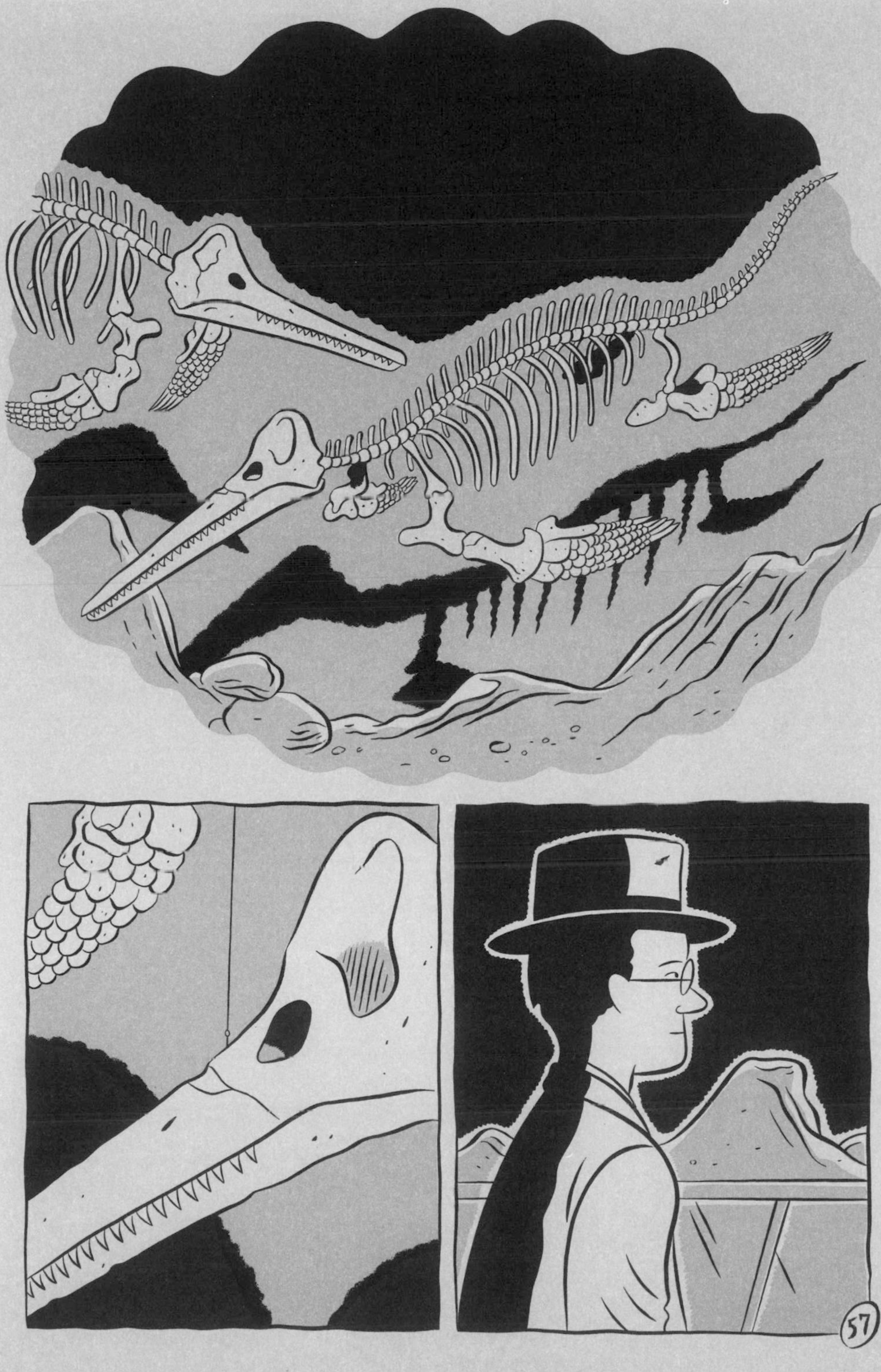

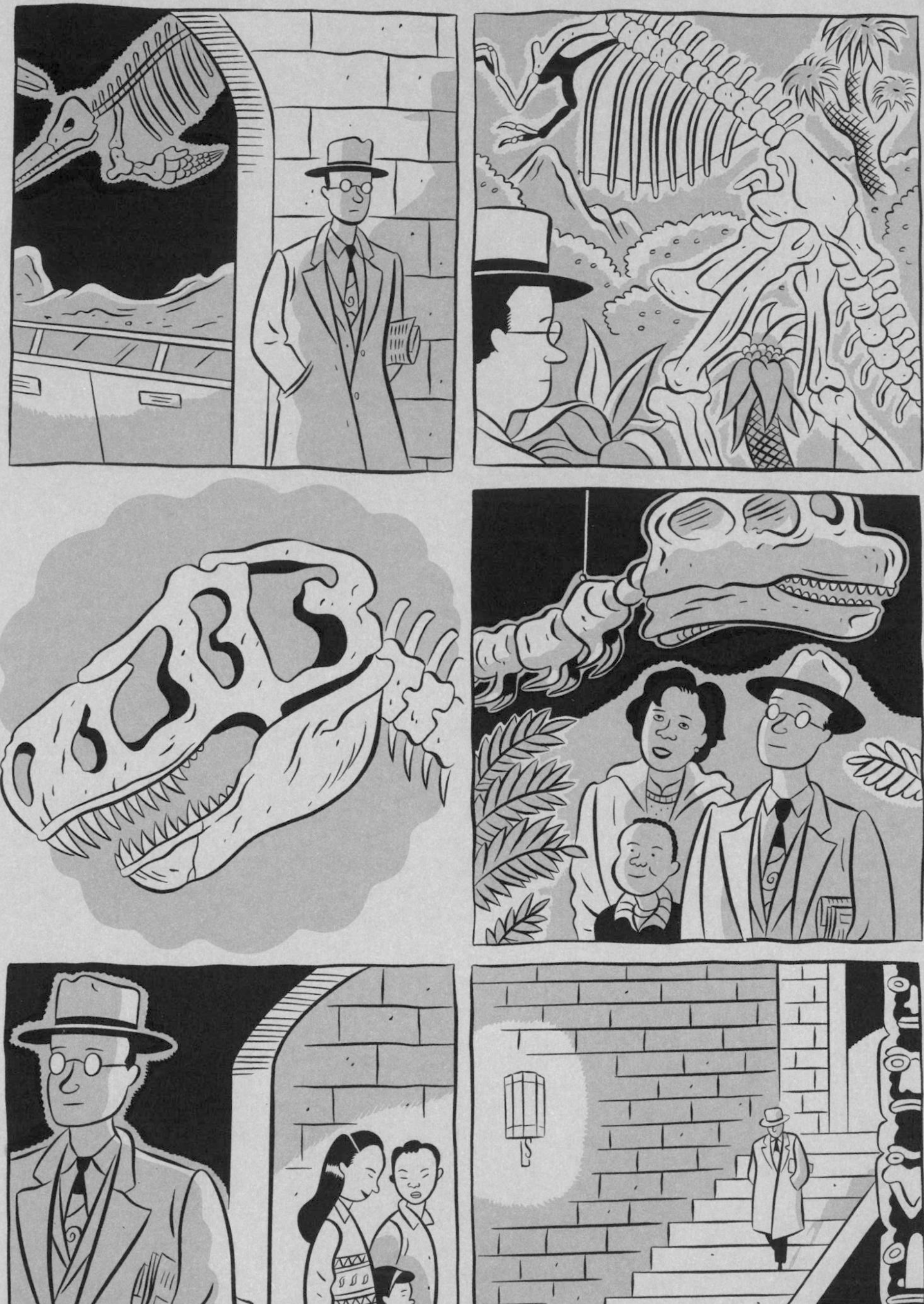

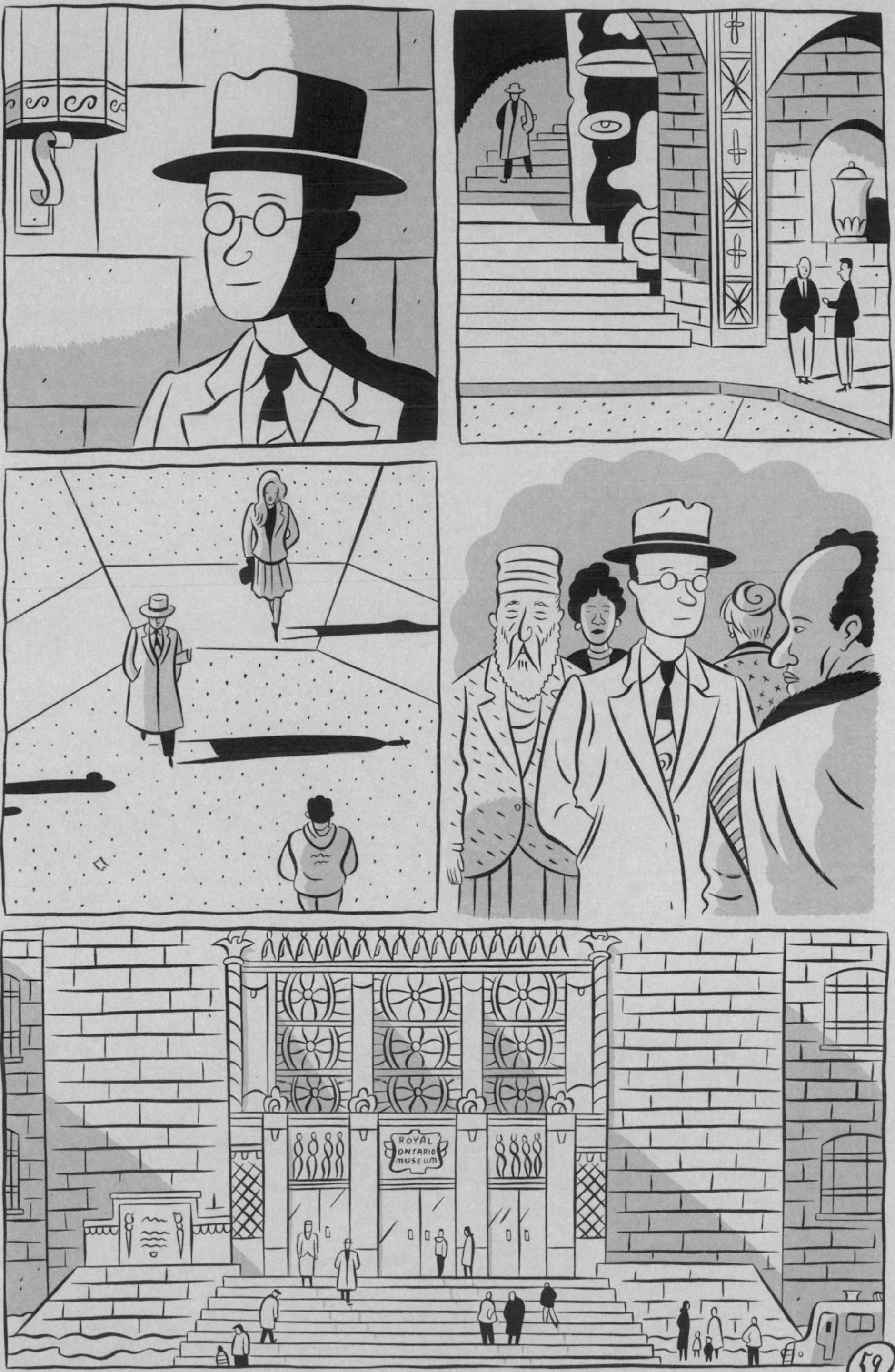
ROYAL ONTARIO MUSEUM

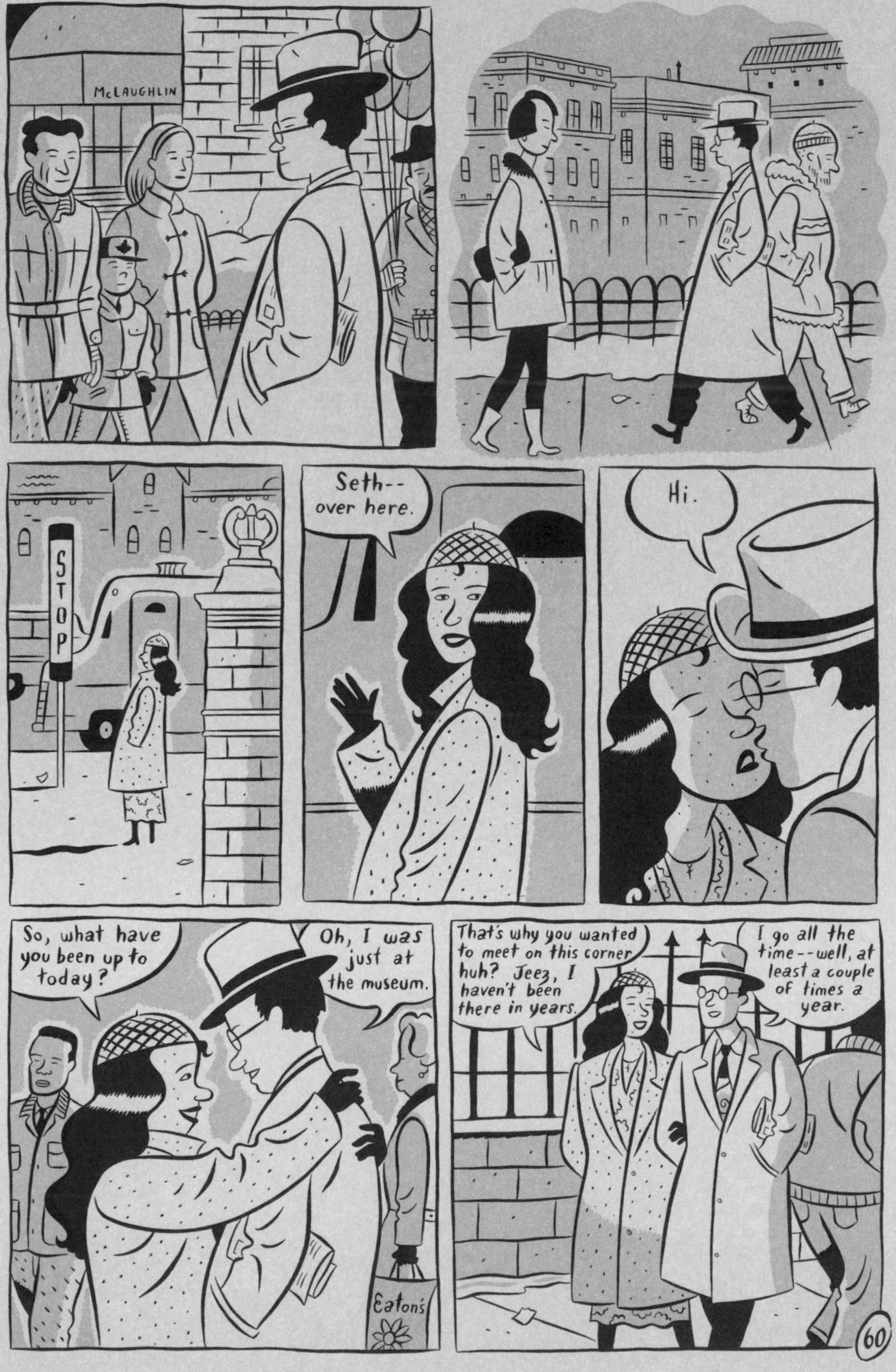
McLAUGHLIN
STOP
Seth-- over here.
Hi.
So, what have you been up to today?
Oh, I was just at the museum.
Eaton's
That's why you wanted to meet on this corner huh? Jeez, I haven't been there in years.
I go all the time--well, at least a couple of times a year.

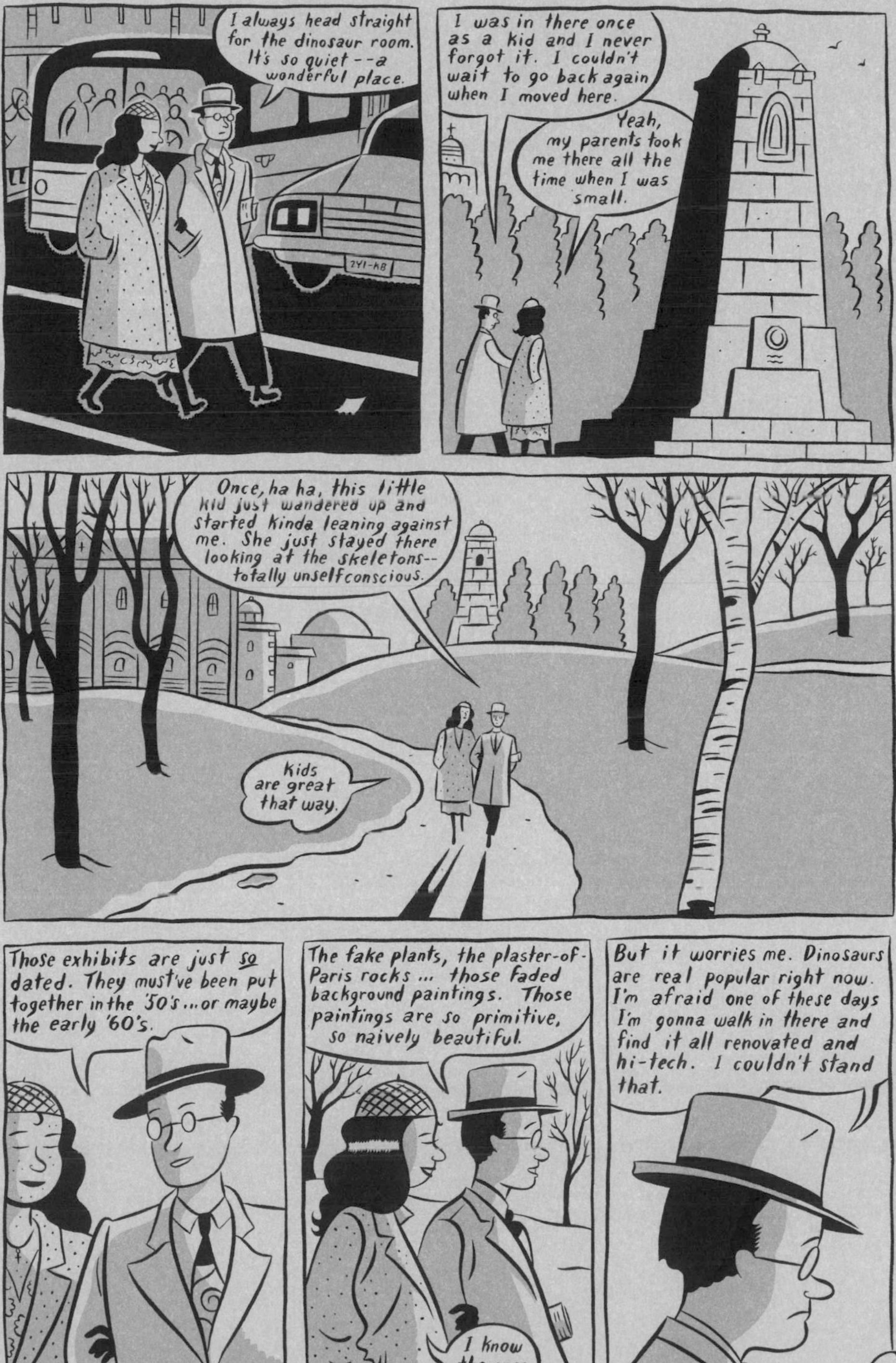
I always head straight for the dinosaur room. It's so quiet --a wonderful place.
I was in there once as a kid and I never forgot it. I couldn't wait to go back again when I moved here.
Yeah, my parents took me there all the time when I was small.
Once, ha ha, this little kid just wandered up and started kinda leaning against me. She just stayed there looking at the skeletons-- totally unselfconscious.
Kids are great that way.
Those exhibits are just so dated. They must've been put together in the '50's ... or maybe the early '60's.
The fake plants, the plaster-of-Paris rocks ... those faded background paintings. Those paintings are so primitive, so naively beautiful.
I know the ones.
But it worries me. Dinosaurs are real popular right now. I'm afraid one of these days I'm gonna walk in there and find it all renovated and hi-tech. I couldn't stand that.

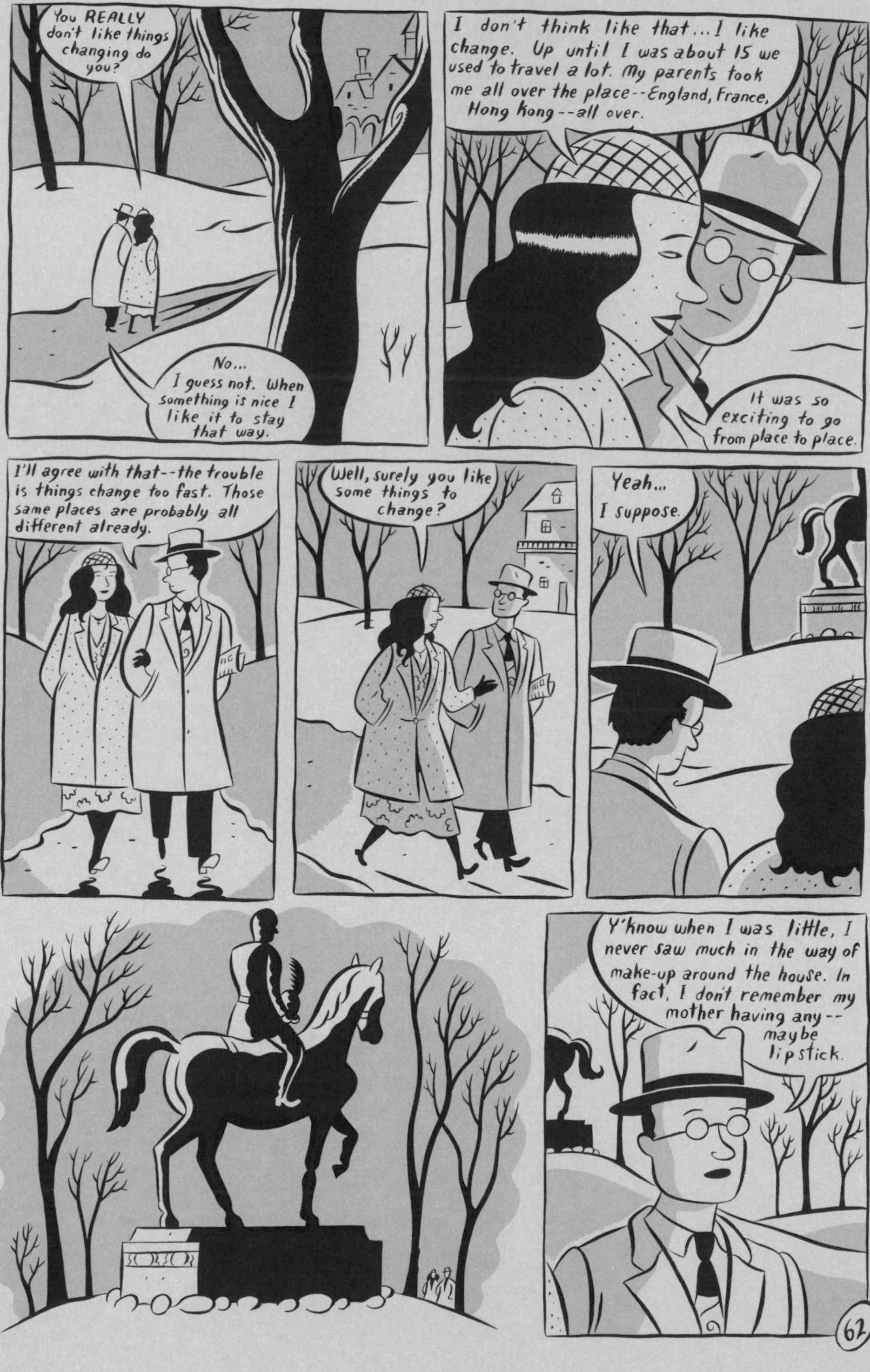
You REALLY don't like things changing do you?
No... I guess not. When something is nice I like it to stay that way.
I don't think like that... I like change. Up until I was about 15 we used to travel a lot. My parents took me all over the place--England, France, Hong Kong--all over.
It was so exciting to go from place to place.
I'll agree with that--the trouble is things change too fast. Those same places are probably all different already.
Well, surely you like some things to change?
Yeah... I suppose.
Y'know when I was little, I never saw much in the way of make-up around the house. In fact, I don't remember my mother having any--maybe lipstick.

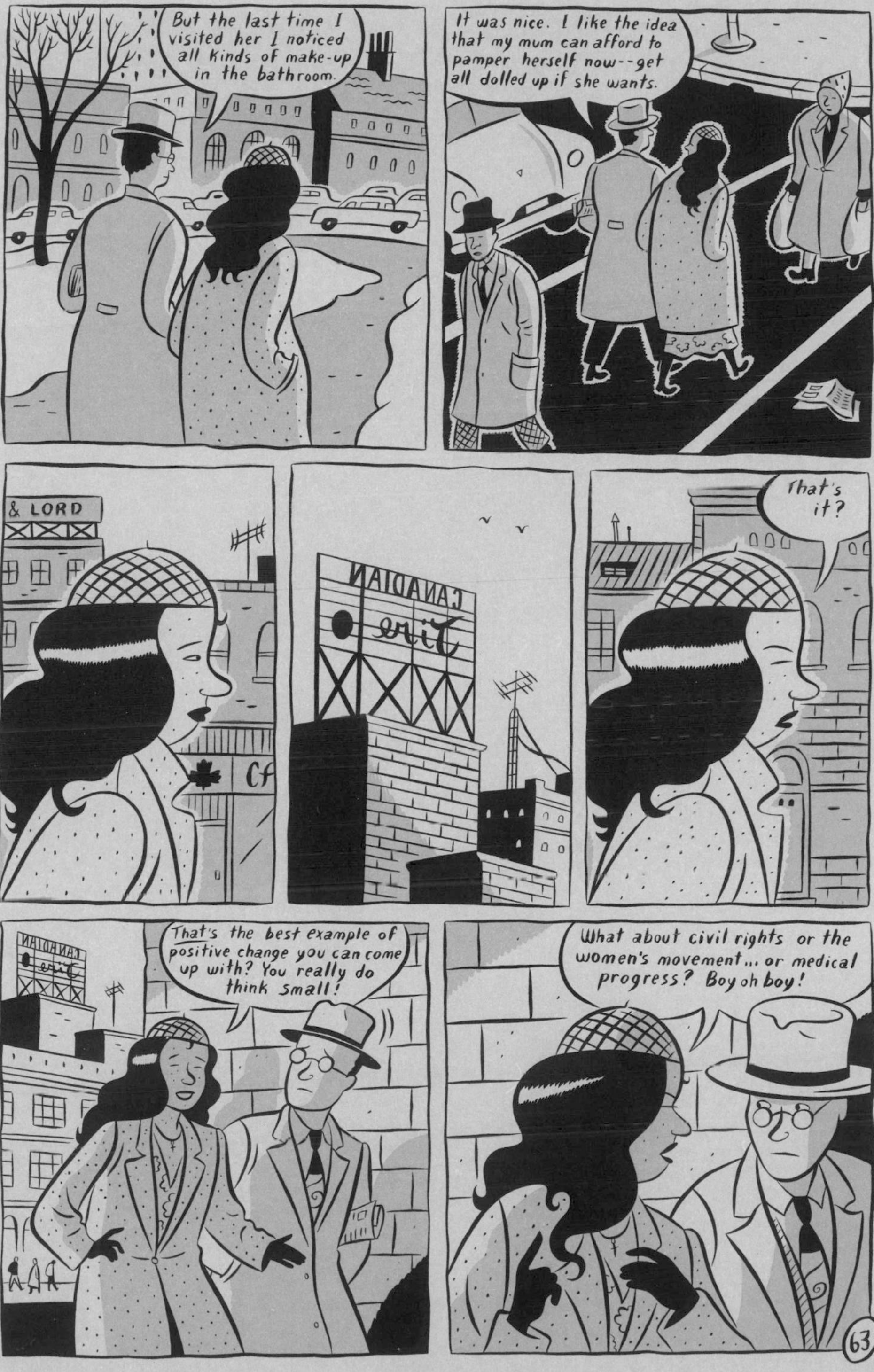
But the last time I visited her I noticed all kinds of make-up in the bathroom.
It was nice. I like the idea that my mum can afford to pamper herself now--get all dolled up if she wants.
& LORD
CANADIAN Tire
That's it?
That's the best example of positive change you can come up with? You really do think small!
What about civil rights or the women's movement... or medical progress? Boy oh boy!

Well sure, that goes without saying. Jeez, I...

Life is about change. I mean, don't you get excited just thinking about the future?

So much will have changed by the time we're old--it'll be amazing! Think of the old people today and how much change they've seen.

Don't even talk about it.

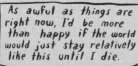

I look forward to the future with nothing but dread. Things are getting worse and worse every year.

As awful as things are right now, I'd be more than happy if the world would just stay relatively like this until I die.

I can't face the next fifty years.

64

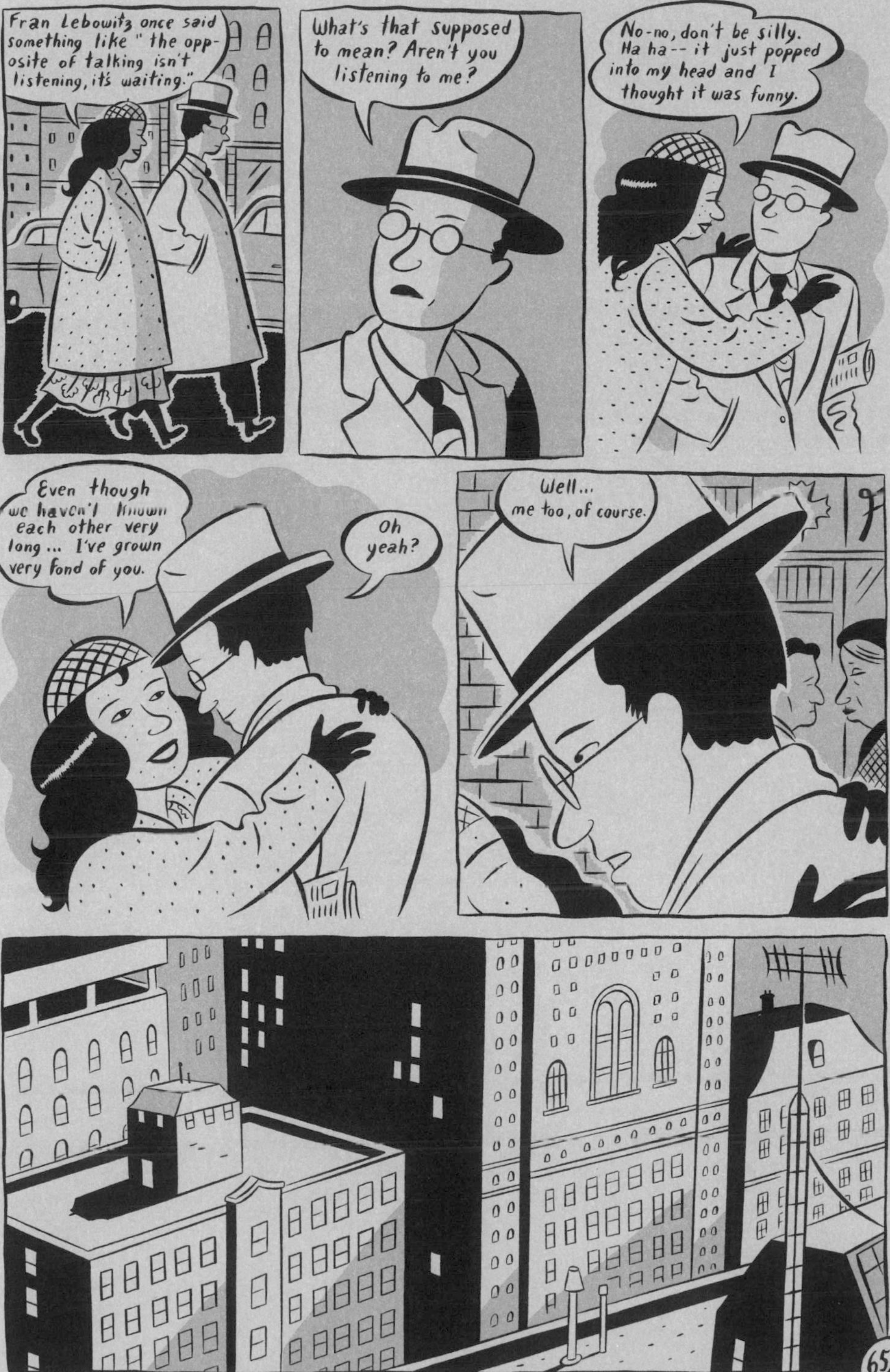
Fran Lebowitz once said something like "the opposite of talking isn't listening, it's waiting."
What's that supposed to mean? Aren't you listening to me?
No-no, don't be silly. Ha ha-- it just popped into my head and I thought it was funny.
Even though we haven't known each other very long ... I've grown very fond of you.
Oh yeah?
Well... me too, of course.

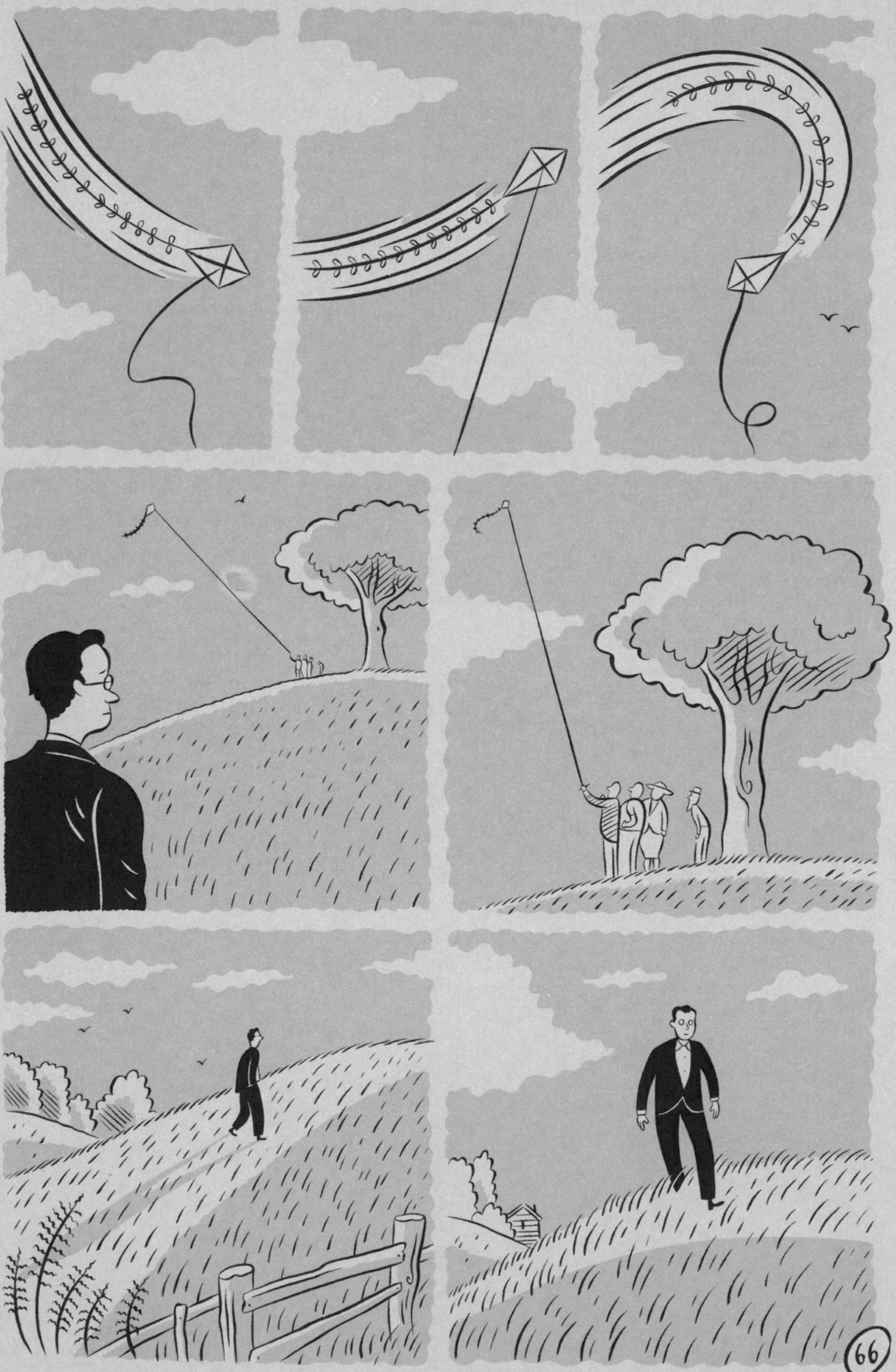

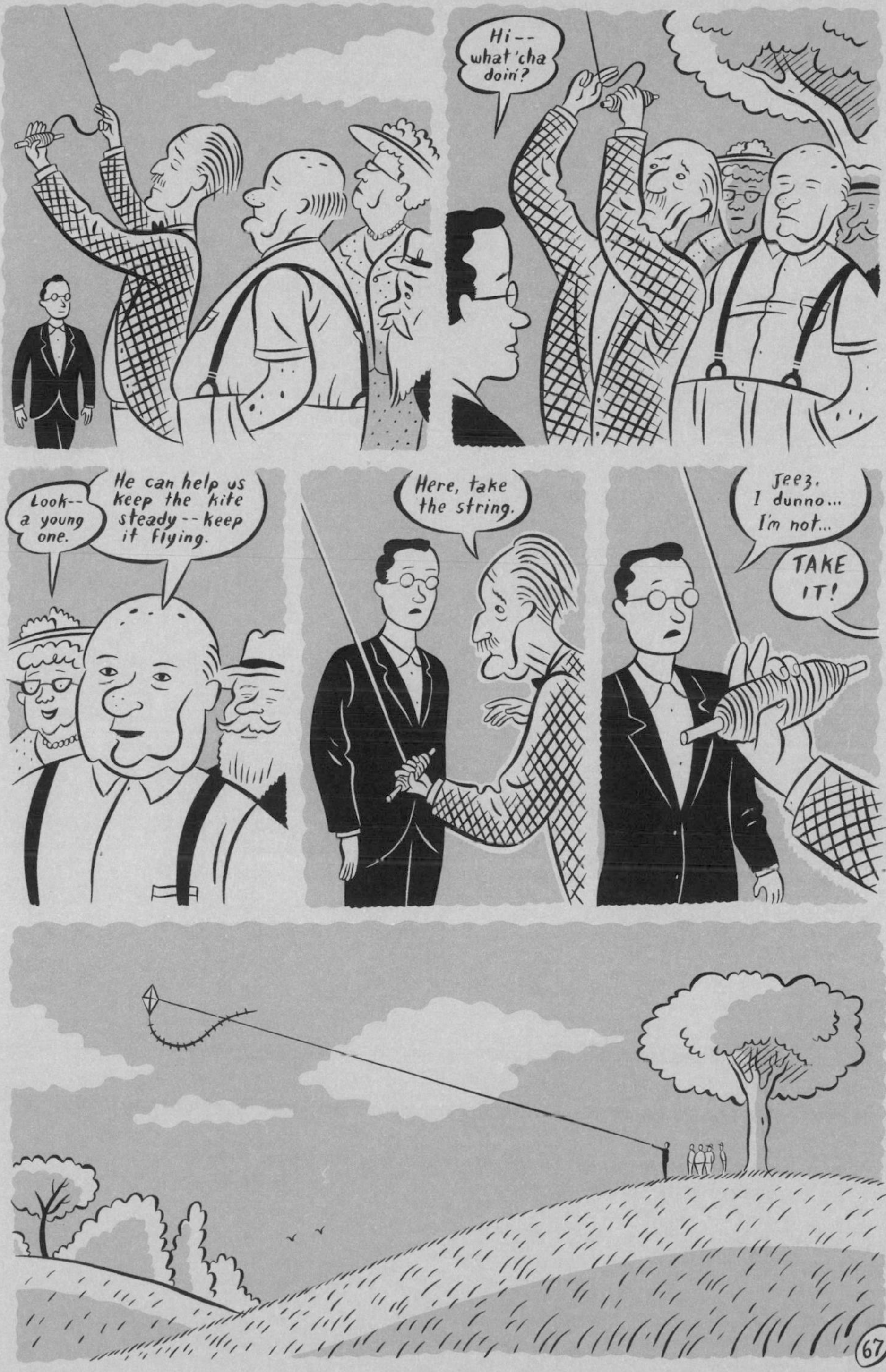
Hi--
what'cha
doin'?
Look--
a young
one.
He can help us
keep the kite
steady--keep
it flying.
Here, take
the string.
Jeez.
I dunno...
I'm not...
TAKE
IT!

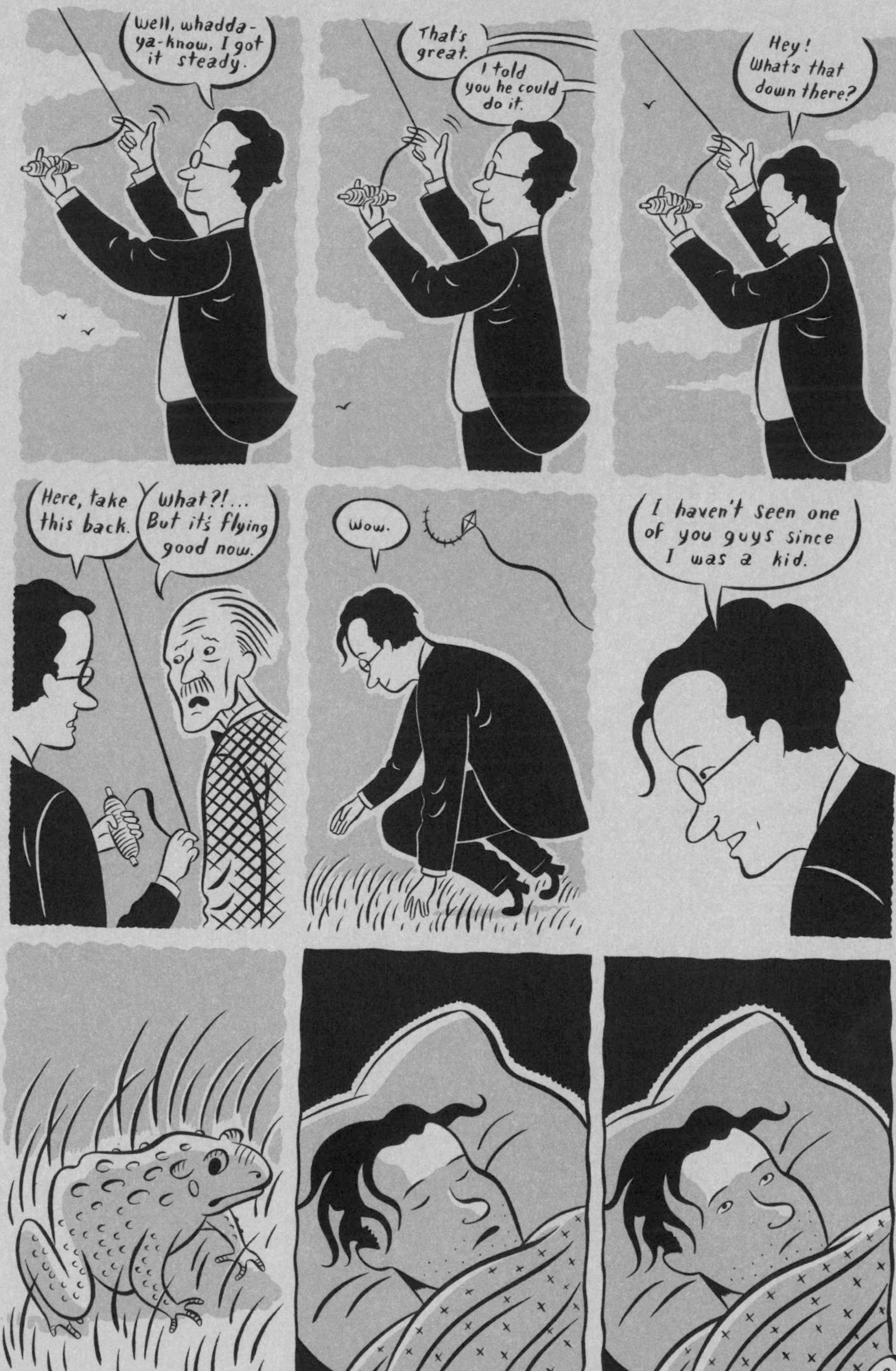
Well, whadda-ya-know, I got it steady.
That's great.
I told you he could do it.
Hey! What's that down there?
Here, take this back.
What?!... But it's flying good now.
Wow.
I haven't seen one of you guys since I was a kid.

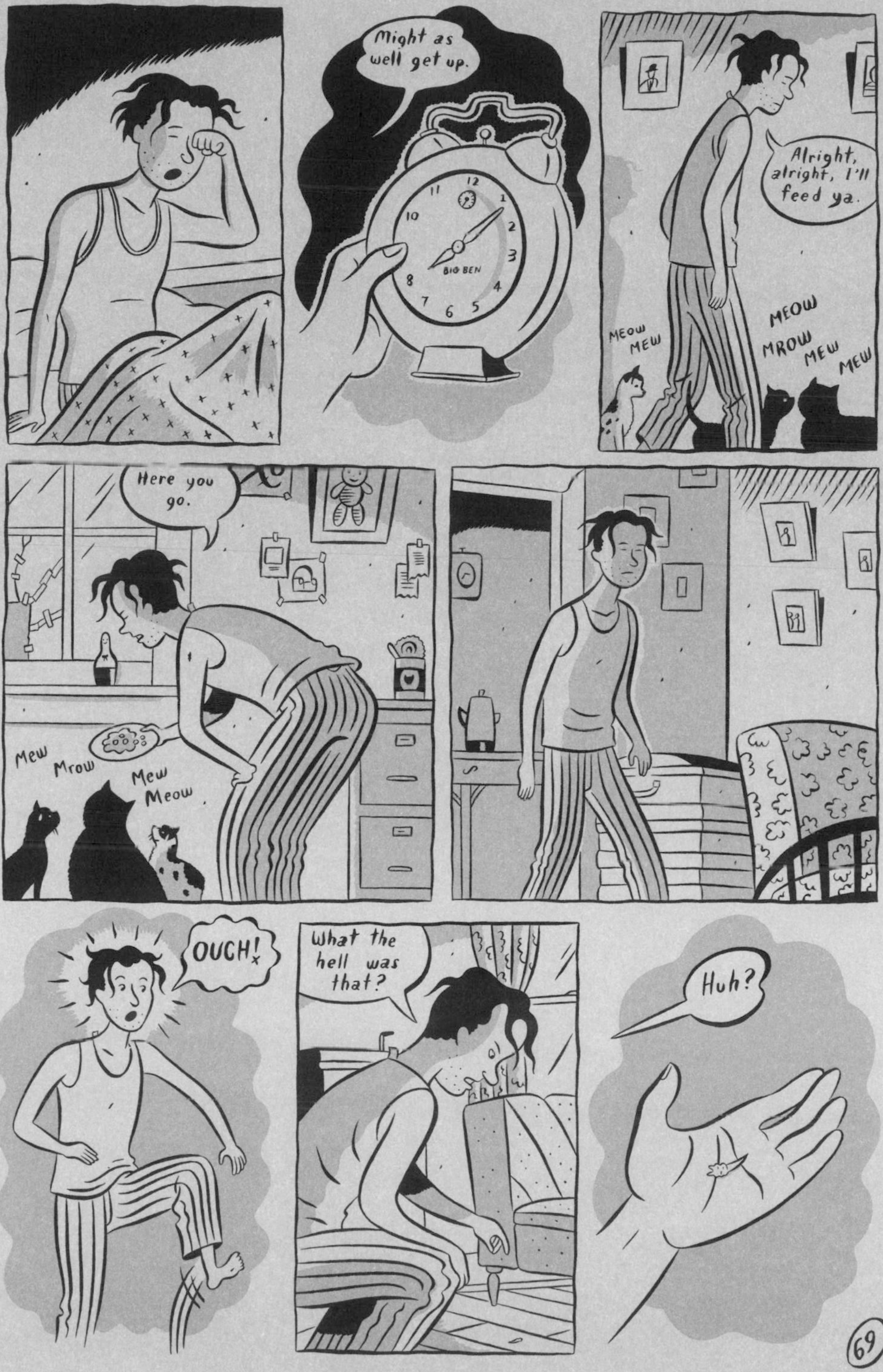
Might as well get up.
BIG BEN
Alright, alright, I'll feed ya.
MEOW MEW
MEOW MROW MEW MEW
Here you go.
Mew Mrow Mew Meow
OUCH!
What the hell was that?
Huh?

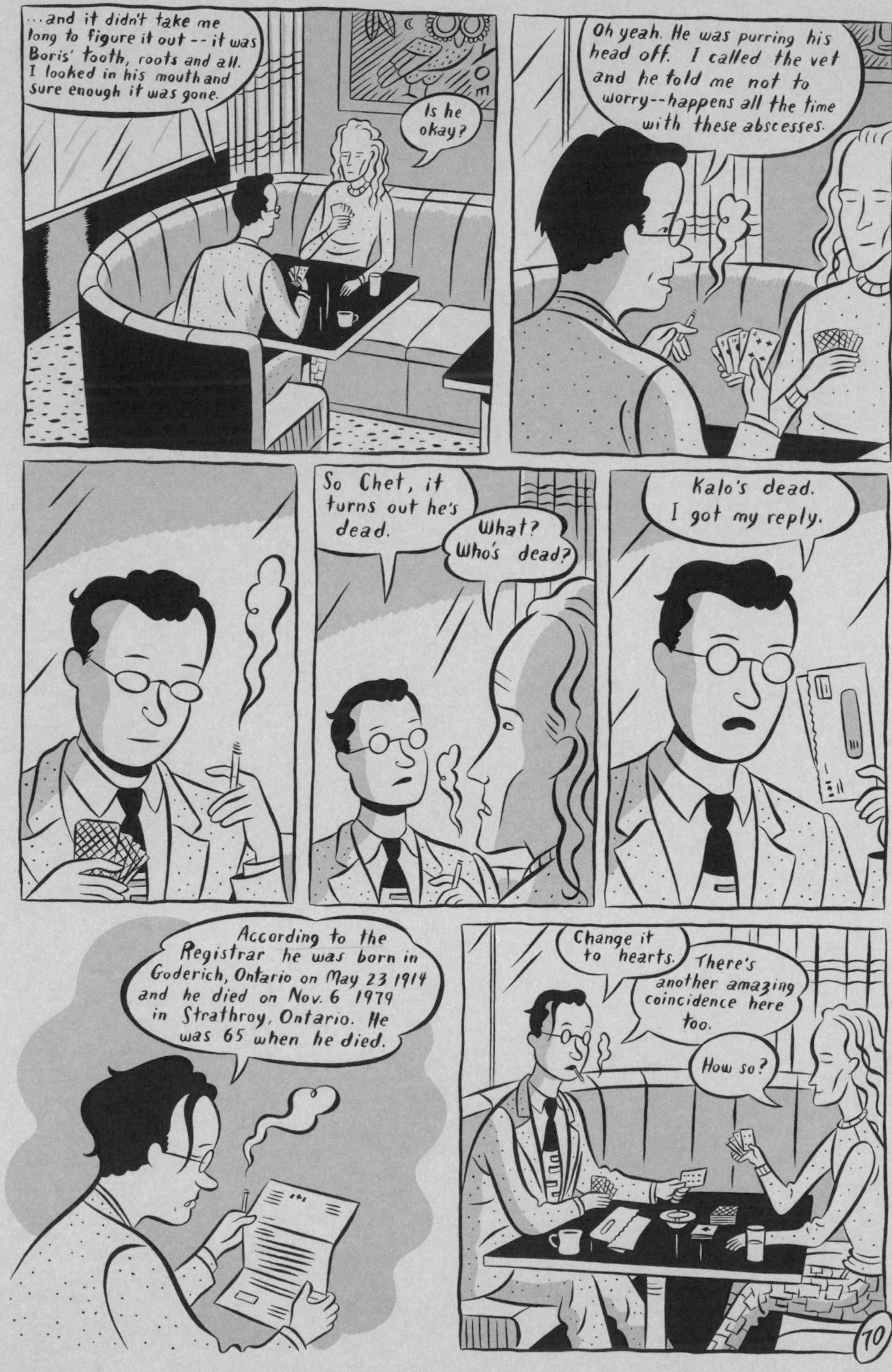
...and it didn't take me long to figure it out -- it was Boris' tooth, roots and all. I looked in his mouth and sure enough it was gone.
Is he okay?
Oh yeah. He was purring his head off. I called the vet and he told me not to worry--happens all the time with these abscesses.
So Chet, it turns out he's dead.
What? Who's dead?
Kalo's dead. I got my reply.
According to the Registrar he was born in Goderich, Ontario on May 23 1914 and he died on Nov. 6 1979 in Strathroy, Ontario. He was 65 when he died.
Change it to hearts.
There's another amazing coincidence here too.
How so?

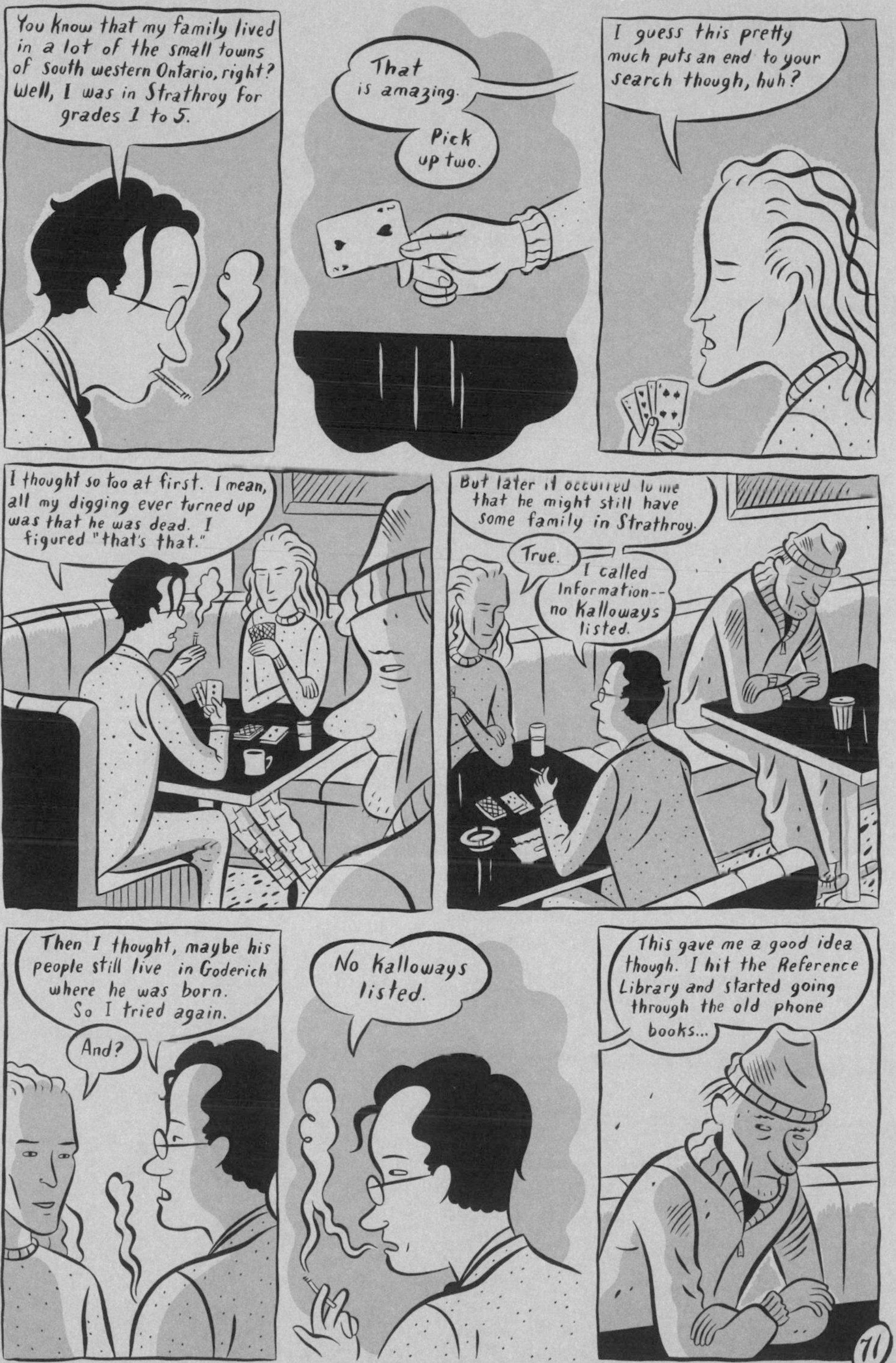
You know that my family lived in a lot of the small towns of south western Ontario, right? Well, I was in Strathroy for grades 1 to 5.
That is amazing.
Pick up two.
I guess this pretty much puts an end to your search though, huh?
I thought so too at first. I mean, all my digging ever turned up was that he was dead. I figured "that's that."
But later it occurred to me that he might still have some family in Strathroy.
True.
I called Information--no Kalloways listed.
Then I thought, maybe his people still live in Goderich where he was born. So I tried again.
And?
No Kalloways listed.
This gave me a good idea though. I hit the Reference Library and started going through the old phone books...

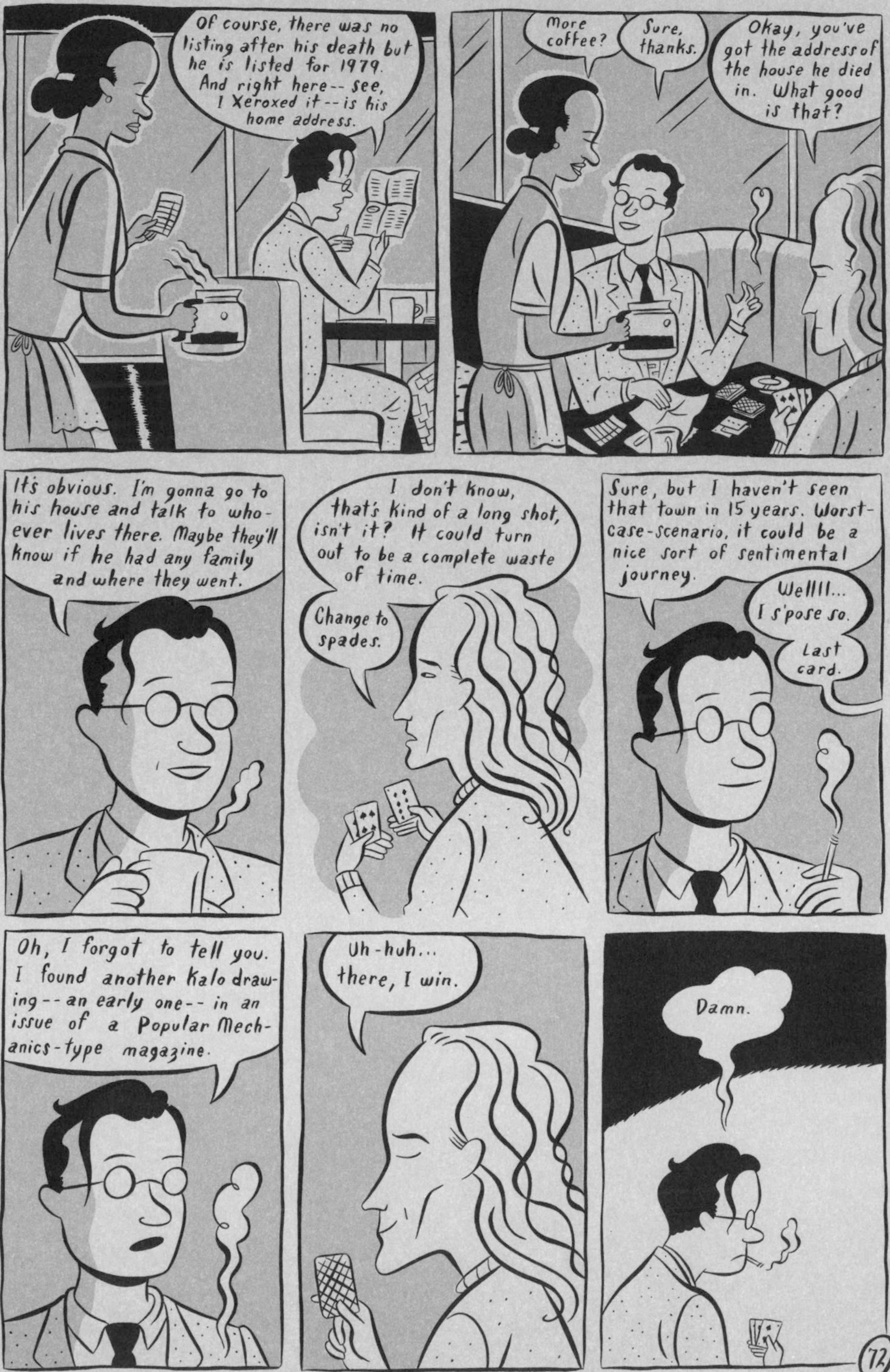
Of course, there was no listing after his death but he is listed for 1979. And right here-- see, I Xeroxed it--is his home address.
More coffee?
Sure, thanks.
Okay, you've got the address of the house he died in. What good is that?
It's obvious. I'm gonna go to his house and talk to who-ever lives there. Maybe they'll know if he had any family and where they went.
I don't know, that's kind of a long shot, isn't it? It could turn out to be a complete waste of time.
Change to spades.
Sure, but I haven't seen that town in 15 years. Worst-case-scenario, it could be a nice sort of sentimental journey.
Wellll... I s'pose so.
Last card.
Oh, I forgot to tell you. I found another Kalo draw-ing--an early one--in an issue of a Popular Mech-anics-type magazine.
Uh-huh... there, I win.
Damn.

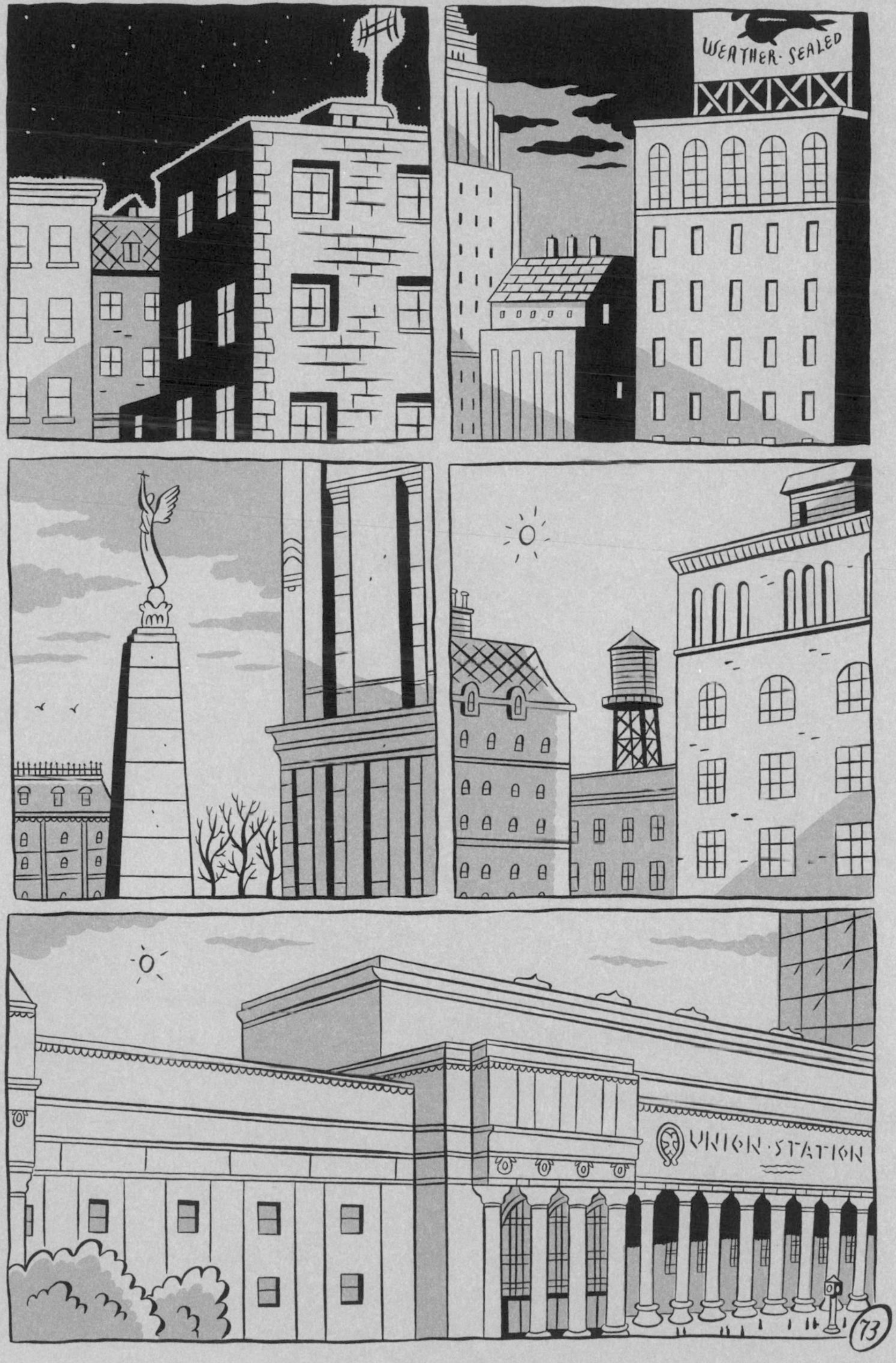
WEATHER-SEALED
UNION·STATION

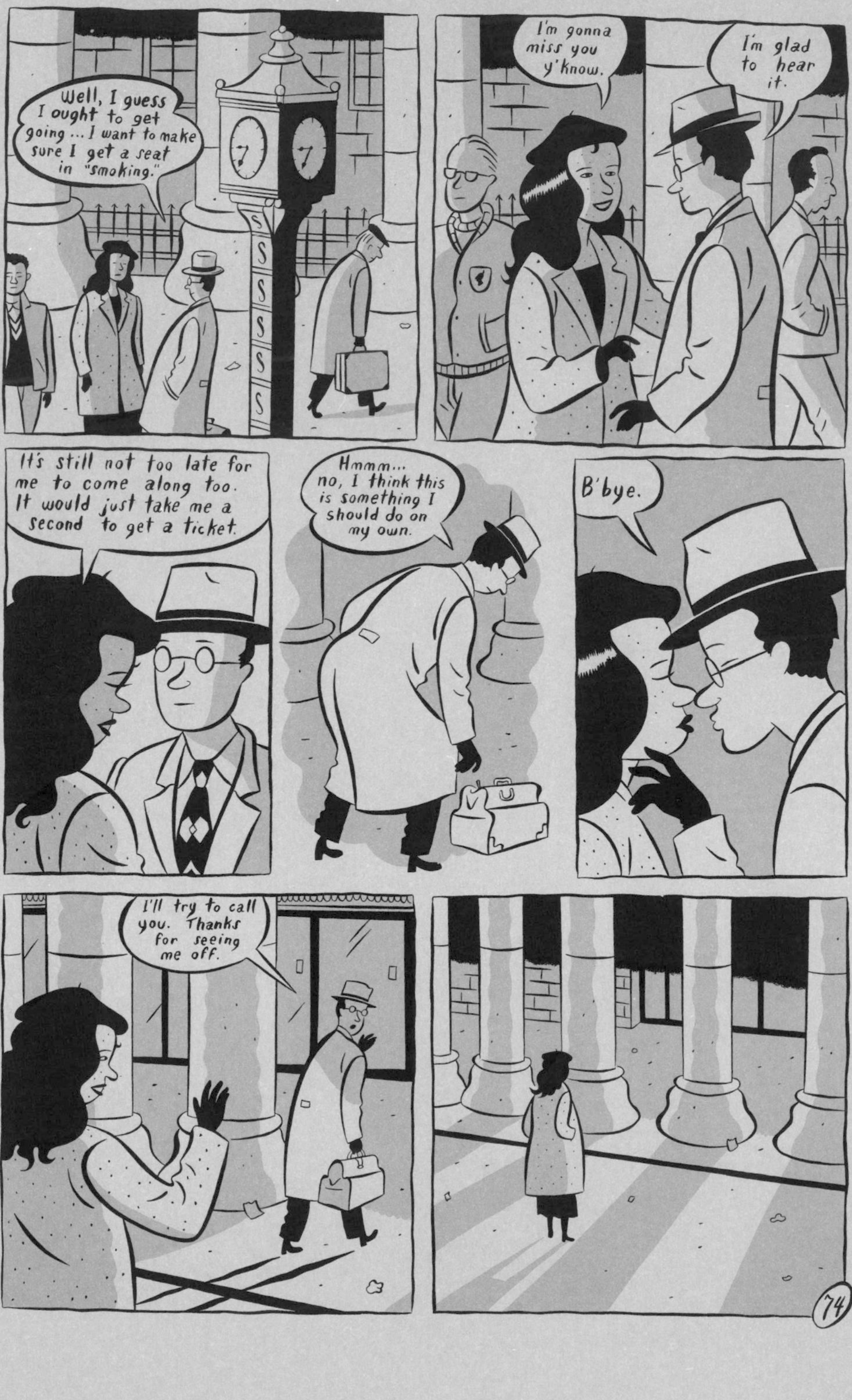
Well, I guess I ought to get going ... I want to make sure I get a seat in "smoking."
I'm gonna miss you y'know.
I'm glad to hear it.
It's still not too late for me to come along too. It would just take me a second to get a ticket.
Hmmm... no, I think this is something I should do on my own.
B'bye.
I'll try to call you. Thanks for seeing me off.
74

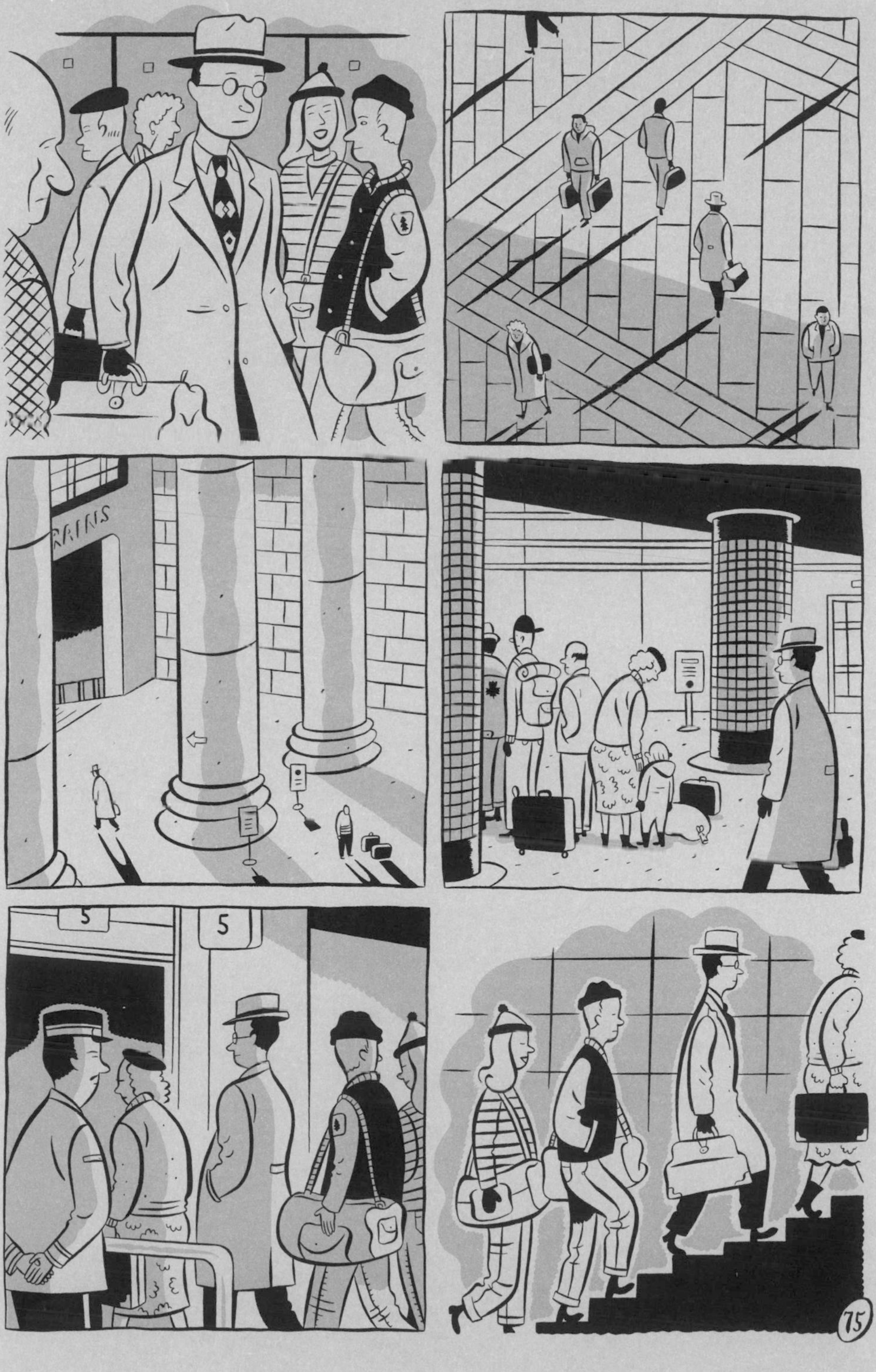
RAINS
5
5

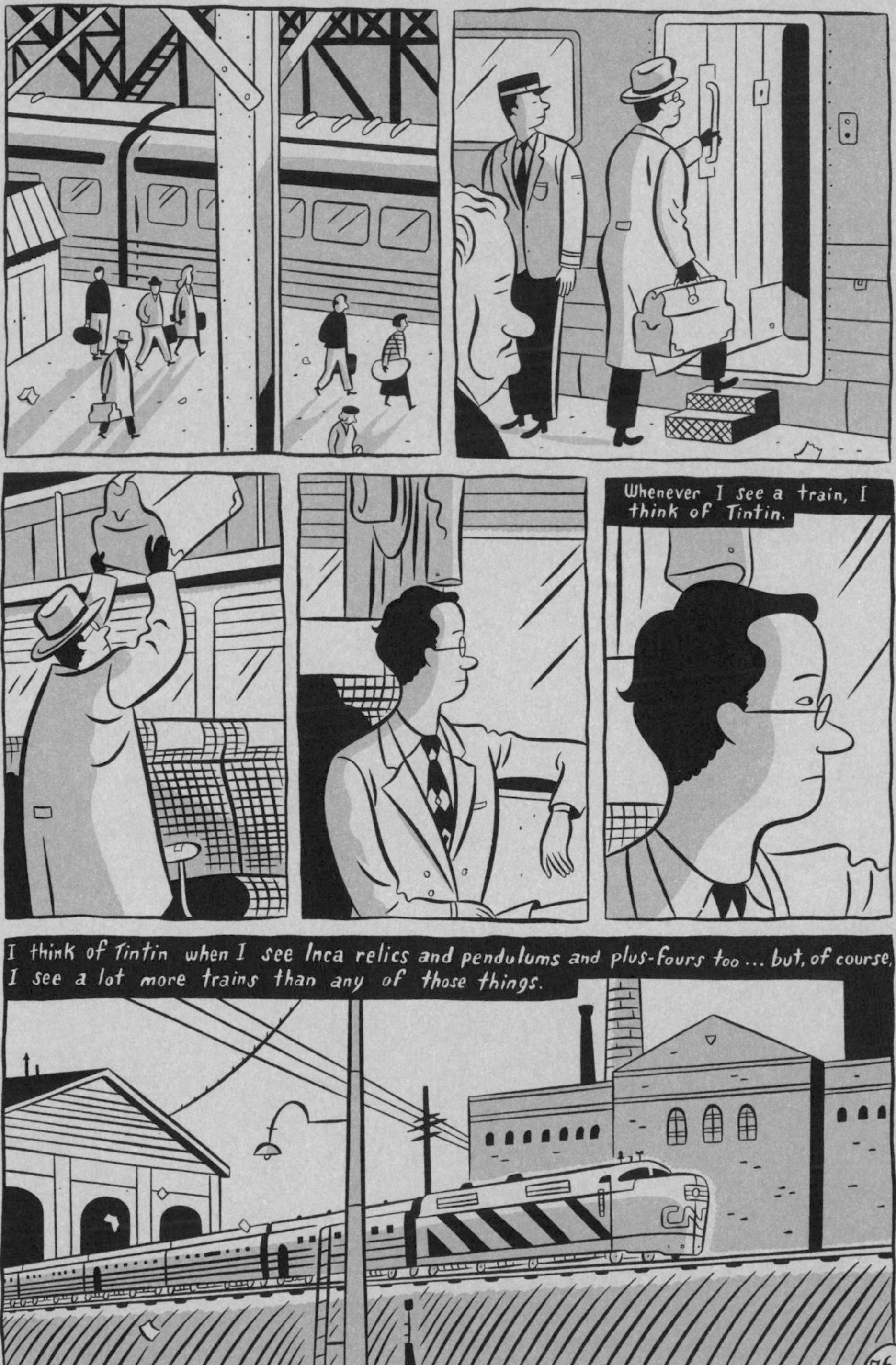
Whenever I see a train, I think of Tintin.
I think of Tintin when I see Inca relics and pendulums and plus-fours too ... but, of course, I see a lot more trains than any of those things.
CN

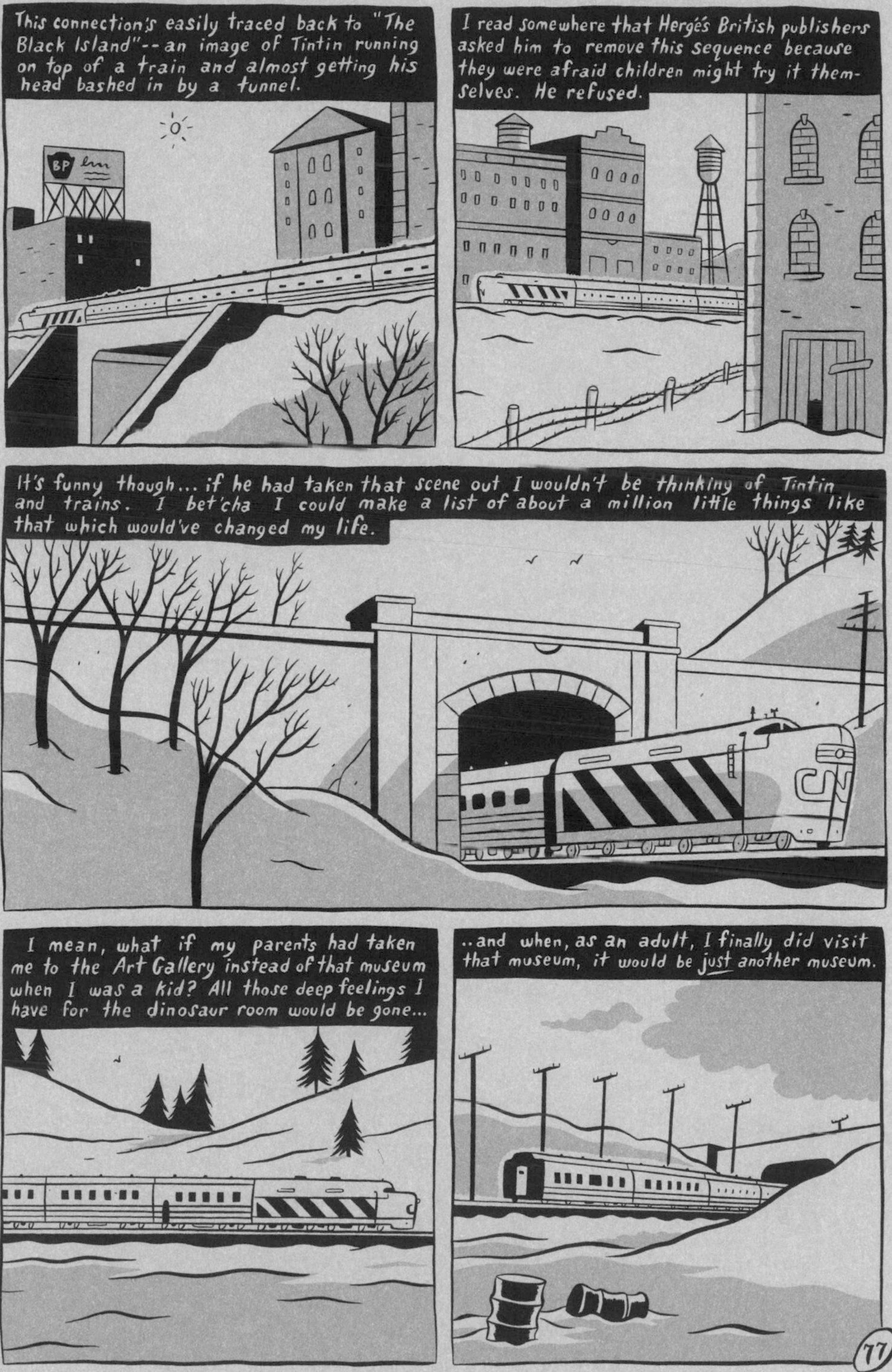
This connection's easily traced back to "The Black Island"-- an image of Tintin running on top of a train and almost getting his head bashed in by a tunnel.
I read somewhere that Hergé's British publishers asked him to remove this sequence because they were afraid children might try it themselves. He refused.
It's funny though... if he had taken that scene out I wouldn't be thinking of Tintin and trains. I bet'cha I could make a list of about a million little things like that which would've changed my life.
I mean, what if my parents had taken me to the Art Gallery instead of that museum when I was a kid? All those deep feelings I have for the dinosaur room would be gone...
..and when, as an adult, I finally did visit that museum, it would be just another museum.

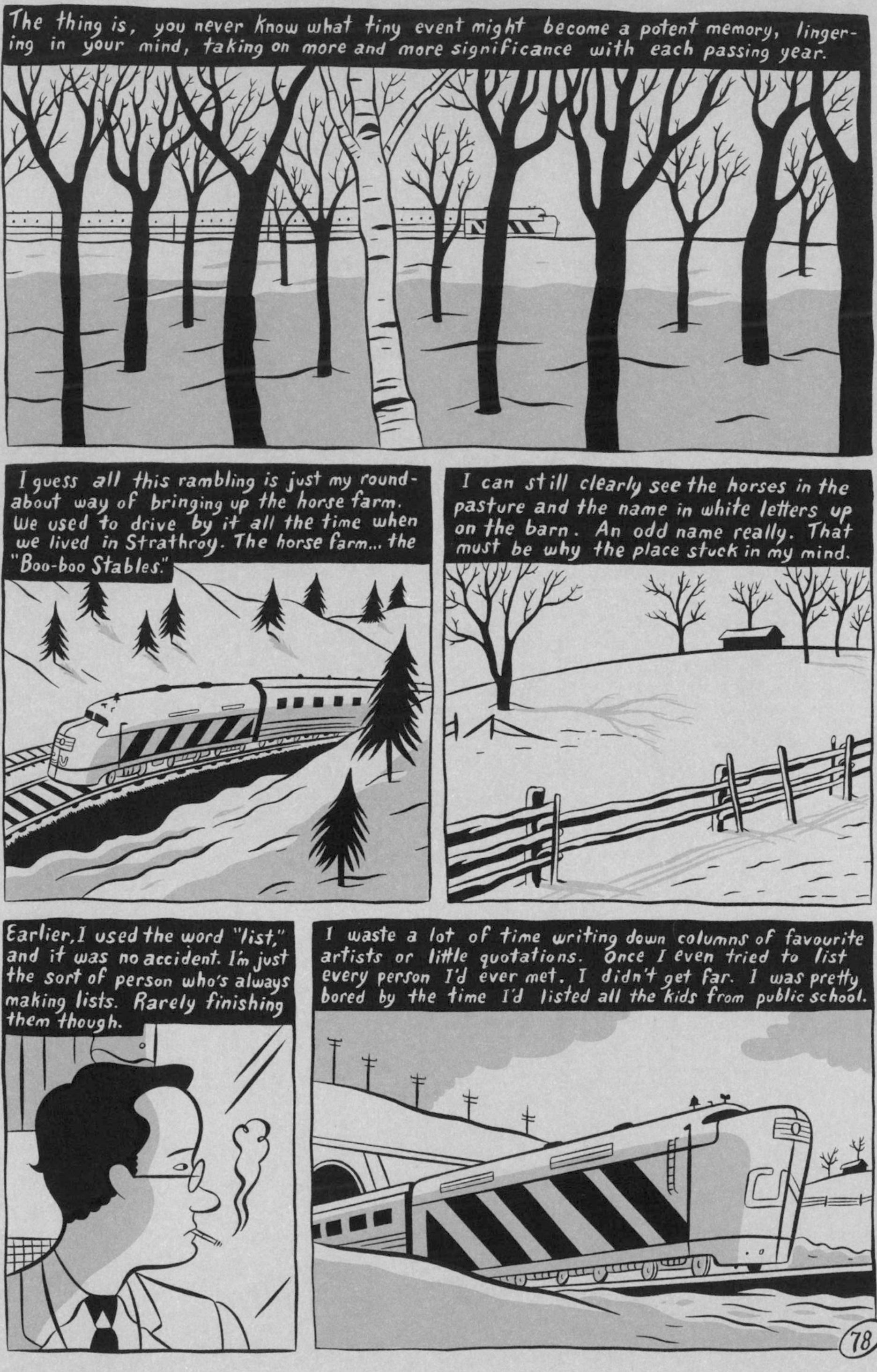
The thing is, you never know what tiny event might become a potent memory, lingering in your mind, taking on more and more significance with each passing year.
I guess all this rambling is just my roundabout way of bringing up the horse farm. We used to drive by it all the time when we lived in Strathroy. The horse farm... the "Boo-boo Stables."
I can still clearly see the horses in the pasture and the name in white letters up on the barn. An odd name really. That must be why the place stuck in my mind.
Earlier, I used the word "list," and it was no accident. I'm just the sort of person who's always making lists. Rarely finishing them though.
I waste a lot of time writing down columns of favourite artists or little quotations. Once I even tried to list every person I'd ever met. I didn't get far. I was pretty bored by the time I'd listed all the kids from public school.

Not too long ago, I wrote out a huge list under the title "Good Things". I KNOW, I KNOW, a real sappy "Hallmark" kind of idea but what do you think made the top ten? That's right, the "Boo-boo Stables."
Oh sure, the rest of the list was mostly cartoonists. That's to be expected. The question is -- why were those stables on the list at all? We never once stopped the car there.
CN STRATHROY
Here's what kills me. Whenever I'm travelling around Ontario I'm really keeping my eyes open for them. Where do I think I'll see them? I'm not even sure where they're located. I guess near Strathroy... but maybe not. Maybe London. Or Grand Bend. They're probably long gone anyway.
CN STRATHROY
It's not like I'm expecting some grand epiphany or anything...
.. but it would be nice to wander into some town or turn a corner and find them there, still standing.
That would be nice.
79

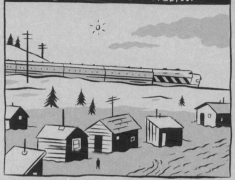

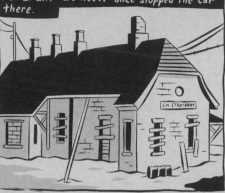

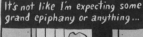

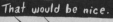

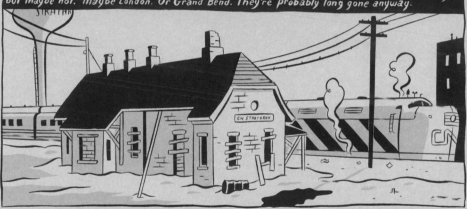

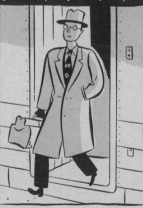

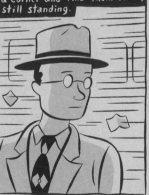

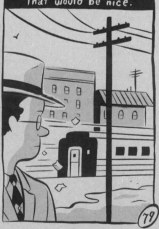

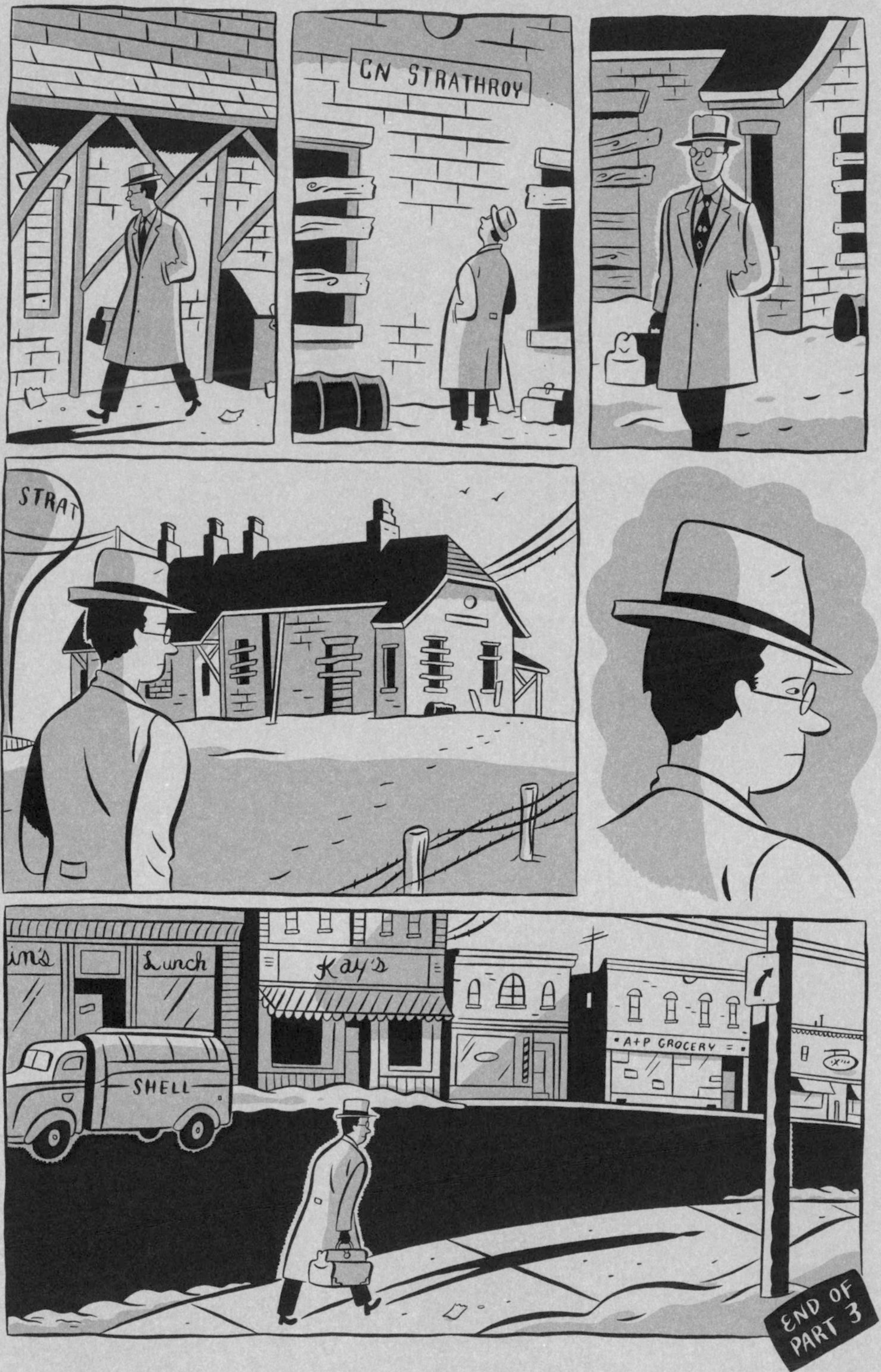

CN STRATHROY
STRAT
in's Lunch
Kay's
SHELL
A+P GROCERY
END OF PART 3

Part Four

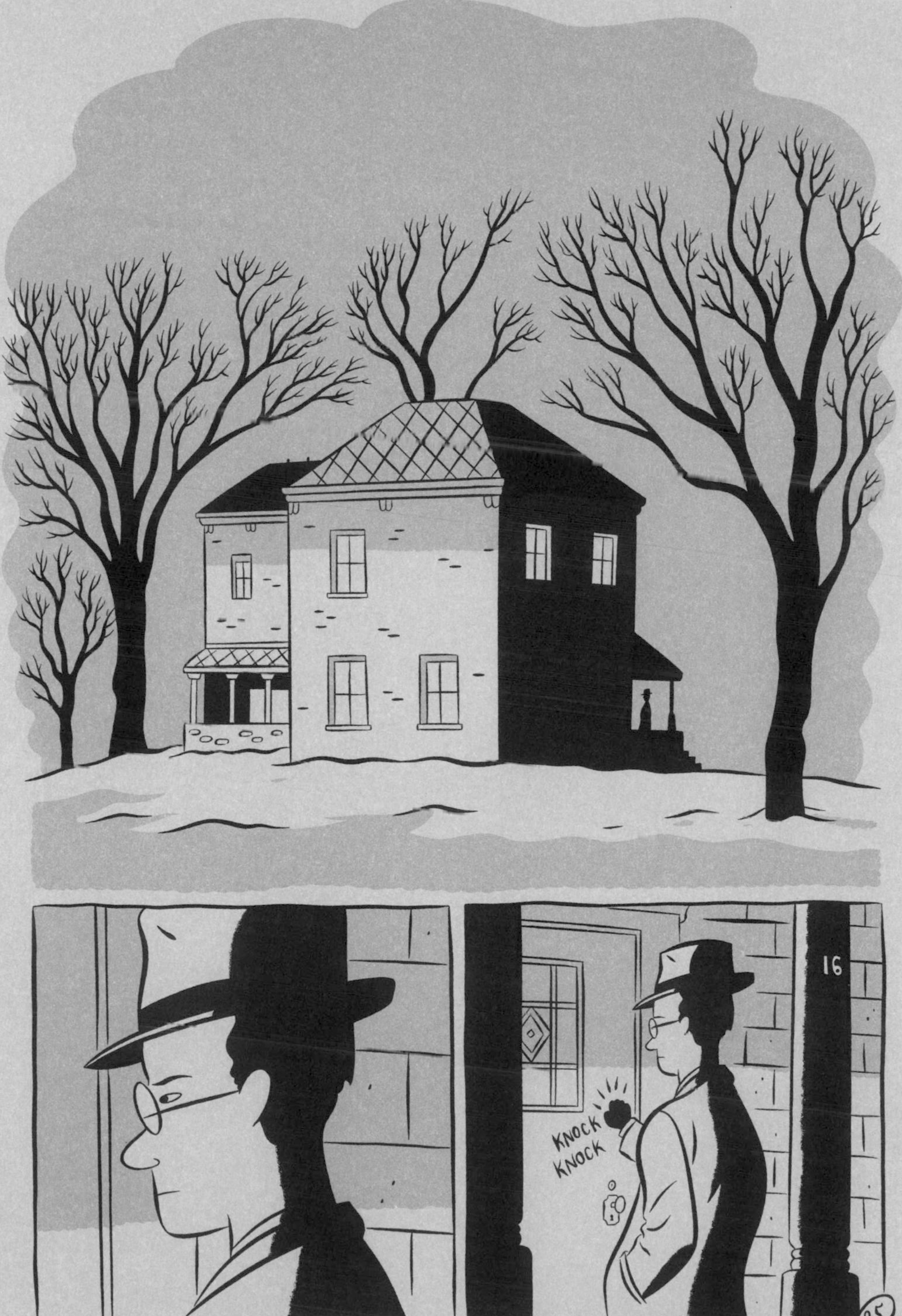
16
KNOCK
KNOCK

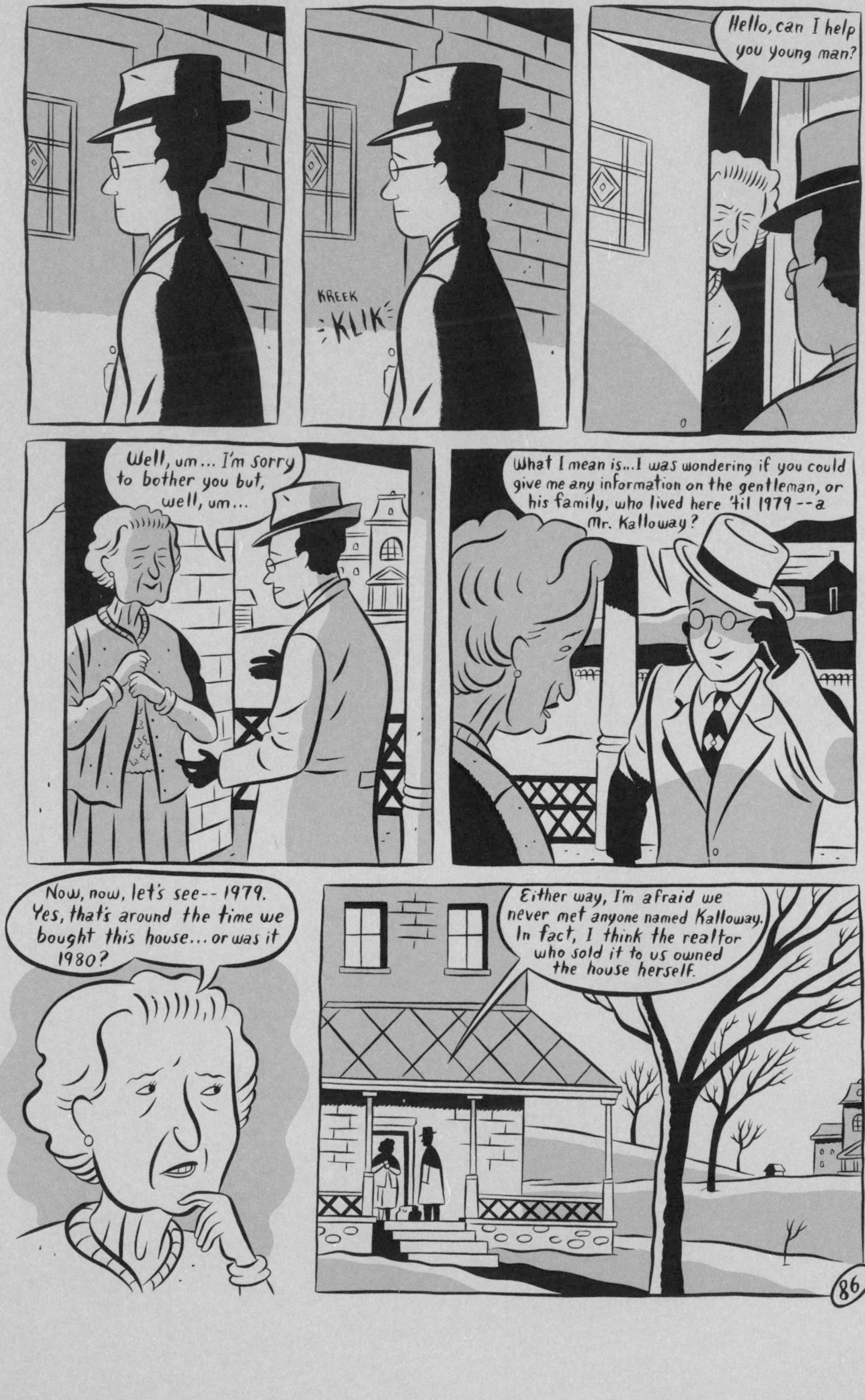

Hello, can I help you young man?
KREEK
KLIK
Well, um... I'm sorry to bother you but, well, um...
What I mean is...I was wondering if you could give me any information on the gentleman, or his family, who lived here 'til 1979 -- a Mr. Kalloway?
Now, now, let's see-- 1979. Yes, that's around the time we bought this house... or was it 1980?
Either way, I'm afraid we never met anyone named Kalloway. In fact, I think the realtor who sold it to us owned the house herself.

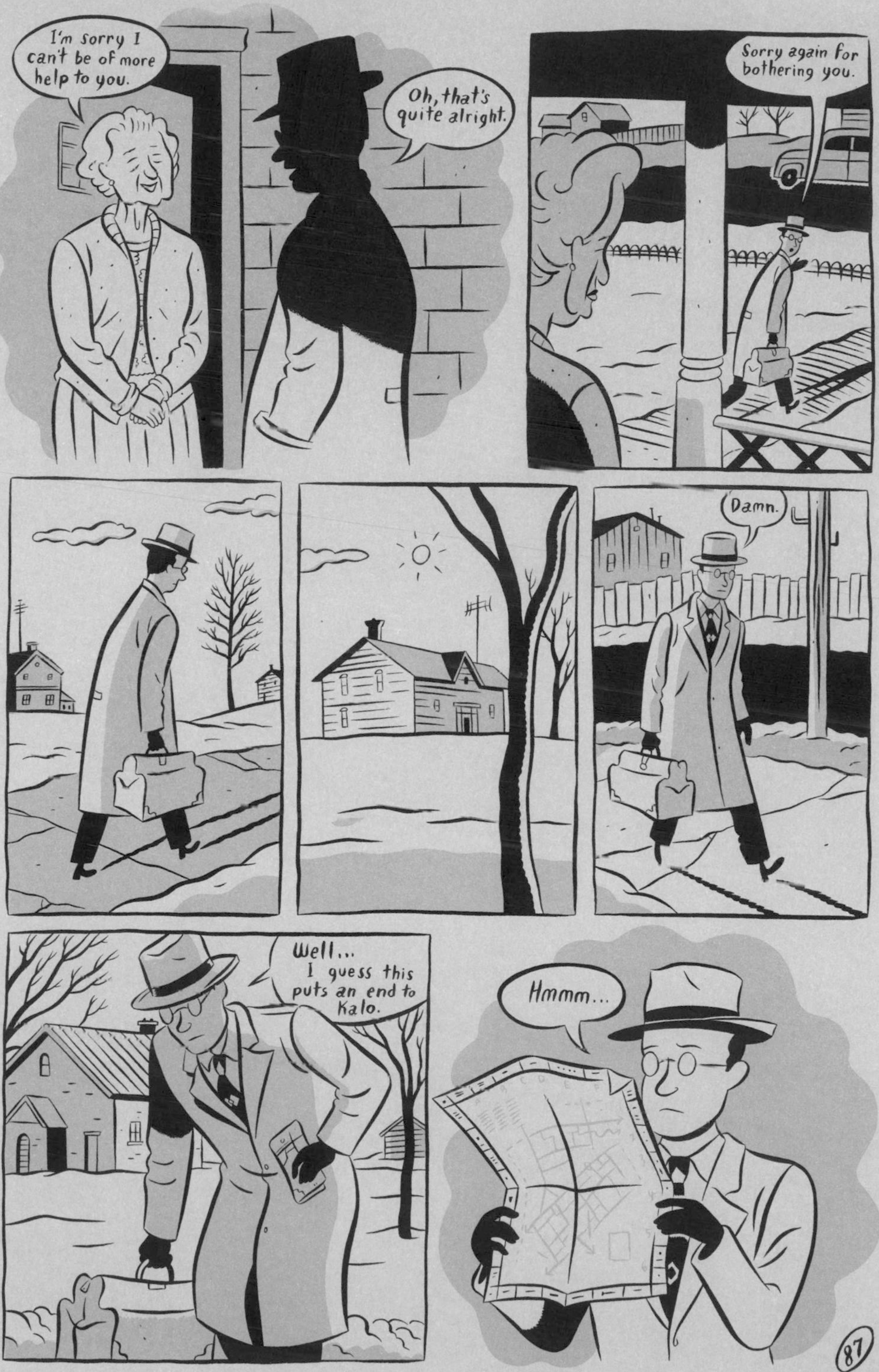
I'm sorry I can't be of more help to you.
Oh, that's quite alright.
Sorry again for bothering you.
Damn.
Well... I guess this puts an end to Kalo.
Hmmm...

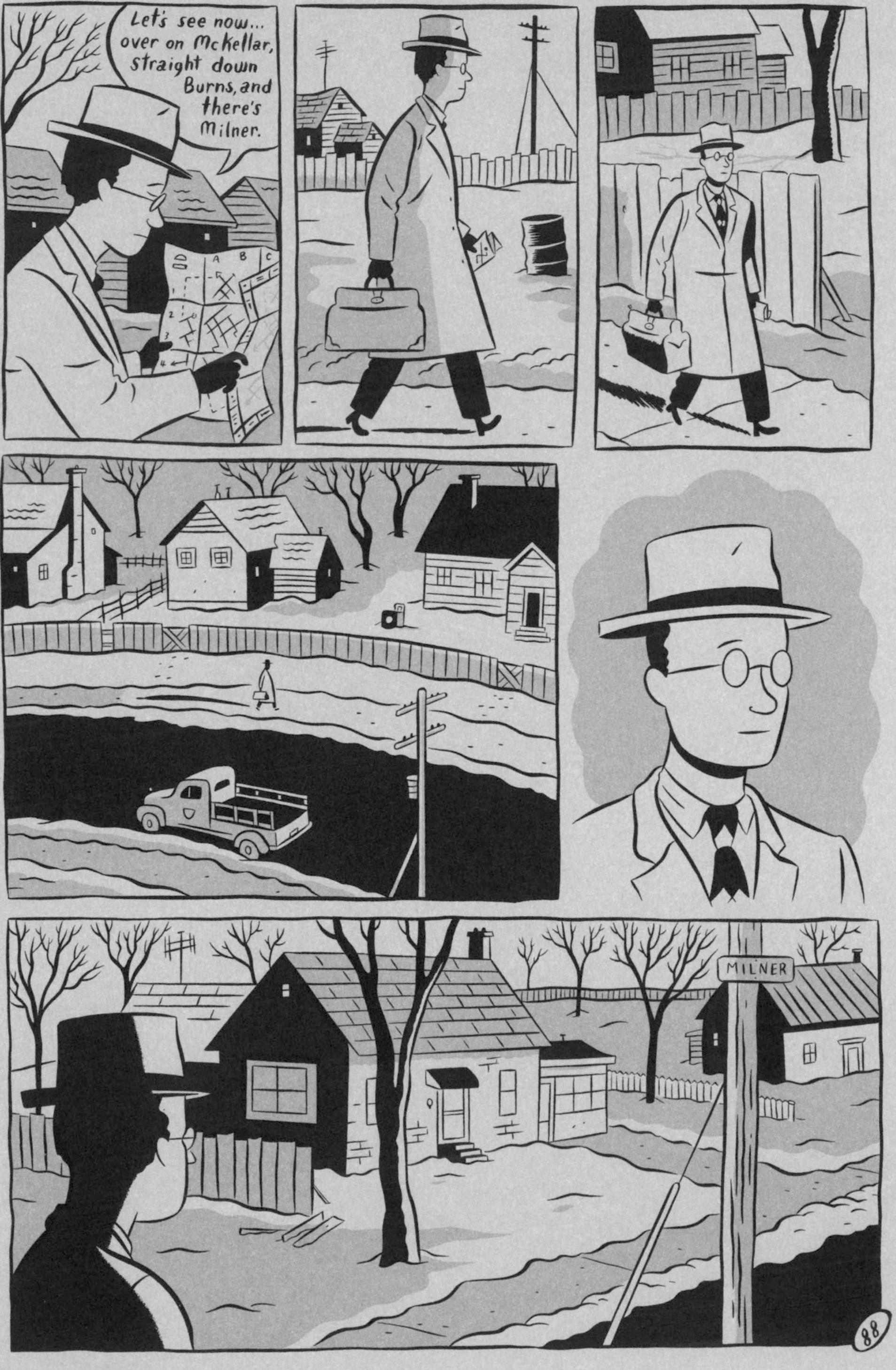
Let's see now... over on McKellar, straight down Burns, and there's Milner.
MILNER

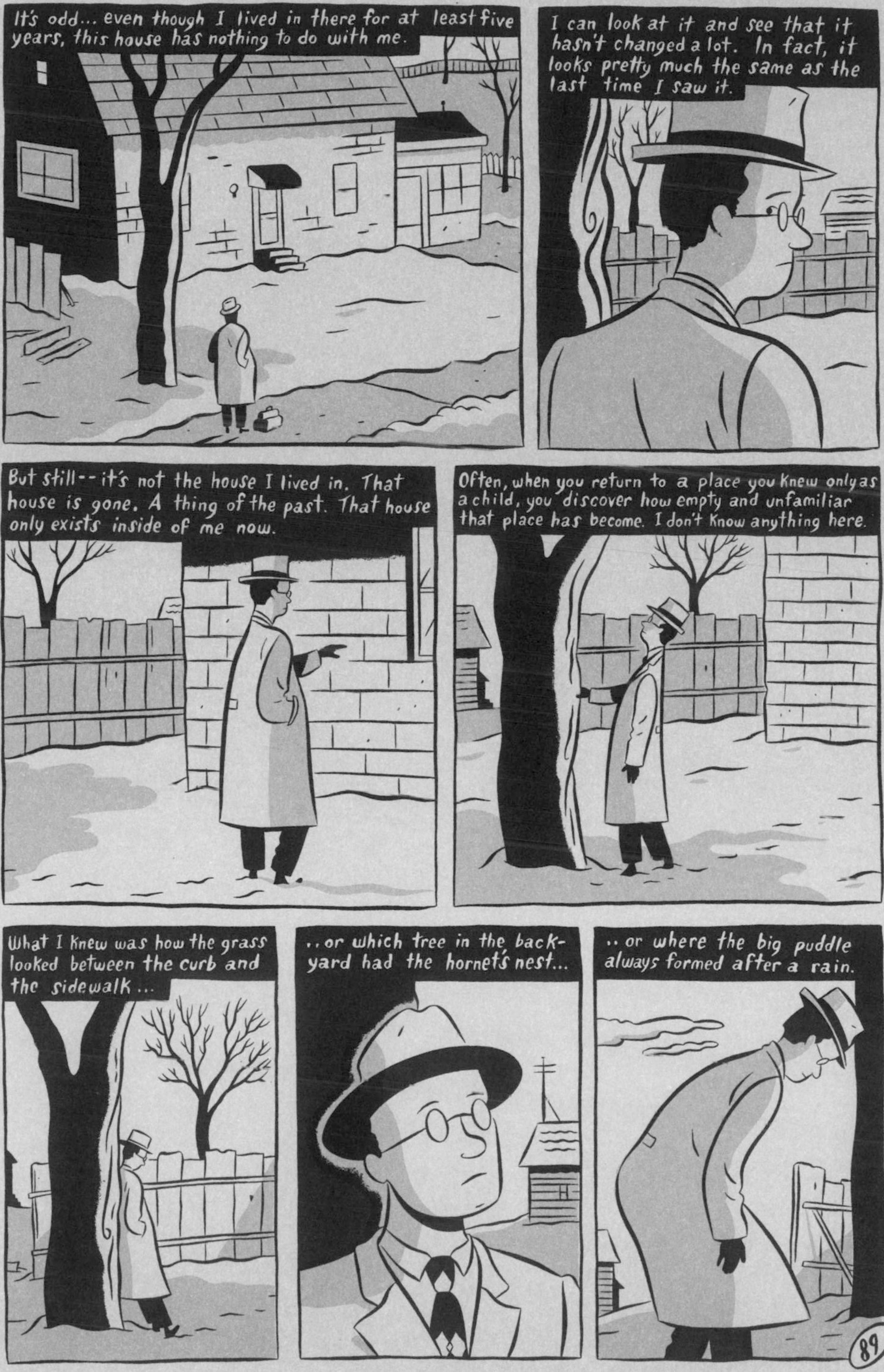
It's odd... even though I lived in there for at least five years, this house has nothing to do with me.
I can look at it and see that it hasn't changed a lot. In fact, it looks pretty much the same as the last time I saw it.
But still-- it's not the house I lived in. That house is gone. A thing of the past. That house only exists inside of me now.
Often, when you return to a place you knew only as a child, you discover how empty and unfamiliar that place has become. I don't know anything here.
What I knew was how the grass looked between the curb and the sidewalk...
..or which tree in the back-yard had the hornet's nest...
..or where the big puddle always formed after a rain.
89

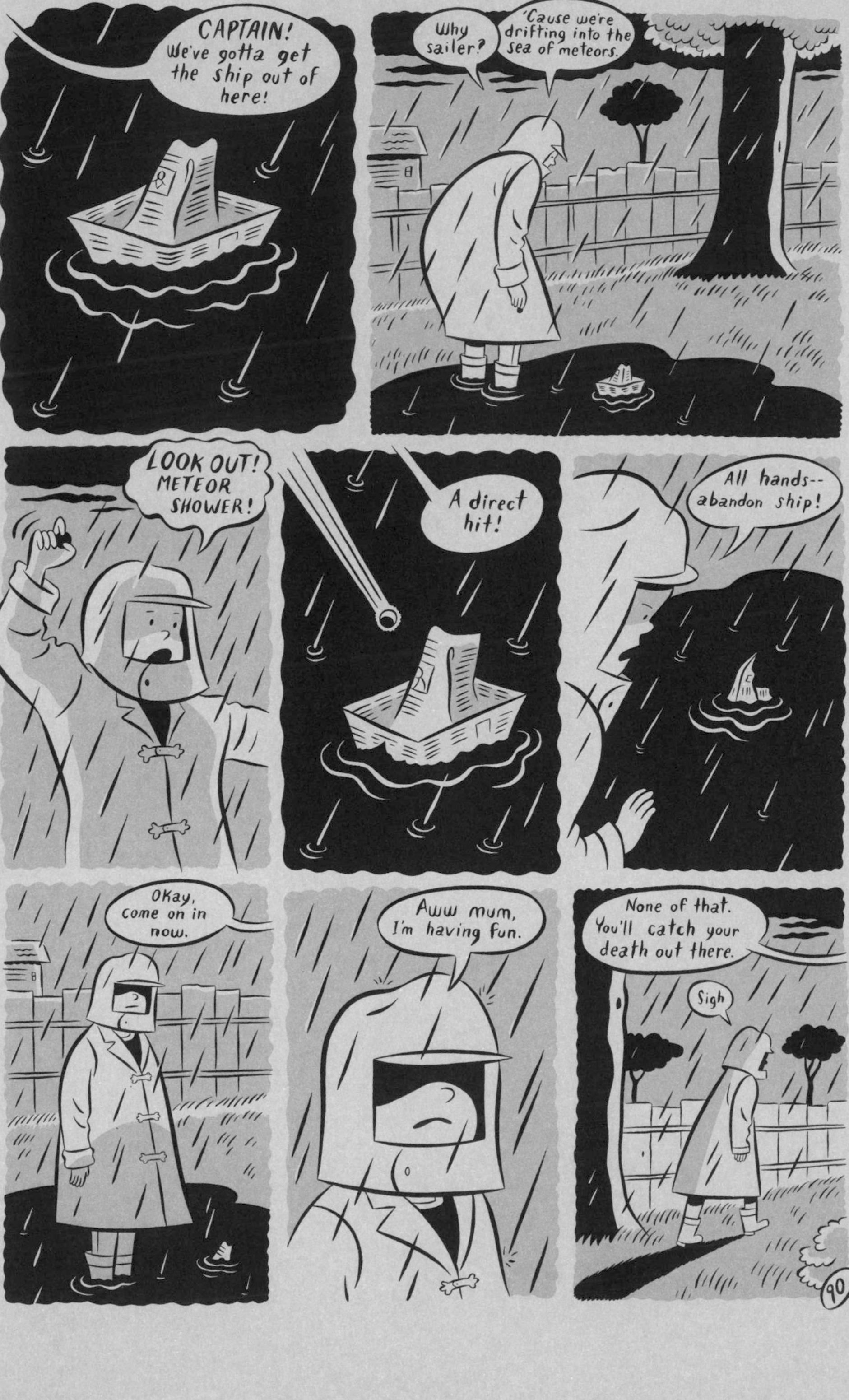
CAPTAIN! We've gotta get the ship out of here!
Why sailer?
'Cause we're drifting into the sea of meteors.
LOOK OUT! METEOR SHOWER!
A direct hit!
All hands-- abandon ship!
OKay, come on in now.
Aww mum, I'm having fun.
None of that. You'll catch your death out there.
Sigh

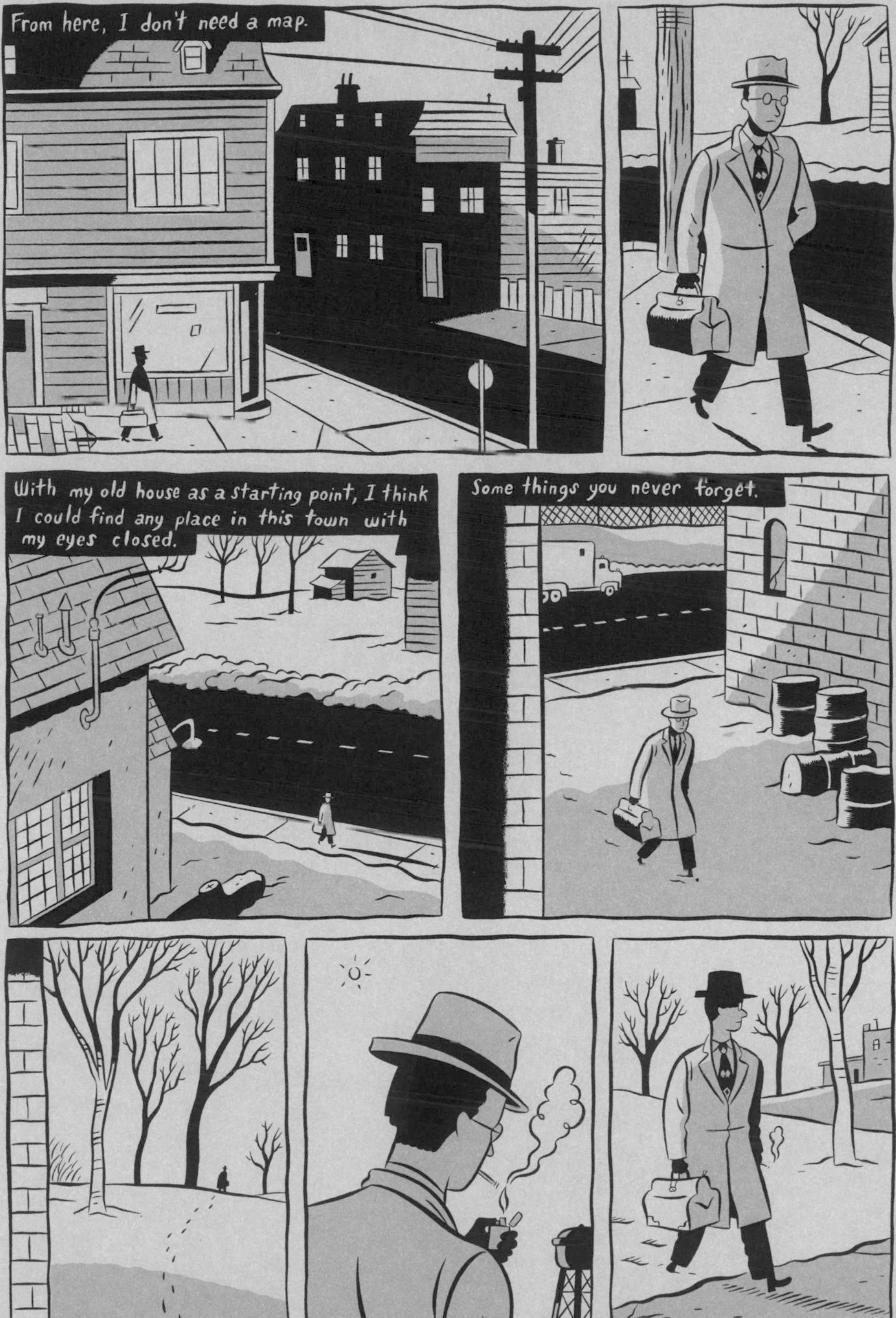
From here, I don't need a map.
With my old house as a starting point, I think I could find any place in this town with my eyes closed.
Some things you never forget.

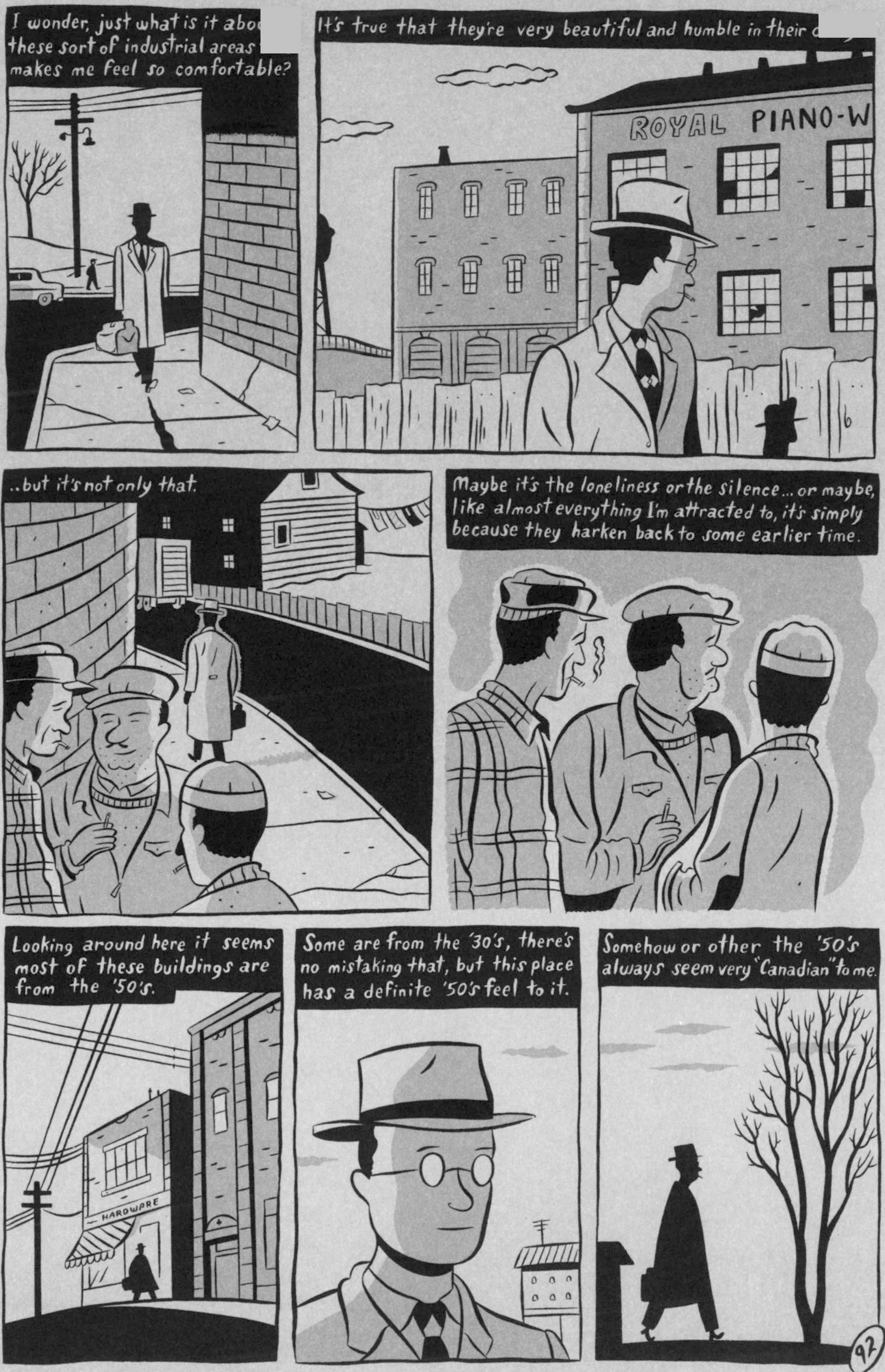
I wonder, just what is it abo
these sort of industrial areas
makes me feel so comfortable?
It's true that they're very beautiful and humble in their
ROYAL PIANO-W
..but it's not only that.
Maybe it's the loneliness or the silence... or maybe, like almost everything I'm attracted to, it's simply because they harken back to some earlier time.
Looking around here it seems most of these buildings are from the '50's.
HARDWARE
Some are from the '30's, there's no mistaking that, but this place has a definite '50's feel to it.
Somehow or other the '50's always seem very "Canadian" to me.

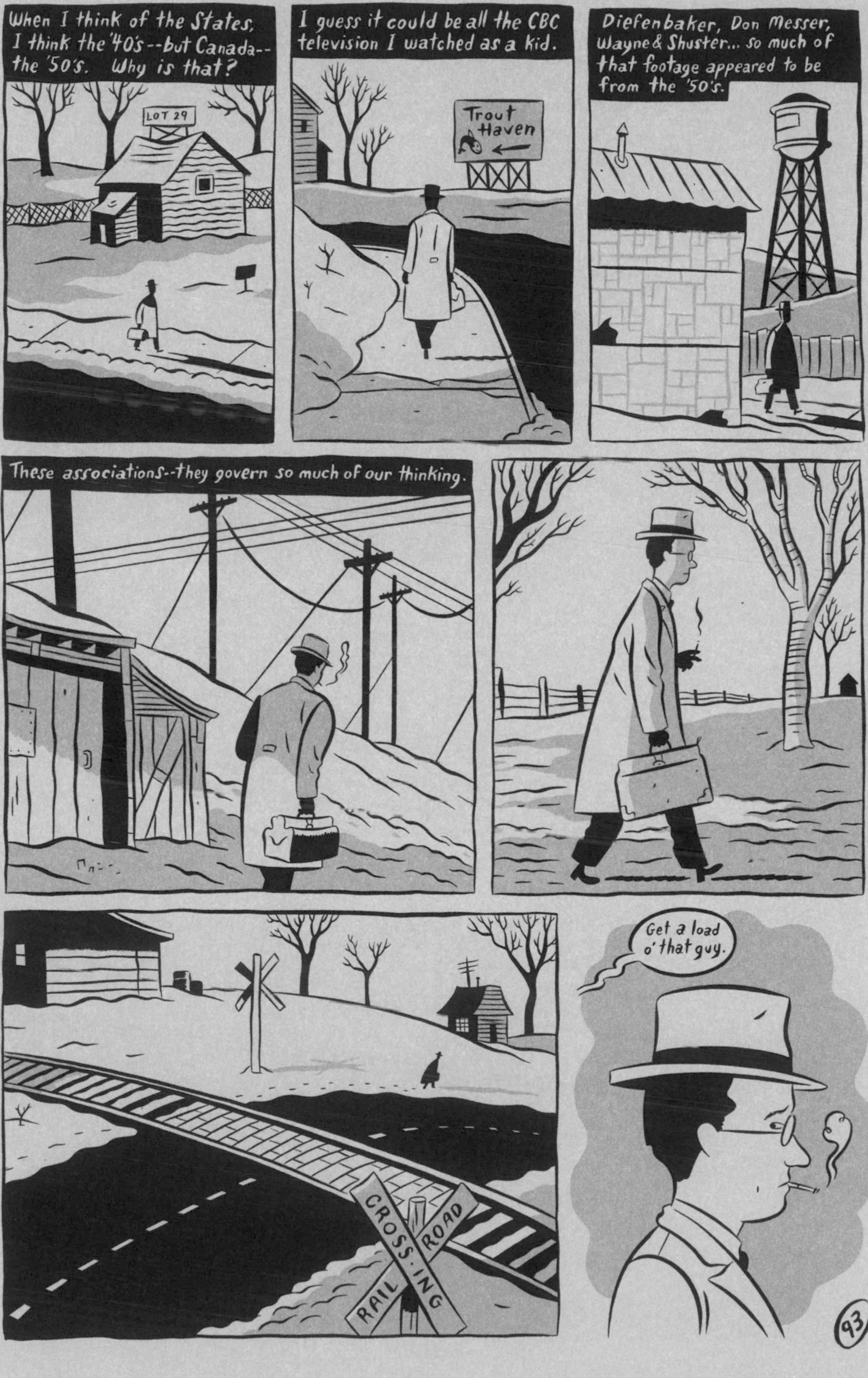
When I think of the States, I think the '40's--but Canada--the '50's. Why is that?
LOT 29
I guess it could be all the CBC television I watched as a kid.
Trout Haven
Diefenbaker, Don Messer, Wayne & Shuster... so much of that footage appeared to be from the '50's.
These associations--they govern so much of our thinking.
RAIL ROAD CROSS-ING
Get a load o' that guy.

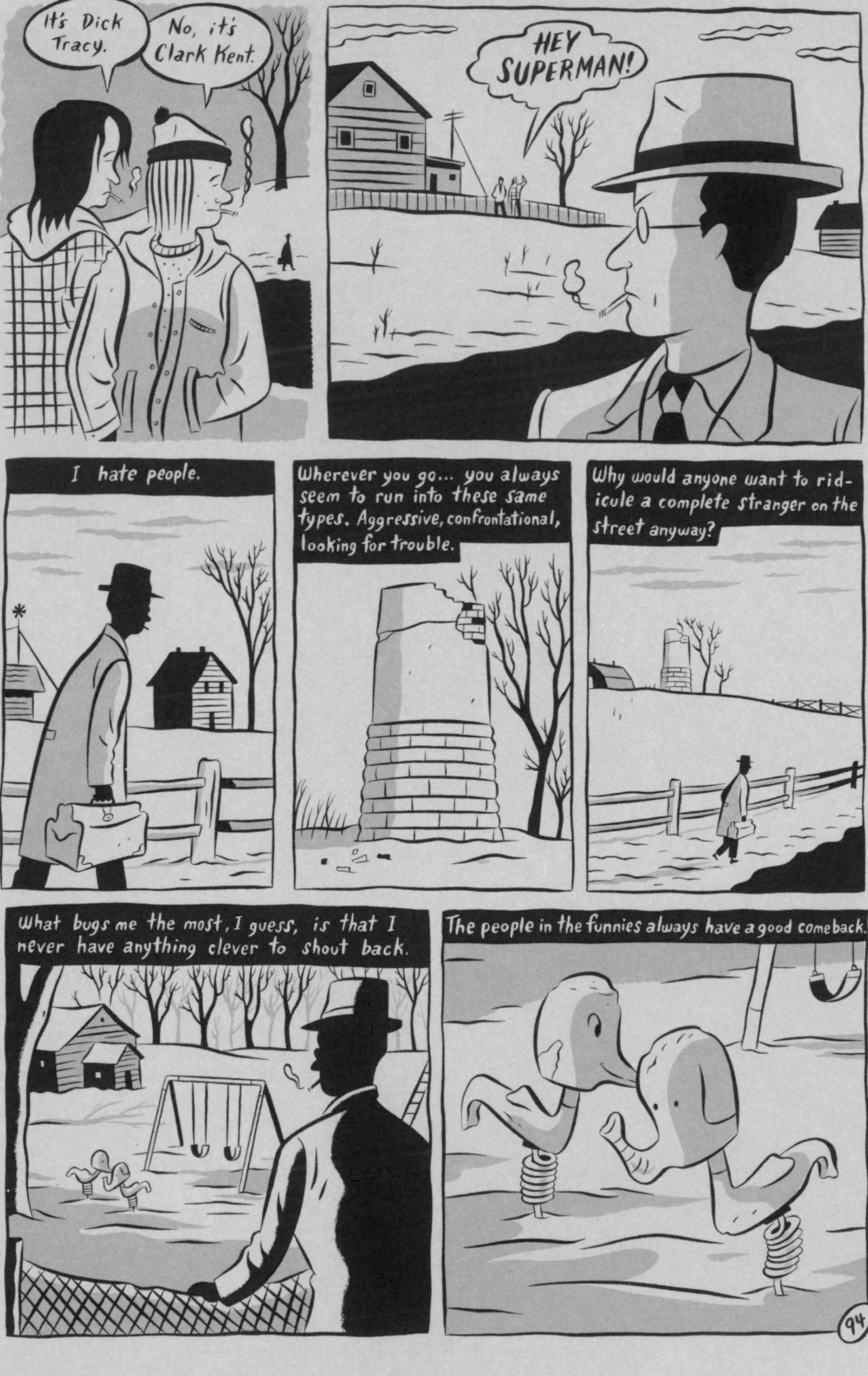
It's Dick Tracy.
No, it's Clark Kent.
HEY SUPERMAN!
I hate people.
Wherever you go... you always seem to run into these same types. Aggressive, confrontational, looking for trouble.
Why would anyone want to ridicule a complete stranger on the street anyway?
What bugs me the most, I guess, is that I never have anything clever to shout back.
The people in the funnies always have a good comeback.

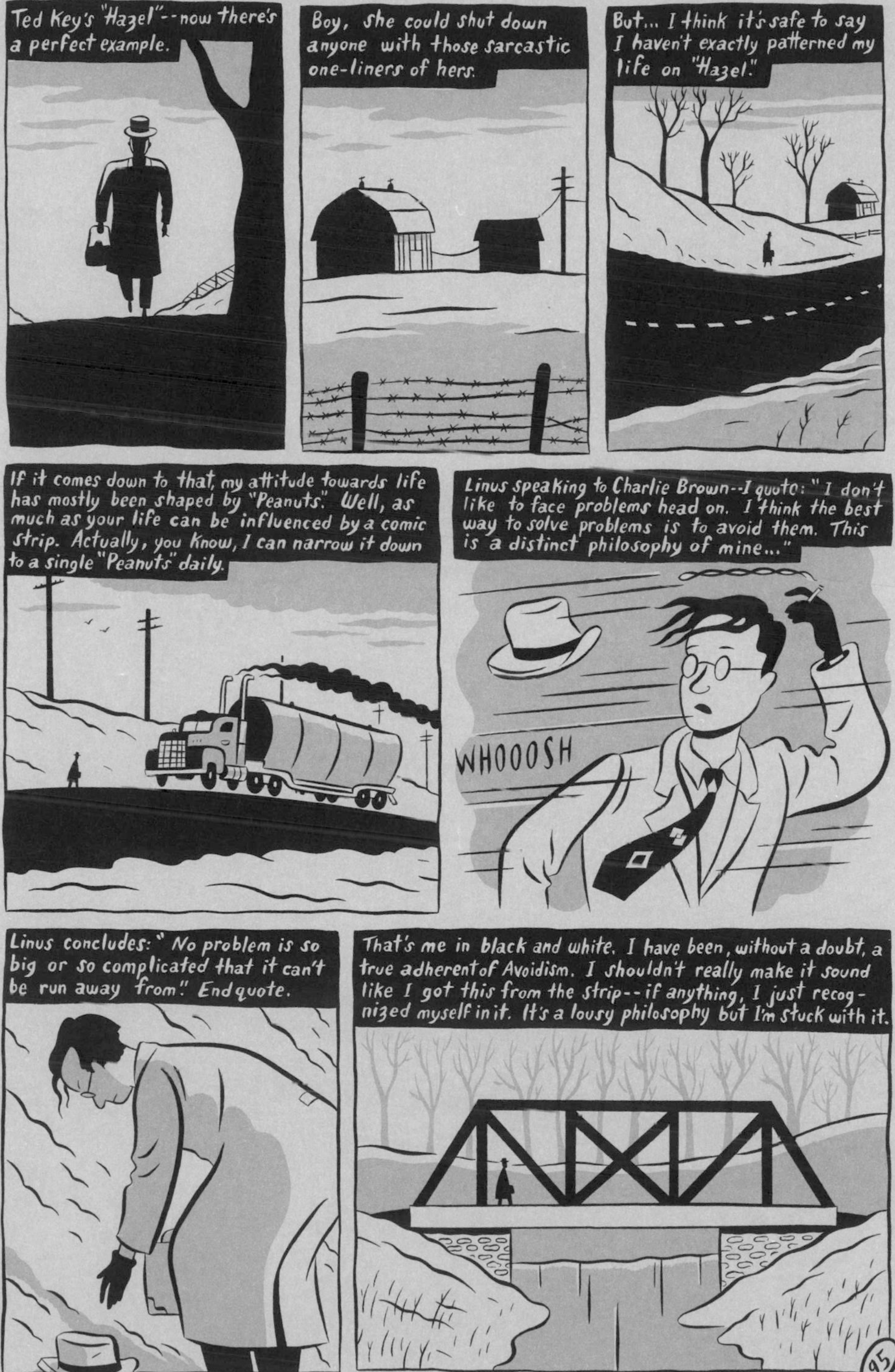
Ted Key's "Hazel"--now there's a perfect example.
Boy, she could shut down anyone with those sarcastic one-liners of hers.
But... I think it's safe to say I haven't exactly patterned my life on "Hazel."
If it comes down to that, my attitude towards life has mostly been shaped by "Peanuts." Well, as much as your life can be influenced by a comic strip. Actually, you know, I can narrow it down to a single "Peanuts" daily.
Linus speaking to Charlie Brown--I quote: "I don't like to face problems head on. I think the best way to solve problems is to avoid them. This is a distinct philosophy of mine..."
WHOOOSH
Linus concludes: "No problem is so big or so complicated that it can't be run away from." End quote.
That's me in black and white. I have been, without a doubt, a true adherent of Avoidism. I shouldn't really make it sound like I got this from the strip--if anything, I just recognized myself in it. It's a lousy philosophy but I'm stuck with it.

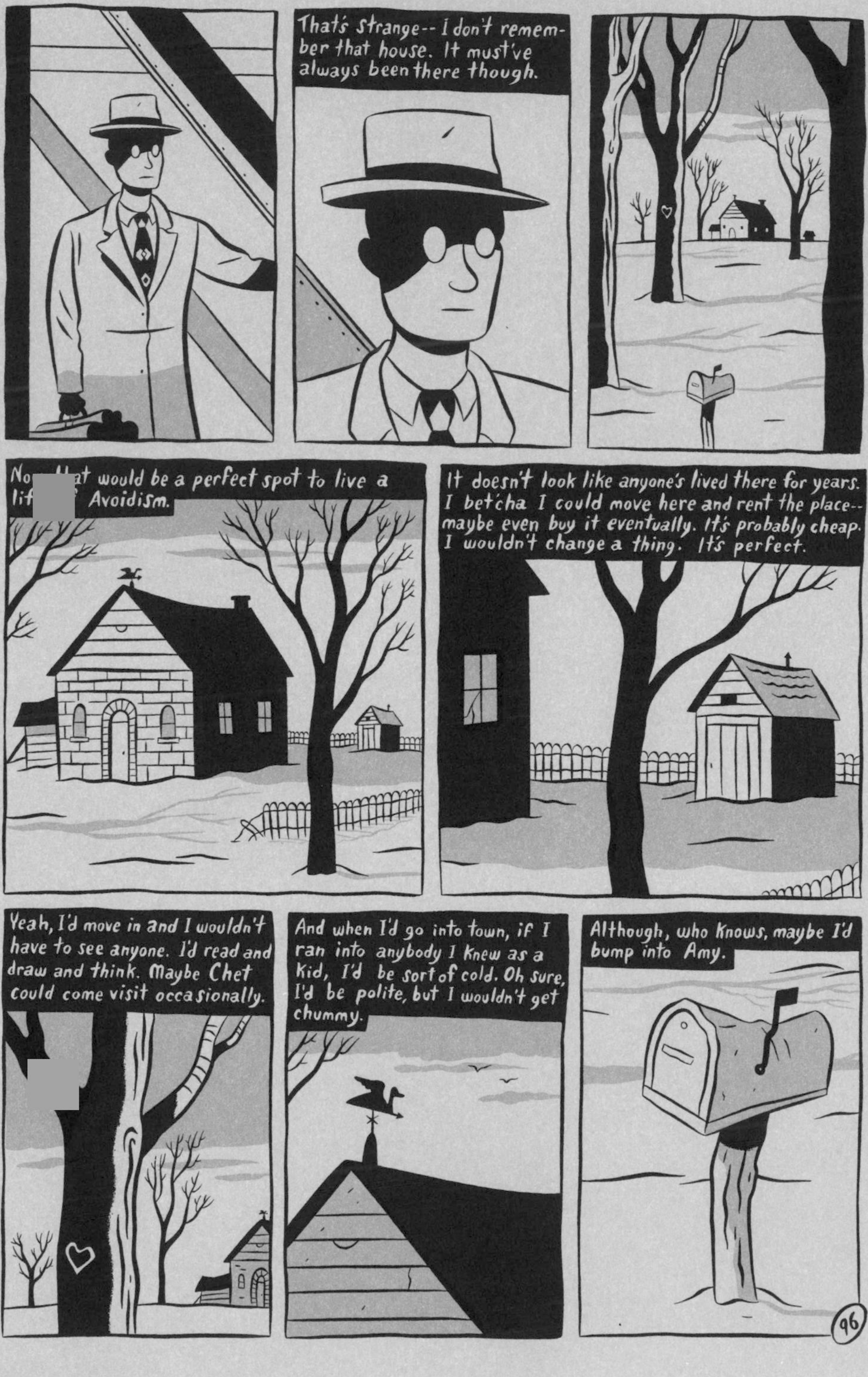
That's strange-- I don't remember that house. It must've always been there though.
No[redacted]at would be a perfect spot to live a lif[redacted] Avoidism.
It doesn't look like anyone's lived there for years. I bet'cha I could move here and rent the place-- maybe even buy it eventually. It's probably cheap. I wouldn't change a thing. It's perfect.
Yeah, I'd move in and I wouldn't have to see anyone. I'd read and draw and think. Maybe Chet could come visit occasionally.
And when I'd go into town, if I ran into anybody I knew as a kid, I'd be sort of cold. Oh sure, I'd be polite, but I wouldn't get chummy.
Although, who knows, maybe I'd bump into Amy.

Now, why would I think of her? Isn't it odd that your brain can dredge up a girl you spent a single afternoon with when you were both seven years old? What keeps her name in my memory when I can barely recall her features?

Still, maybe she'd be beautiful now... and maybe she'd remember me too and we'd fall in love and...

LOT·53

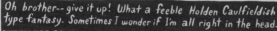

Oh brother-- give it up! What a feeble Holden Caulfieldish type fantasy. Sometimes I wonder if I'm all right in the head.

Besides, if I'm not crazy now, I would be after six months alone in there.

97

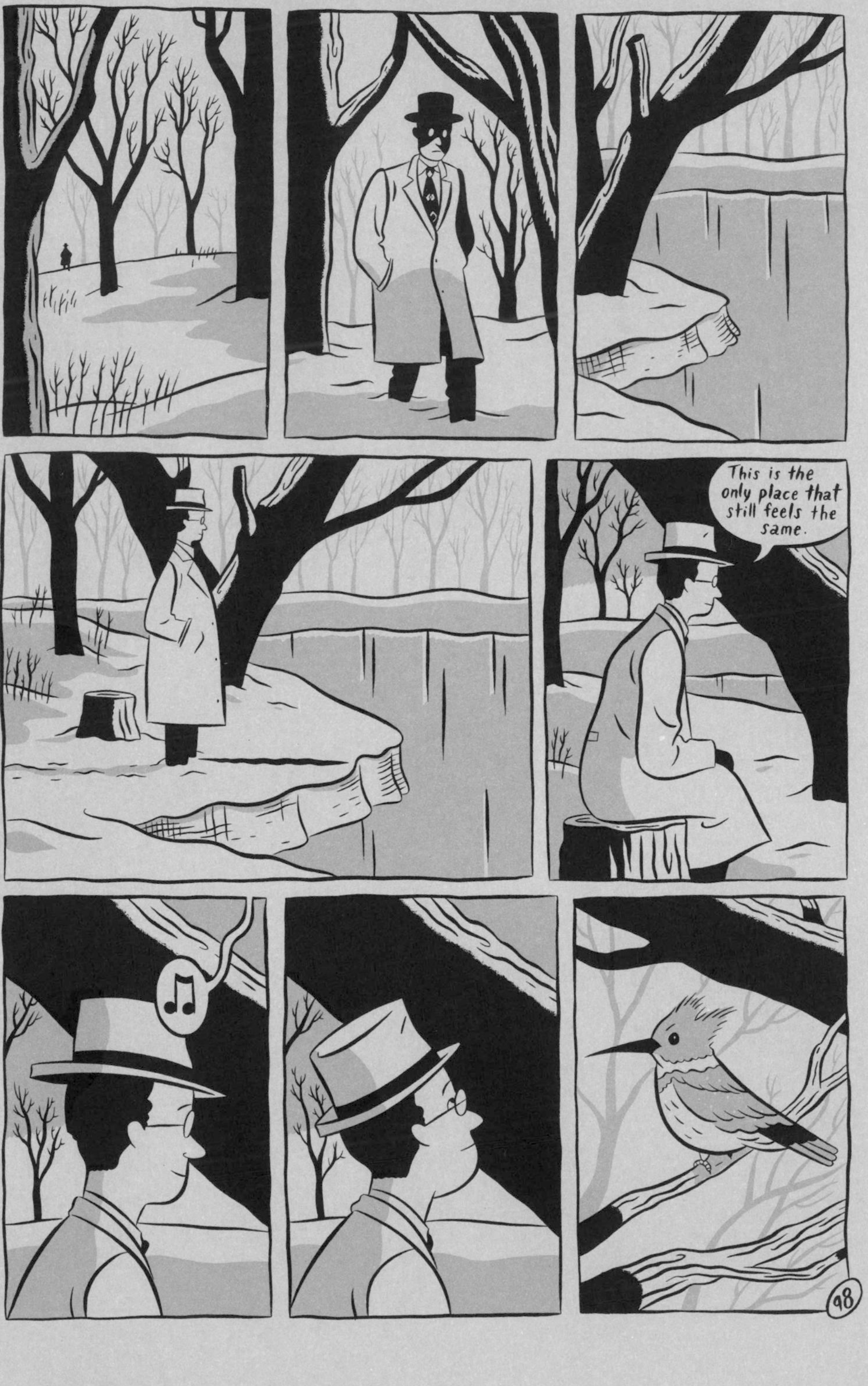
This is the only place that still feels the same.
98

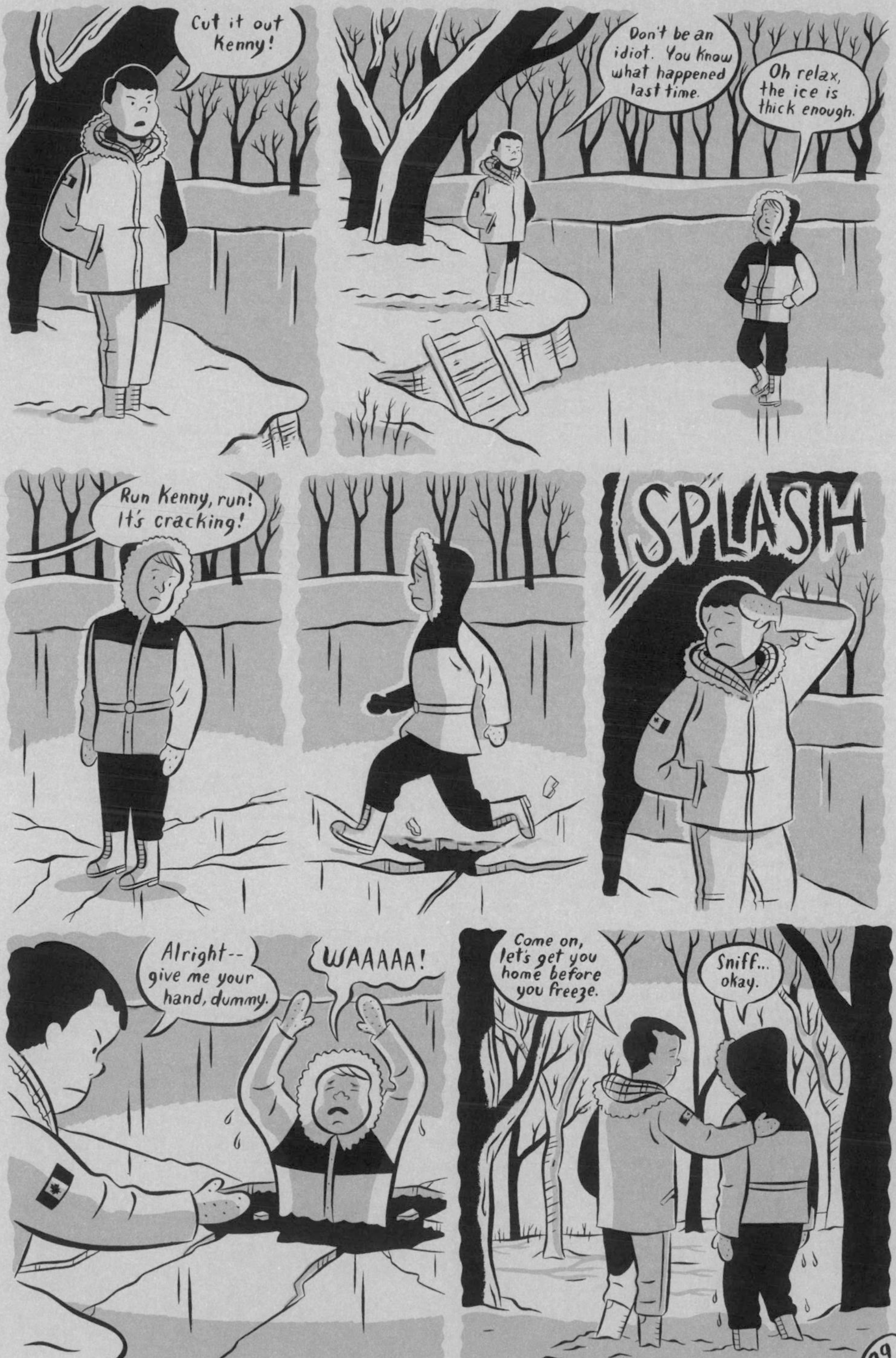
Cut it out Kenny!
Don't be an idiot. You know what happened last time.
Oh relax, the ice is thick enough.
Run Kenny, run! It's cracking!
SPLASH
Alright-- give me your hand, dummy.
WAAAAA!
Come on, let's get you home before you freeze.
Sniff... okay.

If memory serves-- Oak St. should be around here.

Hey, a little junk shop.

USED GOODS

Mennonites. I don't recall any Mennonites in this area. At least I think they're Mennonites--maybe they're Hutterites.

I guess they're waiting for a ride. I wonder if it's a horse and buggy or a car? Some sects allow cars, some don't. You gotta ask though-- how do they decide which modern things are evil and which aren't? I can't.

Once, in a bus station, a guy asked me if I was a Mennonite, I was pleased with the mix-up. I guess I liked being mistakenly lumped into a group that has rejected modern ways.

Hello.

Hello.

The Mennonites wouldn't make that mistake though. I'd be considered as lost as the rest of this miserable society.

Hmm... nothing but crap.

100

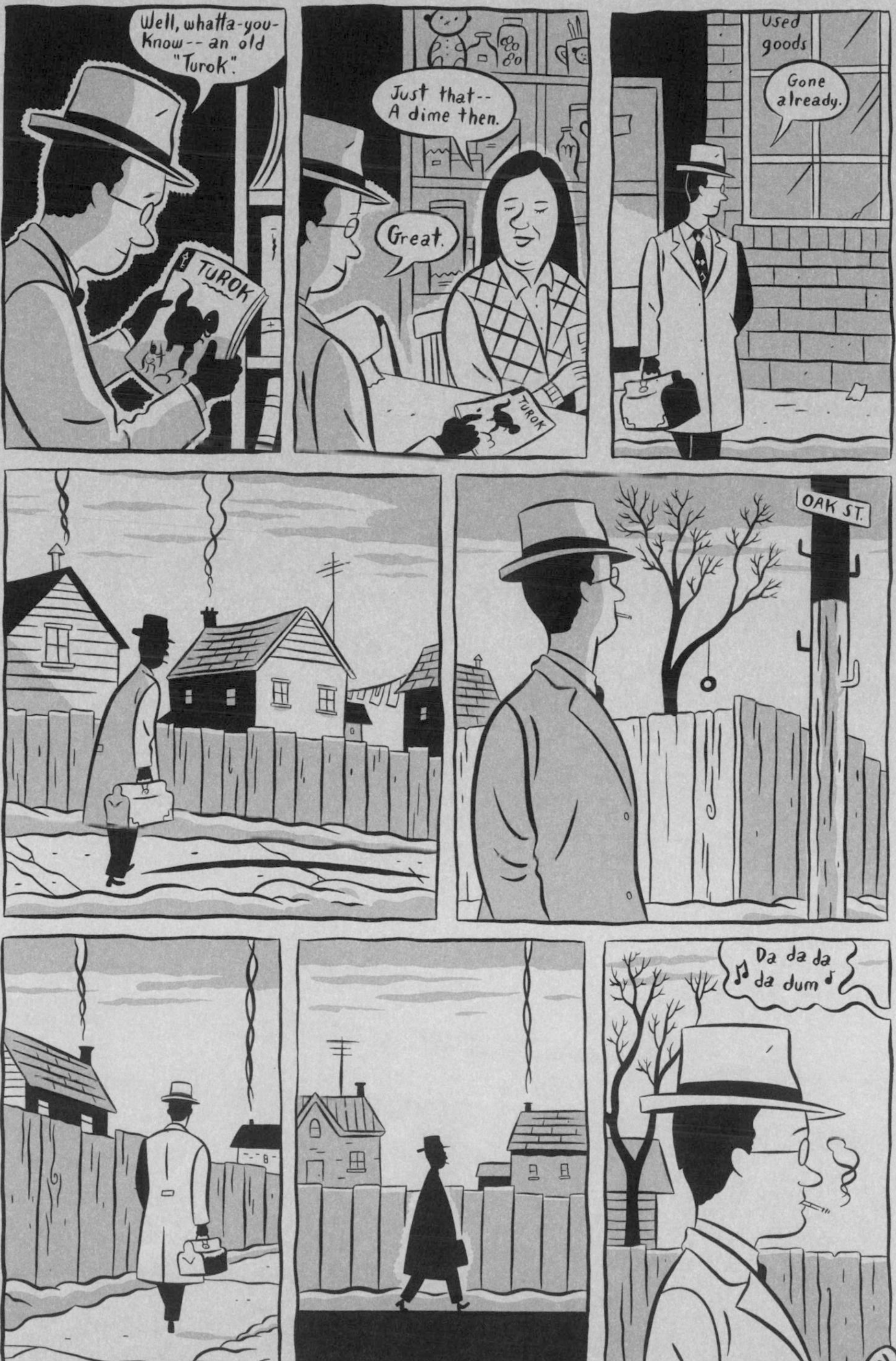

Well, whatta-you-know-- an old "Turok".
TUROK
Just that-- A dime then.
Great.
TUROK
Used goods
Gone already.
OAK ST.
Da da da da dum
101

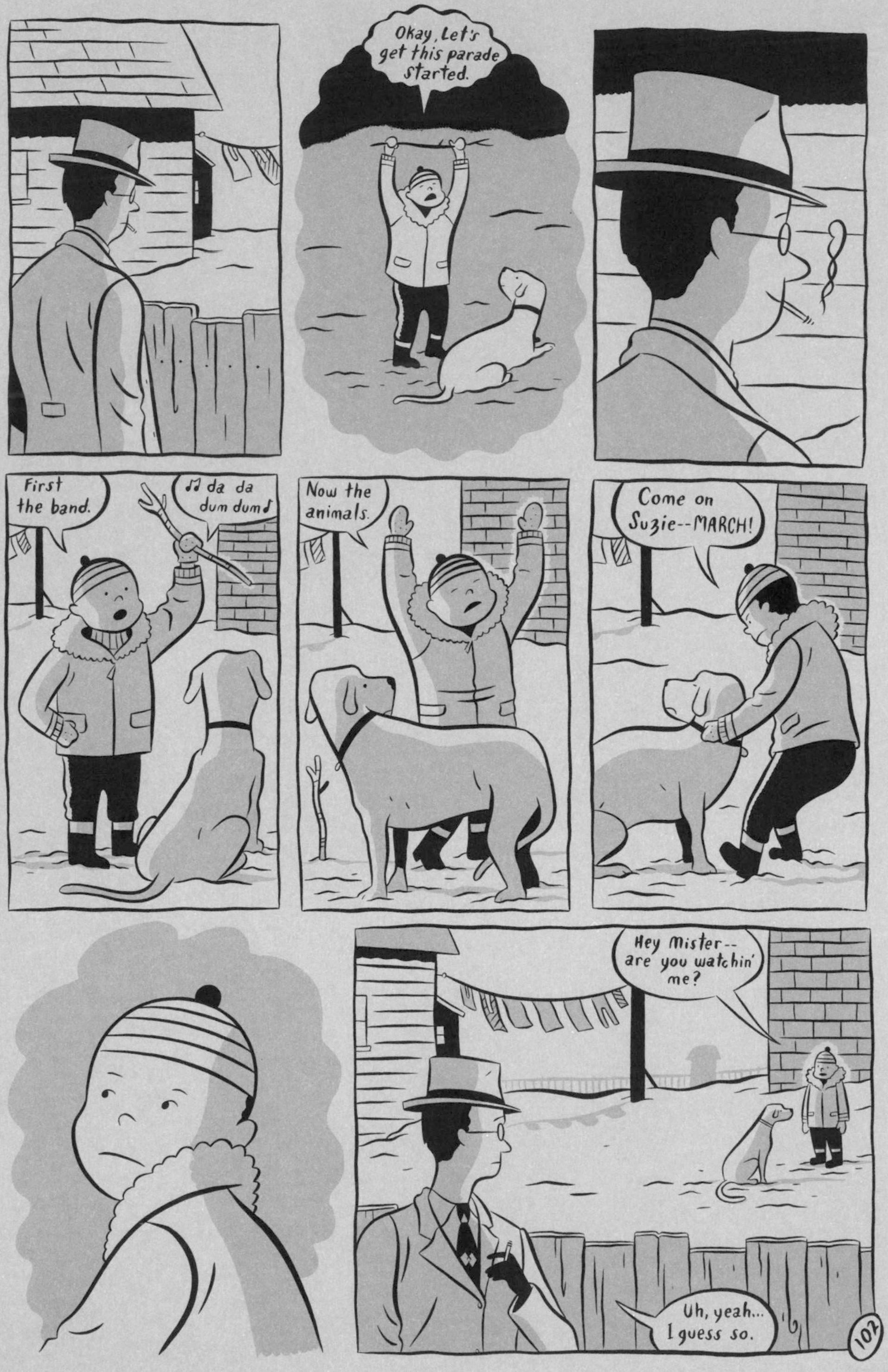
Okay, Let's get this parade started.
First the band.
♫ da da dum dum♪
Now the animals.
Come on Suzie--MARCH!
Hey Mister-- are you watchin' me?
Uh, yeah... I guess so.

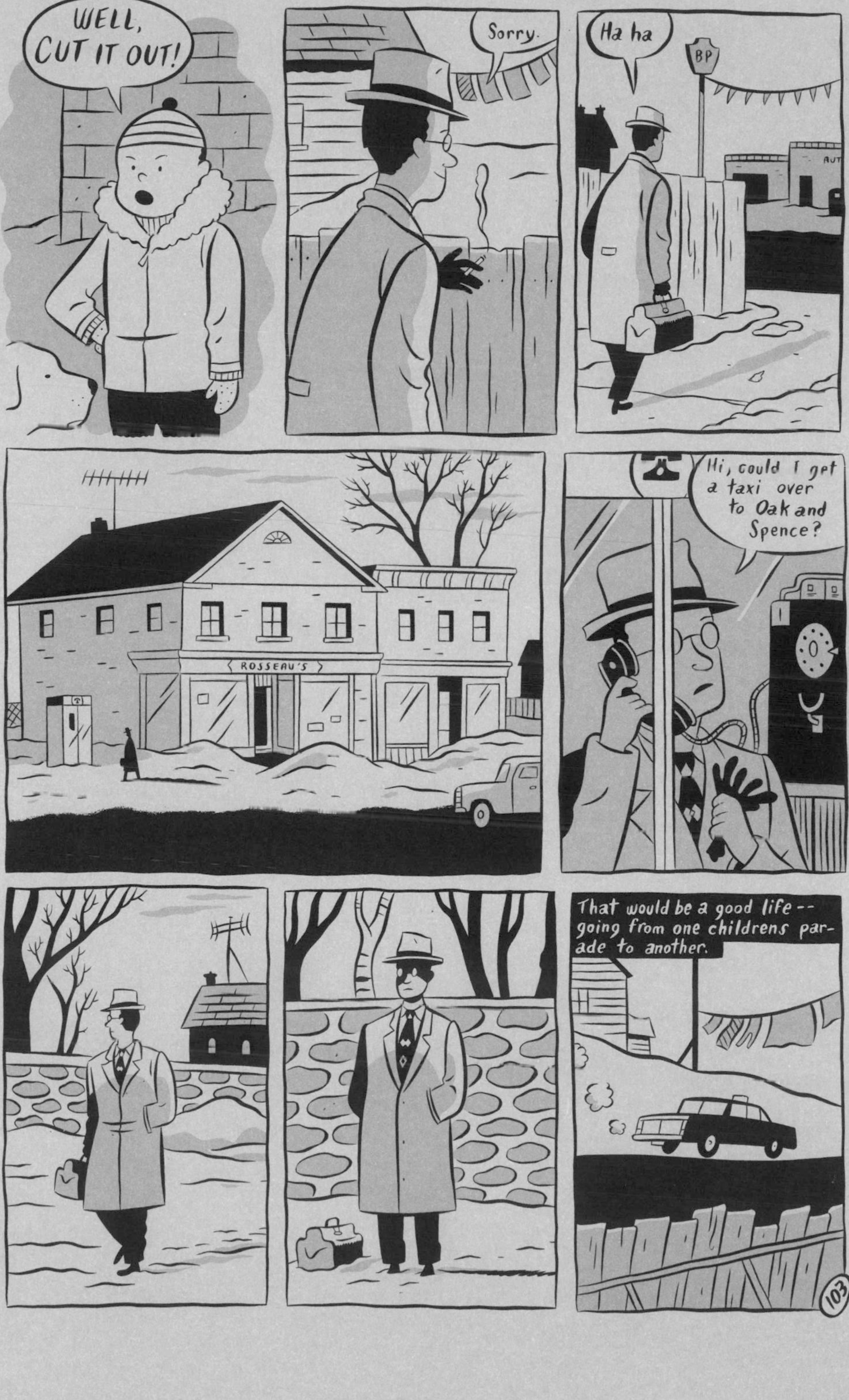
WELL, CUT IT OUT!
Sorry.
Ha ha
BP
ROSSEAU'S
Hi, could I get a taxi over to Oak and Spence?
That would be a good life -- going from one childrens parade to another.

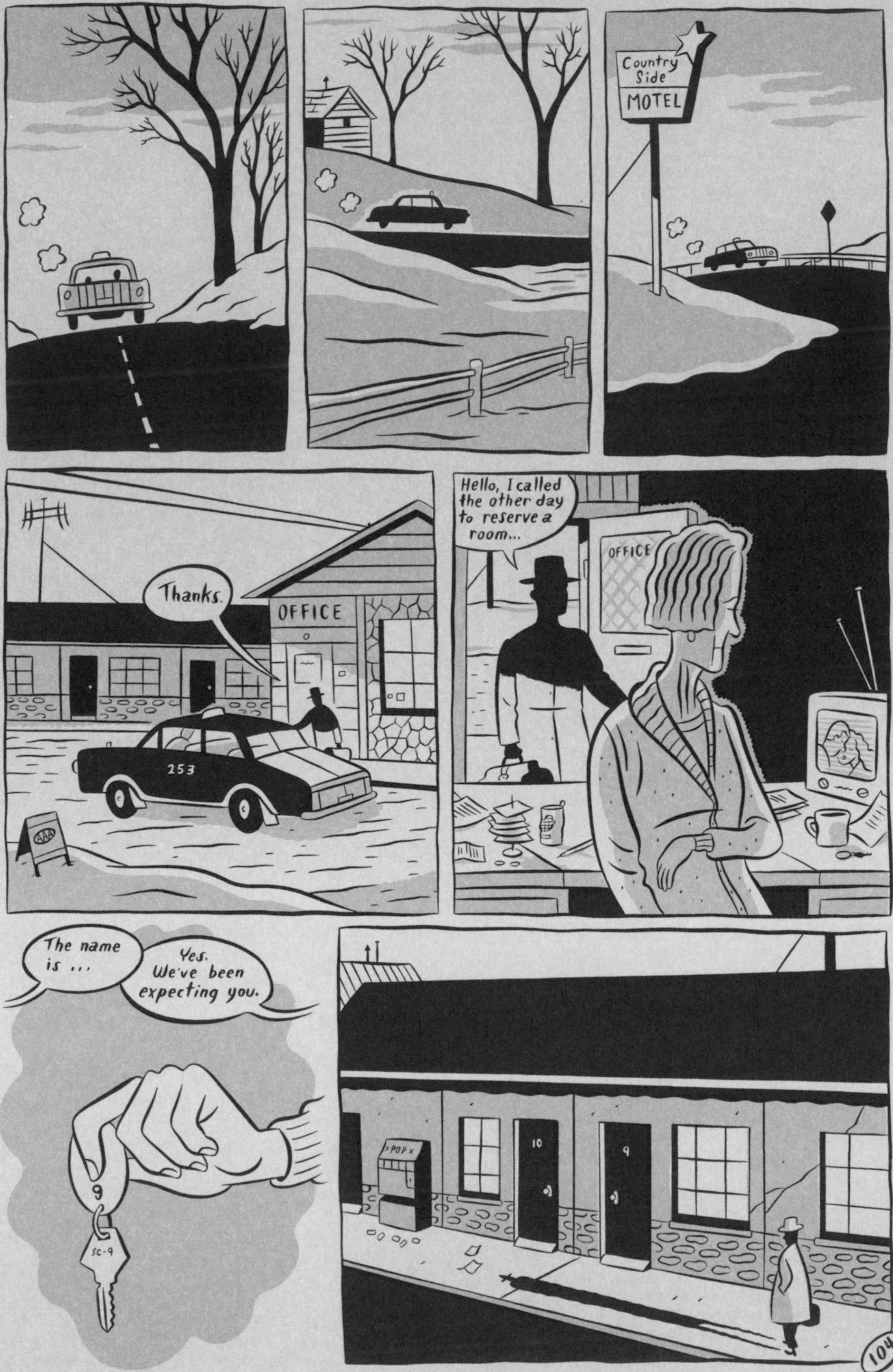
Country Side MOTEL
Thanks.
OFFICE
253
Hello, I called the other day to reserve a room...
OFFICE
The name is ...
Yes. We've been expecting you.
9
SC-9
POP
10
9

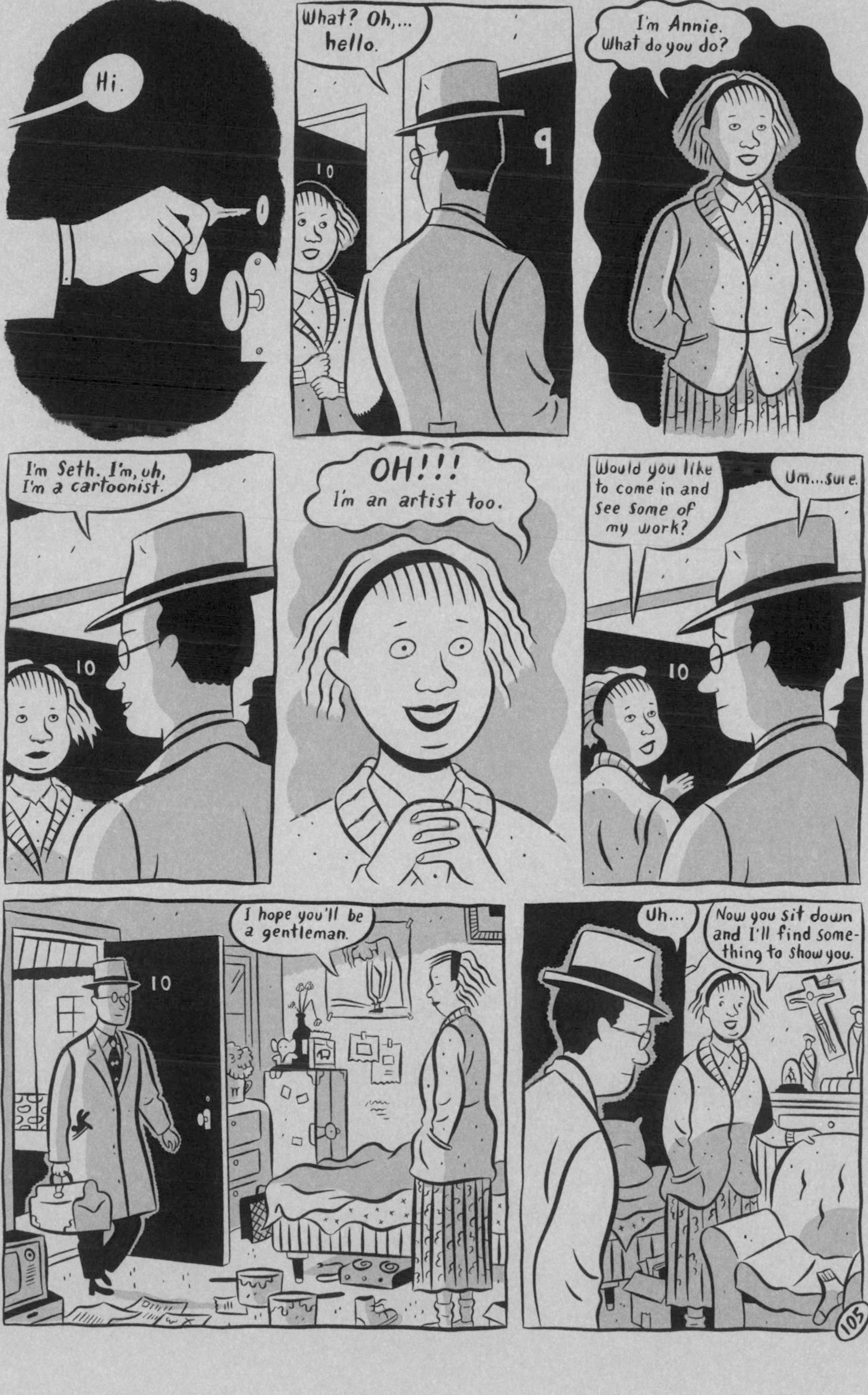
Hi.
What? Oh,... hello.
I'm Annie. What do you do?
I'm Seth. I'm, uh, I'm a cartoonist.
OH!!! I'm an artist too.
Would you like to come in and see some of my work?
Um...sure.
I hope you'll be a gentleman.
Uh...
Now you sit down and I'll find something to show you.

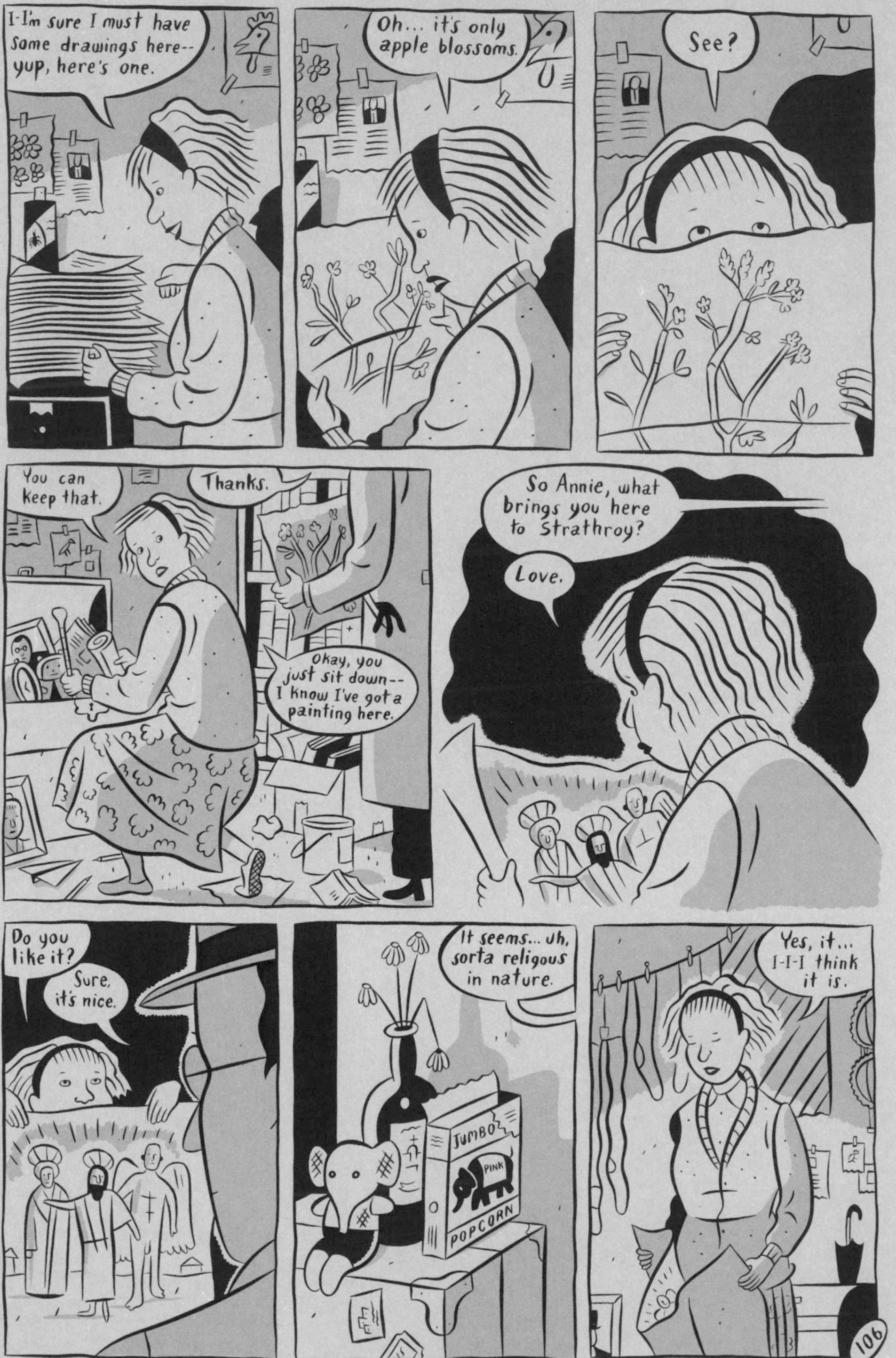
I-I'm sure I must have some drawings here-- yup, here's one.
Oh... it's only apple blossoms.
See?
You can keep that.
Thanks.
Okay, you just sit down-- I know I've got a painting here.
So Annie, what brings you here to Strathroy?
Love.
Do you like it?
Sure, it's nice.
It seems... uh, sorta religous in nature.
JUMBO
PINK
POPCORN
Yes, it... I-I-I think it is.

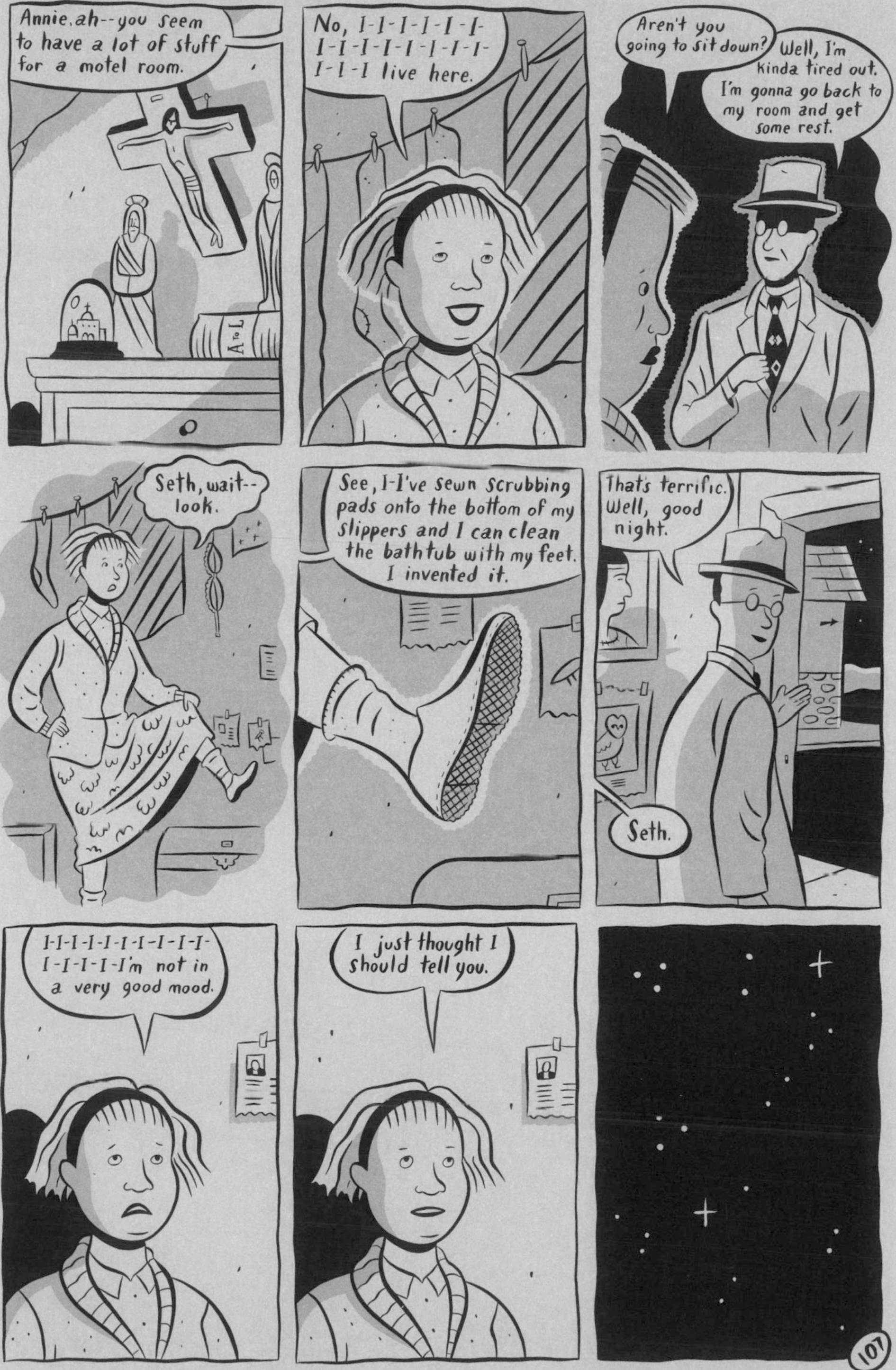
Annie, ah--you seem to have a lot of stuff for a motel room.
No, I-I-I-I-I-I-I-I-I-I-I-I-I-I-I-I-I live here.
Aren't you going to sit down?
Well, I'm kinda tired out. I'm gonna go back to my room and get some rest.
Seth, wait-- look.
See, I-I've sewn scrubbing pads onto the bottom of my slippers and I can clean the bathtub with my feet. I invented it.
That's terrific. Well, good night.
Seth.
I-I-I-I-I-I-I-I-I-I-I-I-I-I-I-I'm not in a very good mood.
I just thought I should tell you.

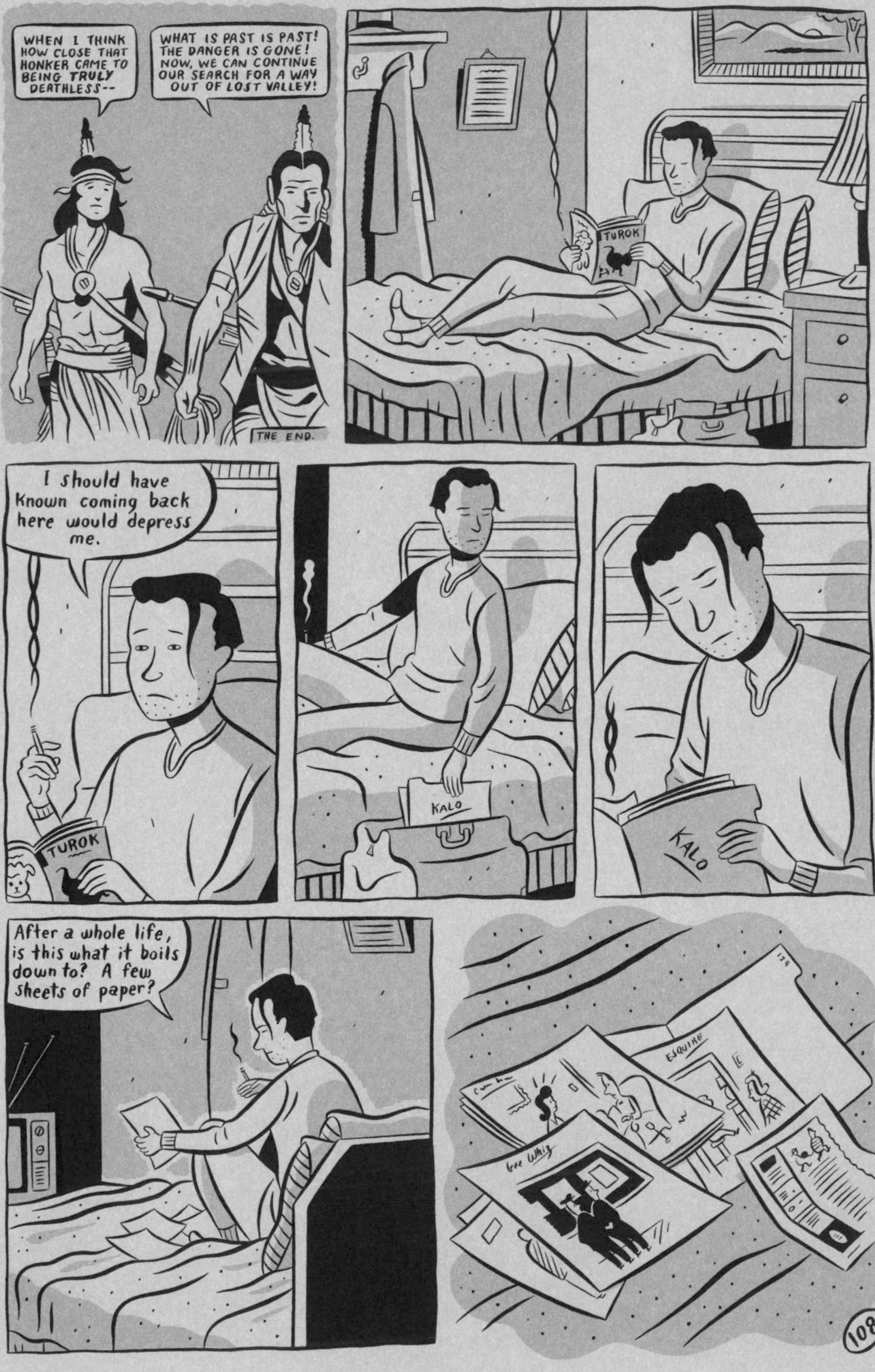
WHEN I THINK HOW CLOSE THAT HONKER CAME TO BEING TRULY DEATHLESS--
WHAT IS PAST IS PAST! THE DANGER IS GONE! NOW, WE CAN CONTINUE OUR SEARCH FOR A WAY OUT OF LOST VALLEY!
THE END.
TUROK
I should have Known coming back here would depress me.
TUROK
KALO
KALO
After a whole life, is this what it boils down to? A few sheets of paper?
ESQUIRE
Gee Whiz

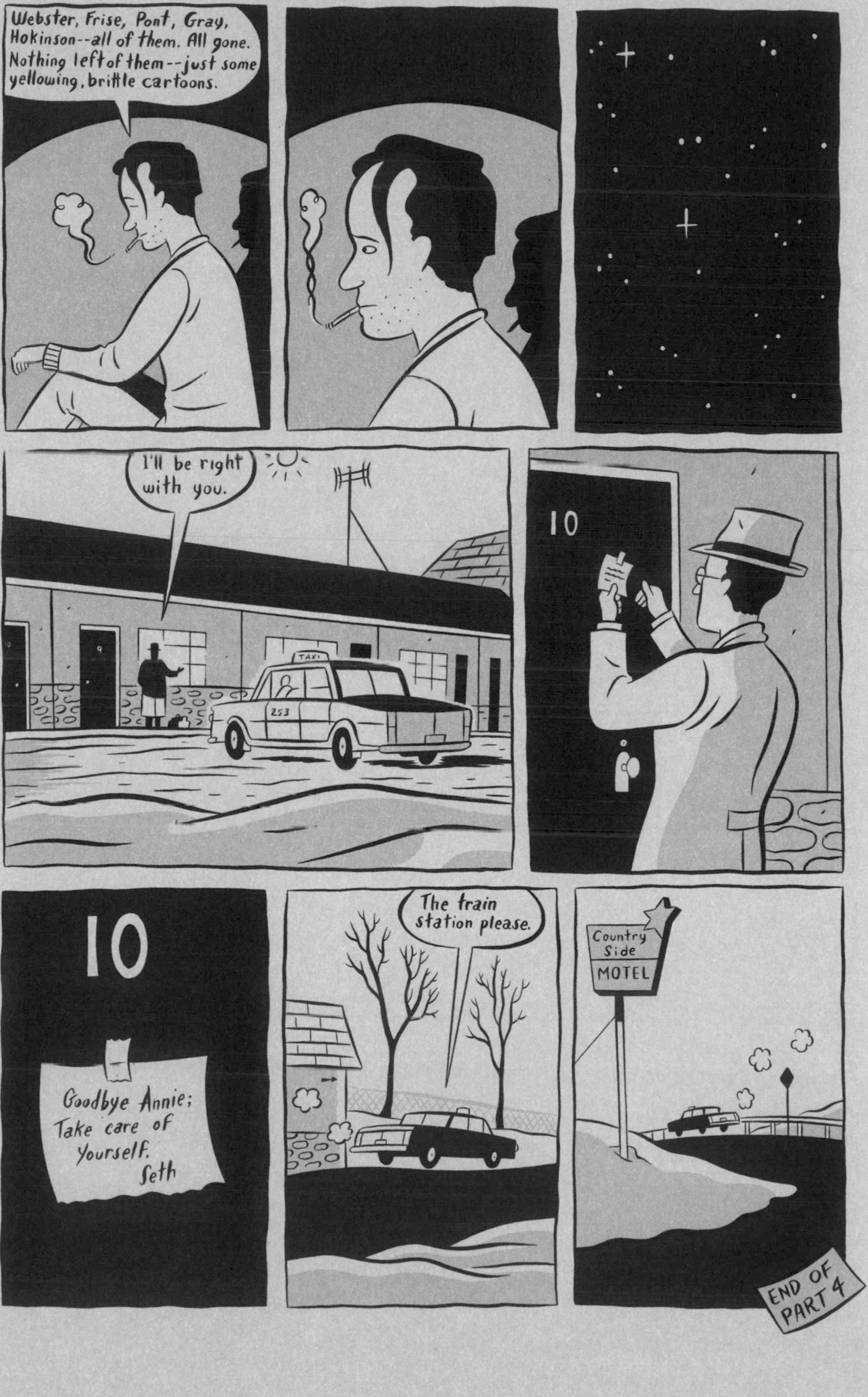
Webster, Frise, Pont, Gray, Hokinson--all of them. All gone. Nothing left of them--just some yellowing, brittle cartoons.
I'll be right with you.
TAXI
253
10
10
Goodbye Annie; Take care of yourself. Seth
The train station please.
Country Side MOTEL
END OF PART 4

Part Five

113

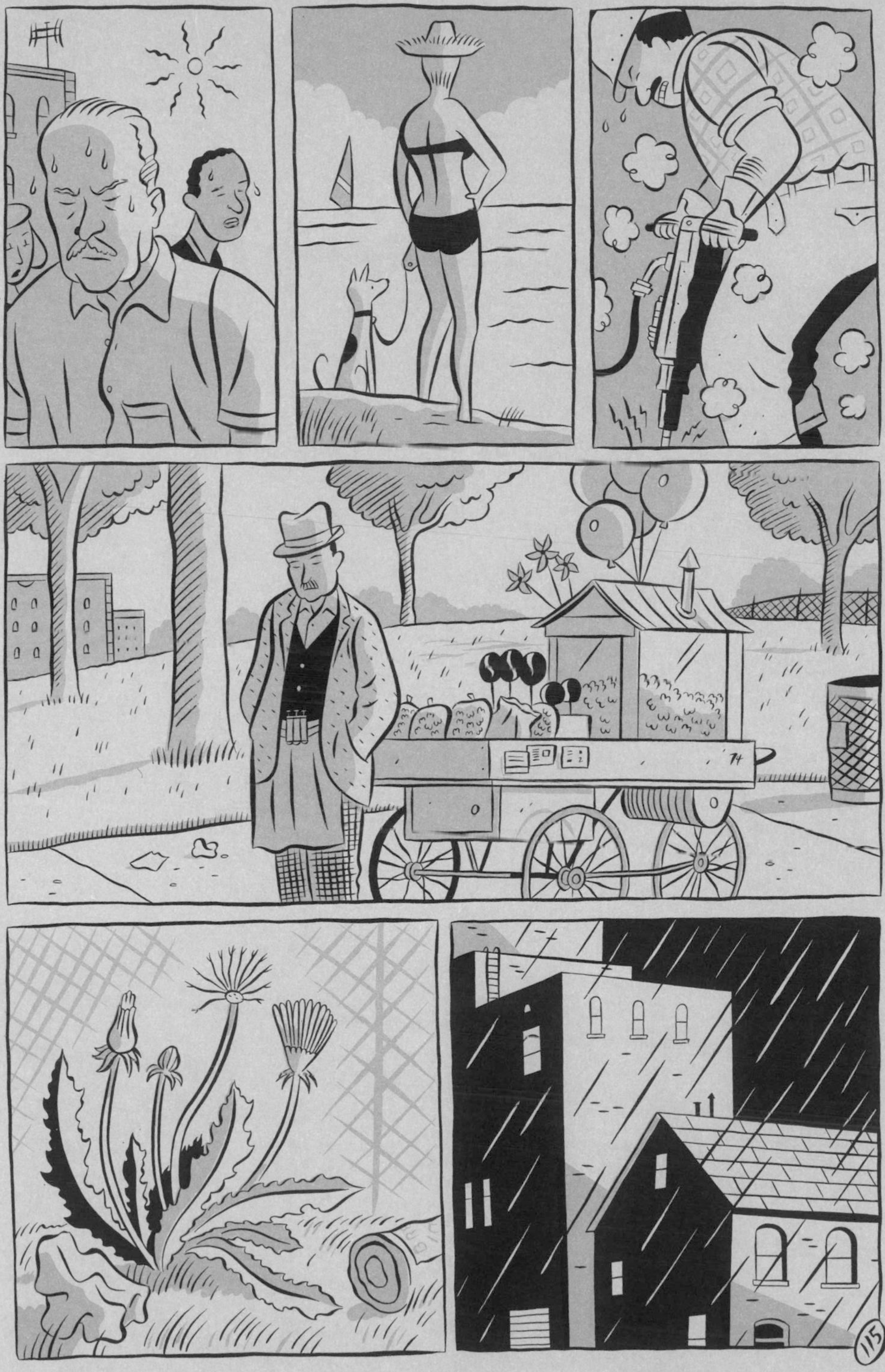

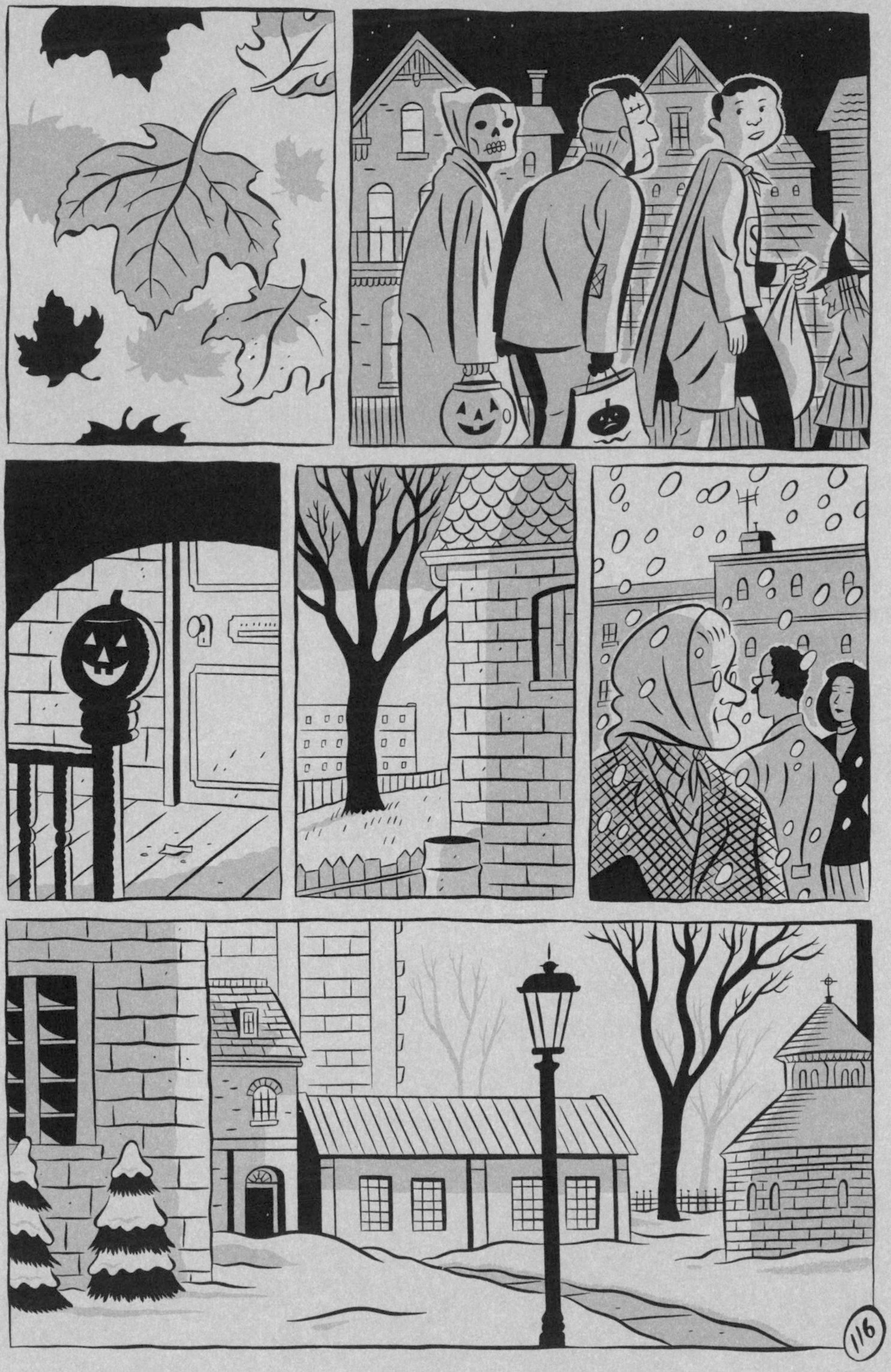
116

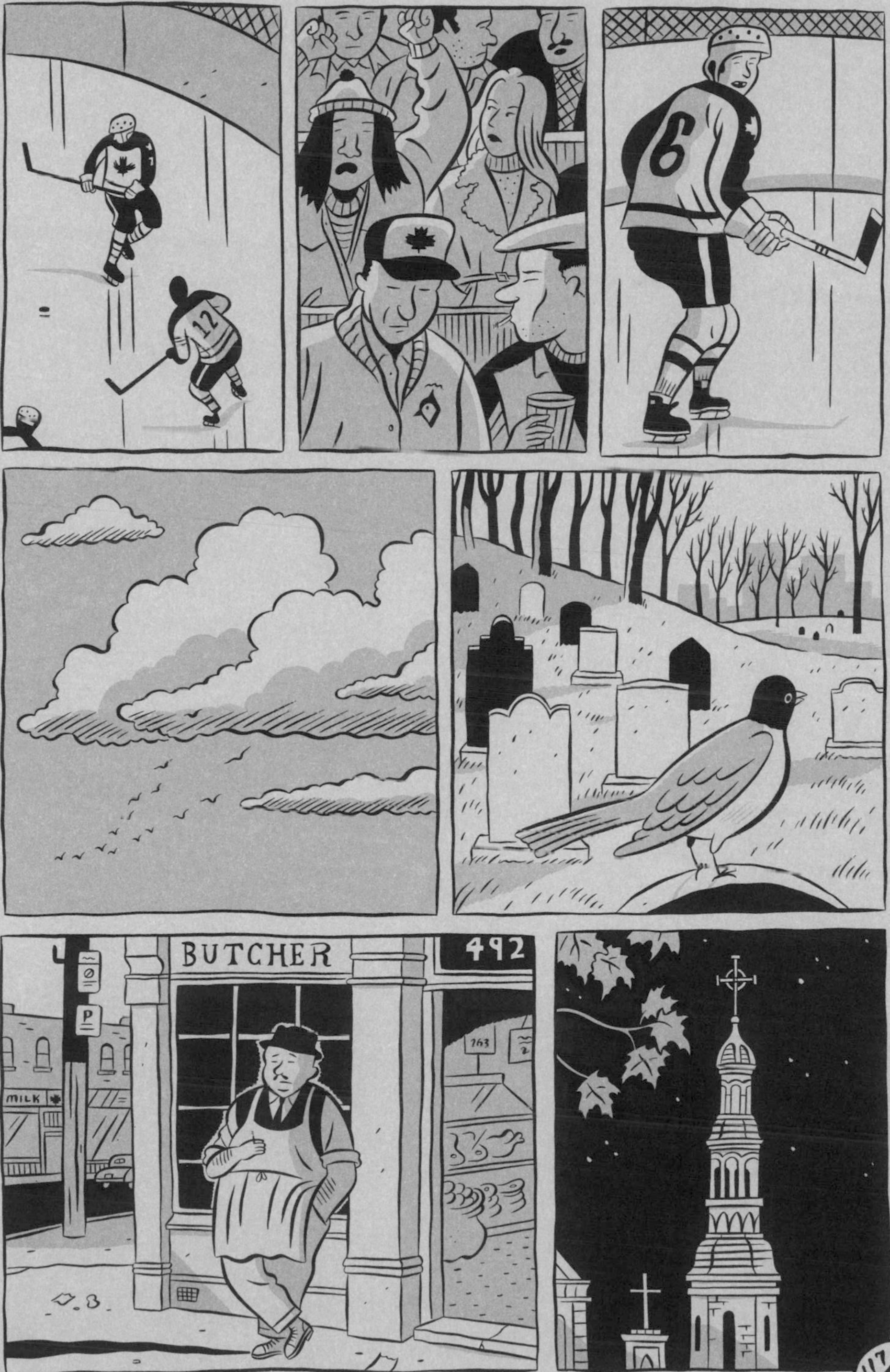
12
6
BUTCHER
492
MILK
P

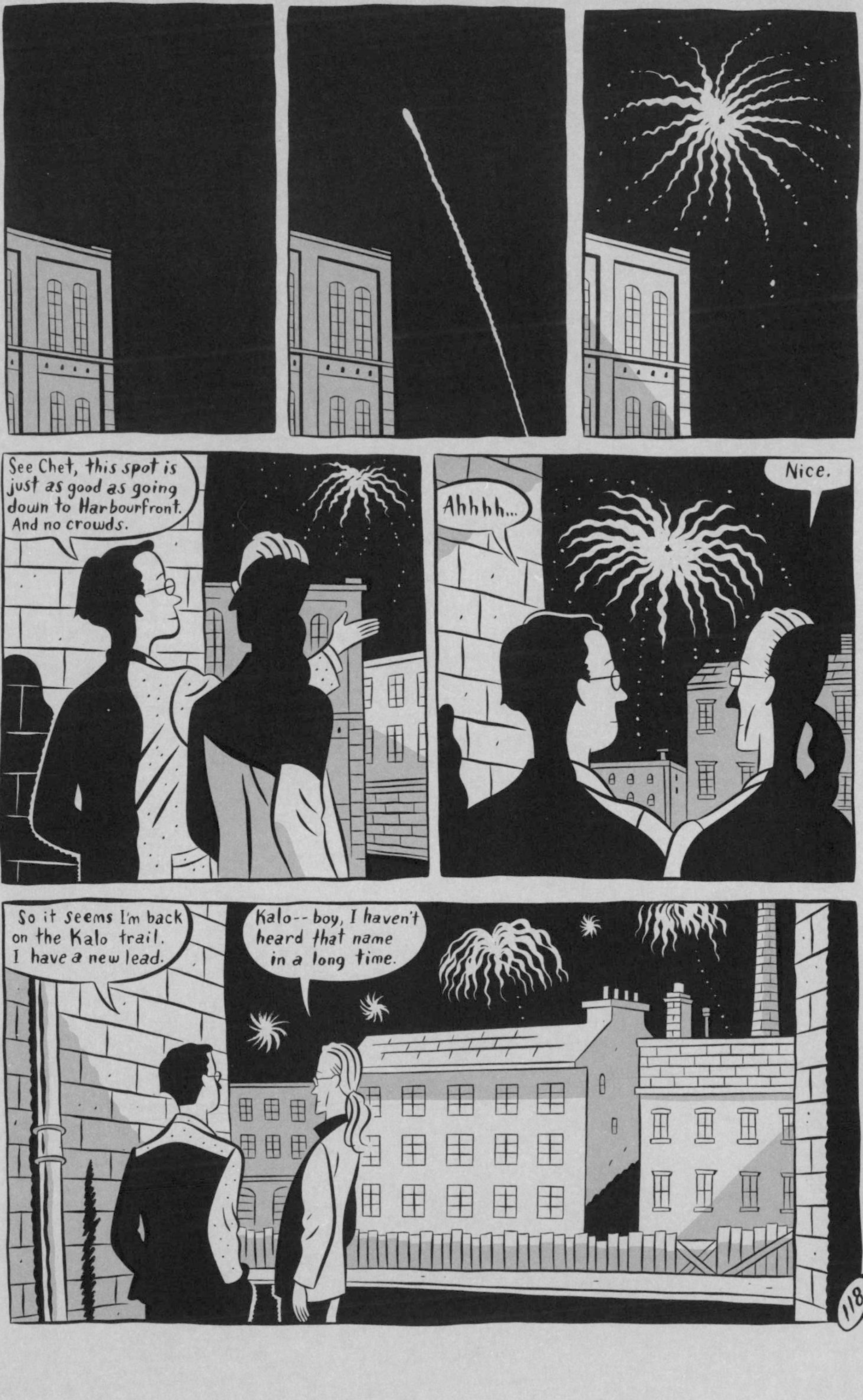
See Chet, this spot is just as good as going down to Harbourfront. And no crowds.
Ahhhh...
Nice.
So it seems I'm back on the Kalo trail. I have a new lead.
Kalo-- boy, I haven't heard that name in a long time.
118

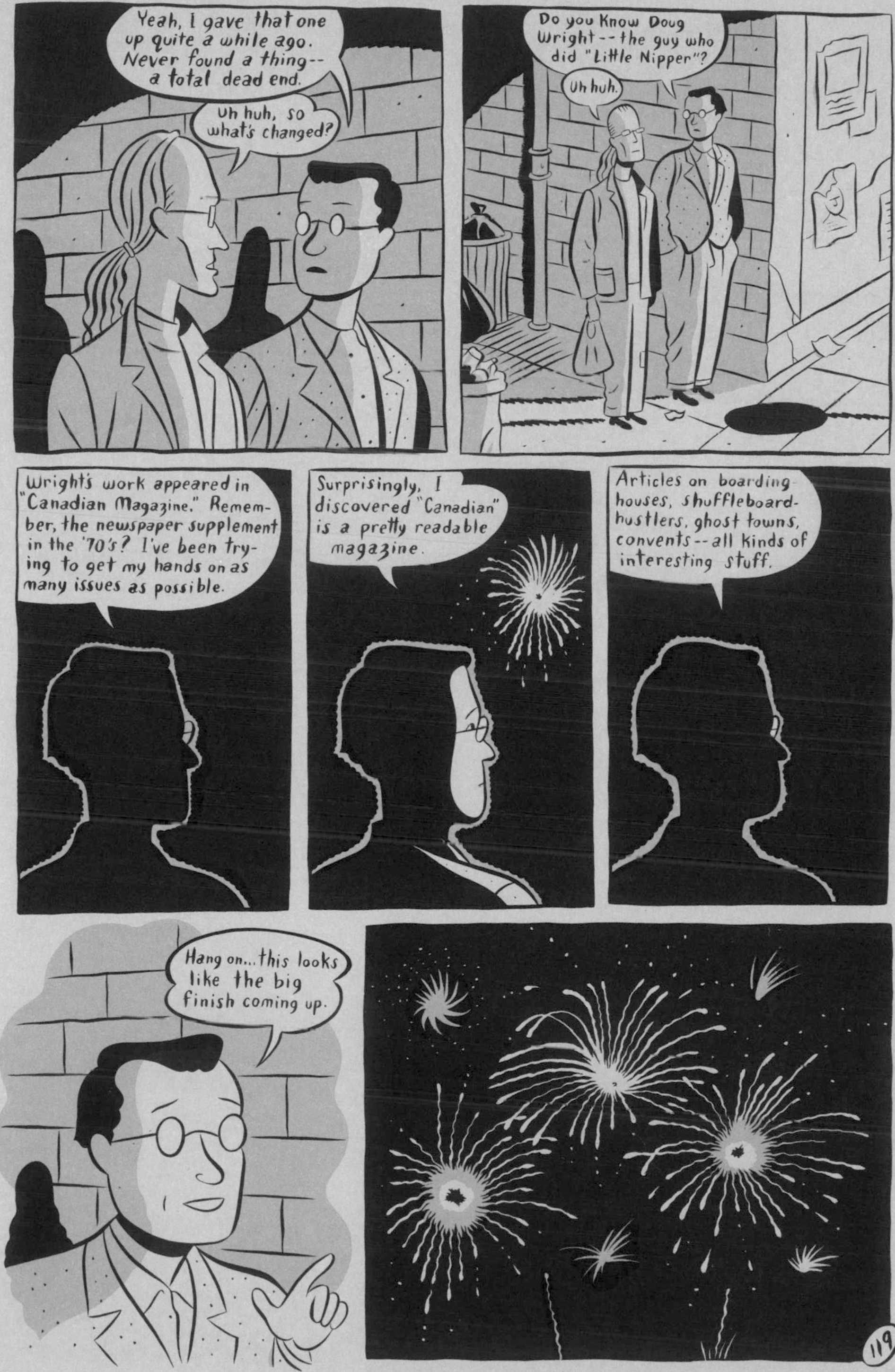

Yeah, I gave that one up quite a while ago. Never found a thing-- a total dead end.
Uh huh, so what's changed?
Do you know Doug Wright -- the guy who did "Little Nipper"?
Uh huh.
Wright's work appeared in "Canadian Magazine." Remember, the newspaper supplement in the '70's? I've been trying to get my hands on as many issues as possible.
Surprisingly, I discovered "Canadian" is a pretty readable magazine.
Articles on boarding houses, shuffleboard-hustlers, ghost towns, convents -- all kinds of interesting stuff.
Hang on... this looks like the big finish coming up.

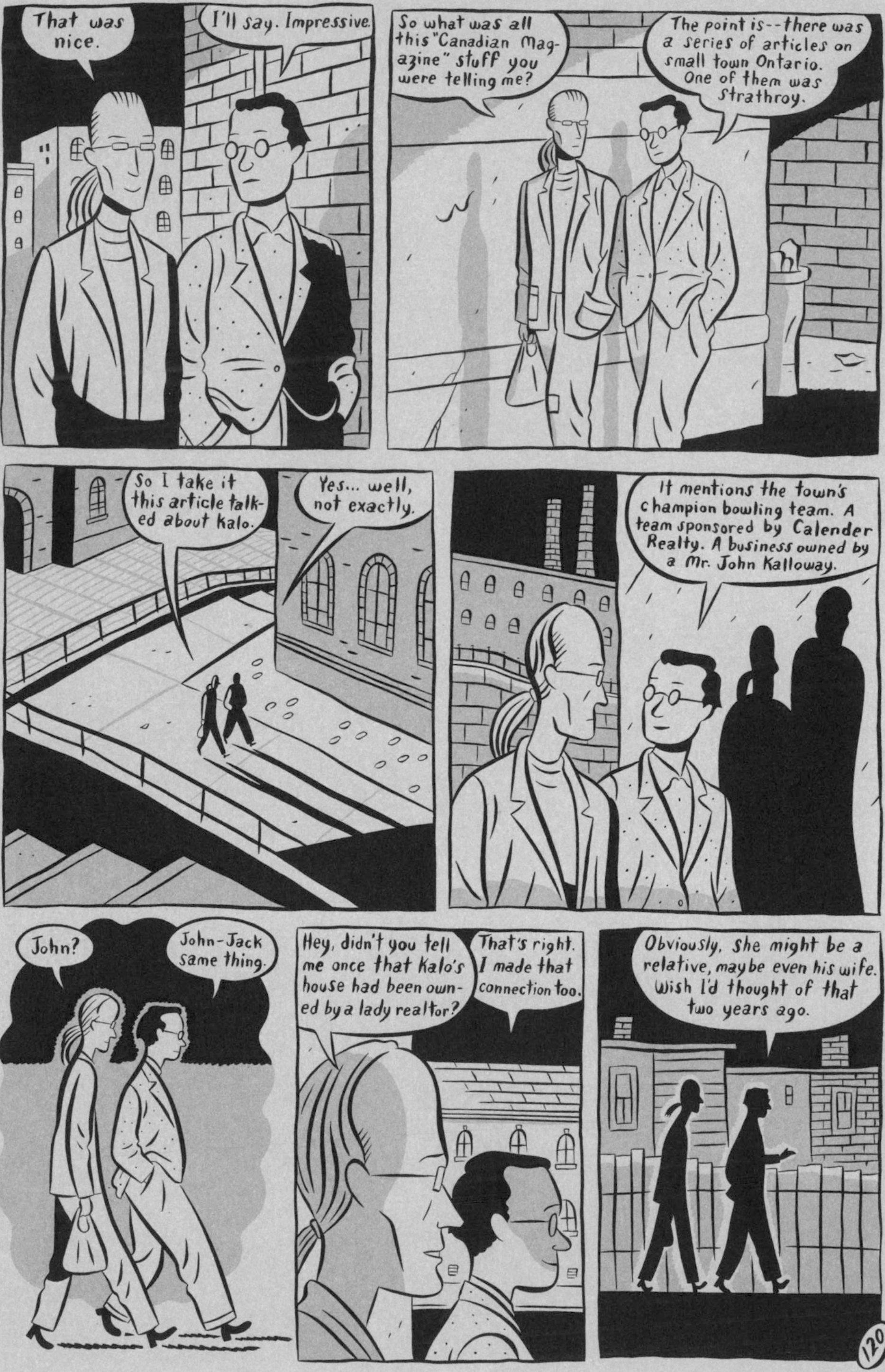
That was nice.
I'll say. Impressive.
So what was all this "Canadian Magazine" stuff you were telling me?
The point is--there was a series of articles on small town Ontario. One of them was Strathroy.
So I take it this article talked about Kalo.
Yes... well, not exactly.
It mentions the town's champion bowling team. A team sponsored by Calender Realty. A business owned by a Mr. John Kalloway.
John?
John-Jack same thing.
Hey, didn't you tell me once that Kalo's house had been owned by a lady realtor?
That's right. I made that connection too.
Obviously, she might be a relative, maybe even his wife. Wish I'd thought of that two years ago.

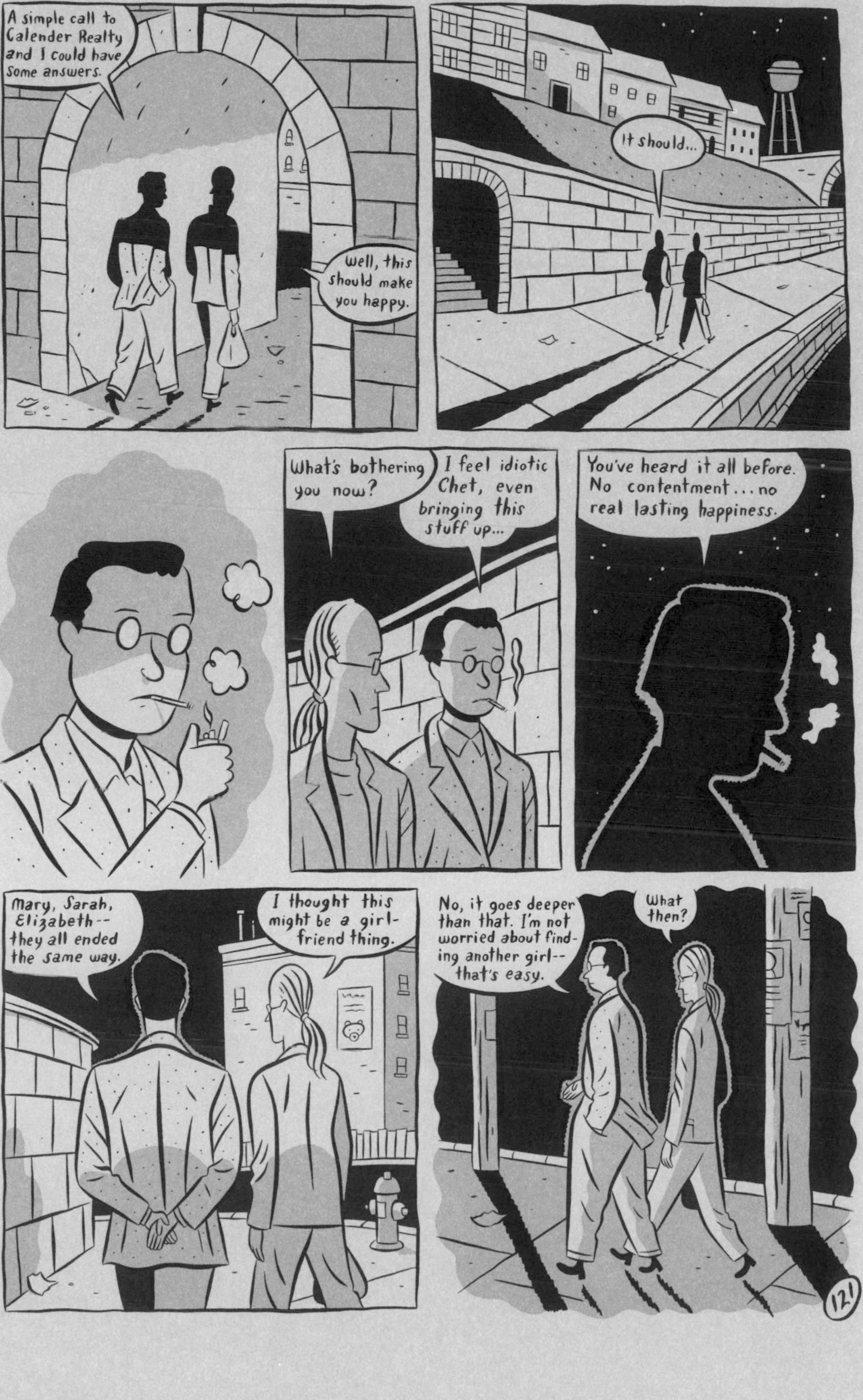
A simple call to Calender Realty and I could have some answers.
Well, this should make you happy.
It should...
What's bothering you now?
I feel idiotic Chet, even bringing this stuff up...
You've heard it all before. No contentment... no real lasting happiness.
Mary, Sarah, Elizabeth-- they all ended the same way.
I thought this might be a girl-friend thing.
No, it goes deeper than that. I'm not worried about find-ing another girl-- that's easy.
What then?

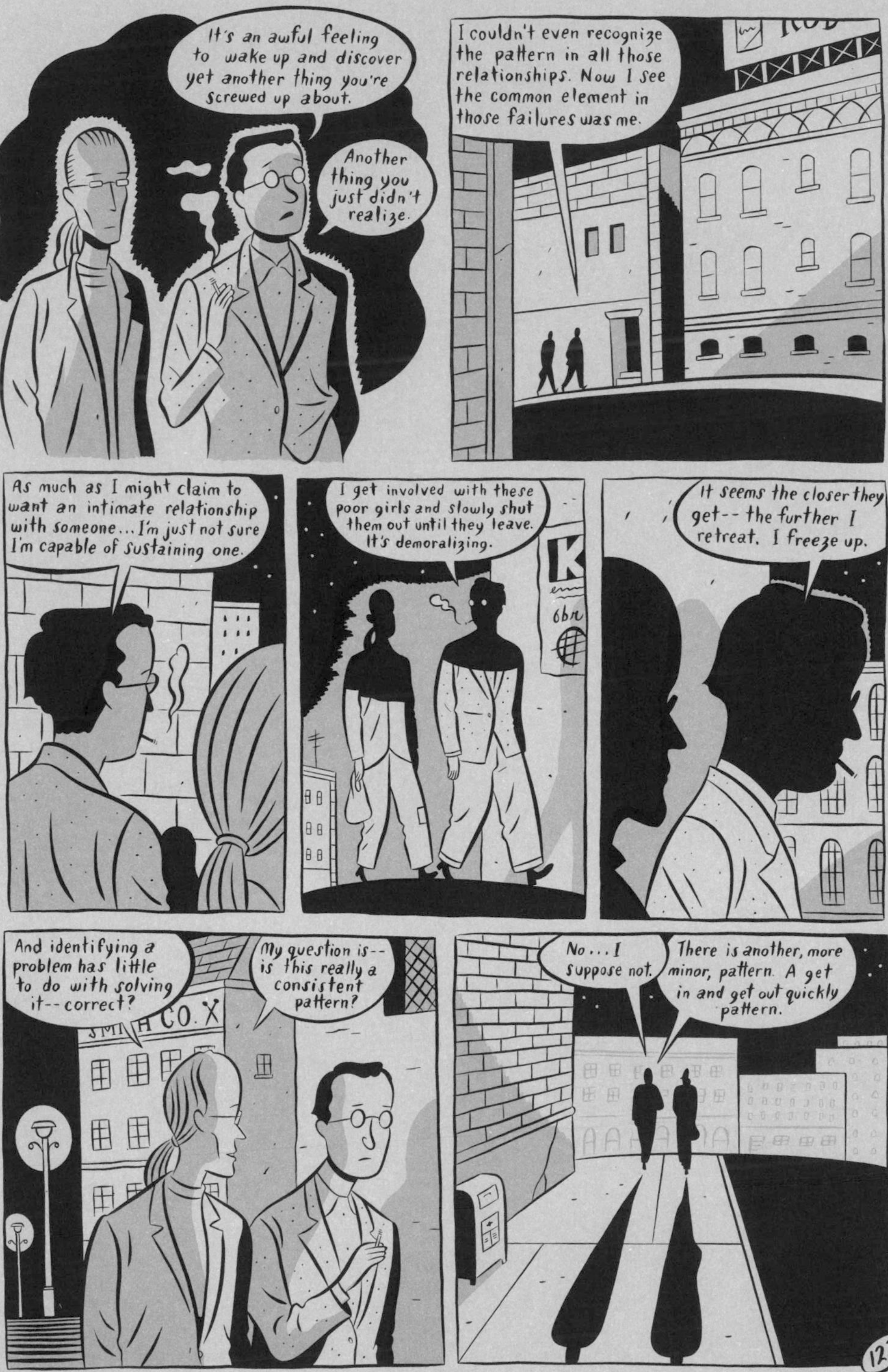
It's an awful feeling to wake up and discover yet another thing you're screwed up about.
Another thing you just didn't realize.
I couldn't even recognize the pattern in all those relationships. Now I see the common element in those failures was me.
As much as I might claim to want an intimate relationship with someone... I'm just not sure I'm capable of sustaining one.
I get involved with these poor girls and slowly shut them out until they leave. It's demoralizing.
It seems the closer they get-- the further I retreat. I freeze up.
And identifying a problem has little to do with solving it--correct?
My question is-- is this really a consistent pattern?
No... I suppose not.
There is another, more minor, pattern. A get in and get out quickly pattern.

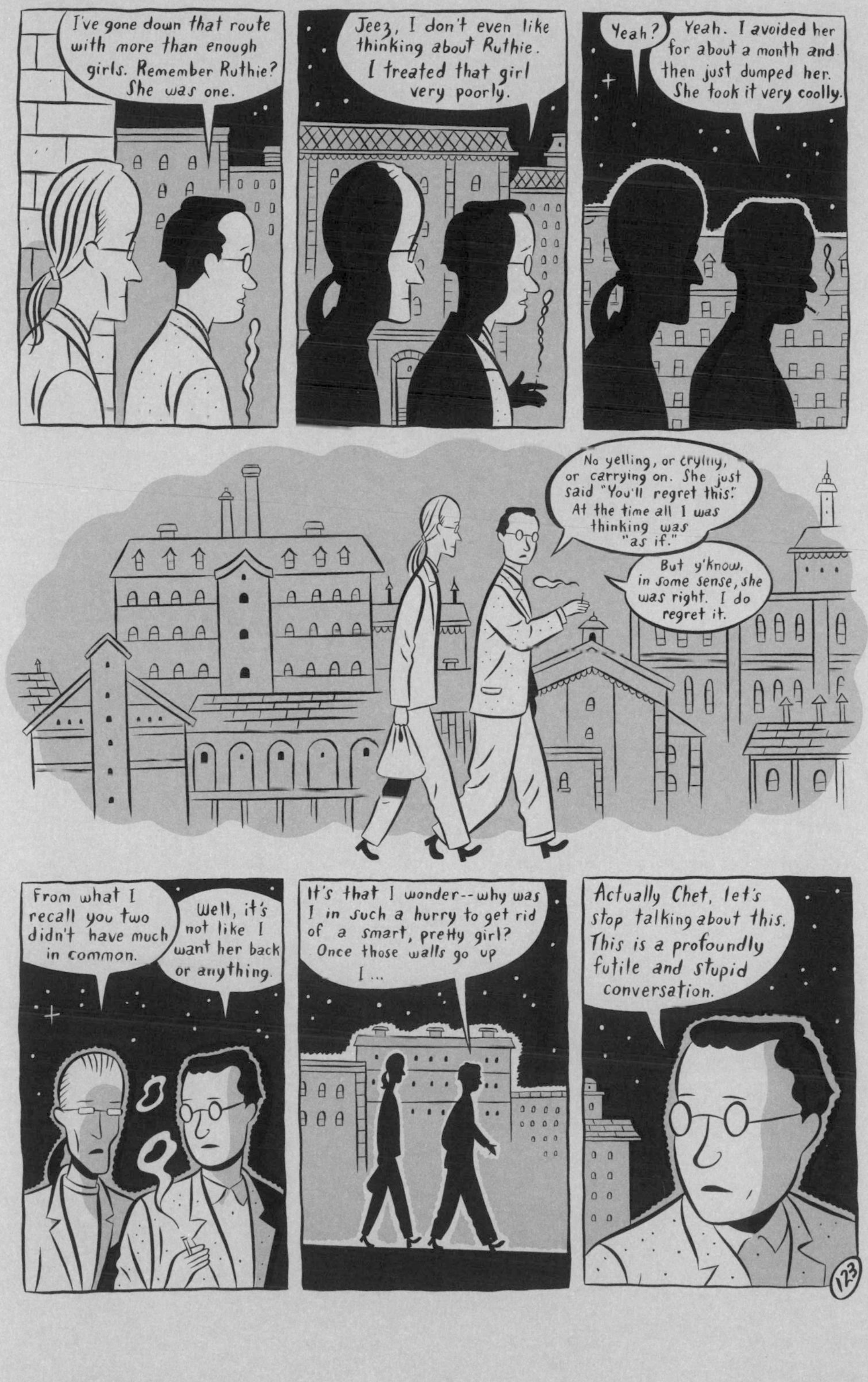
I've gone down that route with more than enough girls. Remember Ruthie? She was one.
Jeez, I don't even like thinking about Ruthie. I treated that girl very poorly.
Yeah?
Yeah. I avoided her for about a month and then just dumped her. She took it very coolly.
No yelling, or crying, or carrying on. She just said "You'll regret this." At the time all I was thinking was "as if."
But y'know, in some sense, she was right. I do regret it.
From what I recall you two didn't have much in common.
Well, it's not like I want her back or anything.
It's that I wonder--why was I in such a hurry to get rid of a smart, pretty girl? Once those walls go up I...
Actually Chet, let's stop talking about this. This is a profoundly futile and stupid conversation.
123

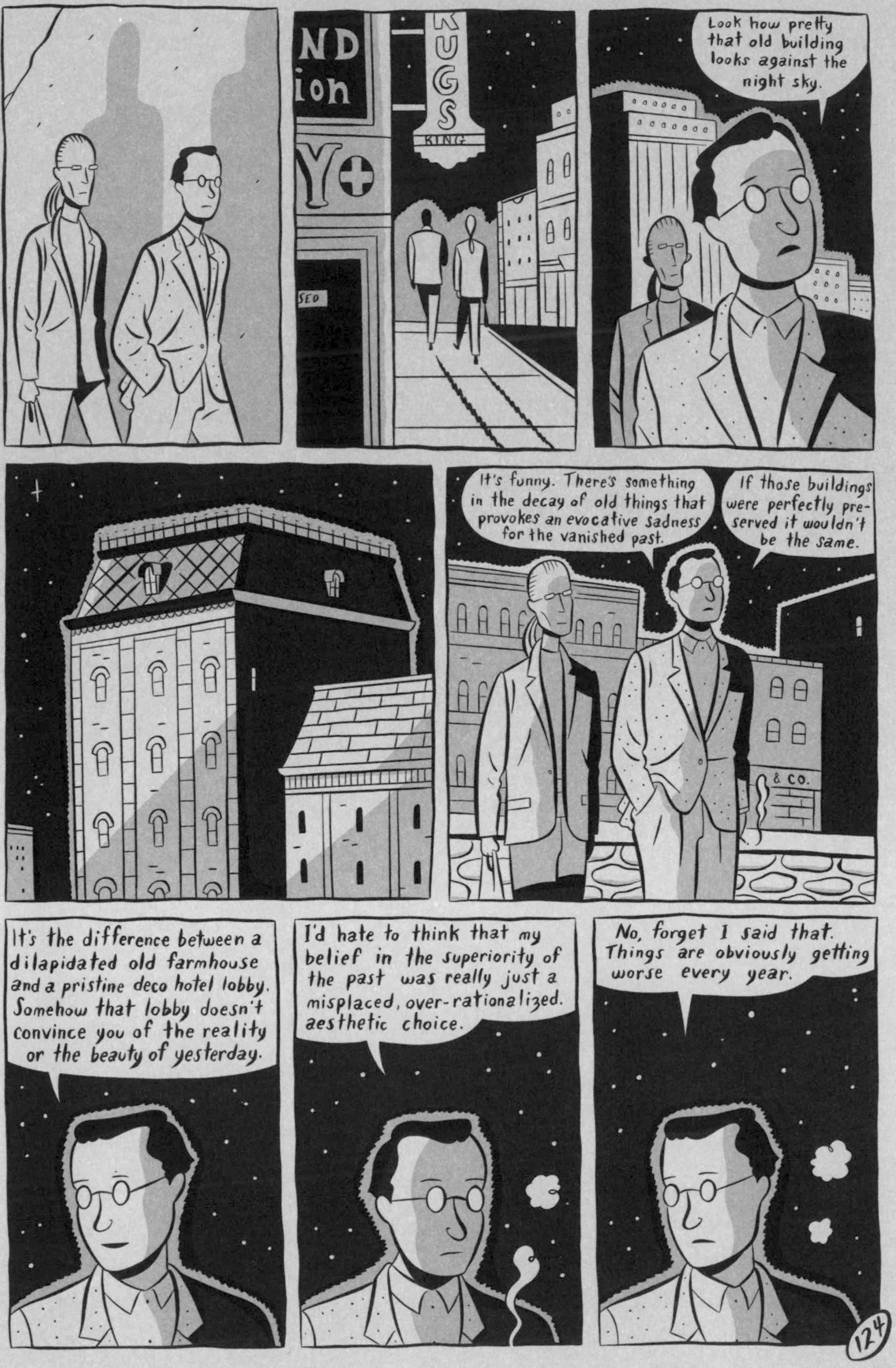
ND
ion
Y
KUGS
KING
SED
Look how pretty that old building looks against the night sky.
It's funny. There's something in the decay of old things that provokes an evocative sadness for the vanished past.
If those buildings were perfectly preserved it wouldn't be the same.
& CO.
It's the difference between a dilapidated old farmhouse and a pristine deco hotel lobby. Somehow that lobby doesn't convince you of the reality or the beauty of yesterday.
I'd hate to think that my belief in the superiority of the past was really just a misplaced, over-rationalized aesthetic choice.
No, forget I said that. Things are obviously getting worse every year.
124

It occurred to me the other day that maybe I'm wasting my time looking for Kalo. He's kind of a nobody--a one-hit wonder.

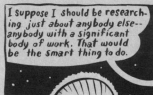

I suppose I should be researching just about anybody else-- anybody with a significant body of work. That would be the smart thing to do.

WORKS EST 1933

125

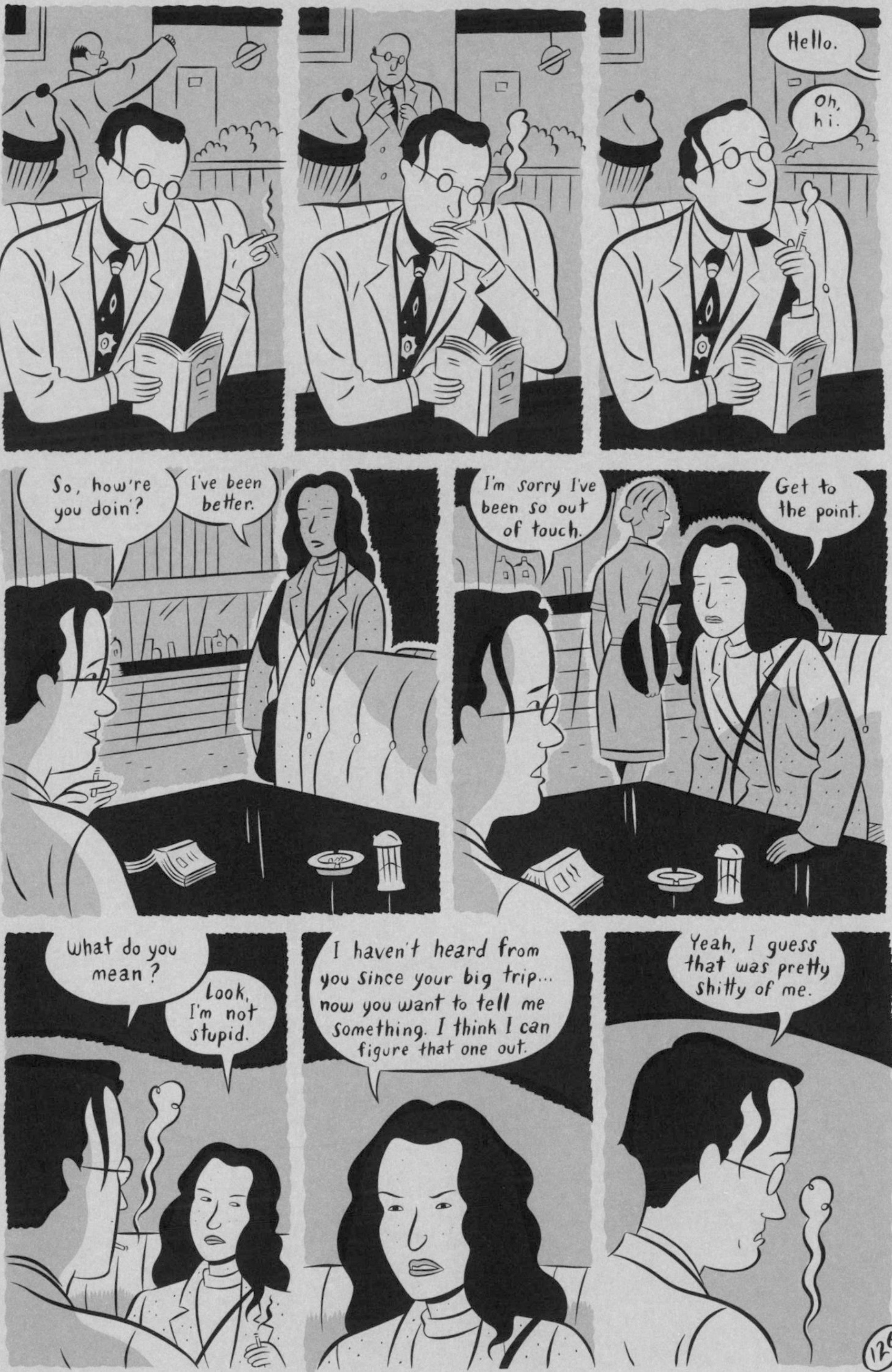
Hello.
Oh, hi.
So, how're you doin'?
I've been better.
I'm sorry I've been so out of touch.
Get to the point.
What do you mean?
Look, I'm not stupid.
I haven't heard from you since your big trip... now you want to tell me something. I think I can figure that one out.
Yeah, I guess that was pretty shitty of me.
126

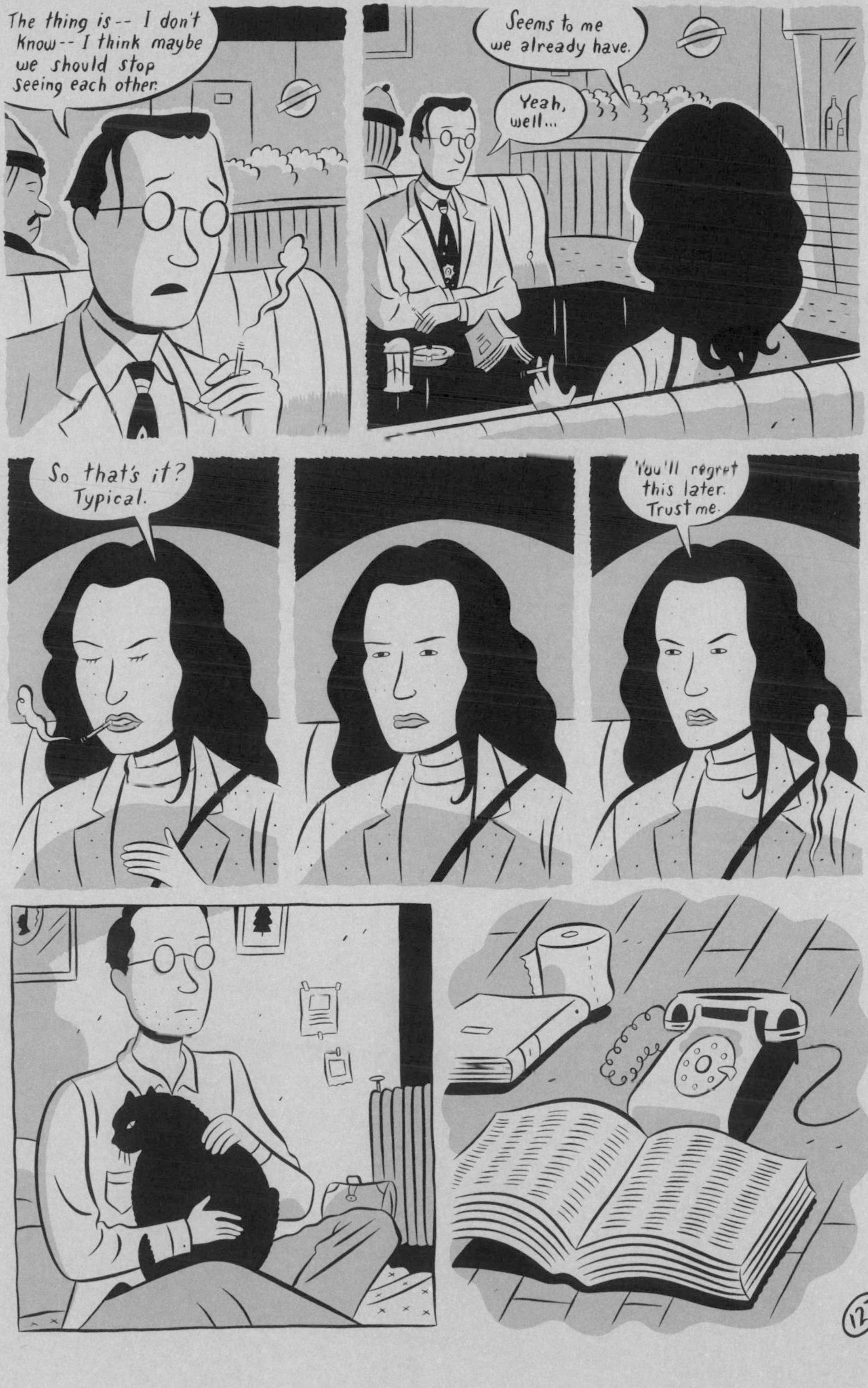

The thing is -- I don't know -- I think maybe we should stop seeing each other.
Seems to me we already have.
Yeah, well...
So that's it? Typical.
You'll regret this later. Trust me.

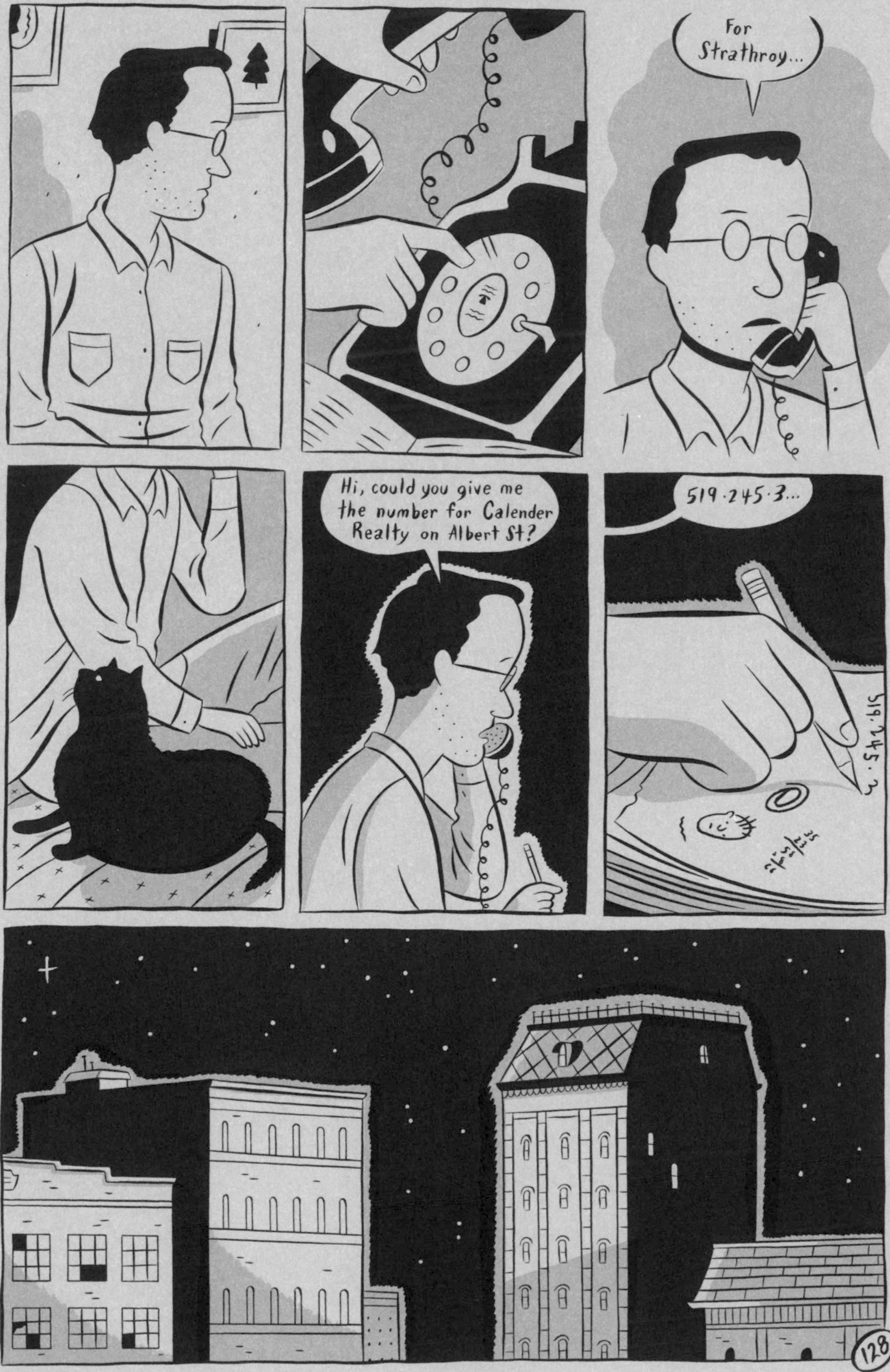
For Strathroy...
Hi, could you give me the number for Calender Realty on Albert St?
519·245·3...
519·245·3

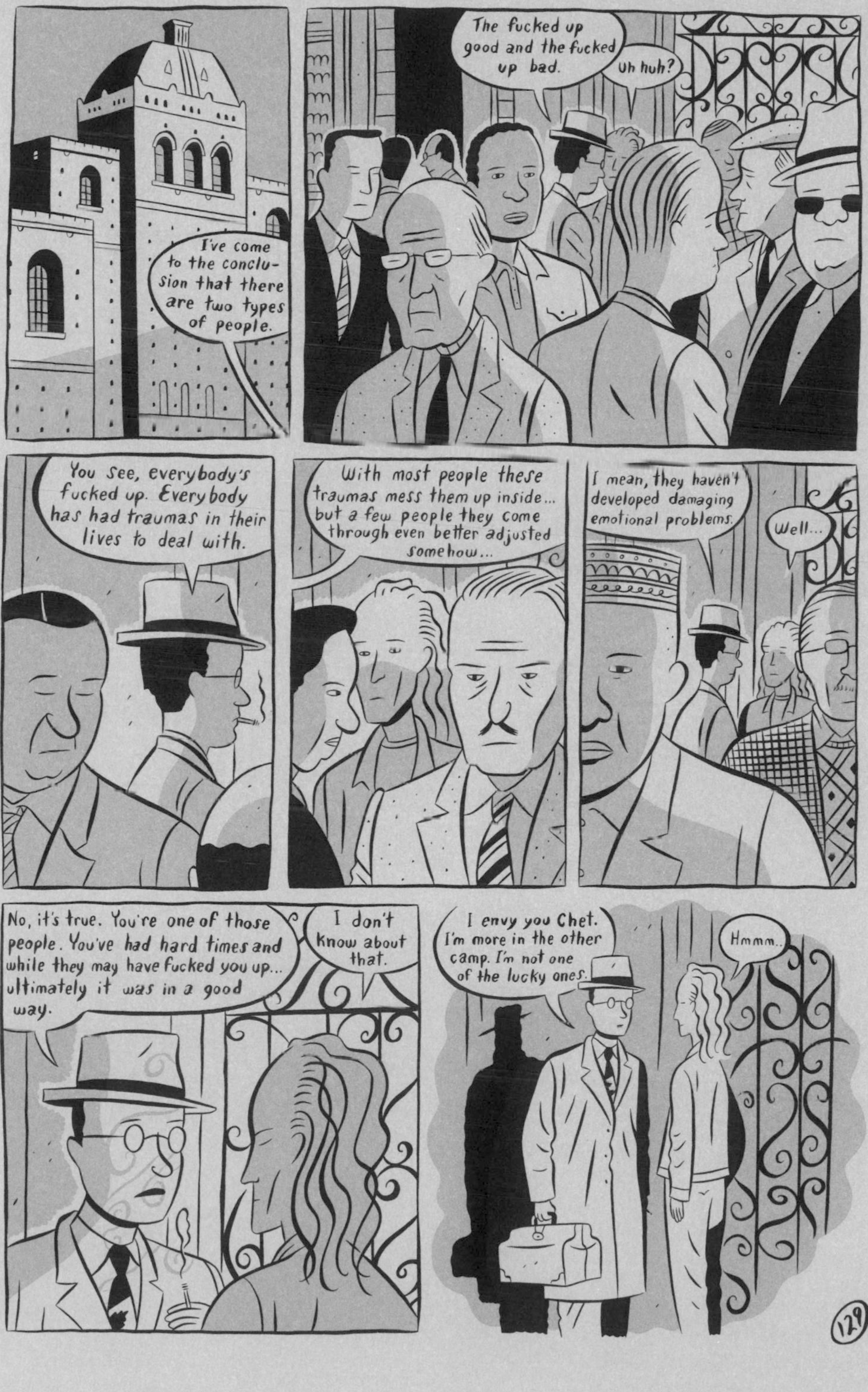
I've come to the conclusion that there are two types of people.
The fucked up good and the fucked up bad.
Uh huh?
You see, everybody's fucked up. Everybody has had traumas in their lives to deal with.
With most people these traumas mess them up inside... but a few people they come through even better adjusted somehow...
I mean, they haven't developed damaging emotional problems.
Well...
No, it's true. You're one of those people. You've had hard times and while they may have fucked you up... ultimately it was in a good way.
I don't know about that.
I envy you Chet. I'm more in the other camp. I'm not one of the lucky ones.
Hmmm..

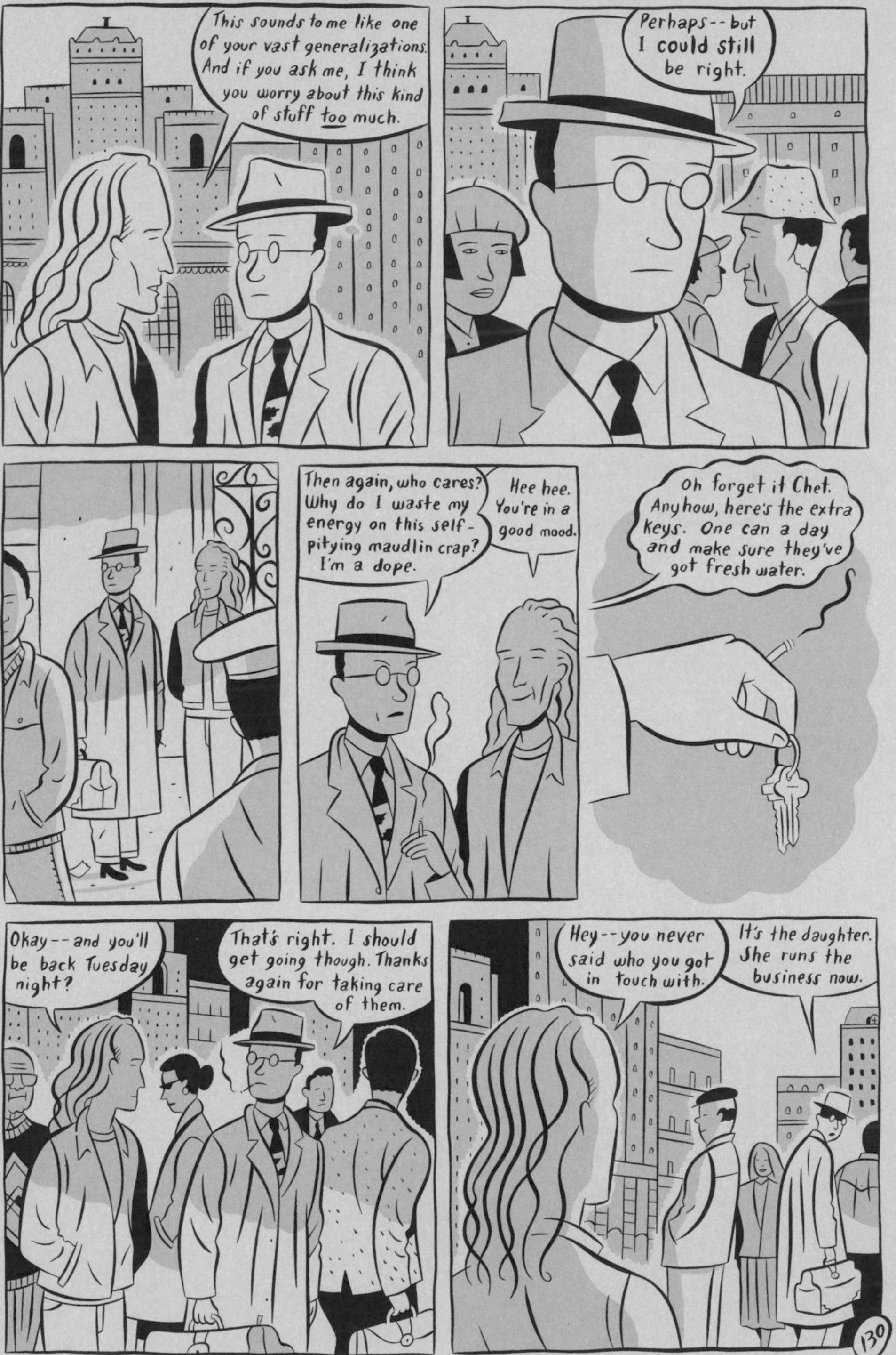
This sounds to me like one of your vast generalizations. And if you ask me, I think you worry about this kind of stuff too much.
Perhaps--but I could still be right.
Then again, who cares? Why do I waste my energy on this self-pitying maudlin crap? I'm a dope.
Hee hee. You're in a good mood.
Oh forget it Chet. Anyhow, here's the extra keys. One can a day and make sure they've got fresh water.
Okay--and you'll be back Tuesday night?
That's right. I should get going though. Thanks again for taking care of them.
Hey--you never said who you got in touch with.
It's the daughter. She runs the business now.
130

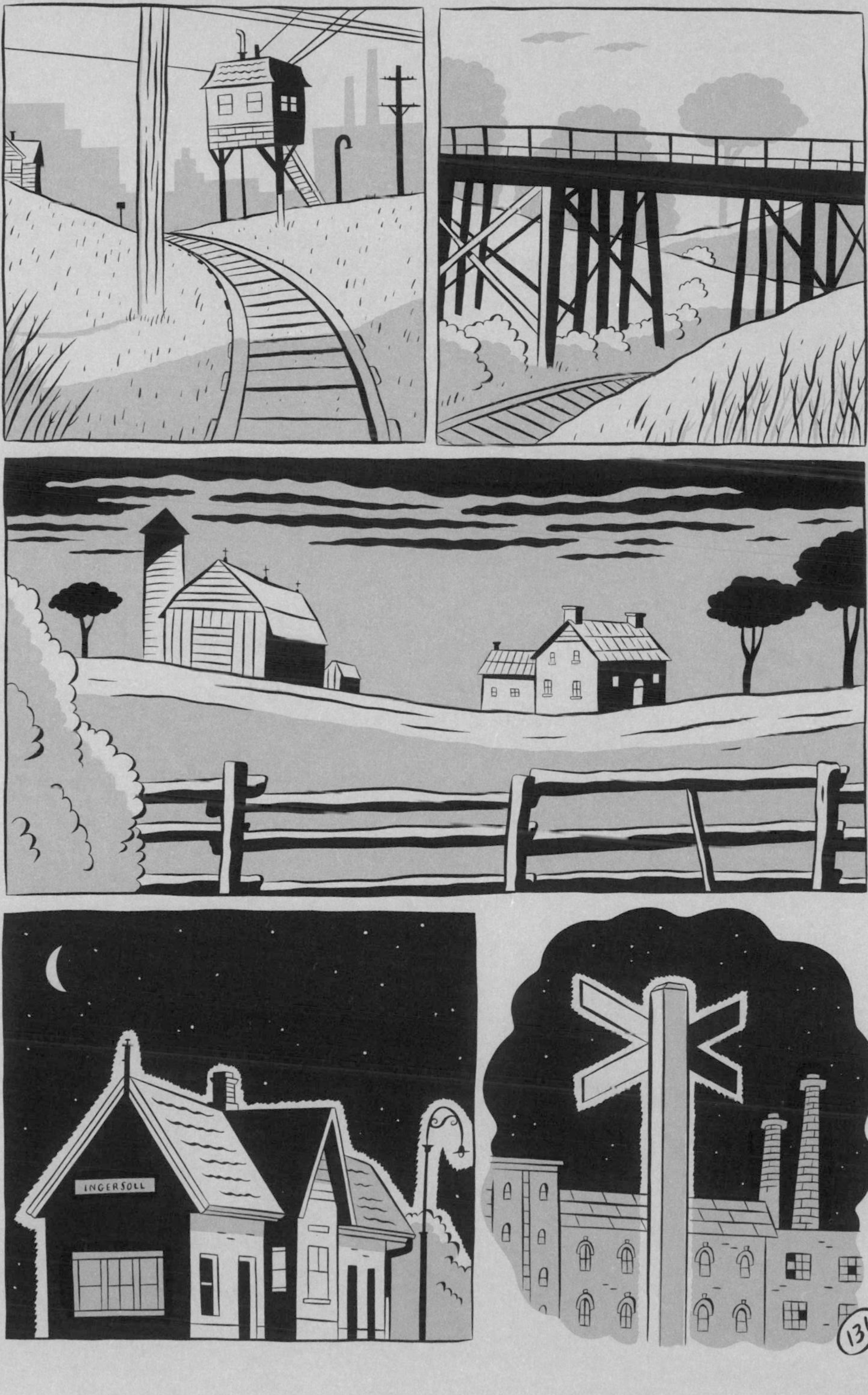
INGERSOLL

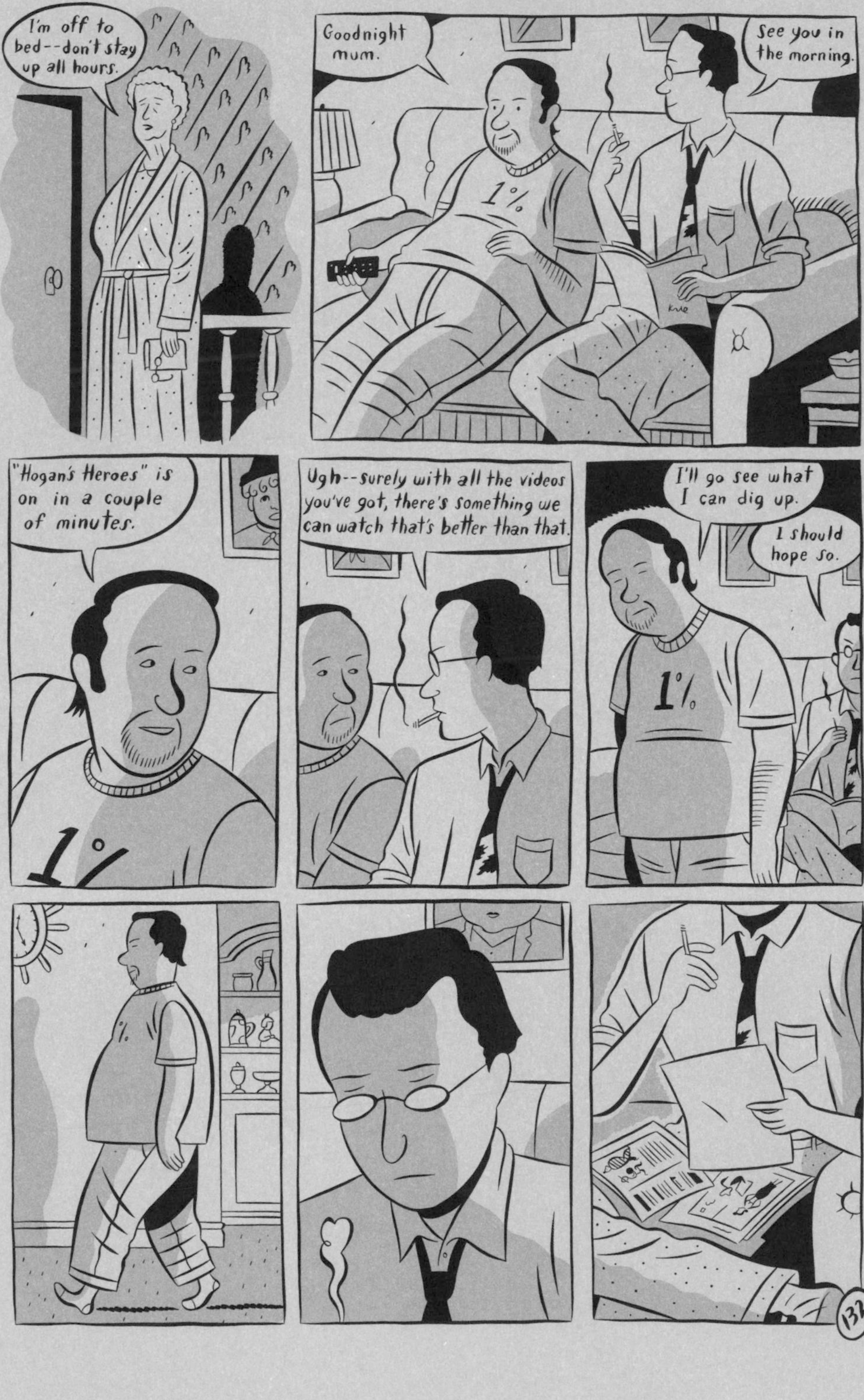
I'm off to bed--don't stay up all hours.
Goodnight mum.
See you in the morning.
"Hogan's Heroes" is on in a couple of minutes.
Ugh--surely with all the videos you've got, there's something we can watch that's better than that.
I'll go see what I can dig up.
I should hope so.

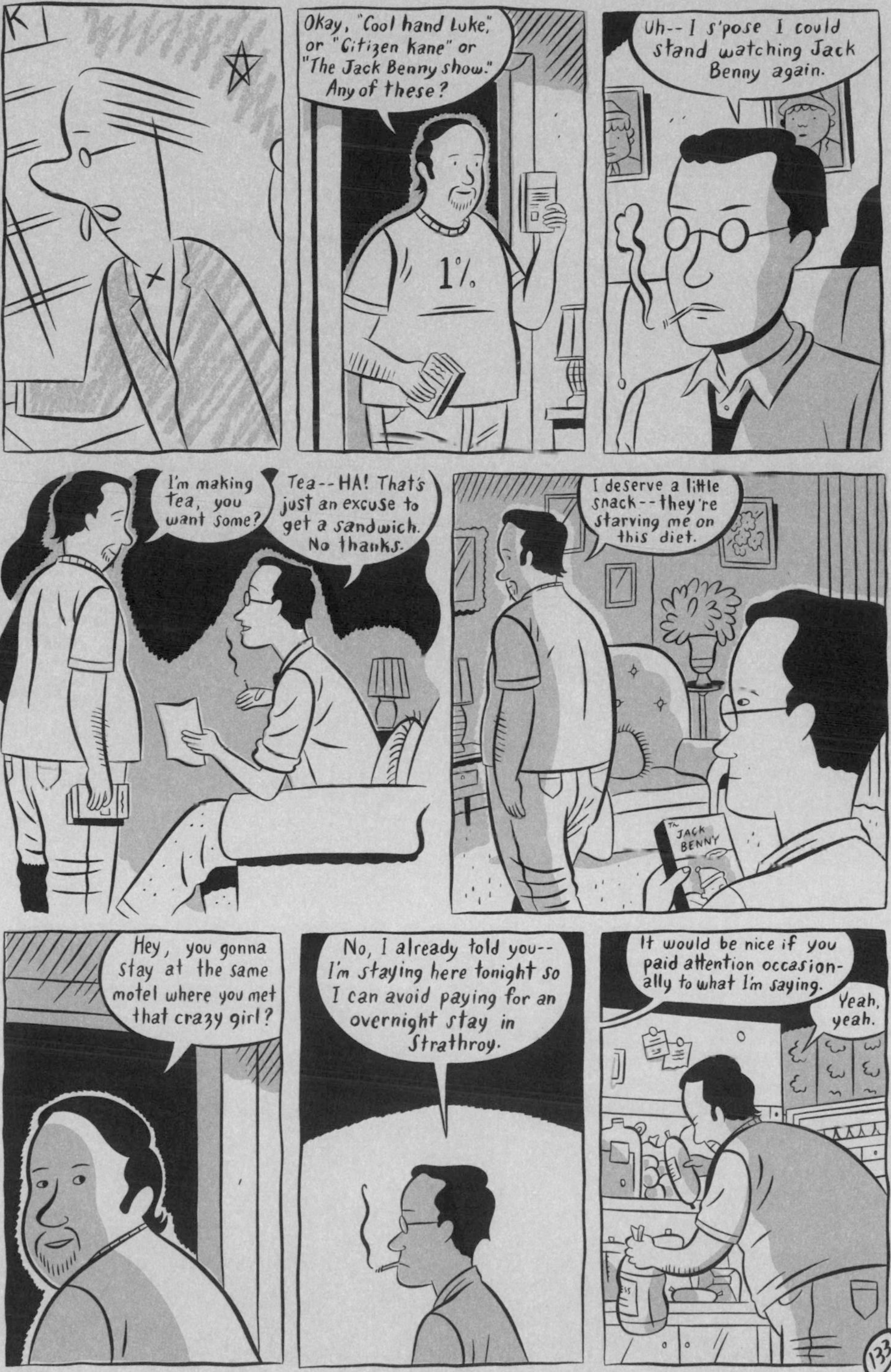
Okay, "Cool hand Luke," or "Citizen kane" or "The Jack Benny show." Any of these?
Uh-- I s'pose I could stand watching Jack Benny again.
I'm making tea, you want some?
Tea--HA! That's just an excuse to get a sandwich. No thanks.
I deserve a little snack--they're starving me on this diet.
Hey, you gonna stay at the same motel where you met that crazy girl?
No, I already told you-- I'm staying here tonight so I can avoid paying for an overnight stay in Strathroy.
It would be nice if you paid attention occasionally to what I'm saying.
Yeah, yeah.

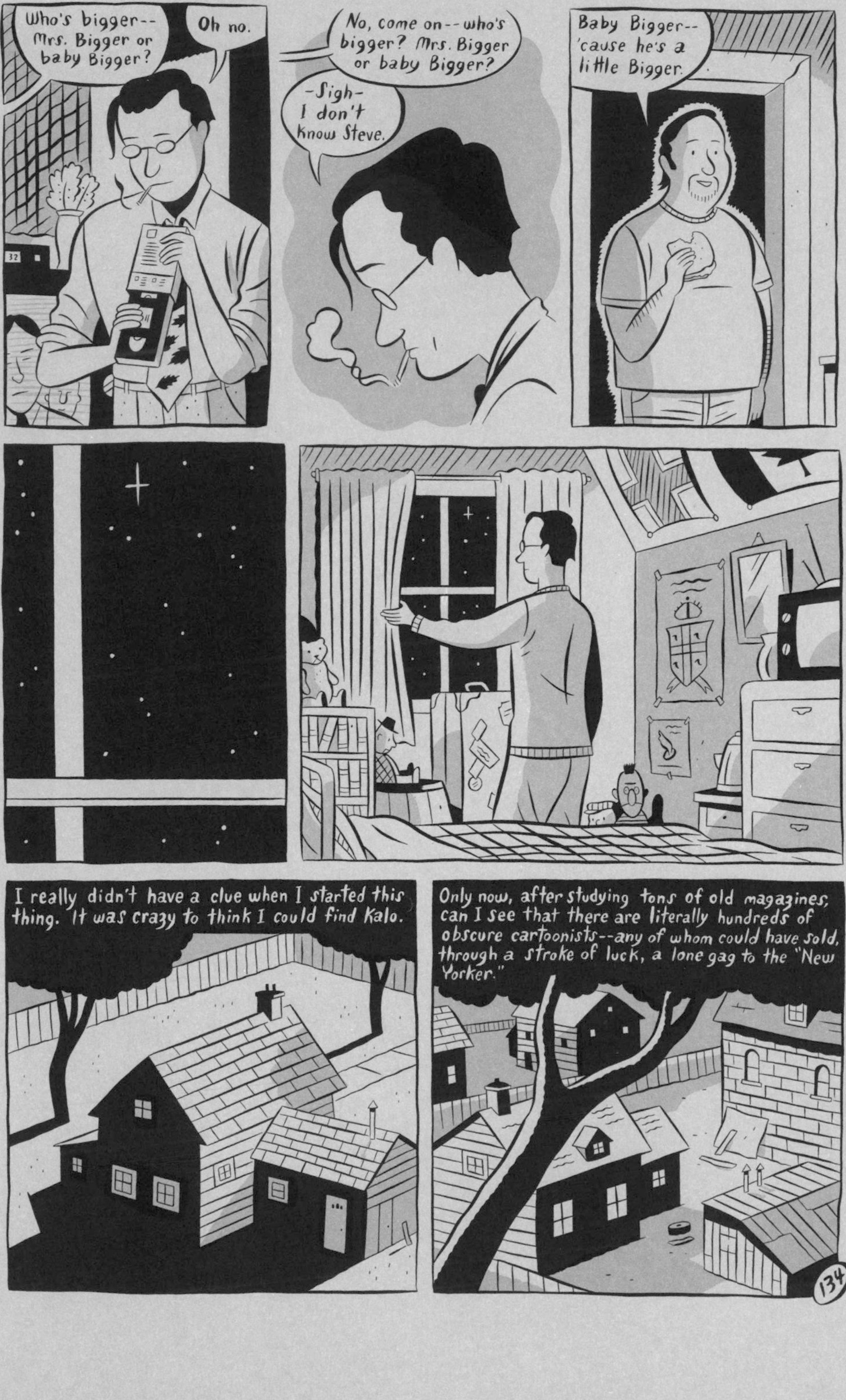
Who's bigger-- Mrs. Bigger or baby Bigger?
Oh no.
No, come on--who's bigger? Mrs. Bigger or baby Bigger?
-Sigh- I don't know Steve.
Baby Bigger-- 'cause he's a little Bigger.
I really didn't have a clue when I started this thing. It was crazy to think I could find Kalo.
Only now, after studying tons of old magazines, can I see that there are literally hundreds of obscure cartoonists--any of whom could have sold, through a stroke of luck, a lone gag to the "New Yorker."

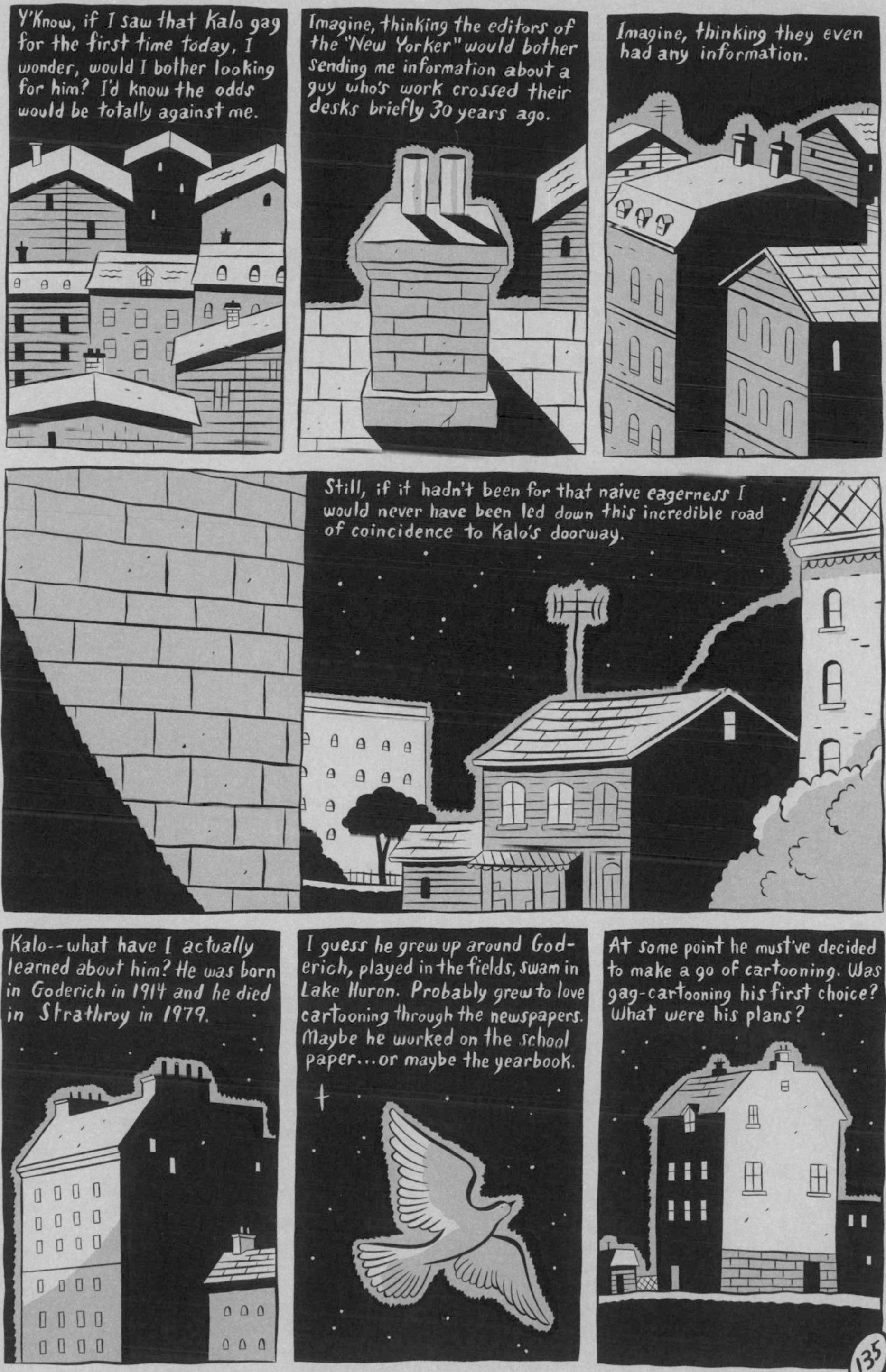
Y'Know, if I saw that Kalo gag for the first time today, I wonder, would I bother looking for him? I'd know the odds would be totally against me.
Imagine, thinking the editors of the "New Yorker" would bother sending me information about a guy who's work crossed their desks briefly 30 years ago.
Imagine, thinking they even had any information.
Still, if it hadn't been for that naive eagerness I would never have been led down this incredible road of coincidence to Kalo's doorway.
Kalo--what have I actually learned about him? He was born in Goderich in 1914 and he died in Strathroy in 1979.
I guess he grew up around Goderich, played in the fields, swam in Lake Huron. Probably grew to love cartooning through the newspapers. Maybe he worked on the school paper...or maybe the yearbook.
At some point he must've decided to make a go of cartooning. Was gag-cartooning his first choice? What were his plans?

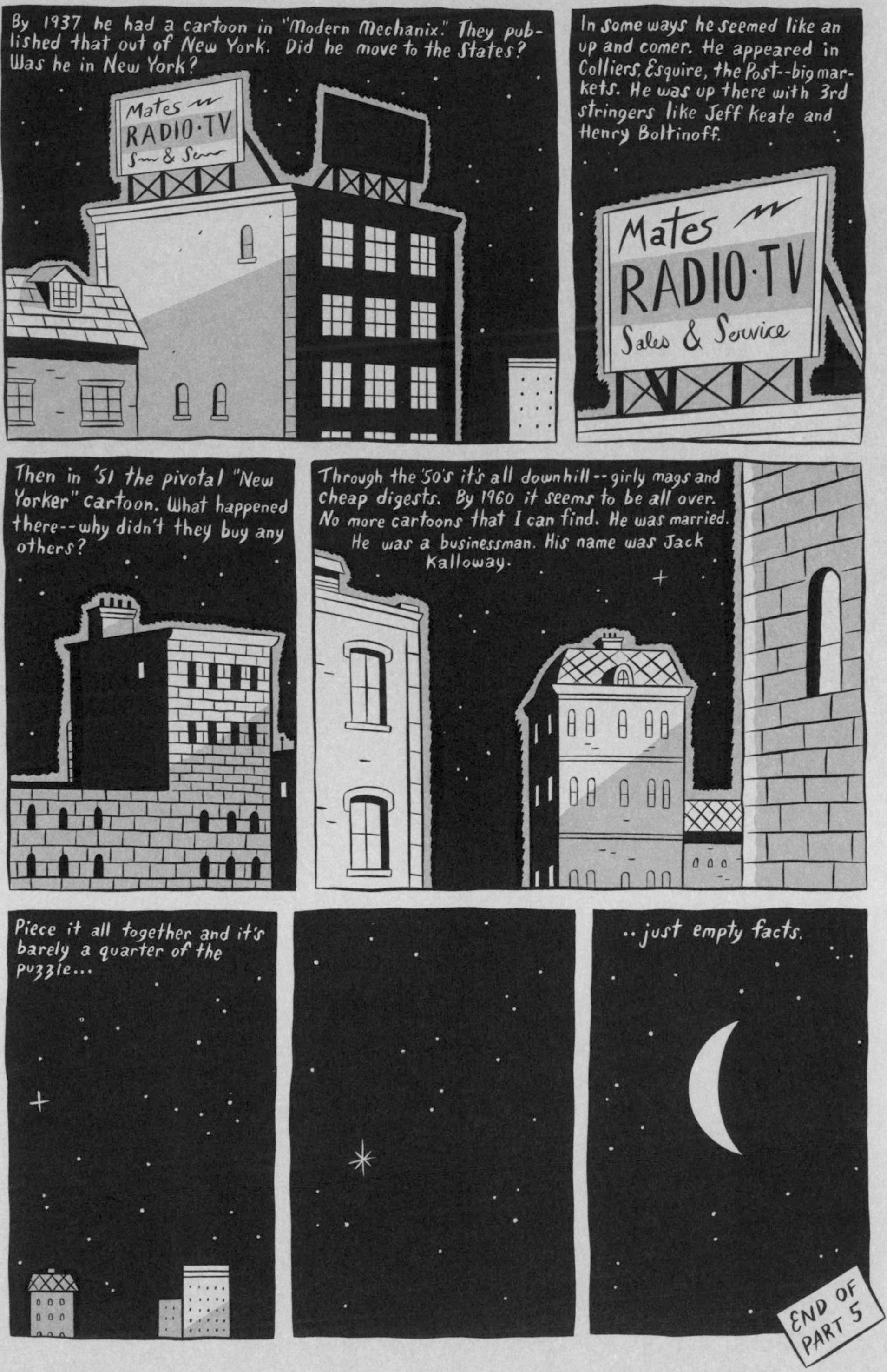
By 1937 he had a cartoon in "Modern Mechanix." They published that out of New York. Did he move to the States? Was he in New York?
Mates RADIO·TV
In some ways he seemed like an up and comer. He appeared in Colliers, Esquire, the Post--big markets. He was up there with 3rd stringers like Jeff Keate and Henry Boltinoff.
Mates RADIO·TV Sales & Service
Then in '51 the pivotal "New Yorker" cartoon. What happened there--why didn't they buy any others?
Through the '50's it's all downhill--girly mags and cheap digests. By 1960 it seems to be all over. No more cartoons that I can find. He was married. He was a businessman. His name was Jack Kalloway.
Piece it all together and it's barely a quarter of the puzzle...
..just empty facts.
END OF PART 5

Part Six

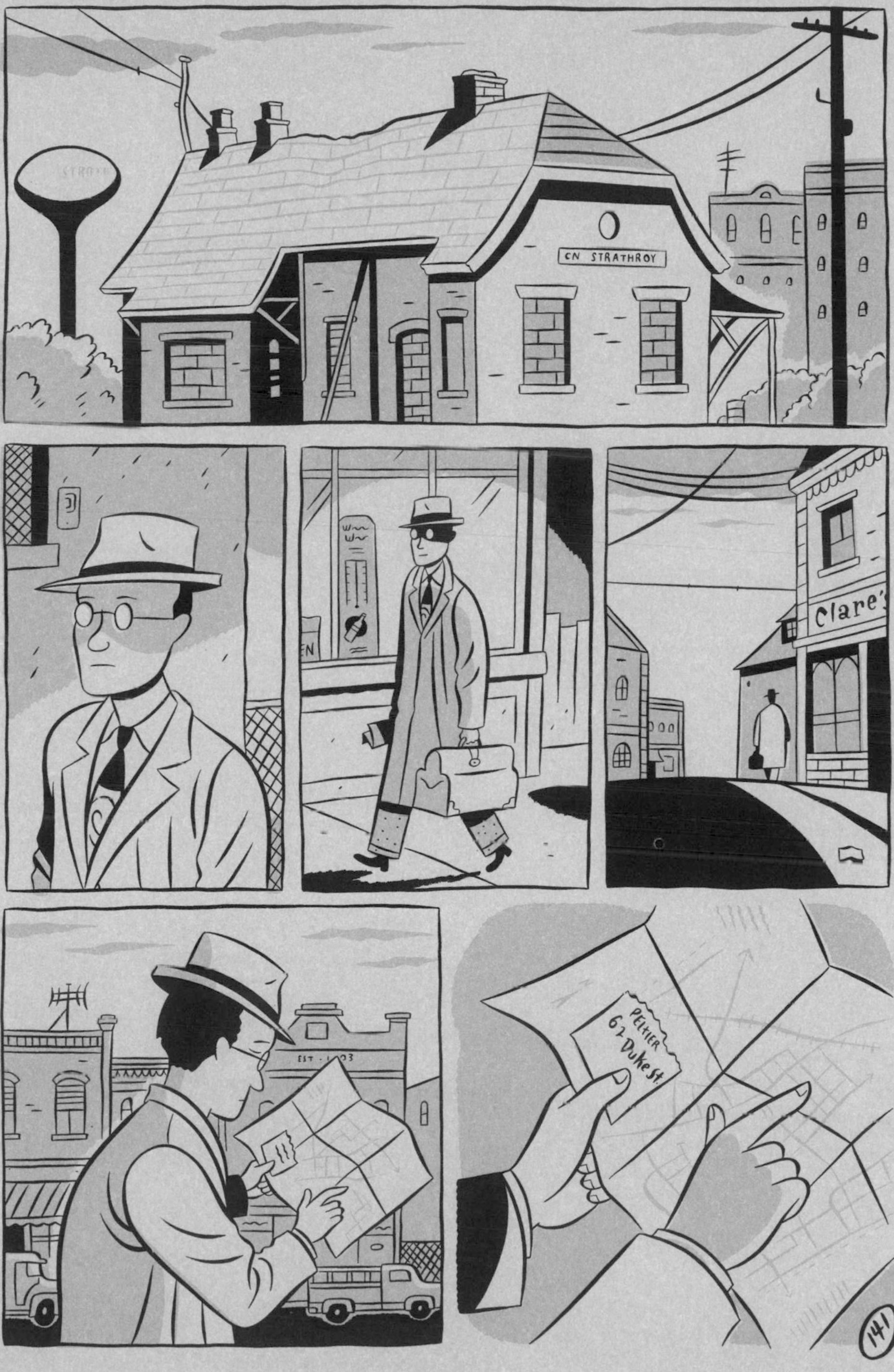
CN STRATHROY
Clare'
PELTIER
62 Duke St

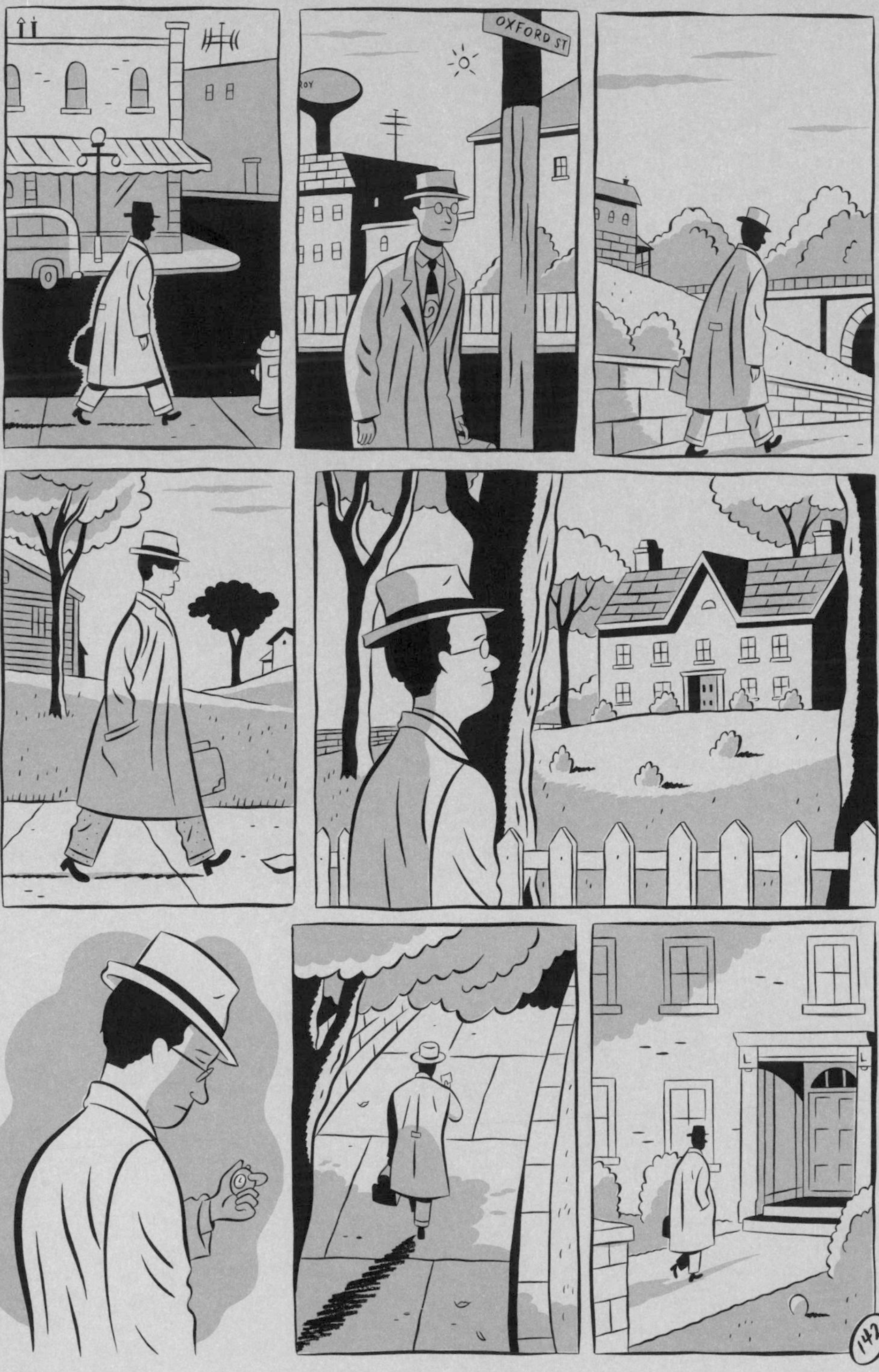
OXFORD ST

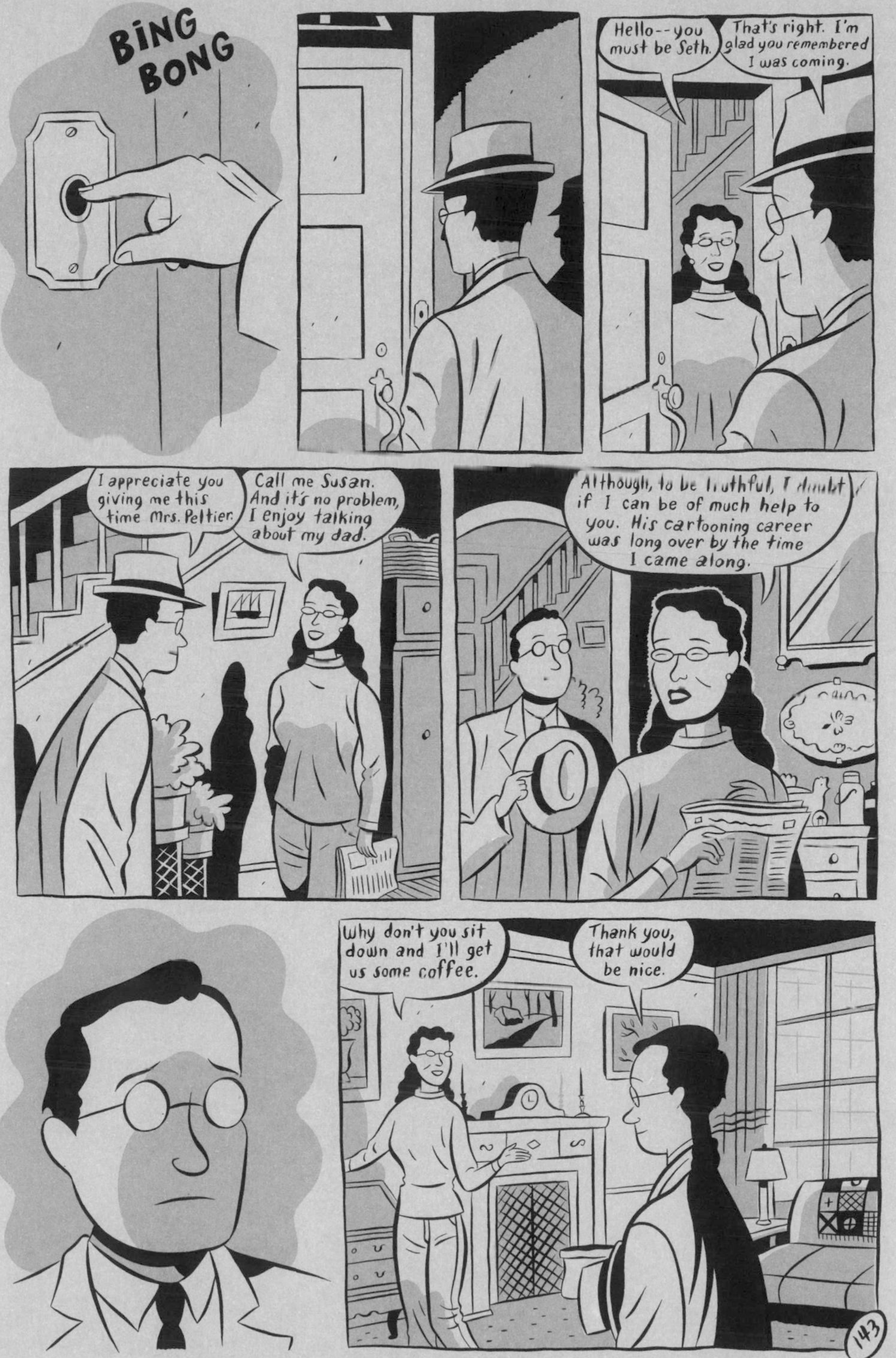
BING BONG
Hello--you must be Seth.
That's right. I'm glad you remembered I was coming.
I appreciate you giving me this time Mrs. Peltier.
Call me Susan. And it's no problem, I enjoy talking about my dad.
Although, to be truthful, I doubt if I can be of much help to you. His cartooning career was long over by the time I came along.
Why don't you sit down and I'll get us some coffee.
Thank you, that would be nice.

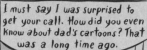

I must say I was surprised to get your call. How did you even know about dad's cartoons? That was a long time ago.

Oh, I do a lot of digging around in old books and magazines. I'm pretty interested in old cartooning.

KALLOWAY

I see you've discovered dad's painting.

It's the only piece of his artwork that I have. Pretty isn't it?

Um, yeah.

154

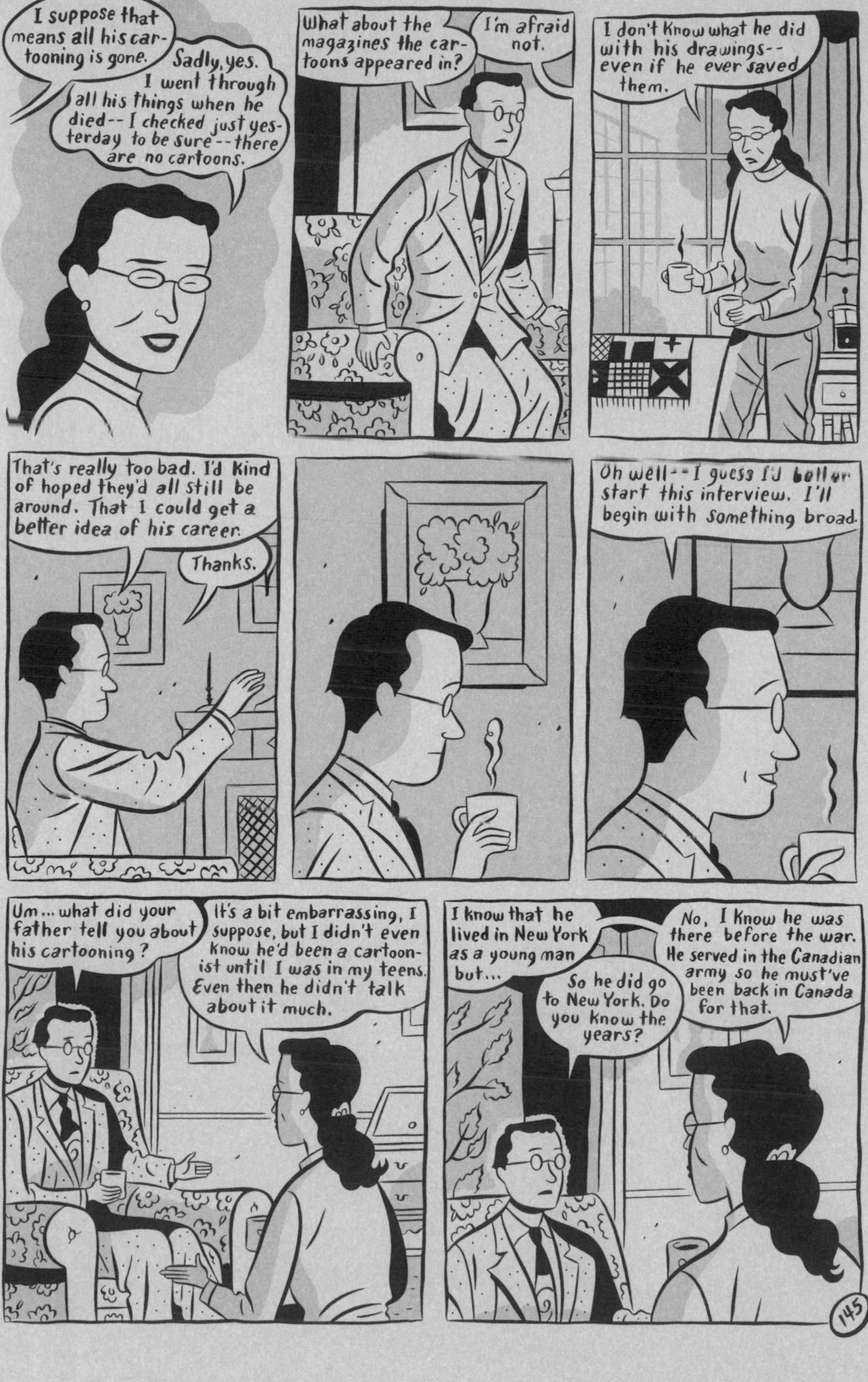
I suppose that means all his cartooning is gone.
Sadly, yes. I went through all his things when he died-- I checked just yesterday to be sure--there are no cartoons.
What about the magazines the cartoons appeared in?
I'm afraid not.
I don't know what he did with his drawings--even if he ever saved them.
That's really too bad. I'd kind of hoped they'd all still be around. That I could get a better idea of his career.
Thanks.
Oh well--I guess I'd better start this interview. I'll begin with something broad.
Um... what did your father tell you about his cartooning?
It's a bit embarrassing, I suppose, but I didn't even know he'd been a cartoonist until I was in my teens. Even then he didn't talk about it much.
I know that he lived in New York as a young man but...
No, I know he was there before the war. He served in the Canadian army so he must've been back in Canada for that.
So he did go to New York. Do you know the years?

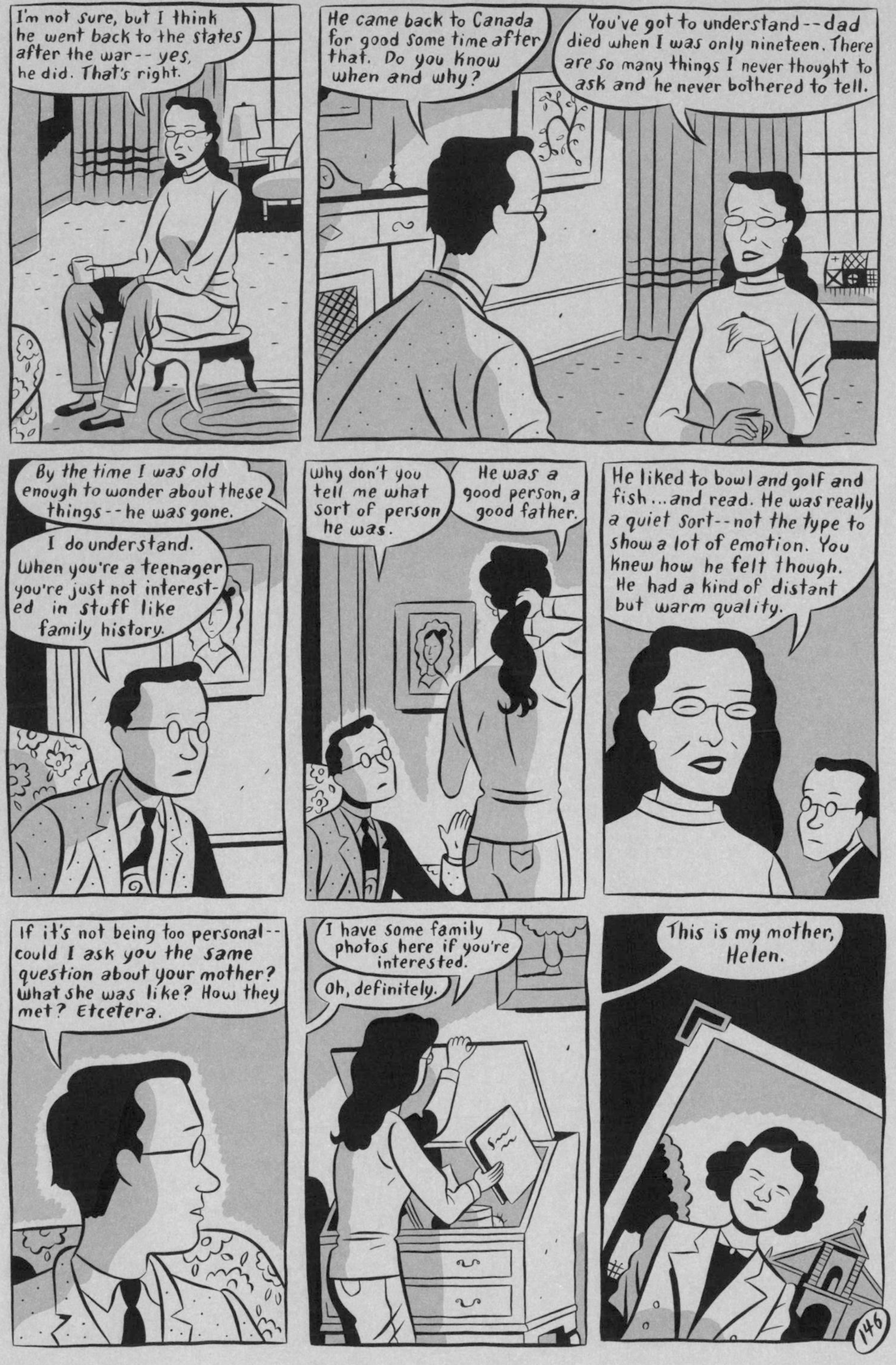
I'm not sure, but I think he went back to the states after the war-- yes, he did. That's right.
He came back to Canada for good some time after that. Do you know when and why?
You've got to understand--dad died when I was only nineteen. There are so many things I never thought to ask and he never bothered to tell.
By the time I was old enough to wonder about these things--he was gone.
I do understand. When you're a teenager you're just not interested in stuff like family history.
Why don't you tell me what sort of person he was.
He was a good person, a good father.
He liked to bowl and golf and fish...and read. He was really a quiet sort--not the type to show a lot of emotion. You knew how he felt though. He had a kind of distant but warm quality.
If it's not being too personal--could I ask you the same question about your mother? What she was like? How they met? Etcetera.
I have some family photos here if you're interested.
Oh, definitely.
This is my mother, Helen.

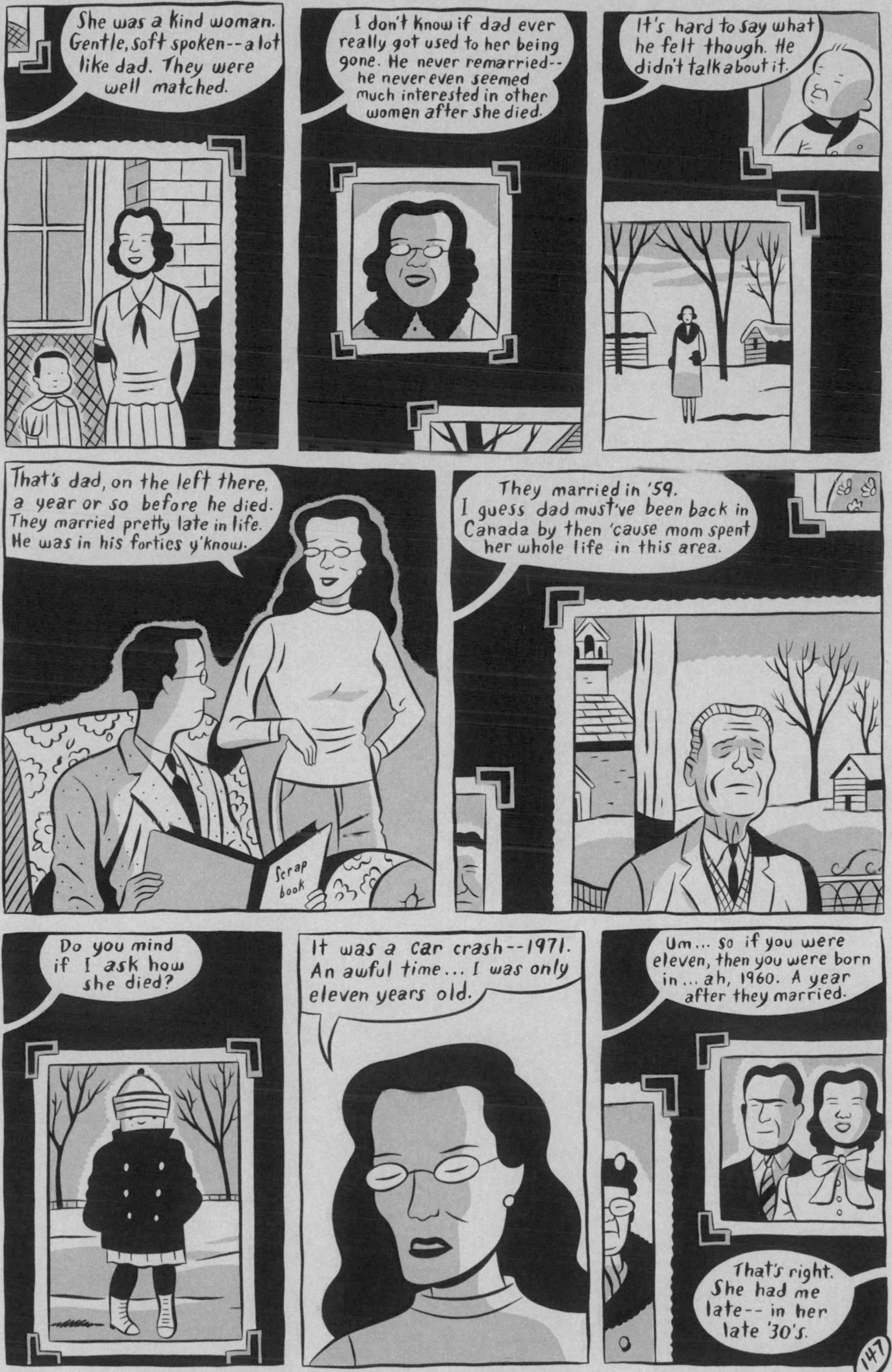
She was a kind woman. Gentle, soft spoken--a lot like dad. They were well matched.
I don't know if dad ever really got used to her being gone. He never remarried--he never even seemed much interested in other women after she died.
It's hard to say what he felt though. He didn't talk about it.
That's dad, on the left there, a year or so before he died. They married pretty late in life. He was in his forties y'know.
Scrap book
They married in '59. I guess dad must've been back in Canada by then 'cause mom spent her whole life in this area.
Do you mind if I ask how she died?
It was a car crash--1971. An awful time... I was only eleven years old.
Um... so if you were eleven, then you were born in... ah, 1960. A year after they married.
That's right. She had me late-- in her late '30's.

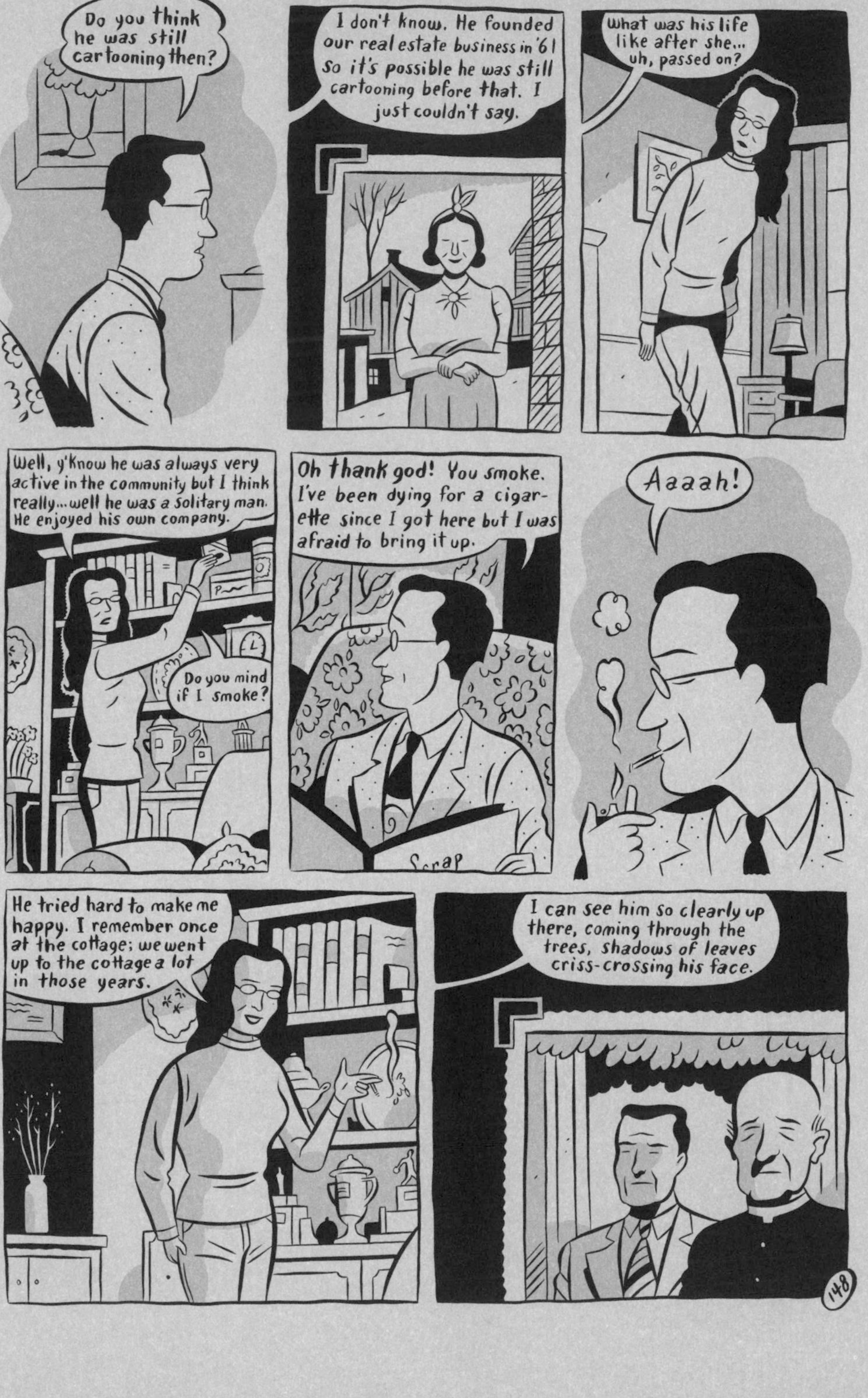
Do you think he was still cartooning then?
I don't know. He founded our real estate business in '61 so it's possible he was still cartooning before that. I just couldn't say.
What was his life like after she... uh, passed on?
Well, y'know he was always very active in the community but I think really...well he was a solitary man. He enjoyed his own company.
Do you mind if I smoke?
Oh thank god! You smoke. I've been dying for a cigarette since I got here but I was afraid to bring it up.
Scrap
Aaaah!
He tried hard to make me happy. I remember once at the cottage; we went up to the cottage a lot in those years.
I can see him so clearly up there, coming through the trees, shadows of leaves criss-crossing his face.

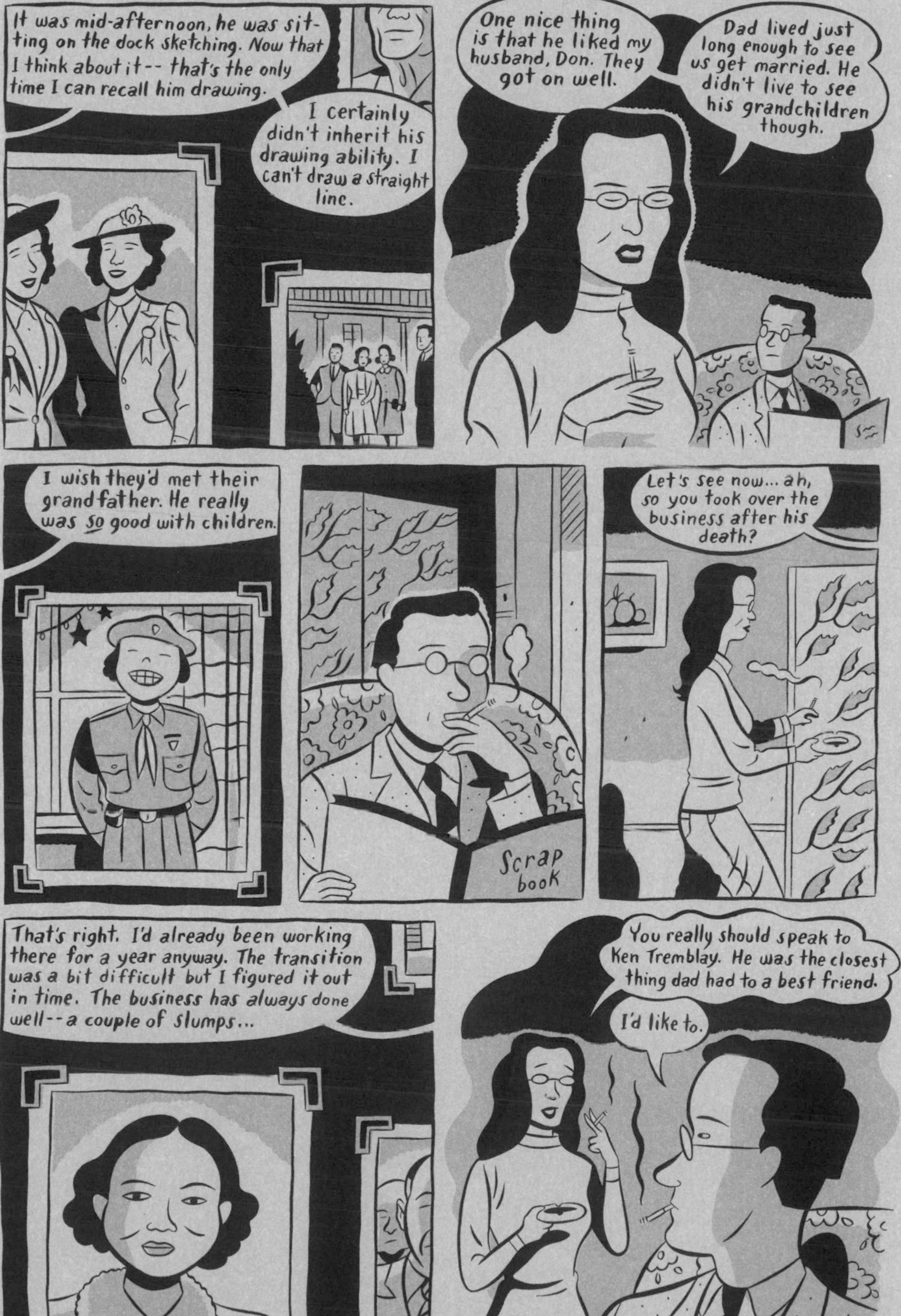
It was mid-afternoon, he was sitting on the dock sketching. Now that I think about it-- that's the only time I can recall him drawing.
I certainly didn't inherit his drawing ability. I can't draw a straight line.
One nice thing is that he liked my husband, Don. They got on well.
Dad lived just long enough to see us get married. He didn't live to see his grandchildren though.
I wish they'd met their grandfather. He really was so good with children.
Scrap book
Let's see now... ah, so you took over the business after his death?
That's right. I'd already been working there for a year anyway. The transition was a bit difficult but I figured it out in time. The business has always done well--a couple of slumps...
You really should speak to Ken Tremblay. He was the closest thing dad had to a best friend.
I'd like to.
149

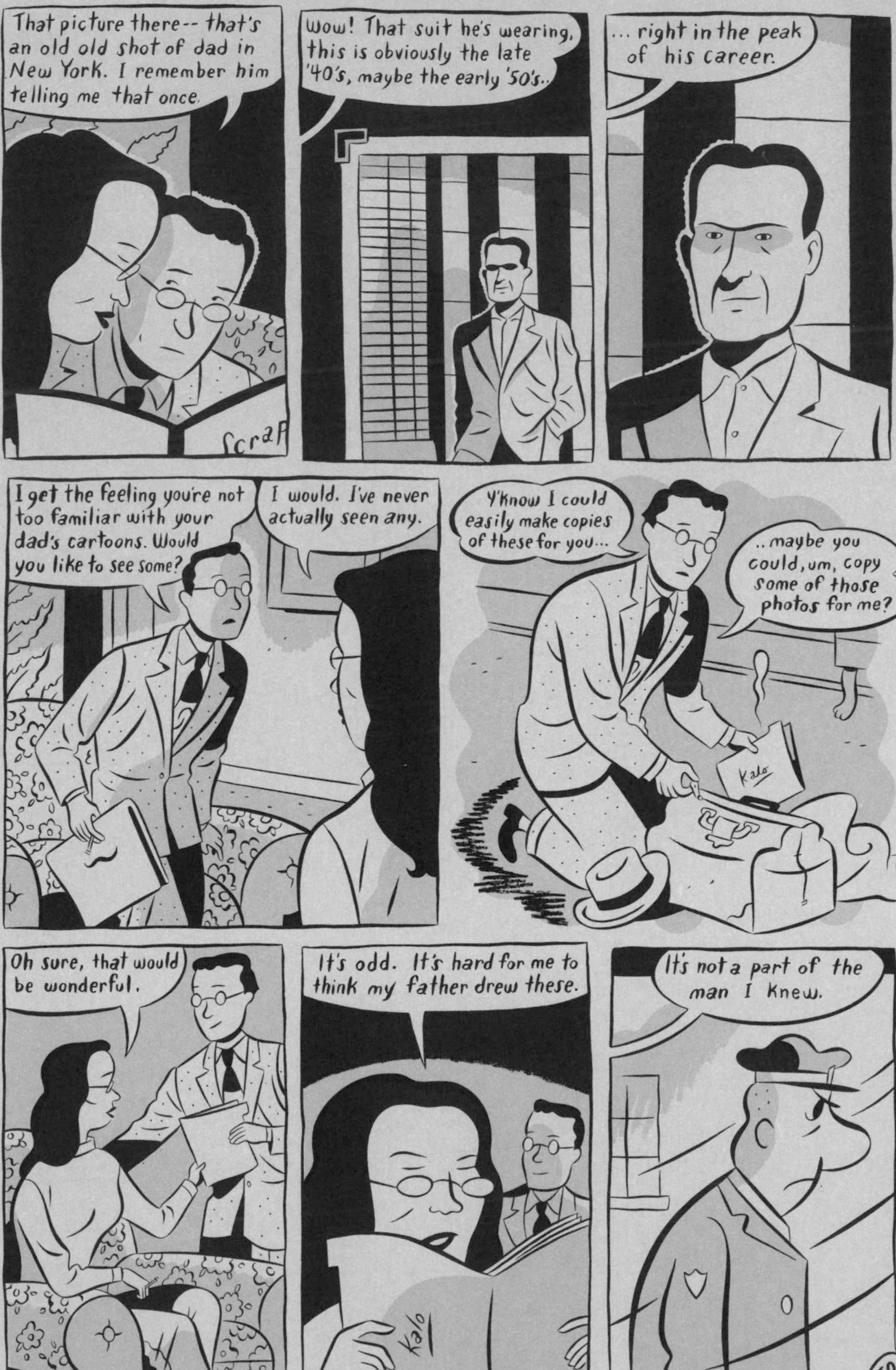
That picture there-- that's an old old shot of dad in New York. I remember him telling me that once.
Scrap
Wow! That suit he's wearing, this is obviously the late '40's, maybe the early '50's..
... right in the peak of his career.
I get the feeling you're not too familiar with your dad's cartoons. Would you like to see some?
I would. I've never actually seen any.
Y'know I could easily make copies of these for you...
..maybe you could, um, copy some of those photos for me?
Kalo
Oh sure, that would be wonderful.
It's odd. It's hard for me to think my father drew these.
Kalo
It's not a part of the man I knew.

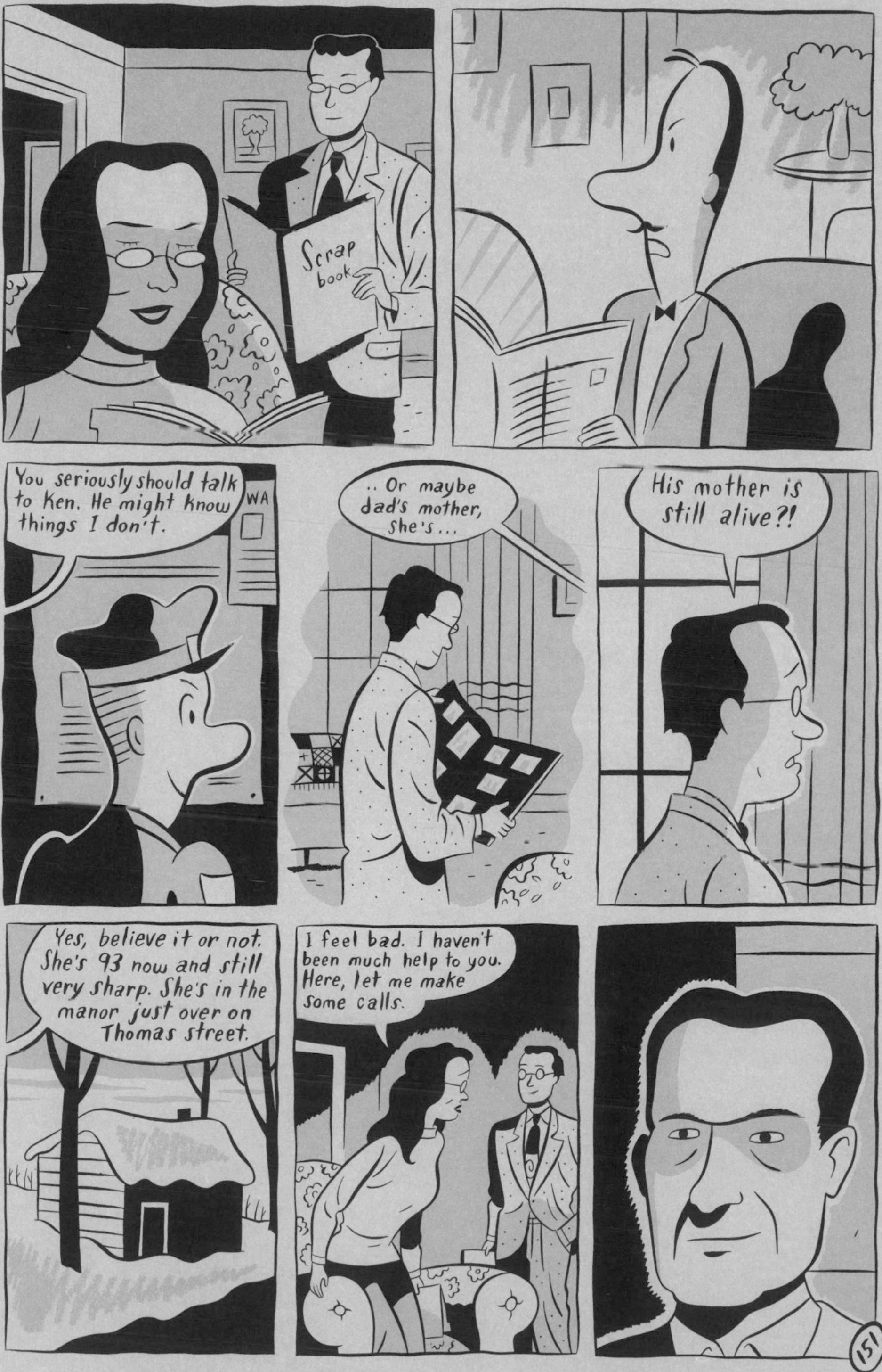
Scrap book
You seriously should talk to Ken. He might know things I don't.
WA
.. Or maybe dad's mother, she's...
His mother is still alive?!
Yes, believe it or not. She's 93 now and still very sharp. She's in the manor just over on Thomas street.
I feel bad. I haven't been much help to you. Here, let me make some calls.

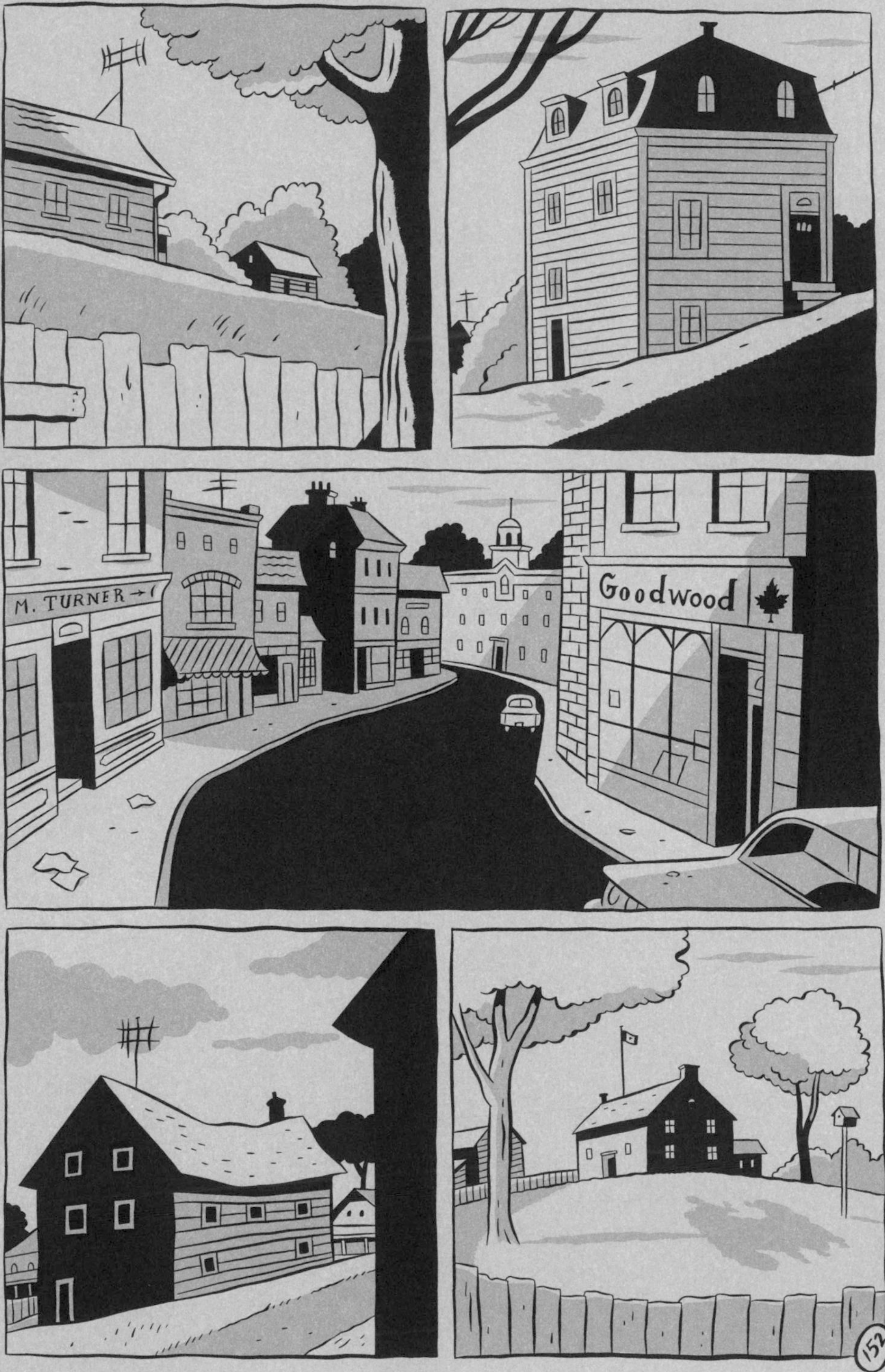
M. TURNER →
Goodwood

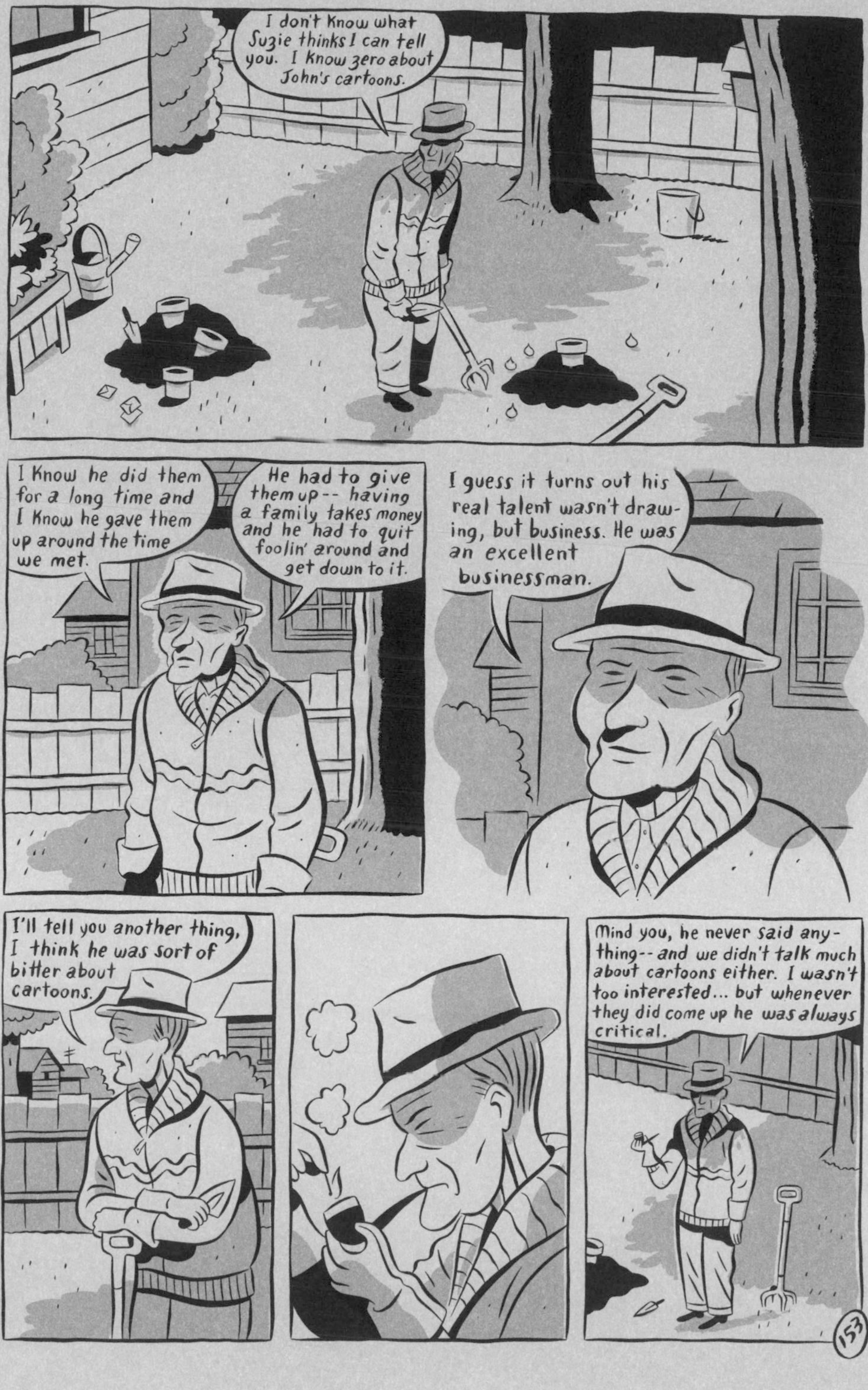
I don't know what Suzie thinks I can tell you. I know zero about John's cartoons.
I know he did them for a long time and I know he gave them up around the time we met.
He had to give them up -- having a family takes money and he had to quit foolin' around and get down to it.
I guess it turns out his real talent wasn't drawing, but business. He was an excellent businessman.
I'll tell you another thing, I think he was sort of bitter about cartoons.
Mind you, he never said anything -- and we didn't talk much about cartoons either. I wasn't too interested... but whenever they did come up he was always critical.

He'd tell me how the drawing was getting worse or how the humour was getting cruder... or something. But it was always negative.

So what did go wrong with his cartooning career?

I don't know, he just wasn't making any money on it. He had to move on.

Do you think that's why he came back to Canada?

Maybe. He was still doing it for awhile after he got back. Things couldn't have been going too well in the States though or he'd have stayed there.

It's a good thing he did come back or he wouldn't have met Helen. That was a piece of luck for him.

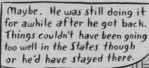

John and I used to spend many a Saturday afternoon talking at the Legion-- well, I did most of the talking. John was a quiet type.

He wasn't the type of quiet that made you awkward. No, he was the type you could talk to for hours. Just babble on and it didn't matter what crap was coming out of your mouth.

You didn't feel he was judging you. And that's saying a lot-- 'cause he was a smart guy and he could've judged someone like me quite a bit.

154

Did he ever mention the "New Yorker?"

Yes. I think so.

Nothing important enough for me to remember though.

Do you think it mattered-- I mean, do you think he suffered about letting go of the cartooning?

Sure it mattered.

When you get to my age you discover that everything mattered.

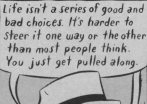

Life isn't a series of good and bad choices. It's harder to steer it one way or the other than most people think. You just get pulled along.

You look back and you wonder "could I have changed the course of my life?" Maybe you could've ... but it would probably have taken a tremendous force of will.

155

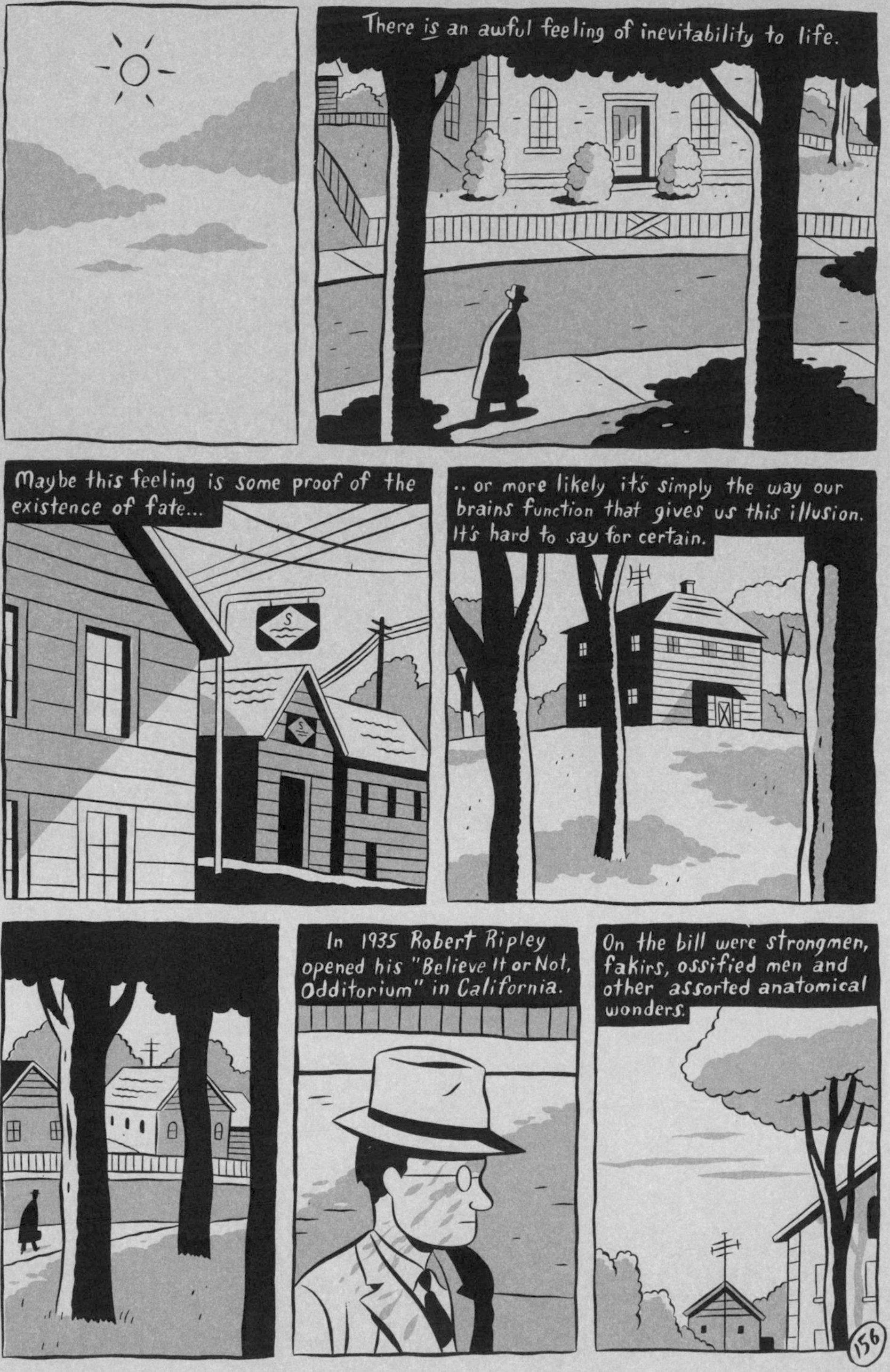
There is an awful feeling of inevitability to life.
Maybe this feeling is some proof of the existence of fate...
.. or more likely it's simply the way our brains function that gives us this illusion. It's hard to say for certain.
In 1935 Robert Ripley opened his "Believe It or Not, Odditorium" in California.
On the bill were strongmen, fakirs, ossified men and other assorted anatomical wonders.
156

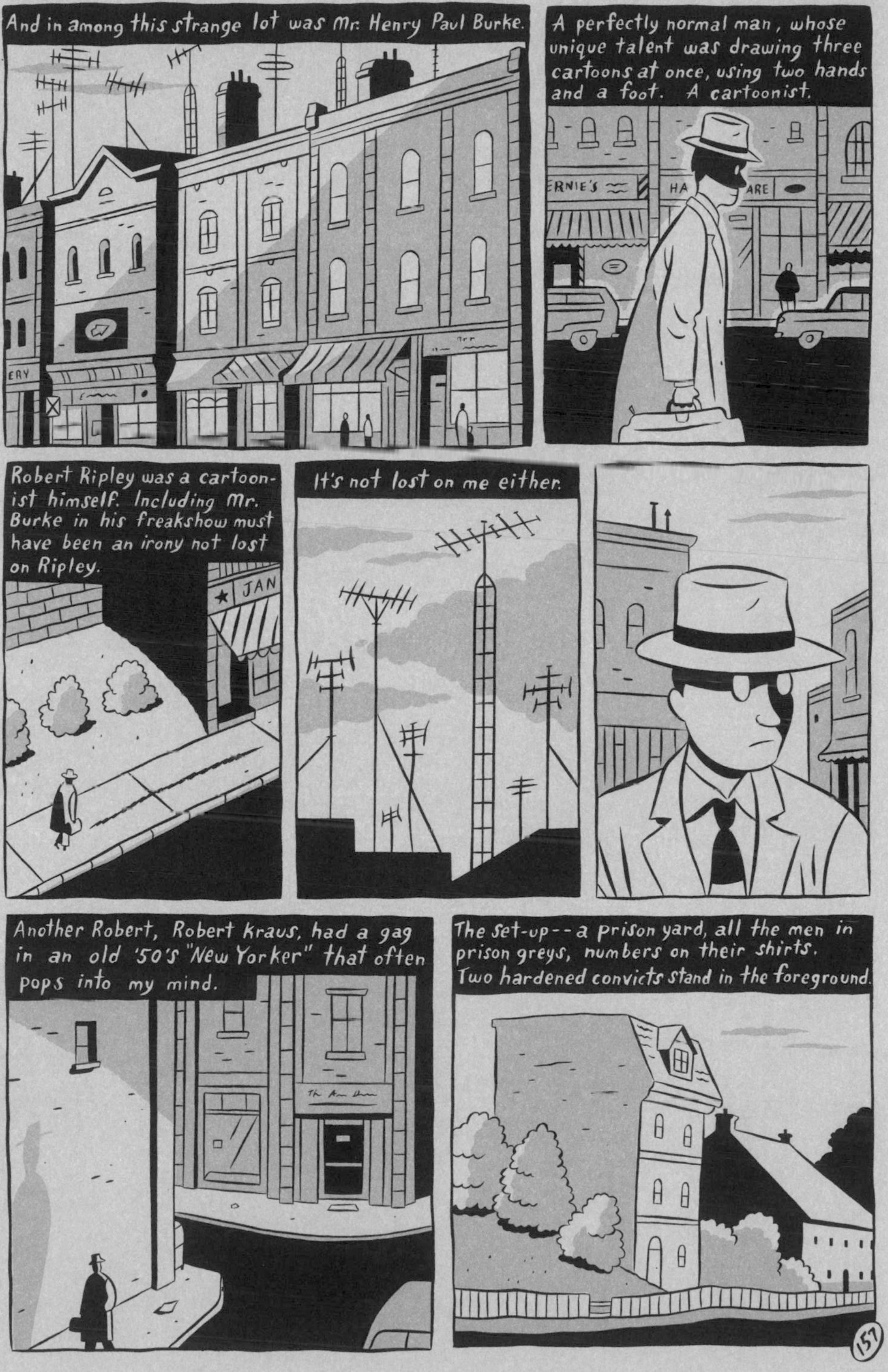

And in among this strange lot was Mr. Henry Paul Burke.
A perfectly normal man, whose unique talent was drawing three cartoons at once, using two hands and a foot. A cartoonist.
ERNIE'S
Robert Ripley was a cartoonist himself. Including Mr. Burke in his freakshow must have been an irony not lost on Ripley.
JAN
It's not lost on me either.
Another Robert, Robert Kraus, had a gag in an old '50's "New Yorker" that often pops into my mind.
The set-up--a prison yard, all the men in prison greys, numbers on their shirts. Two hardened convicts stand in the foreground.

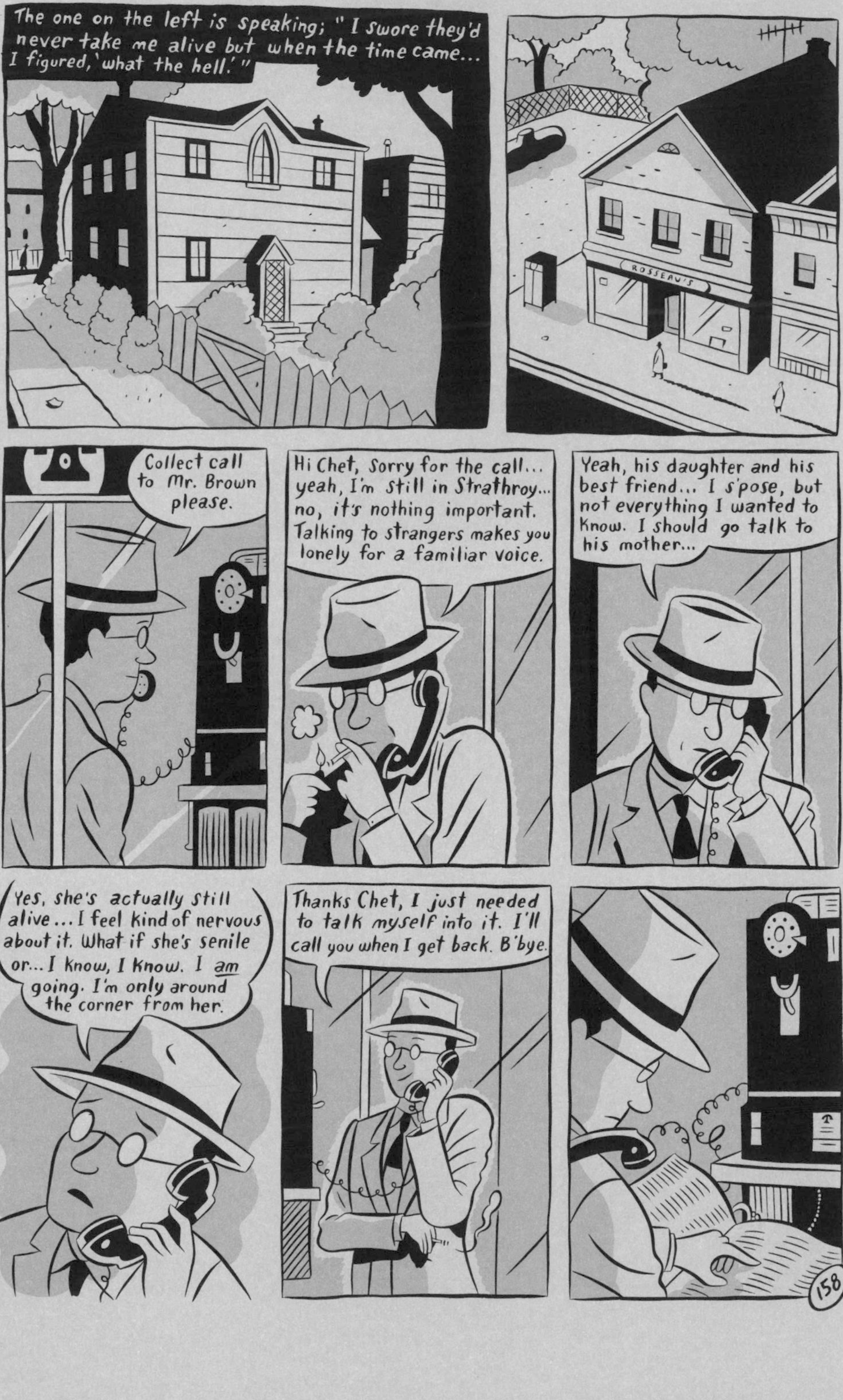

The one on the left is speaking; "I swore they'd never take me alive but when the time came... I figured, 'what the hell.'"
ROSSEAU'S
Collect call to Mr. Brown please.
Hi Chet, sorry for the call... yeah, I'm still in Strathroy... no, it's nothing important. Talking to strangers makes you lonely for a familiar voice.
Yeah, his daughter and his best friend... I s'pose, but not everything I wanted to know. I should go talk to his mother...
Yes, she's actually still alive... I feel kind of nervous about it. What if she's senile or... I know, I know. I am going. I'm only around the corner from her.
Thanks Chet, I just needed to talk myself into it. I'll call you when I get back. B'bye.

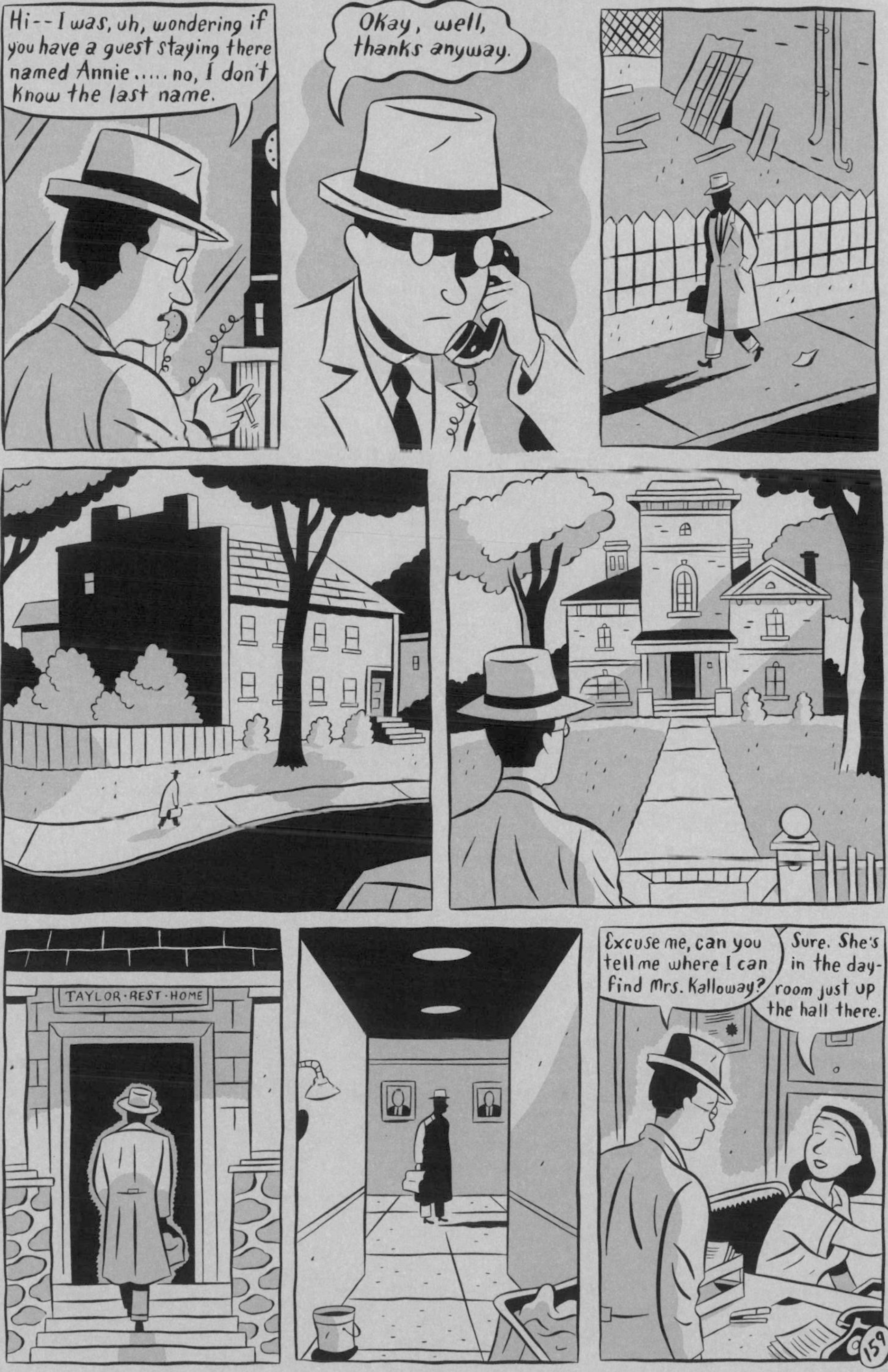
Hi--I was, uh, wondering if you have a guest staying there named Annie..... no, I don't know the last name.
Okay, well, thanks anyway.
TAYLOR·REST·HOME
Excuse me, can you tell me where I can find Mrs. Kalloway?
Sure. She's in the day-room just up the hall there.

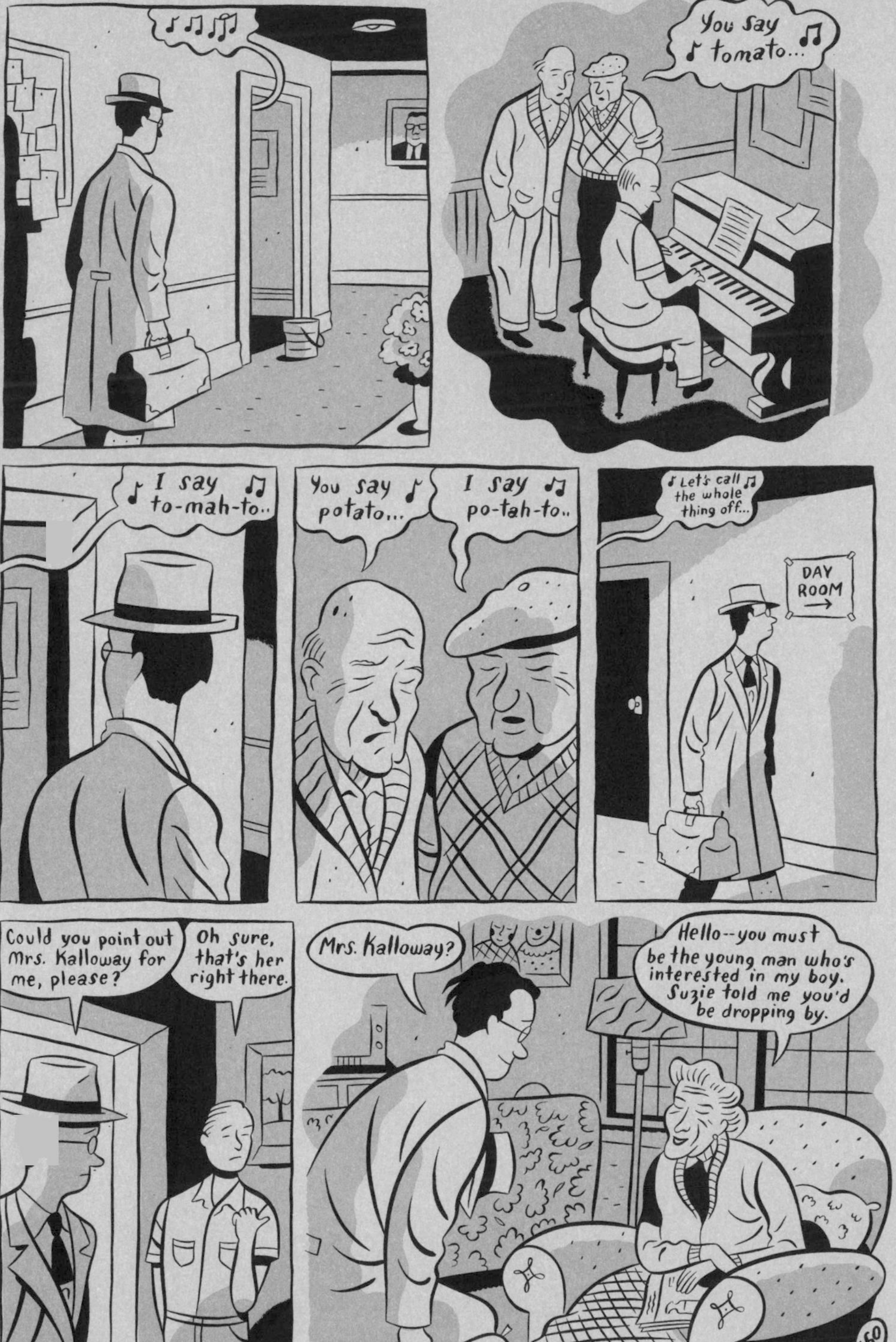

You say tomato...
I say to-mah-to..
You say potato...
I say po-tah-to..
Let's call the whole thing off...
DAY ROOM →
Could you point out Mrs. Kalloway for me, please?
Oh sure, that's her right there.
Mrs. Kalloway?
Hello--you must be the young man who's interested in my boy. Suzie told me you'd be dropping by.

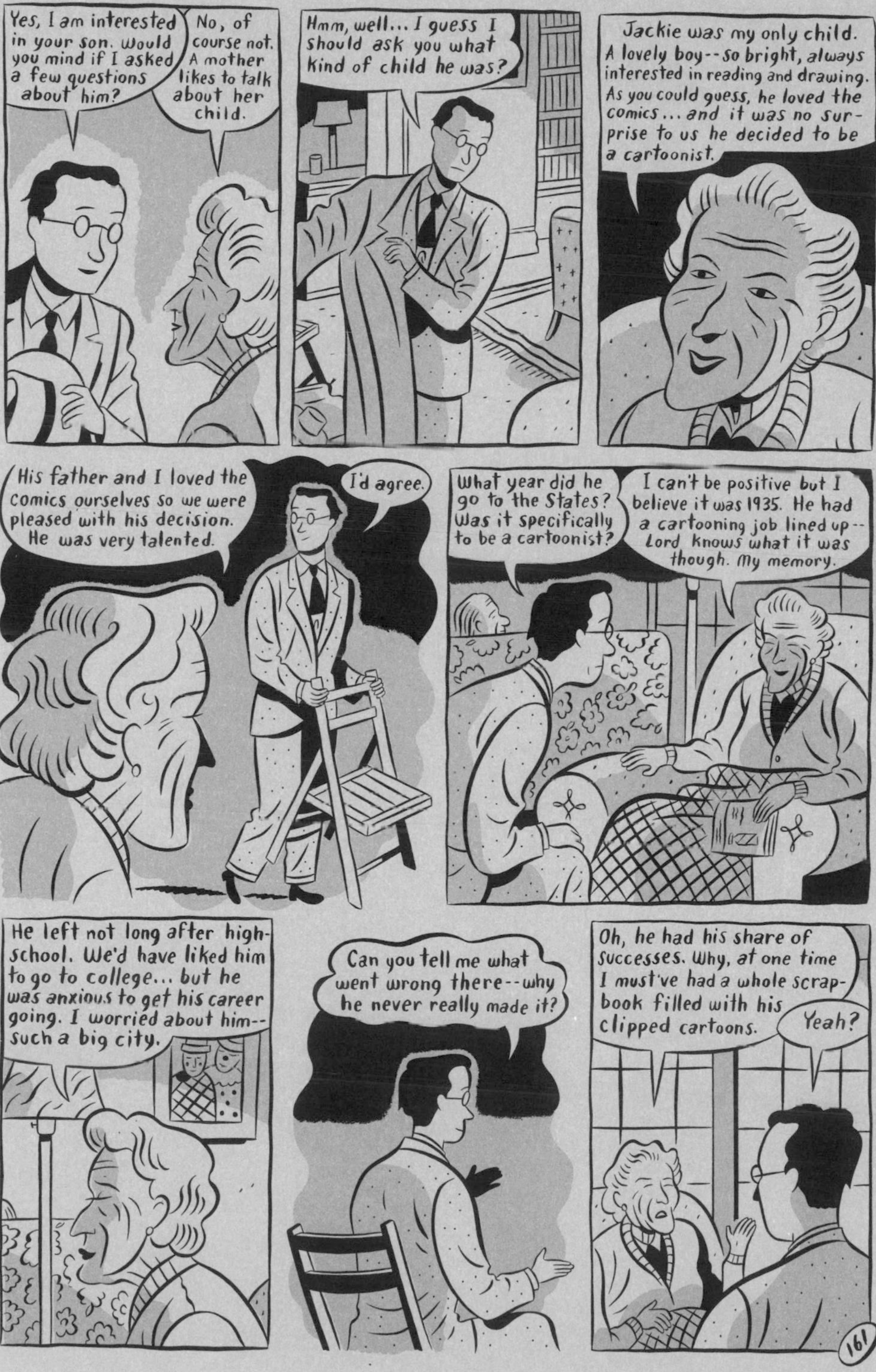
Yes, I am interested in your son. Would you mind if I asked a few questions about him?
No, of course not. A mother likes to talk about her child.
Hmm, well... I guess I should ask you what kind of child he was?
Jackie was my only child. A lovely boy--so bright, always interested in reading and drawing. As you could guess, he loved the comics... and it was no surprise to us he decided to be a cartoonist.
His father and I loved the comics ourselves so we were pleased with his decision. He was very talented.
I'd agree.
What year did he go to the States? Was it specifically to be a cartoonist?
I can't be positive but I believe it was 1935. He had a cartooning job lined up--Lord knows what it was though. My memory.
He left not long after high-school. We'd have liked him to go to college... but he was anxious to get his career going. I worried about him--such a big city.
Can you tell me what went wrong there--why he never really made it?
Oh, he had his share of successes. Why, at one time I must've had a whole scrap-book filled with his clipped cartoons.
Yeah?
161

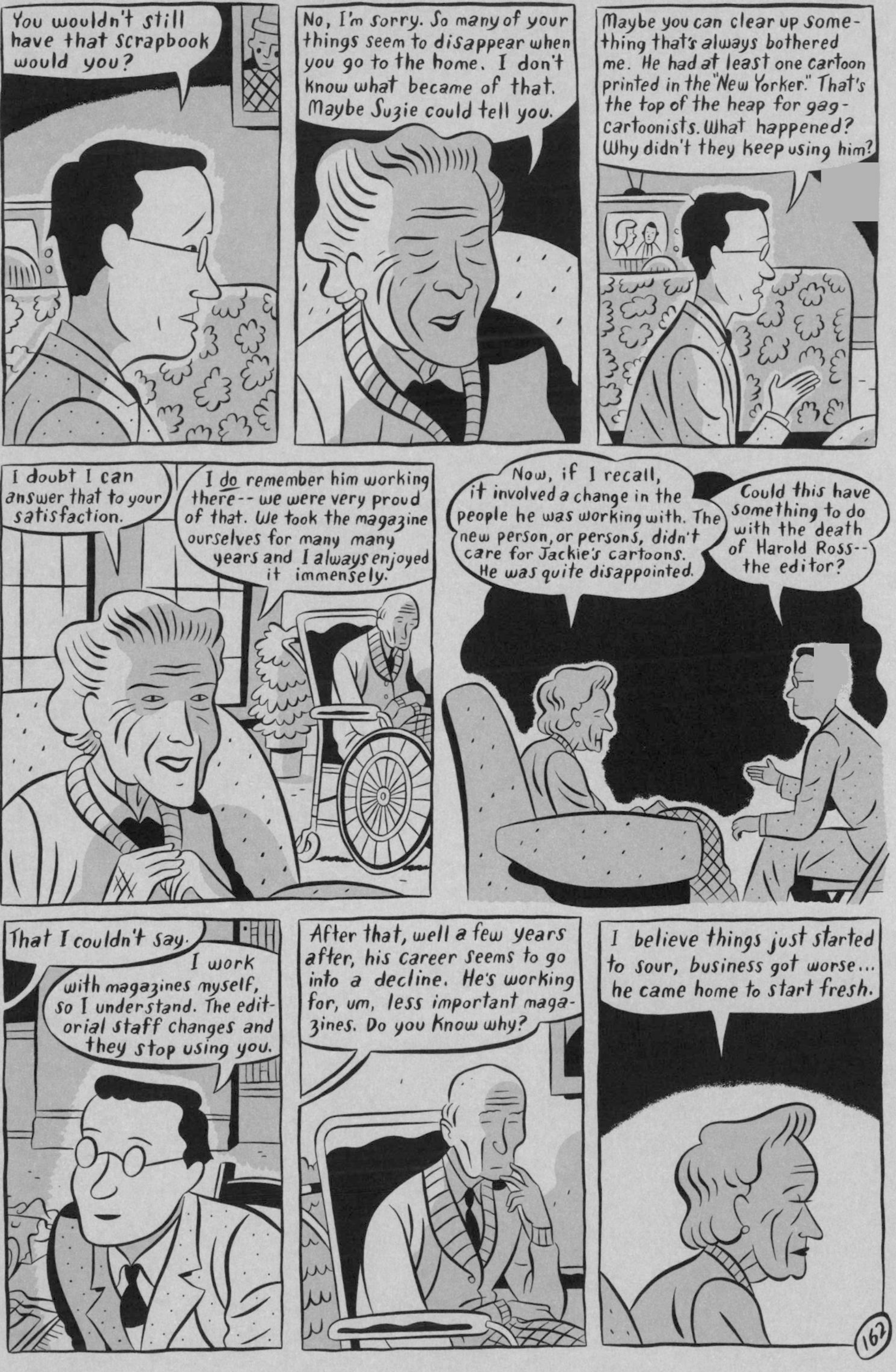
You wouldn't still have that scrapbook would you?
No, I'm sorry. So many of your things seem to disappear when you go to the home. I don't know what became of that. Maybe Suzie could tell you.
Maybe you can clear up something that's always bothered me. He had at least one cartoon printed in the "New Yorker." That's the top of the heap for gag-cartoonists. What happened? Why didn't they keep using him?
I doubt I can answer that to your satisfaction.
I do remember him working there-- we were very proud of that. We took the magazine ourselves for many many years and I always enjoyed it immensely.
Now, if I recall, it involved a change in the people he was working with. The new person, or persons, didn't care for Jackie's cartoons. He was quite disappointed.
Could this have something to do with the death of Harold Ross-- the editor?
That I couldn't say.
I work with magazines myself, so I understand. The editorial staff changes and they stop using you.
After that, well a few years after, his career seems to go into a decline. He's working for, um, less important magazines. Do you know why?
I believe things just started to sour, business got worse... he came home to start fresh.

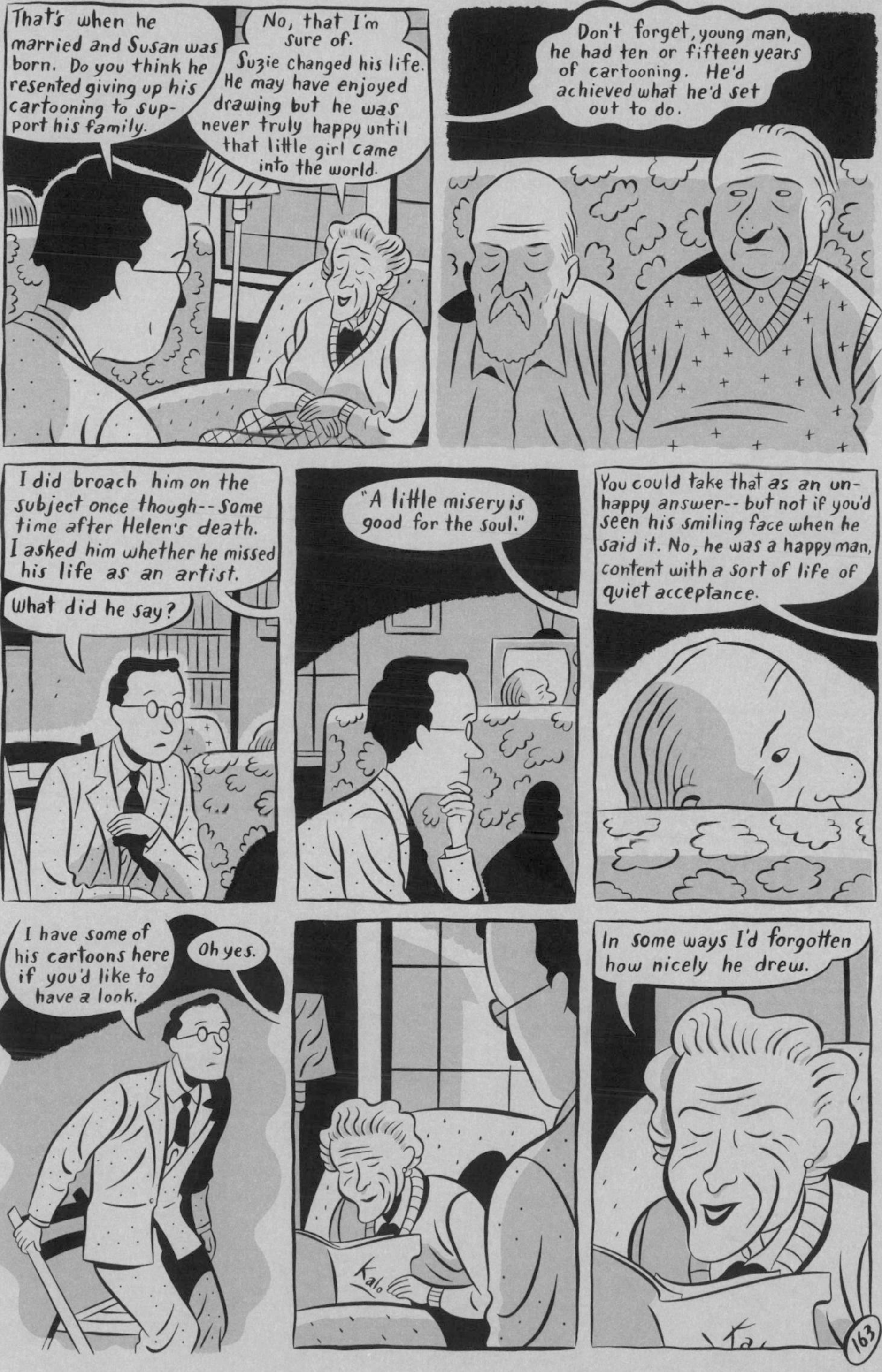
That's when he married and Susan was born. Do you think he resented giving up his cartooning to support his family.
No, that I'm sure of. Suzie changed his life. He may have enjoyed drawing but he was never truly happy until that little girl came into the world.
Don't forget, young man, he had ten or fifteen years of cartooning. He'd achieved what he'd set out to do.
I did broach him on the subject once though-- some time after Helen's death. I asked him whether he missed his life as an artist.
What did he say?
"A little misery is good for the soul."
You could take that as an unhappy answer-- but not if you'd seen his smiling face when he said it. No, he was a happy man, content with a sort of life of quiet acceptance.
I have some of his cartoons here if you'd like to have a look.
Oh yes.
Kalo
In some ways I'd forgotten how nicely he drew.
Ka

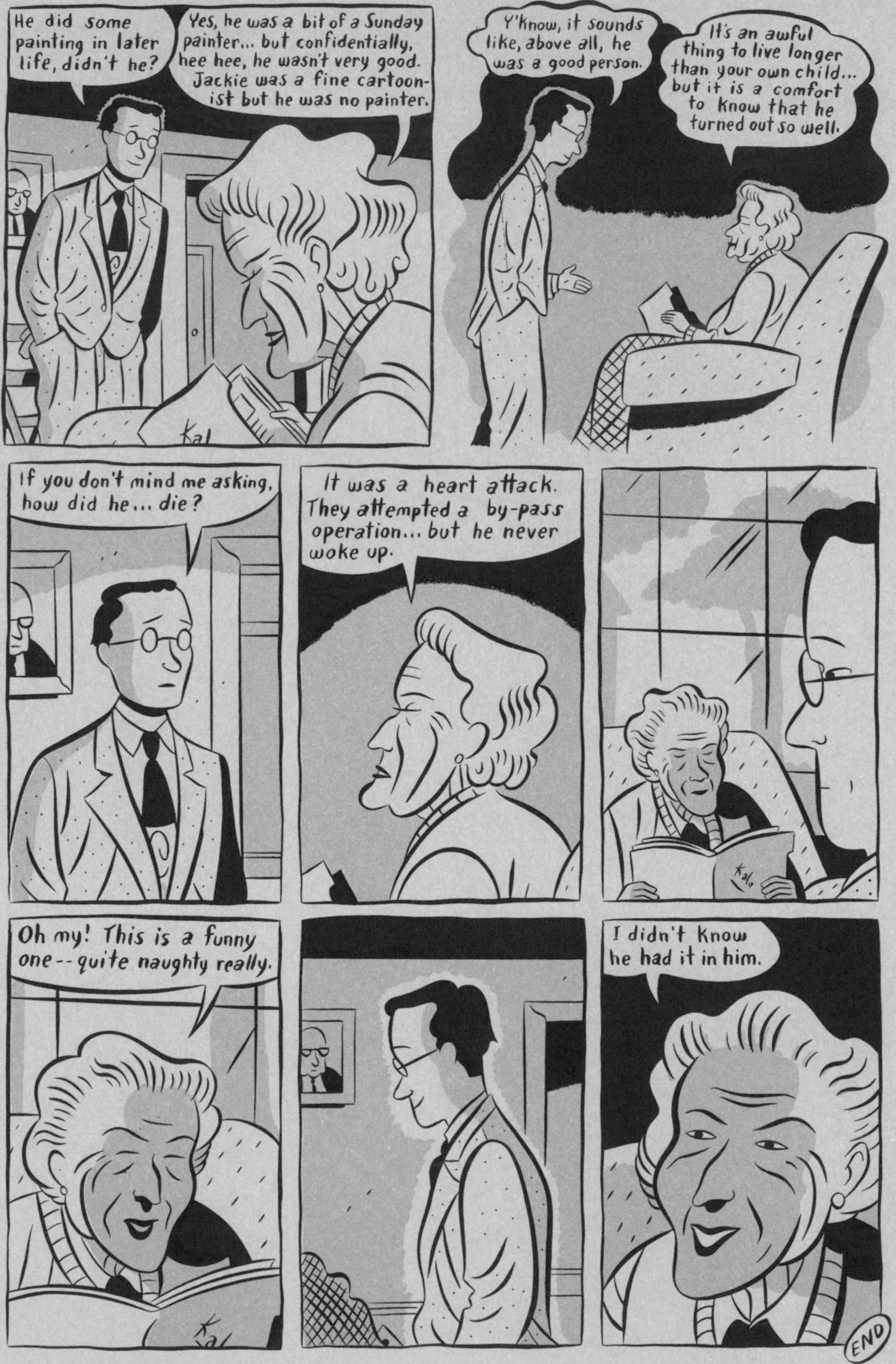
He did some painting in later life, didn't he?
Yes, he was a bit of a Sunday painter... but confidentially, hee hee, he wasn't very good. Jackie was a fine cartoonist but he was no painter.
Kal
Y'know, it sounds like, above all, he was a good person.
It's an awful thing to live longer than your own child... but it is a comfort to know that he turned out so well.
If you don't mind me asking, how did he... die?
It was a heart attack. They attempted a by-pass operation... but he never woke up.
Kal
Oh my! This is a funny one--quite naughty really.
Kal
I didn't know he had it in him.
END

For over a decade now I've been actively looking for "Kalo" cartoons. Sadly, my successes have been few and far between. In fact, I haven't come across a new one in several years. On the following pages you will find my meagre collection-- less than a dozen.

The Famous ELEVEN

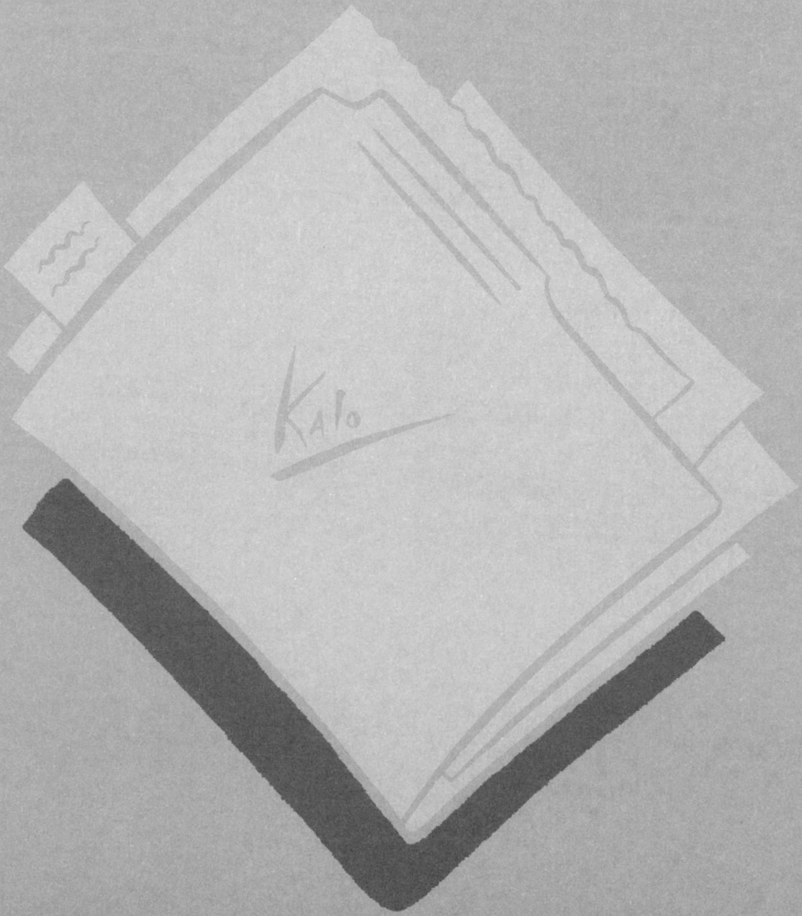
Kato

KALO

Called "The Lady Edison"

[*Continued from page* 147]

One of her inventions for women was the snap-on parasol. Through this novel idea milady may have an umbrella to match any frock. The frame or handle of this umbrella is not limited to one cover but you may have any number and in new colors as fashion dictates. One can take off the cover to dry, and the cover and frame both benefit. If the cover becomes soiled it may be snapped off and dipped in gasoline. It is indeed a versatile umbrella, simple, clever, and practical —a "snap" and off comes the cover; a "snap" and on goes a new one.

The radio and even toys and dolls have not escaped Miss Henry's quest. Her patented method of making toy animals and dolls with inflatable rubber inner tubes replacing the old interior stuffings, has revolutionized this particular business. The idea lends a life-like reality to the toys and greatly reduces their weight. Large dolls, formerly weighing as much as five pounds, are greatly reduced in weight under her method of manufacture. The dolls or animals may be inflated or deflated at will by means of a bulb concealed in the dolls or animals.

It has been stated that Miss Henry is "psychic" because inventions appear to her suddenly, complete in almost every detail. Instead of working out her inventions step by step, as most inventors do, they seem to appear to Miss Henry right out of the air, as a completed vision. She then directs workmen in making the product, often designing machinery to accomplish this task. After inventing the rubber sponge which holds a cake of soap, she invented a machine which would cut the opening in ten thousand sponges a day. Lest one suppose that all Miss Henry's inventions are but the result of happy thoughts, however, it may be stated that the model for the Protograph, including time and money expended in its perfection

 Accept No Substitutes! Always Insist on the Advertised Brand!

Earliest discovered Kalo
MODERN MECHANIX, May, 1937.
(Note the atypical signature.)

you all drunk, all sing... about words. Jus' sing an' laugh. Yvonne an' Henri weel teach you on zee way. Here."

She handed him a small piece of paper. "Eef you need more help from people in France, show thees paper. Eef Nazis gat you, eat eet! You promise?"

Leo nodded, and they all kissed him again, poured more wine on him, and pushed him into the cart on a floor of hay, with Yvonne. "Some day you weel come back, to a free France," the woman told him. But before he could even say, "Thanks," the cart started moving, and the people disappeared in the woods.

Right from the beginning, Yvonne lay close to him, her arm around his neck. Leo didn't know if it was all right, but he was

...n't been ... be been enjoying himself. They ... stopped, inspected, and passed three times. The third time Yvonne kissed him full on the lips, while the German soldiers watched and laughed at some joke. (If he had been at home, Leo would have taken a poke at both of them.) Then right after that, Leo could smell the ocean. He knew it was close because the hay in the cart was sweet, the smell of wine was heavy, and Yvonne—well, he couldn't decide which was more fragrant, her hair or her lips. At that second, he was sure she was the most beautiful girl he had ever seen. By far.

As the cart began rolling over sand, they both sat up. They were heading along a sandy road behind some dunes. Over the dunes, Leo could see the masts of boats and tops of wooden shacks and he could feel a small pulse beating in Yvonne's hand. Five

sour wine ... and didn't even care when they missed by a prowling Nazi patro... wouldn't have cared if they hit ... fact, he couldn't even show any ... when the Frenchmen stopped ... minesweeper, and motioned for hi... aboard it up a ladder. He just b... the deck, and got even sicker all... the way to England.

All the while the English Inte... cer was questioning him at Dover, ... a daze. He could still feel the wi... ached, he had a running nose, and ... stop burping. All he wanted wa... even a floor to go to sleep on, s... officer got excited after the questi... ordered a plane to take them to ... Headquarters, Leo only felt more ... Too much had happened for one ... one day. He wished he were hom...

"Of all the men who were shot ... that airfield," the Englishman s... him along, "you're the first to get ... you know what that means!" Leo ... didn't care. He was dying to sle...

A sergeant gave him some h... two doughnuts at Supreme Hea... fore he was questioned. But ... couldn't make up for the waiti... rough flight, and Leo could hard... eyes open. He barely got his ar... salute to the general and colon... been called in to hear his story.

WHAT he told them got ... excited than it had t... They looked at the clothes h... smelled for the wine, and insp... hundred times the small piec... Frenchwoman had given him. ... —for hours—Leo was trying ... tention, and not to burp.

"It's incredible," the general ... "The underground must have ju... that area. Incredible!" He looke... the other brass hats. "Washin... hear this immediately."

Leo just shuddered.

Six hours and a thousand q... after they had given him ... (without his Tech Sergeant ... wear, and strict orders not ... a soul before he got to W... found himself in a refitted fi... back to the States. They cr... in less than nine hours, bu... so he didn't get any sle... wouldn't stop running.

At the field in Washingt... the pilot were waiting for ... bled a postcard to his foll... hadn't said a word about ... not to talk.) "Am back in... wrote. "Can't say more. ... mailed it just before they w... Intelligence Headquarters. .

Back in Pennsylvania, th...

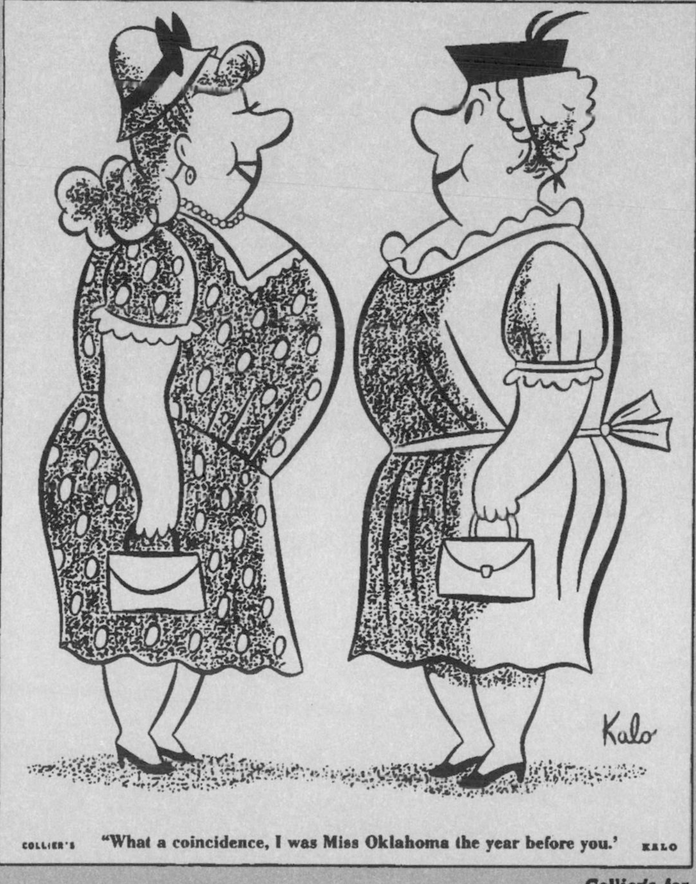
Kalo

COLLIER'S "What a coincidence, I was Miss Oklahoma the year before you.' KALO

COLLIER'S, May 1947

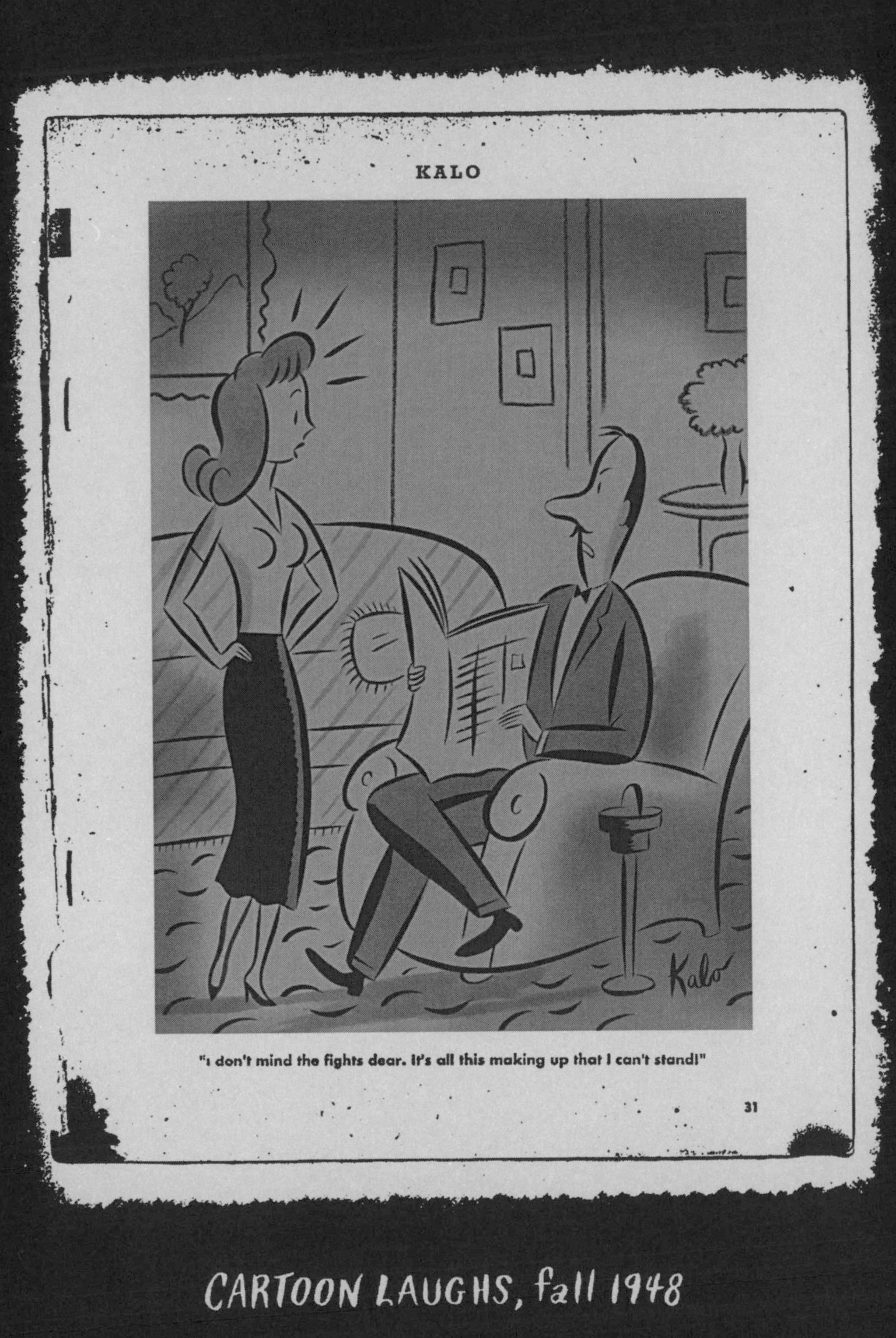
Kalo

"I don't mind the fights dear. It's all this making up that I can't stand!"

CARTOON LAUGHS, fall 1948

KALO

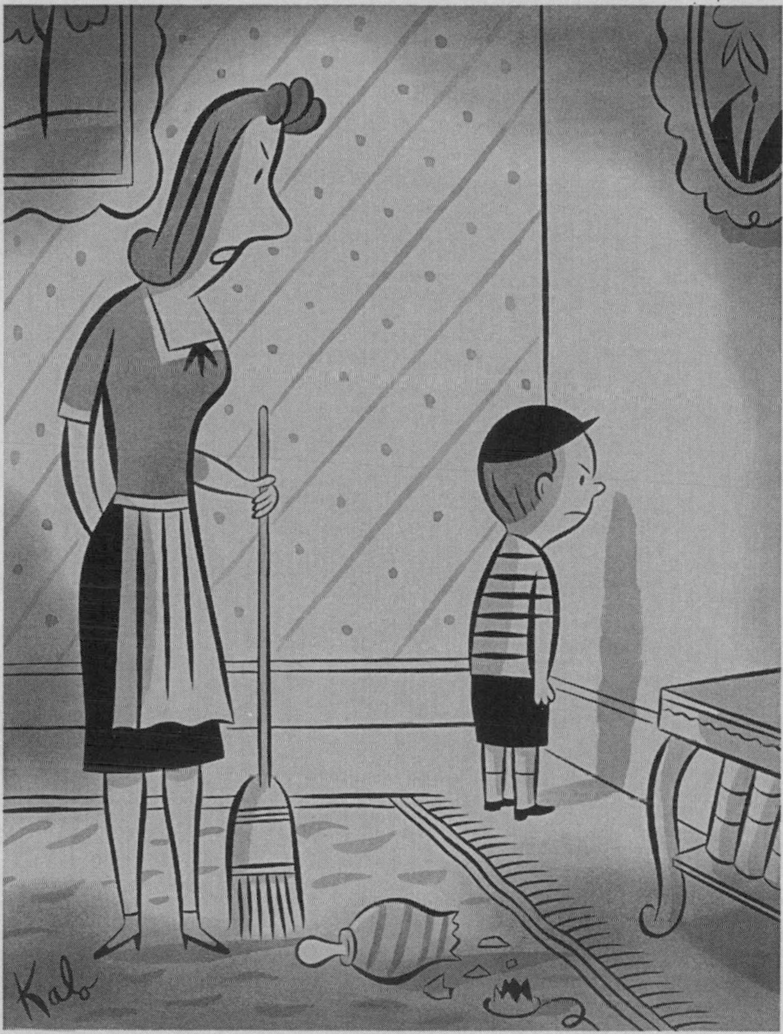
Kalo

"I am not drunk with power!"

CARTOON LAUGHS, fall 1948

KALO

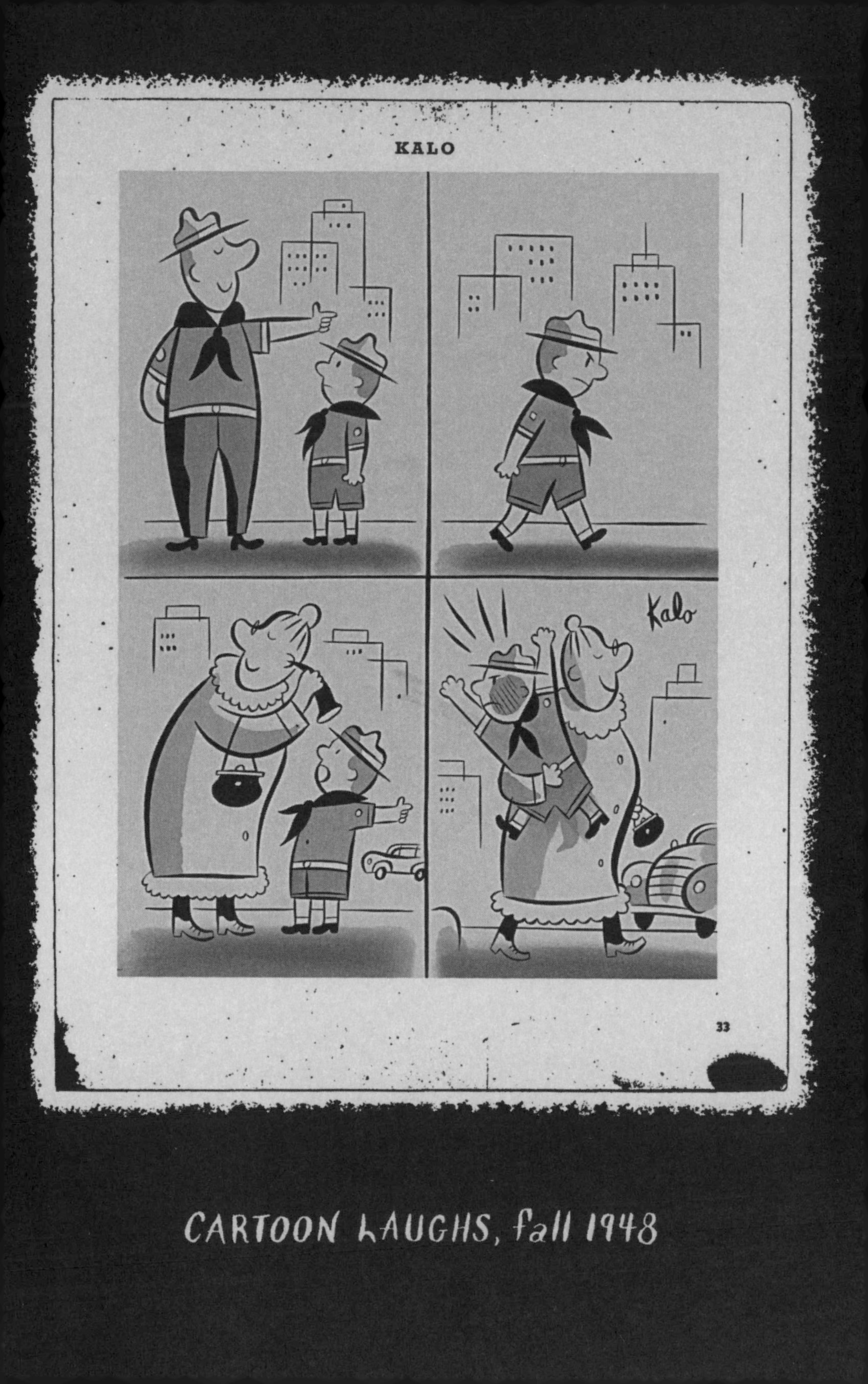
Kalo

33

CARTOON LAUGHS, fall 1948

see why you're so damn sure

it is inevitable. They would
ken her otherwise. They will
before you go elsewhere. I
y taken steps to have the call
I fear it will not help. They
clever. Excuse. They know
ove with her, Mr. Rhyce."
ırds came out brutally in the
oom, and Jack felt his face
-red, but he knew he had no
angry.
mistake," he said. "We both
were damn fools—not that it
ood."
I am not criticizing," Mr.

it is necessary," Jack Rhyce
ust as soon not bring this sub-
ain."
oto's manner was considerate
answered. "I do not wish to
only speak because I think you
ready. I think they will be
o make you an interesting pro-
. Rhyce."
sort?"
ot know. So much of our work
in the dark, but I think you
e close to finding something
es them, Mr. Rhyce."
rue about working in the dark,
Moto's words had aroused a
in Jack Rhyce that gripped him
fingers. "Do you think they're
propose a swap?" he asked.

Mr. Moto answered, his voice
nd measured. "Yes, Mr. Rhyce,"
I believe they will offer to bring
art safely back if you will agree
here. You see, I think they are
u know too much."
hyce felt a spasm in the pit of his
and his heart was beating faster,
he could notice that Mr. Moto
hing him very carefully.
will have to make a decision as
her to leave or whether to stay,"
"and I am so very much afraid I
elp you, Mr. Rhyce."
urse, he had to make up his mind,
ad the training to do it.
en the telephone rang. Mr. Moto
he earphones over his head.
wer quickly, please," he whis-
Seem to be anxious, please."
Jack picked up the telephone, he
dier. He even felt a spasm of an-

...damness could n...
have been lost on Mr. Pender.

"Thanks for letting me know," he said. "I was beginning to be worried about her."

There was a good-natured laugh on the other end of the wire. "We thought you might be. Well, take it easy, Jack. She's right here, and we wish you were too. And she's happy and comfortable as of now, Jack. I'll let you speak to her in a minute."

"Why, thanks," Jack Rhyce said, "thanks a lot."

remember him exactly. I don't think I ever saw him, but I'm sure I'd recognize him."

"Well, he remembers you, boy. He saw you in Moscow, back in '47. He was a waiter at one of those big parties, and passed you caviar. Just as soon as I described you, he clicked. You were talking to Molotov, back in '47. You were saying all men are brothers."

Jack exchanged a glance with Mr. Moto. The chief had said it was a damn-

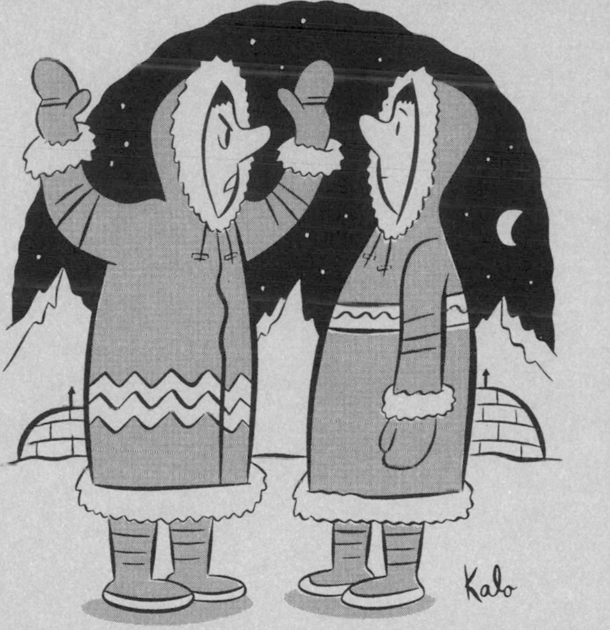

Kalo

"Why didn't you tell me you weren't a girl before we were married?"

THE SATURDAY EVENING POST

THE SATURDAY EVENING POST, Jan. 1951

I'm really worried about. They learn the Communist theories in school, and when they come home, their parents tell them something different. After a while, the poor kids don't know where they're at. They get confused and frightened. Everybody is frightened. Coming home on the streetcar tonight, I was frightened. A man sitting across from me gave me a funny look. I looked back at him, and almost automatically the questions came to my mind."

"What questions?" I asked.

"I suppose everybody has some reason to be afraid," Janda said. "Everybody is hiding something. You become afraid that your doubts and intentions show in your face. I looked at this man and I said to myself, 'Now, where does he belong? He's not wearing a Party badge. You might say, then, that he's not a Communist, but on the other hand he may be such an important Communist that he doesn't *have* to wear a badge. He may be a member of the central committee. Or a member of the secret police. Or perhaps he's a reactionary. Does he know that I am just an opportunist? Why does he keep looking at me? Have I done anything that might get me into trouble—today, yesterday, last week, last year? Could it be because an American friend called me on the phone?' "

"I'm sorry, Karel," I said. "I didn't think—"

"No, no," Janda said. "I'm just trying to explain our nationwide anxiety neurosis. You go to bed with fear in your bones, and when you get up in the morning the fear is still there. The fear is constantly there. During the German Occupation, it wasn't any fun to ride on a streetcar, with all those S.S. men and German soldiers around, but in those days I was never afraid. I would get on a streetcar and sit or stand beside a Czech. I wouldn't talk to him, but just his presence seemed warm and reassuring. I knew I wasn't alone. We Czechs were all together then. Before the war, we'd had fifteen political parties in Parliament and they fought each other tooth and nail. There was always much talk about national unity but nobody did anything about it. Then the Germans occupied the country, and suddenly the nation was truly united. The much-talked-about dream of unity had at last come true. But today?" Janda's tone became bitter. "It's brother against brother. They take you to Pankrác Prison, and when you get there, Czechs—your own people—beat you up. That's what's so hard to take. You walk up to a shopwindow where two women are talking, and as you approach, they become silent and back away. They are afraid of you. They think you're a secret one. You're all alone now, more alone than ever before in your life. And there is no hope that it will be over someday."

Janda turned from the window abruptly. "Remember that evening early in May, 1945, when you were here?" he asked with a warm smile. "You were sitting exactly where you're sitting now. And that girl in the white blouse, with a gun in a holster and the armband of the Republican Guard, was sitting next to you—"

I remembered. The evening he spoke of was the second after the Liberation. There was still sporadic gunfire in the nearby Olšany Cemetery, but the sound of the shots was soon drowned out by joyous shouts from the street. Boys and girls came riding by on trucks, singing Czech songs that had been *verboten* for six years, like the red, white, and blue Czech flag they were carrying. I was an American sergeant at the time, and had entered Prague in a jeep. The Russians were already in the city, but I had no difficulty getting through their lines. Everybody was everybody else's friend. The difficulty was to make my way through the throngs to Janda's apartment. When I finally got there, the living room was a melee of excited, exultant people. Most of them were drunk—as much, I imagine, from joy as from beer and wine. A thin-lipped Czech lieutenant colonel kissed me on both cheeks. Marta's younger sister, Jarmila, was dancing a gypsy dance, and singing and laughing and kissing everybody. Mrs. P., the slovenly janitress, sat on the couch, and Mr. K., the

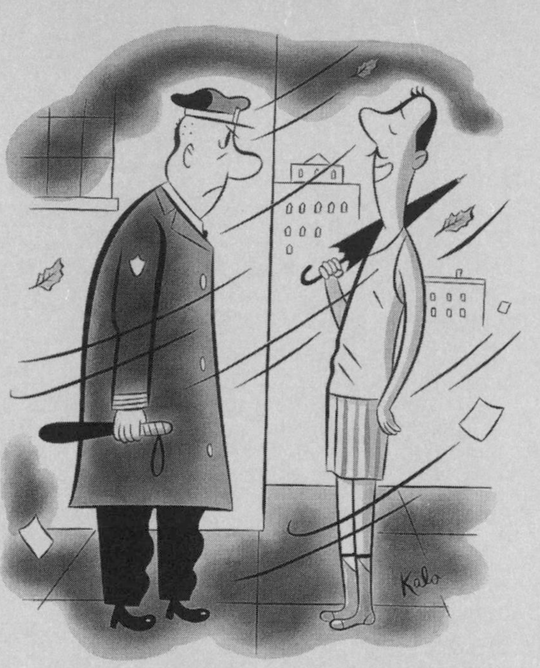
Kalo

"It's actually quite an amusing story, first my hat blew off..."

THE NEW YORKER, Apr. 1951

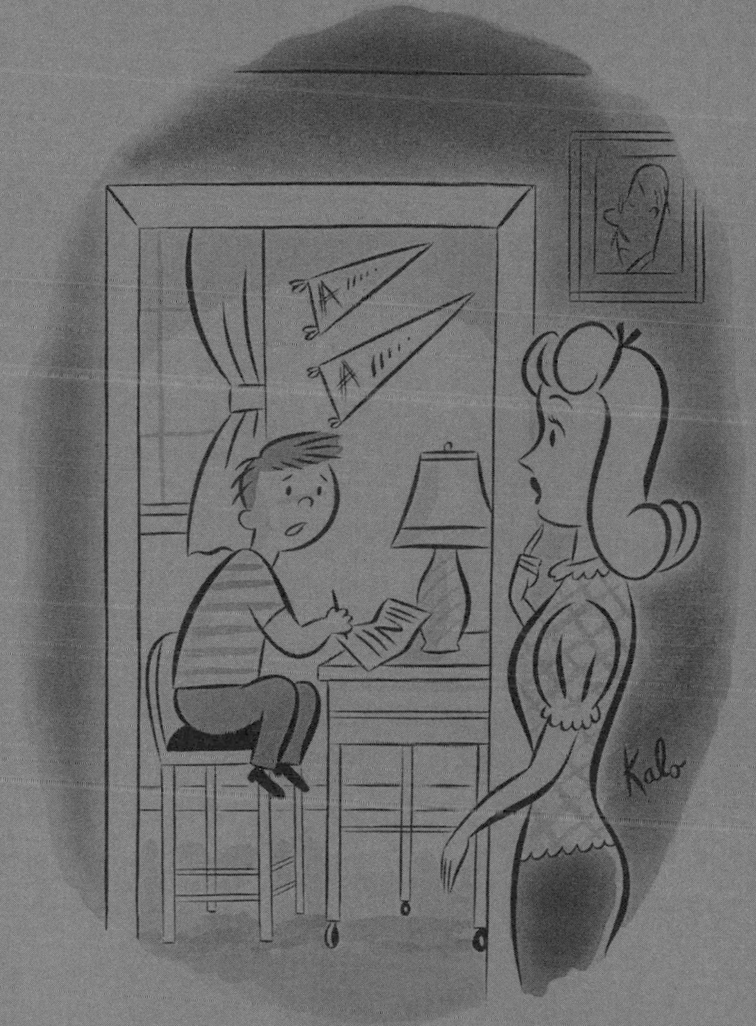
Kalo

"No, I don't want privacy, just leave me alone."

Cartoon Screamers! Gags! Jokes!

GEE-WHIZ! IT'S A RIOT — EYE IT!

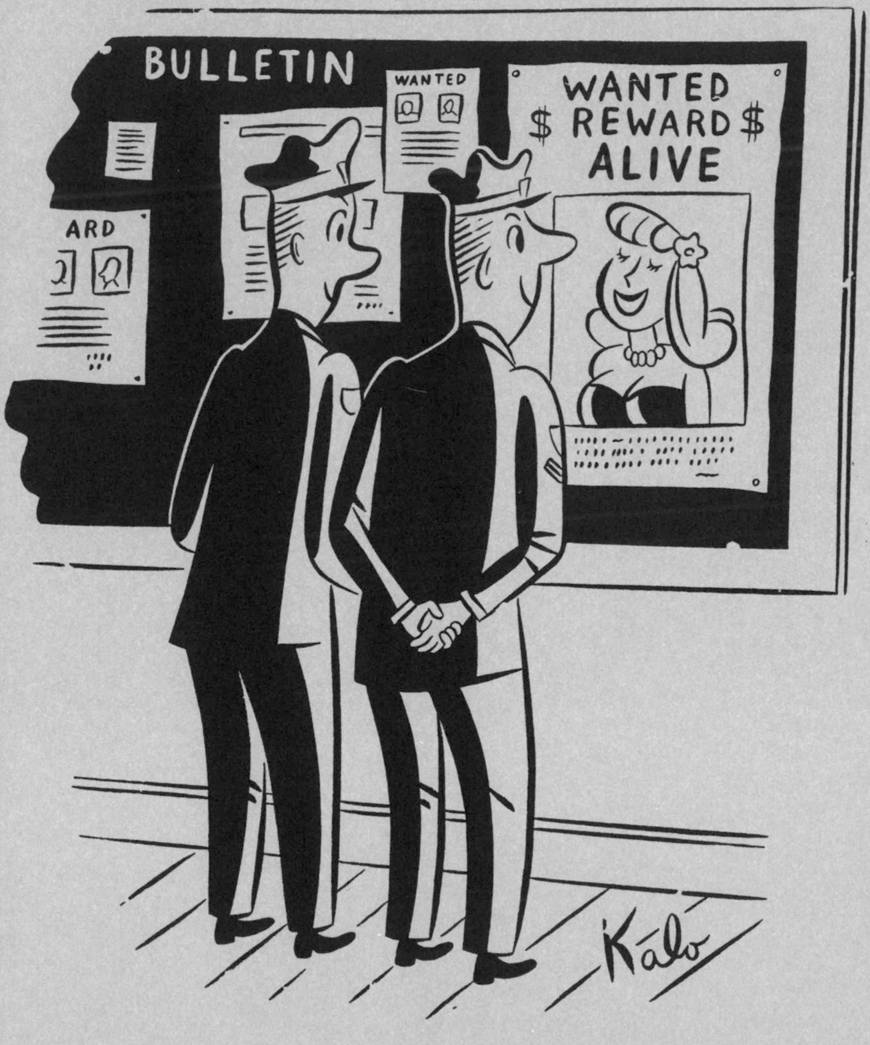
BULLETIN
WANTED
WANTED
$ REWARD $
ALIVE
ARD
Kalo

97

GEE-WHIZ, Sept. 1956

HOT DRINK
HANDLE CUPS
COLD DRINK CUPS
PLATES
DESSERT DISHES
INDOORS — OUTDOORS

this

and NEXT

Double Parkin

John C. Parkin, whose provocative comments on the state of Canadian architecture begin on page 2, comes from a long line of Parkins. His father, of course, was a Parkin, whose family came from England. But his mother was a Parkin, too, the seventh generation of an old Canadian family.

And in Toronto, in 1944, John C. Parkin, architect, formerly of Winnipeg, met the man with whom he is now in partnership — John B. Parkin, architect, formerly of Hamilton. To carry the coincidence one stage further, both Parkins were married to Toronto girls named Jean — though John B's wife spells her name Jeanne. To no one's surprise, when sons arrived in each family, they were named John, Jr.

In the early days of the Parkin partnership, trying to get the right John by telephone was enough to make customers give up and design their own home or factory. But within the office there is no confusion: John C. is the firm's architectural chief and John B. is in charge of administration.

The Editors

4B
4C
Kalo

"It's something about two bucks, dear."

WEEKEND MAGAZINE, 1961

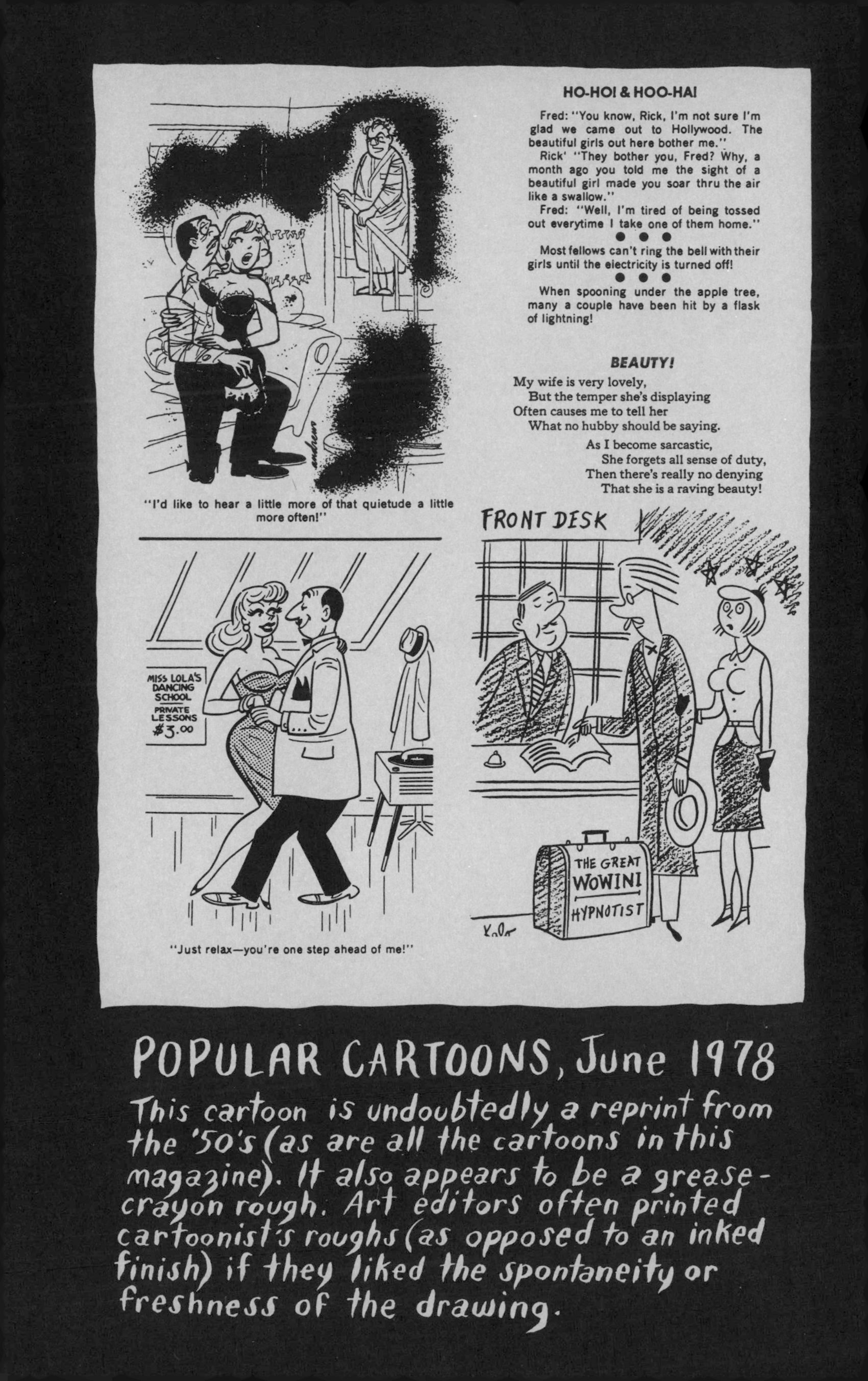
HO-HO! & HOO-HA!

Fred: "You know, Rick, I'm not sure I'm glad we came out to Hollywood. The beautiful girls out here bother me."

Rick' "They bother you, Fred? Why, a month ago you told me the sight of a beautiful girl made you soar thru the air like a swallow."

Fred: "Well, I'm tired of being tossed out everytime I take one of them home."

● ● ●

Most fellows can't ring the bell with their girls until the electricity is turned off!

● ● ●

When spooning under the apple tree, many a couple have been hit by a flask of lightning!

BEAUTY!

My wife is very lovely,
But the temper she's displaying
Often causes me to tell her
What no hubby should be saying.

As I become sarcastic,
She forgets all sense of duty,
Then there's really no denying
That she is a raving beauty!

"I'd like to hear a little more of that quietude a little more often!"

MISS LOLA'S DANCING SCHOOL
PRIVATE LESSONS
$3.00

"Just relax—you're one step ahead of me!"

FRONT DESK
THE GREAT WOWINI HYPNOTIST

POPULAR CARTOONS, June 1978

This cartoon is undoubtedly a reprint from the '50's (as are all the cartoons in this magazine). It also appears to be a grease-crayon rough. Art editors often printed cartoonist's roughs (as opposed to an inked finish) if they liked the spontaneity or freshness of the drawing.

glossary

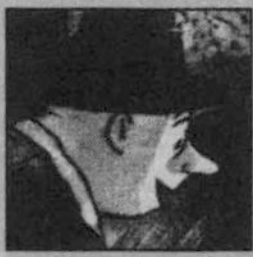
Addams, Charles (1912 to 1988). *The New Yorker's* king of the Macabre. His black humour cartoons are very beautifully rendered and still timelessly funny. Most people today are still familiar with his "Addams Family".

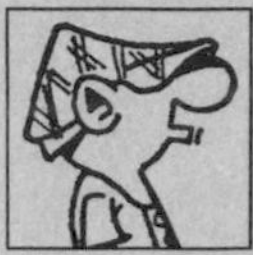
Andy Capp — The wife-beating, selfish, drunken layabout Mr. Capp and his long-suffering wife Flo have appeared in papers all over the world since 1957. Created by Reg Smythe.

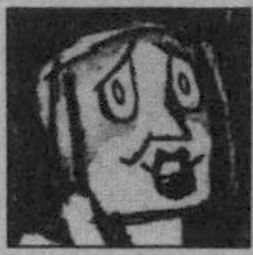
Arno, Peter (1904 to 1968). One of the early pioneers of the one-line gag cartoon which replaced the tedious he/she captions, Arno was pure modernity—bold lines, masterful compositions. Possibly *The New Yorker's* greatest stylist.

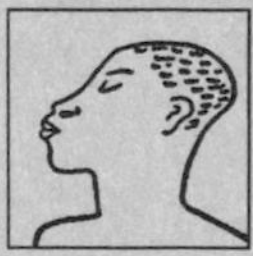
Bemelmans, Ludwig (1898 to 1962). Writer/painter/children's book author. He not only illustrated for *The New Yorker,* he also wrote for them. He's mostly known today for the *Madeline* children's book series.

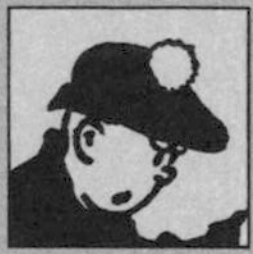
"The Black Island" — Tintin's Scottish adventure. First published in 1938 and then redrawn in 1966. A good album, but I think my favourite would be *The Castifiore Emerald*.

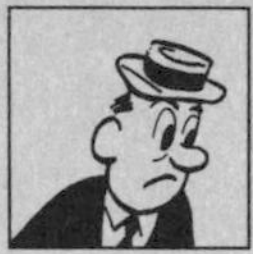
Boltinoff, Henry (1914 to 2001). Highly prolific cartoonist. His work appeared in just about every major market from the 1930s to the 60s. His strips often appeared as filler in most DC comic books during the 1960s.

CBC — Canadian Broadcasting Corporation.

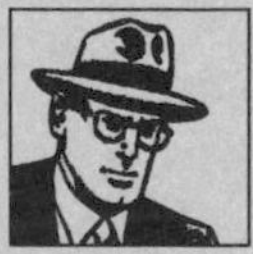
Clark Kent — Superman's mild-mannered alter-ego.

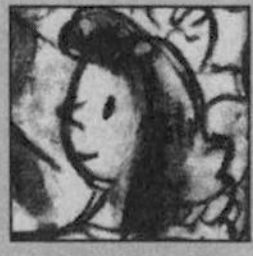
Darrow Jr., Whitney (1909 to 1999). One of the great *New Yorker* cartoonists. He had a scratchy yet solid style that was very appealing to the eye. He was a successful commercial artist, illustrating books, ad campaigns, etc.

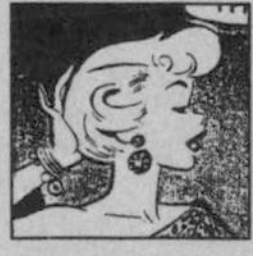
DeCarlo, Dan (1919 to 2001). The artist who has drawn *Archie* comics for forty years. He also did some great stuff for Marvel/Atlas previous to that including some beautiful girly cartoons for their *Humorama* line of magazines.

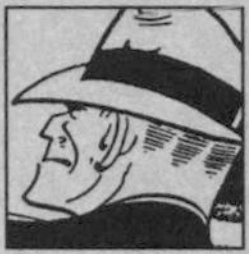
Dick Tracy — Chester Gould's brilliant and very readable detective strip. Started in 1931.

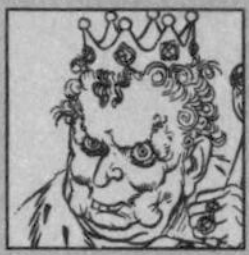
Diefenbaker, John — The thirteenth Prime Minister of Canada. A political cartoonist's dream. He served from 1957 to 1963.

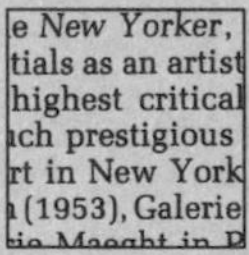
e New Yorker,
tials as an artist
highest critical
ich prestigious
rt in New York
(1953), Galerie

The Encyclopedia of Cartoonists — Actually *The World Encyclopedia of Comics* edited by M. Horn. A good source of information but a much more comprehensive listing of North American cartoonists is needed.

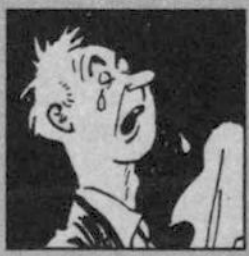
Frise, Jimmie (1891 to 1948). Undoubtably the finest Canadian cartoonist of the past. Unfortunately, his strip, *Birdseye Center* (191? to 1948) is largely forgotten today. Like Hokinson, he died at the height of powers.

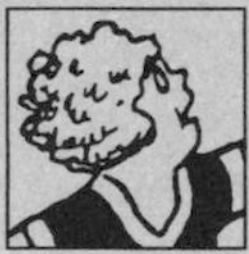
Gray, Harold (1894 to 1968). The creator of one of the greatest newspaper strips of all time—*Little Orphan Annie*.

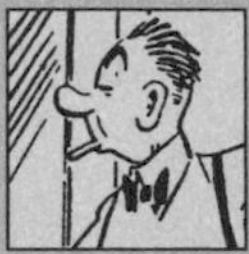
Hatlo, Jimmie (1898 to 1963). One of the great screwball cartoonists. His *They'll Do It Every Time* newspaper panel was enormously popular for over thirty years.

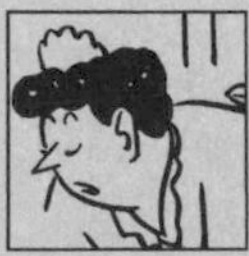
Hazel — Wise-cracking maid who rules the household. Started as a regular panel in *The Saturday Evening Post* in 1943. Later syndicated by King Features. It inspired a popular 1960s TV series.

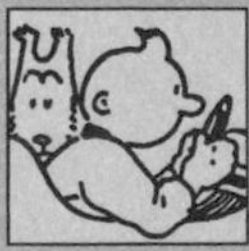
Hergé (1907 to 1983). The father of European cartooning. His beautiful "clear line" style has influenced generations of cartoonists. A master.

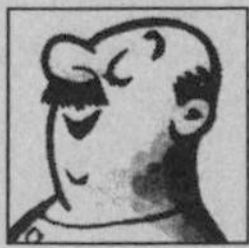
Hoff, Syd (1912 to 2004). He was *The New Yorker's* potato-nose cartoonist. His subject matter was usually Brooklyn/ethnic types. Funny stuff. An amazing, prolific cartoonist who authored countless children's books.

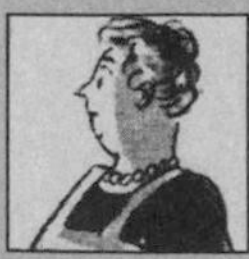
Hokinson, Helen (1893 to 1949). *New Yorker* cartoonist almost forgotten today. Hokinson produced a beautiful body of work from the 1920s to the 40s. A personal favourite of mine, she died tragically in a plane crash in 1949.

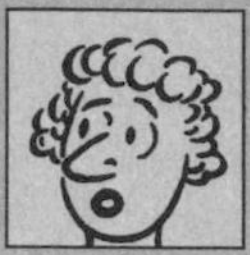

Keate, Jeff (1914 to ?). Vancouver-born, New York-based gag cartoonist whose work appeared in all major markets of the 1940s and 50s. A simple but slightly ugly style of drawing. strangely appealing, though.

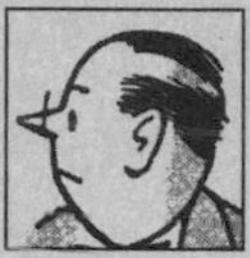

Key, Ted (1912 to ?). Although Key's gag cartoons appeared everywhere, he is mostly known today for his popular character "Hazel". A pleasant drawing style.

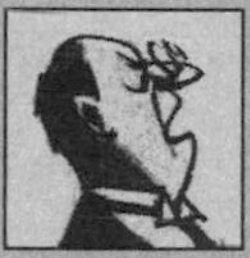

Krause, Robert (? to ?). Gag cartoonist long associated with *The New Yorker*. Not a real favourite of mine but he makes me laugh every so often.

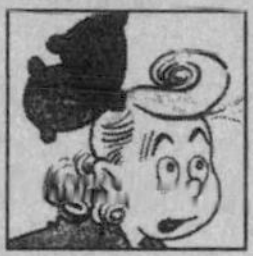

Little Iodine — Hatlo's little terror. She first appeared in *They'll Do It Everytime* and then got her own Sunday strip in 1943. She also appeared in many Dell comics.

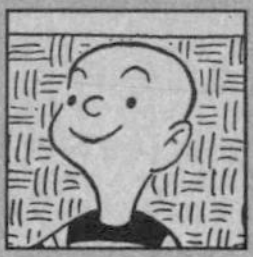

Little Nipper — A strip that every Canadian, born before 1970, knows well. Doug Wright's domestic pantomime strip (starring two bald children) appeared from 1948 to 1980.

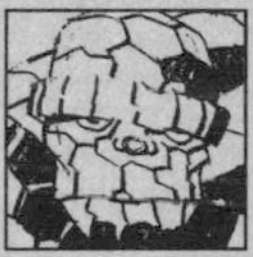

Marvel Comics — Back in the 1960s it was a wonderfully fun line of comic books—especially the Kirby and Ditko stuff. Now, it's a hateful media conglomerate that popularizes bad drawing.

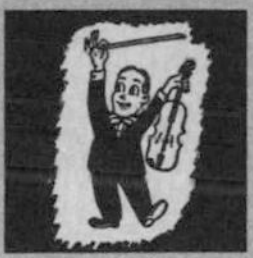

Messer, Don — Don Messer and his Islanders had a long-running Maritime music show (Don Messer's Jubilee) on the CBC until it was unceremoniously cancelled (if I remember correctly) in the 1970s.

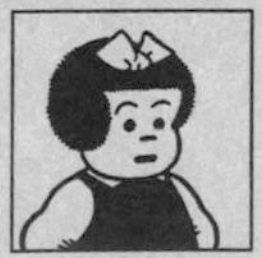

Nancy — Ernie Bushmiller's masterpiece of simplicity. A strip much loved for its precise drawing and dumb gags. It ran for over forty years.

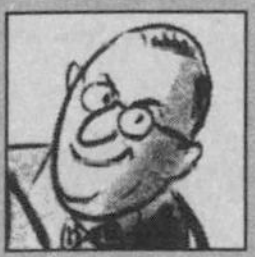

"The Office Party" — Published in 1951 by Doubleday. Written by Corey Ford. Charming.

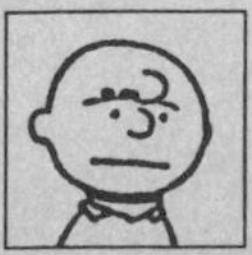

Peanuts — Charlie Brown, Linus, Snoopy, and the whole gang. Charles Schulz's subtle masterpiece began in 1950 and ran daily for fifty years.

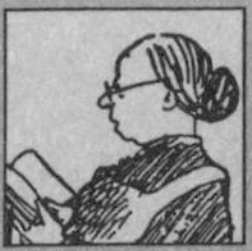

Pont (1908 to 1940). Very dry and sophisticated *Punch* cartoonist. Best known for his series titled *The British Character*. Beautiful, loose, textural, drawing style.

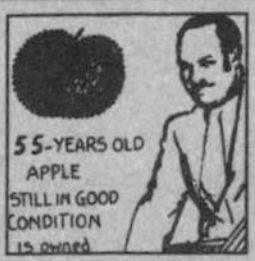
55-YEARS OLD
APPLE
STILL IN GOOD
CONDITION

Ripley, Robert (1893 to 1949). Really, more of a phenomenon than a cartoonist. His *Ripley's Believe It Or Not* odd-facts panel began in 1918 and still runs today (under other hands of course).

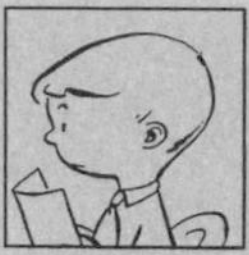

Schulz, Charles (1922 to 2000). The master cartoonist behind *Peanuts*. I can't overemphasize the effect this man's work has had on me.

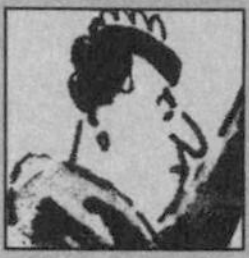

Steig, William (1907 to 2004). Second only to Saul Steinberg for innovative drawing. Steig is the last of the old *New Yorker* cartoonists still working today. He's also produced many lovely children's books.

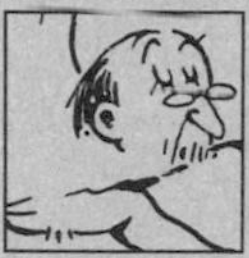

Dr. Seuss (1904 to 1991). The genius of children's books. *Green Eggs and Ham. The Cat in The Hat,* etc, etc—we all know them well.

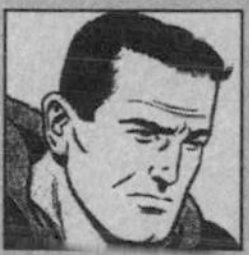

Superman — Jerry Siegal and Joe Shuster's famous superhero. He spawned hundreds of imitations (still does, actually).

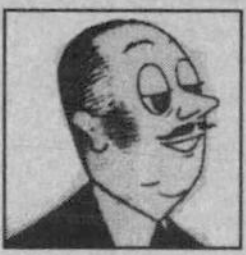

Taylor, Richard (1902 to 1970) Canadian cartoonist who joined the *New Yorker* staff in 1935. Though in general he had an appealing style. I've always disliked the bulging *Garfield*-type eyes he gave all of his characters.

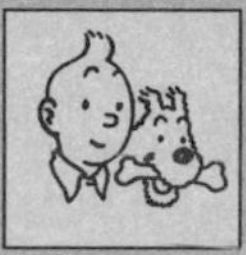

Tintin — The boy reporter (and perpetual boy scout) from Belgium whose twenty-three book-length adventures have thrilled readers the world over for seven decades.

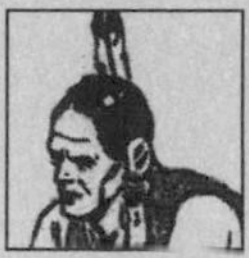

Turok — A comic book with an odd mix of dinosaurs, cavemen, and American Indians. Originally published by Dell, later by Gold Key, it ran for decades (mostly as reprints, though). A perfect thing when you're a child.

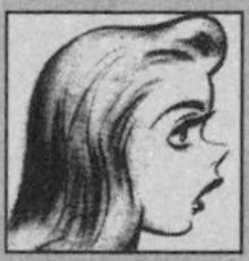

Ward, Bill (1919 to 1998). Known for his girly cartoons of large (!) breasted women and mousy men. Still working today, but his best work seems to be between the 1940s to mid 60s.

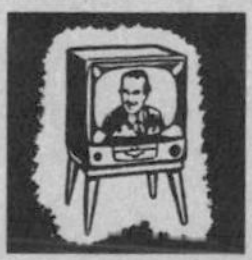

Wayne & Shuster — Canadian comedians who appeared about seventy times on *The Ed Sullivan Show*. Also did <u>many</u> comedy specials in Canada. Frank Shuster was Joe Shuster's cousin.

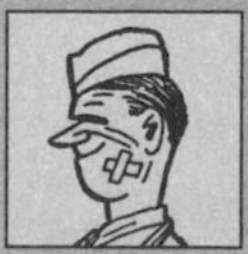

Webster, H.T. (1885 to 1953). Master cartoonist, responsible for many features. Perhaps best remembered for *The Timid Soul*. Breathtaking control of space and line.

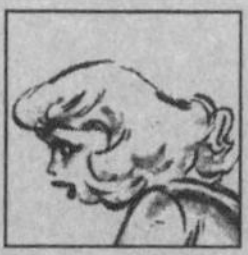

Wenzel, Bill (? to ?). One of the better girly cartoonists of the 1950s and 60s. His work appeared everywhere. In the 1970s he illustrated a series of popular books about sexy stewardesses.

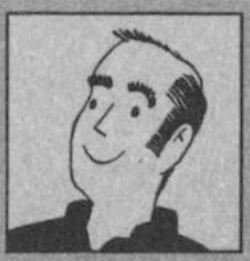

Wright, Doug (1917 to 1983). A popular Canadian cartoonist. His strip *Nipper* (later *Doug Wright's Family)* was extremely well-recalled until recent years. It ended in 1980 and is now almost forgotten.

Kalo in New York
Circa late '40's / early '50's

Seth was born in Clinton, Ontario in 1962. For the first twenty (or so) years he lived under the name his parents had given him; Gregory Gallant. In the 1980's he changed it to his current nom-de-plume. Looking back, this may have been a youthful error... however, little can be done about it now. He has been writing and drawing his comic book series PALOOKAVILLE since 1991 and his illustration work has appeared in numerous publications, including THE WALL ST. JOURNAL, MOTHER JONES, THE NEW YORK TIMES, THE ATLANTIC, FORTUNE, THE NEW YORKER, NICKELODEON, AND SATURDAY NIGHT. He lives in Guelph, Ontario with his wife Tania, and their two cats. He divides his time between two passions--working on PALOOKAVILLE and seeking out the work of old-time cartoonists.

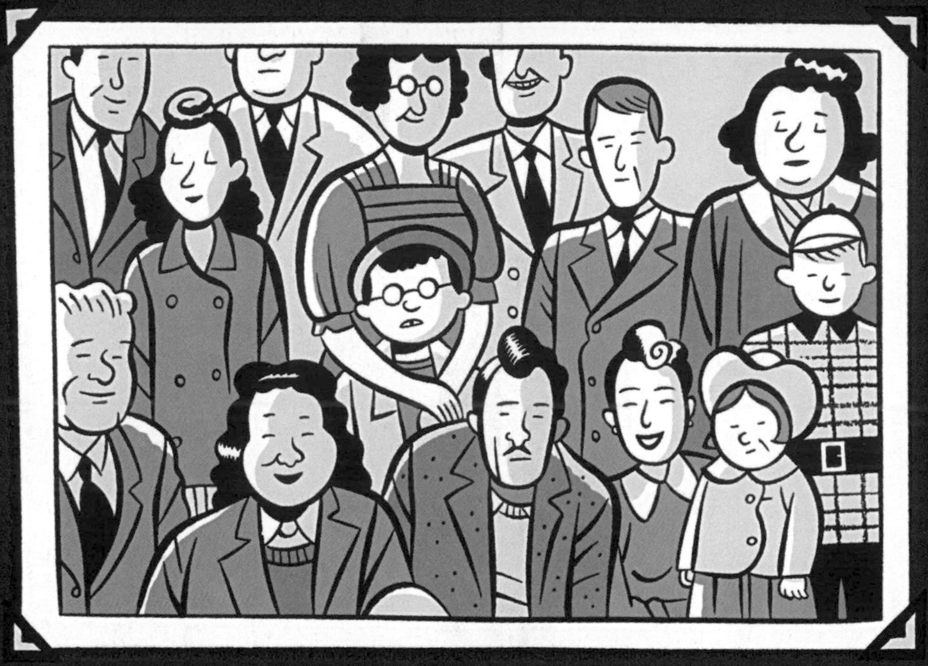

The Whole Clan

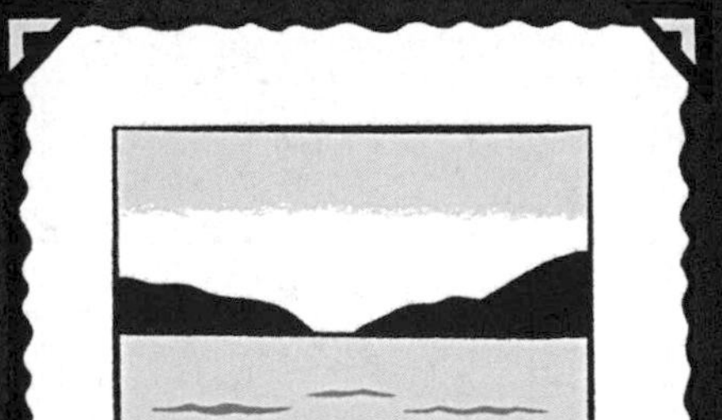

Lake Juniper

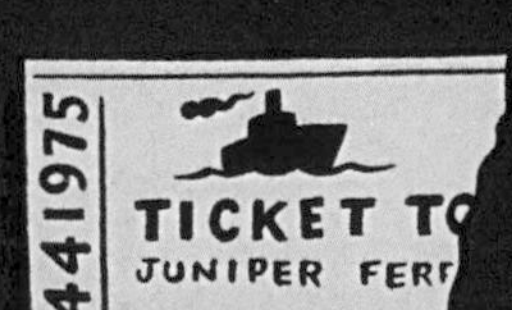
441975
TICKET TO
JUNIPER FER

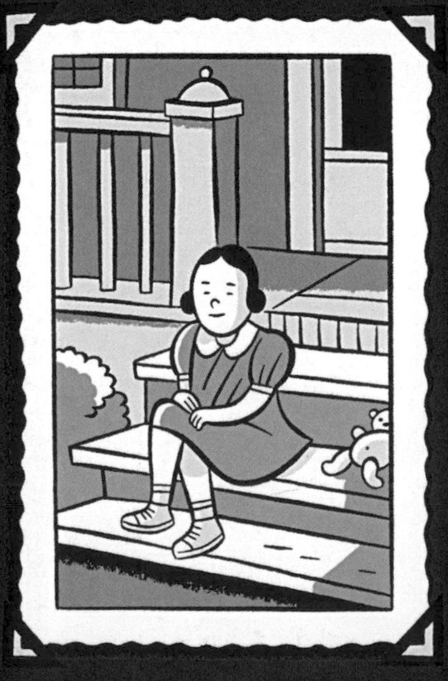

All Alone